MARRIAGE: A TASTE OF HEAVEN

Volume I: APPRECIATING MARRIAGE

by

Patsy Rae Dawson

Cover by Denise Sanford
Illustrations by Lisa Bade

GOSPEL THEMES PRESS
P.O. BOX 1154
SUMNER, WA 98390

Published by:
    Gospel Themes Press
    P. O. Box 69097
    Seattle, WA 98168, U. S. A.

ISBN 0-938855-40-9 Paper
     0-938855-44-1 Set

Library of Congress Cataloging in Publication Data.

Dawson, Patsy Rae, 1945-
    Marriage, a taste of heaven.
    Includes bibliographies and indexes.
    Contents: v. 1. Appreciating marriage -- v. 2. Learning to love (God's people make the best lovers)
    1. Marriage--United States--Religious aspects--Christianity. 2. Love. 3. Sex--Religious aspects--Christianity. I. Title.
HQ734.D34   1987   261.8'3581   86-22746
ISBN 0-938855-44-1 (set)

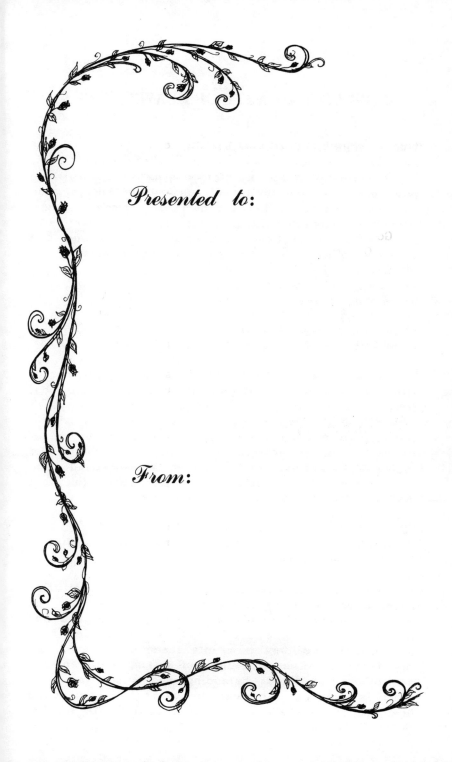

Presented to:

From:

THE
MARRIAGE: A TASTE OF HEAVEN SERIES

VOL. I: APPRECIATING MARRIAGE

Contains the formula for solving every marriage problem from the Bible. Discusses the mental and physical differences between men and women and how they blend together in perfect harmony. A verse-by-verse study of the Song of Solomon contrasts true love with sensuous love. The final section discusses the differences between subjection and leadership vs. servitude and dominion. True biblical subjection brings a blessing instead of a curse.

VOL. II: LEARNING TO LOVE
(GOD'S PEOPLE MAKE THE BEST LOVERS)

Shows how God provides proper sex education for His people at each stage of their sexual development from puberty through the temptation for middle-aged affairs. God pictures the woman as a wonderful initiator of love and an exciting lover in her older years. The origin of Victorian morals are examined and their contradictions to scriptures are exposed. The number-one sexual problem in America today, inhibited desire and pleasure, is examined in detail.

VOL. III: ENJOYING THE HOME
(Scheduled for release in the fall of 1988 if sufficient interest is expressed.)

A beautiful discussion of the woman of great price emphasizes the value of the woman who faces life and solves the normal problems of loving a husband and raising a family. One section shows how to deal with problems before they turn into resentments or chain-reaction wars. The challenges of raising children with a mother and father balancing and supporting each other is examined. An overview of Ecclesiastes shows how God rewards the man with a loving wife for his labors on earth.

VOL. IV: FINDING FULFILLMENT
(Scheduled for release in the fall of 1990 if sufficient interest is expressed.)

Some of the great women of faith come to life as Sarah, Abigail, and Mary and Martha show how to find happiness. I Cor. 11 reveals the splendor behind God's universal law of authority. Since many women don't understand their role in the church, many churches suffer from a lack of their good influence. The open doors for women to serve God are examined. Paralleling the Jewish marriage customs with Christ taking the church for His bride shows how modern marriage should literally be "a taste of heaven."

If you would like to express interest in Volumes III and IV, and to be notified of future publications, please send a postcard with your name, address, and zip code to:

Gospel Themes Press
P.O. Box 69097
Seattle, WA 98168

All books can be ordered direct from the publisher or your local bookstores. Write the publisher at the above address for current ordering information.

Vol. I: Appreciating Marriage

"For everything created by God is good, and
nothing is to be rejected, if it is received
with gratitude: for it is sanctified by means
of the word of God and prayer."

(I Tim. 4:4–5)

TABLE OF CONTENTS

THE PROBLEM:

THE COMMON DELUSION

A young girl grows up reading fairy tales such as *Snow White and the Seven Dwarfs* and *Cinderella* where the handsome prince rescues the maiden from all harm and they live happily ever after. Later she reads thrilling love stories and dreams of a beautiful marriage built upon love and happiness. But as she matures, well-meaning people begin to teach her that life is not that way. Handsome princes do not exist, and even if they did, women do not need to be protected from potential harm. The delusion begins.

Then one day Mr. Wonderful comes along and proposes to her. They begin marriage deliriously happy. She confidently assumes that their union will be blessed and that they will delight in what no one else seems to enjoy--a storybook marriage where "they live happily ever after." The delusion is rejected.

The honeymoon is over. She seeks help with her problems from older and more mature women. They tell her that she expects too much from marriage, for marriage is just not all that great. They advise her to concentrate on her housework, to become absorbed with her children, and to forget her feelings and desires. The delusion begins again.

She reads marriage books which all begin "Too many people enter marriage expecting to live happily ever after. The sooner they realize that life is just not that way, the happier they will be." She becomes more miserable as she loses her hope of marital happiness. The delusion is convincing.

Feminists tell her that a woman does not need a man for anything except to bear children. And they ask her, "What woman, in her right mind, wants to stay home with babies?" They argue that men only make women unhappy by enslaving their minds and bodies. They reason that men were handy to kill bears and snakes in times past, but now women can do anything men can. They explain that a woman cannot expect to live under a man's guidance and be happy. The delusion is encompassing.

She becomes more discouraged as she fails to see any happiness in the marriages of others except for a few select cases. She quickly dismisses these because the woman accidentally got an extra-thoughtful husband. She accepts the assumption that only in fairy tales do men and women live together happily ever after. Thus, she proclaims the evils of marriage and laughs at the foolishness of those who tell her that a marriage can be happy, delightful, and the greatest pleasure on earth. "Just wait until the honeymoon is over!" she tells them. The delusion is perpetuated.

In this way, many a woman yearns for marital happiness in her youth only to find that her chief ambition in life is not a reality for her. The youthful glow of anticipation changes to the dull expression of bitterness and hopelessness as the years pass. But the fantasy of which she is a victim is not the conception that marriages can be blissfully happy. Rather the delusion is the belief that marital happiness is impossible or happens only out of pure chance.

If marriages are such miserable unions only to be endured, then why did the apostle John use the example of marriage as a wonderful promise of heaven? Why did he say through inspiration, "Let us rejoice and be glad and give the glory to Him, for the marriage of the Lamb has come and His bride has made herself ready" (Rev. 19:7)? If happy marriages exist only in fairy tales, why did he try to make people want to go to heaven by saying, "Blessed [happy--PRD] are those who are invited to the marriage supper of the Lamb" (Rev. 19:9)?

Over and over again, God declared the reality of enjoying a happy marriage throughout the Bible. God pronounced His creation "good" in Gen. 1:31 after He joined Adam and Eve together as husband and wife. Through the apostle Paul, God affirmed that marriages are indeed good and to be received with gratefulness in I Tim. 4:3-4. Through the Hebrew writer, God proclaimed that marriages be "held in honor [highly valued--PRD] among all" (Heb. 13:4). God even announced that marriages are patterned after the relationship of Christ to the church in Eph. 5:22-33. Thus, earthly marriages should be a very literal taste of heaven.

However, I am not a marriage counselor nor am I a marriage expert. If that's true, then why do I teach classes on marriage and the woman's role? And why have I written a series of books about marriage? More importantly, why does anyone care what I have to say if I'm not an expert or a counselor?

The answer to these questions comes from the story of how these lessons came about. Nearly twenty years ago in Seattle, my husband and I spent a lot of time with another young couple. The husband acted so overbearing with his wife that my husband often remarked after an outing with them, "I don't see how she stands him." Other people likewise remarked, "I don't see how she stands him."

The husband always spent lots of money on himself buying fancy clothes and whatever he wanted. Yet his wife and son wore hand-me-downs from people who felt sorry for them. A mutual friend who worked where he did told us that one day he came to work bragging about making his pregnant wife get out that morning and thaw all the pipes under their house trailer. To hear him tell it, that feat was something to boast about. Yet the men who heard him gloating gasped in disbelief.

The man was not content to just lord it over his wife, for he soon began to use me as a shining example for her to follow. Once while we all rode down the freeway together, he turned around to his wife, who sat in the back seat with me, and said, "Why aren't you ever quiet like Patsy is quiet?" That embarrassed us both.

Another time when they and several other couples came to our house for farmer's breakfast, he started in on her again. As we were trying to eat, he chewed her out, "Why don't you ever fix ham and eggs and biscuits and gravy like Patsy does? I never get a meal like this!" And on and on he went. Yet the amount of money he gave her to buy groceries would not even allow her to buy napkins, let alone ham.

Then he started something new. One day he asked, "Patsy, do you think that if a husband tells his wife she ought to eat beans seven days a week, she ought to eat beans seven days a week?"

I knew he was trying to use me. He wanted me to say something in front of her that he could use to browbeat her. His manipulation of me and his wife really offended me. Now that he had put me on the spot, I knew I had to do something. But what?

I had read the few verses about women in the Bible that I knew about. But they didn't seem very detailed to me, so I hadn't studied them in depth. However, I knew that if I could answer his questions with scriptures and focus on what he was doing wrong, it would stop him from using me as an excuse to mistreat his wife. It might even make him quit taking advantage of my friend.

So I began searching the Bible for answers--*anything* I could use on him. I soon discovered that the Bible contained some definite teachings about husbands and wives. Then without warning, my efforts to help my friend began backfiring as I started coming face-to-face with the scriptures about subjection. Painfully, I realized that I was not practicing what the Bible said. Yet if somebody had asked me beforehand if I was a submissive wife, I would have answered, "Sure! No doubt about it!" Now I knew better. I'd been violating some of those principles of subjection all along through ignorance. I immediately reacted with, "That's not fair! I shouldn't have to do that. It'll just make my husband take advantage of me!"

This was a serious problem for me. When my husband asked my father for my hand in marriage, my father replied, "You can marry her if you want to. But I want you to understand one thing: Patsy is the most stubborn person I've ever known." And that was the truth. So here was the most stubborn person my father had ever known studying Bible passages that showed that her strong will displeased God.

I cried many tears, and complained a lot to God about how impossible His laws were to obey. But I knew two things: First of all, I knew that I would have to submit myself wholly to my husband to obey God. Secondly, I knew that I would have to *like submitting* or it wouldn't count as obedience to God.

So I went to work on my actions, and I went to work on my attitudes. As I began to work on these things, I quickly forgot about my friend's husband whom I was trying to prove wrong. Now I searched the scriptures to learn things for myself.

Surprisingly, my husband, who I mentally rehearsed a long list of complaints about, turned into the sweetest man a wife could ever want. I quit crying. And I got excited about that! I told my friends, "Guess what I found in the Bible, and it works!" Then they went home and tried subjection. It produced the same effect on their husbands, and they got excited! Sadly, my friend whose husband goaded me into studying moved away and I never got to share what I learned with her.

The next thing I knew, all my other friends started coming to me and asking, "What about this?" and "What does the Bible say about that?" I didn't know, but my previous success aroused my curiosity, so I started studying some more. The more I learned and applied to my marriage, the more I enjoyed my husband which encouraged me to study harder than ever. Thrilled, I shared these new findings with my friends who likewise became even more excited. And the more I shared, the more they asked questions. Soon, just from trying to find out if a wife should eat beans seven days a week if her husband asked her to, I was hooked on studying about the woman's role in the Bible.

Several years later my husband started preaching full time and we moved to Spokane. That decision to preach presented yet other opportunities for me to learn even more as my husband began building a large religious library. Since we didn't have any children for the first ten years of our marriage, I had time to spend in deep study. I checked out each new book as he bought it and read every new commentator's remarks about the passages on marriage. My husband taught me how to look up word definitions in Greek lexicons. Thus, I enjoyed access to books that most women don't even know about. So God gave me some privileges that many women don't experience simply because raising children consumes their time and they don't live right beside a well-stocked religious library.

In time, I developed four two-hour-long classes on marriage which I shared with friends. I naively thought, "That's all the Bible says about marriage and the woman's role. I now know it all." Invariably though, each time I taught the material, someone always asked a question that I didn't know the answer to, so I would study some more. Before I knew it, the set had grown to six lessons.

Then one day as I went through the material with a friend, she said, "Patsy, I know a lady who says she no longer loves her husband. Can a woman learn to love her husband after she's fallen out of love with him?" I didn't know, so I started studying again.

That question added four more lessons on learning to love. And over and over I heard women say after taking the classes, "I'm falling in love all over again with my husband."

Then I had ten two-hour-long classes. Surely, the Bible didn't contain any more information about the man-woman relationship. But while I was teaching what I thought was the final collection of subjects, a student asked some important questions making the total grow to twelve lessons. And to think, when I started with four classes, I thought that was all the Bible said.

Now ten years later after revising the original Vol. I to make it easier to teach in forty-five-minute classes instead of two-hour-long ones like I originally taught, I added two and a half new chapters. I must confess, in all honesty, that I believe that I have not even begun to exhaust the subject of enjoying a happy marriage.

So you see why I say, "I am not a marriage counselor nor am I marriage expert." *God is the supreme, unsurpassed marriage counselor and marriage expert.* And He's not through with me yet. He's still teaching me His marvelous secrets of marital happiness through motivating questions and comments from others. I'm still discovering in His divine word things I've overlooked in the past.

Solomon said it best, "Even though one should never sleep day or night,...I concluded that man cannot discover the work which has been done under the sun. Even though man should seek laboriously, he will not discover; and though the wise man should say, 'I know,' he cannot discover" (Eccl. 8:16-17). Both this revised volume and *Vol. II: Learning to Love* take advantage of many new medical and scientific discoveries of the last ten years to shed light on the eternal truths of the Bible. They also prove beyond all doubt the dependability of God's marriage regulations. Who knows what men will discover in the next ten or twenty years. Truly, God's wonderful word deserves mankind's respect, attention, and obedience.

When women apply God's principles to their marriages, it brings out the best in them. It renews feelings that they felt in courtship, but which grew cold in the interim. The Bible's principles also affect husbands in the same way. Many times, revived love proves more exciting and satisfying than when first kindled.

Some people consider this view of marriage too idealistic and not realistic enough for them. However, the following unsolicited letter demonstrates the power of God's word to help His people find, not an impossible fairy tale ending to their marriages, but a very real, literal taste of heaven:

Dear Patsy,

A preacher gave me a copy of the tapes of the lessons you gave there; I put them on cassettes. I want you to know how much I have enjoyed them! Along with some personal counselling from the preacher, the instructions have saved my marriage, my sanity, my children, and maybe my life and soul as I had considered ending it. I'm sure that sounds a little dramatic, but to me at least it's a reality.

I learned so much about being an individual--a woman and person responsible for my own soul. I tried as hard as I could before, and I was faithful in my study and attendance--yet something was missing! Before, I never thought of the Bible and God talking to me as a *woman*, for I felt everything was unisex or something--that I was an "it", not a woman. This upset me and frustrated me because I knew I had a lot of influence. I felt like something *drastic* was missing somewhere.

I also felt frustrated that somehow my brain was withering which probably sounds crazy. I *did* study my Bible, but I didn't know what to *do* with it. As a woman, I felt useless in that way. Yet it was so important to me.

My children were unhappy and grouchy too. My marriage was miserable, although we, mostly I, tried to hide it. My husband is a big, sweet, grouchy, yet happy, completely devoted honest Christian who drove me crazy (I thought).

I finally wound up with some form of breakdown in the hospital. There were some other difficult pressures, but the personal insecurities and doubts and fears were crumbling from *inside*. The doctors had me taking four tranquilizers a day plus twelve anti-depressants a day plus another pill to up their effectiveness!

I have a friend who was at least as unhappy as I was or worse. I shared your tapes with her and several other women in a home class. After awhile she said, "You know, I've fallen in love with my husband and you know what caused it? The tapes!" They had hated each other and had filed for divorce twice, I think. Yet they were both Christians--sincere, faithful ones. Now, they are really happy, now that she knows how to be happy. Many times I stayed up and tried to talk her into not leaving him. Once when she did, I went and got her and took her back home before he found out. But I didn't know how to help her, except for her not to leave him.

It seems to me that most Christians have been fighting doctrinal disagreements or the social trends in the church world, which all need to be done; but the home has been going down the drain. Many older women complain that they would teach the young women but that we won't listen. Many of these women are wonderful, sweet women, but the young women look at them and know they aren't submissive.

In fact, I can look back in my own life and see where my not being submissive has caused many problems. We all go around and pretend we don't have any problems, but inwardly we are killing ourselves being so lonely and wanting help so badly. I am looking forward so much to the book.

A Student

In view of the need for such a book and with great confidence in the power of the word of God to transform misery into happiness, these lessons are prayerfully dedicated to God's people everywhere. Then someday soon perhaps the pagans will once again exclaim as they did in the first few centuries, "What marriages those Christians have!" Hopefully, observing the personal bliss of God's people will make those outside of Christ want to turn to God, too, for the answers to all of their problems. Truly, everyone can enjoy a marriage that is a taste of the supreme marriage that is to come.

Patsy Rae Dawson
Seattle, Washington

SOLUTION I:

GOD'S WORD

vs.

WORLDLY FABLES

(How to Find the Answers to Marriage Problems)

"Marriage...which God created to be gratefully shared in by those who believe and know the truth."

(I Tim. 4:2–3)

CHAPTER 1

GOD'S PLAN FOR MEN AND WOMEN

Social scientists say that romantic love didn't appear in the world until the Middle Age courtiers discovered it. But alas! Romance was still not for marriage--the courtiers found it only in extramarital affairs. The psychologists say that true romance didn't enter marriage until this century.

Even then, love still lacks fulfillment. Dr. Elaine Hatfield, a specialist on love research, says that feelings of "being in love" only last between six to thirty months. Then the marriage loses its vibrancy as it becomes more a relationship of companionship than love.[1] The rising divorce rate in this country shows that marriages still face a profound crisis. The internal turmoil of husbands and wives drives love far from their lives.

Yet God created romantic love for husbands and wives--not for promiscuous courtiers or starry-eyed newlyweds. For over three thousand years God has patiently taught men and women the secret of lasting love in the Bible. Rather than being an invention of the twentieth century, romantic love is as old as time itself. It's just that men and women have failed to apply God's plan for love to their individual lives.

God designed an important role for women which uses their unique abilities to promote love in the home. Ideally, the women's skill for expressing love should increase with age making them love specialists in their later years. Then God wants the older women

[1] Morton Hunt, "Does Love Really Make the World Go Round?" *Parade Magazine* (2/8/87), p. 16.

and widows to pass their knowledge of love on to the next generation of women. When women follow God's plan for love, the world continually grows more loving.

Essentially, when the social scientists say that love has been absent in centuries past, that is the same as saying that women have failed to follow God's plan for their lives. Thus, God addresses the three stages of a woman's life (young mother, older woman, and widow), and shows women how to promote love. As a result of following God's plan, women leave a lasting mark upon the world that says, "I was here; I was important; I made a difference."

God also has a plan for men. But God's plan for men doesn't revolve around conquering the world, it focuses on loving their families. God is family oriented, and He wants His people, both male and female, to be family oriented, too.

I. GOD'S PLAN FOR OLDER WOMEN

God designed for a woman's later years to be her most productive. Thus, clearly understanding the highlight of a woman's life makes her younger years and days of widowhood take on a new perspective. Once young women comprehend God's overall plan for their lives, they know better how to work toward that goal in their youth.

The Bible contains three important passages that deal specifically with older women. While society often assumes that older women don't care about sexual love, Solomon describes them as exciting lovers who ravish their husbands in ways that young wives cannot:

A. AN EXCITING LOVER

> Prov. 5:18–19: "Let your fountain be blessed, and rejoice in the wife of your youth. As a loving hind and a graceful doe, let her breasts satisfy you at all times; be exhilarated [ravished--KJV] always with her love."

"The wife of your youth" refers to an older woman, the bride a man married in his youth and with whom he has lived all this time. Now they've grown older together. So Solomon tells older men why their older wives can satisfy them night after night in a way that a different youthful body each night cannot.

Solomon entertains no delusions about the honeymoon being the height of a man's sexual delight with his wife. The sexual love of the older couple who have lived a lifetime together far outweighs the joys of their honeymoon period. Thus, Solomon admonishes the husband, "Let your fountain be blessed," as he describes a loving wife as a bubbling spring of love, always ready to revive her husband. Her refreshing waters come forth from her emotional involvement with her husband

Solomon advises, "Rejoice in the wife of your youth." "Rejoice" refers to supreme pleasure and extreme happiness. He continues, "As a loving hind and a graceful doe, let her breasts satisfy you at all times." "Breasts" literally means "breasts, the seat of love." Through molding her feelings and attitudes according to the word of God, the older wife learns through the years how to give her body as an expression of her deep and pure love for her husband.

As a result, together in each other's arms they become exhilarated or ravished with her love. "Exhilarated" means "intoxicated or carried away." Without a doubt, Solomon portrays the older wife as an exciting lover to her husband who both gives pleasure to him and who enjoys the embrace of love for herself.

This section of scripture shows God's love for His people, for it provides safeguards for a sexually dangerous time for both men and women. Psychologists recognize the middle years as the most likely time for a husband or a wife to engage in an affair. Yet God tells them in these passages how to thrive on each other's love.

Unfortunately, today many wives live just on the fringes of Victorian morals. For many older women the teachings of the past deny them their spiritual heritage of being an exciting lover. Instead, they heed the false dogma that "nice women don't enjoy lovemaking." Contrary to these views, spiritually-minded wives not only delight in the physical embrace of their husbands, but they also even initiate the act of love.

Vol. II: Learning to Love discusses how God designed eight different purposes for the sexual relationship, the least important perhaps being procreation. In addition, God created the woman as the man's equal in ability to enjoy the embrace of love. God designed the sexual relationship for His people to use in service of Him, not for the ungodly people of this world to use in service of Satan. When a husband and wife follow God's rules, their lovemaking improves with age. Thus, through the years the older wife becomes an ever more ravishing lover for her older husband.

B. FAMILY ORIENTED

> **Prov. 31:10-11: "An excellent [virtuous--KJV] wife, who can find? For her worth is far above jewels. The heart of her husband trusts in her, and he will have no lack of gain."**

Beginning with the Jews, women have always loved the description of the woman of great price ever since it was first written. But rather than depicting all wives, Proverbs 31:10-31 lists the special attributes of older wives. For example, verse 23 reflects her age by saying that her husband is known in the gates, the place of judgment. The Jews understood that this meant that he was a respected elder, an older man. This implies that the woman of great price was older, too. Thus, the whole section of scripture portrays an older wife.

Essentially, the description tells how an older wife masters the various areas of her life. She lives a balanced, orderly life. Her many activities revolve around her family--she is family oriented. Although she works for extra income, she doesn't neglect her husband, her children, her home, the needy, or even teaching God's word to others.

In like manner, she maintains a healthy relationship with her husband. The word "husband" means "owner, master, possessor, ruler." She gladly submits to her husband as she recognizes him as the head of the family. And as she faces and overcomes the normal problems of life, her husband compares her favorably to the young wives of other men (vs. 28-29). He praises her saying, "Many daughters have done nobly [virtuously--KJV], but you excel them all." The word "daughters" carries the idea of youth or maidens just starting out in marriage in contrast to the older wife. Also, the word "nobly" or "virtuously" is a form of the word "excellent" or "virtuous" in verse 10 which describes the woman of great price. "Virtuous" basically refers to the strength of an army. The main difference? The older wife has reached her goal of becoming all that God desires, while the young wives still struggle toward mastery of their lives.

Through devoting herself to her family through the years, the older woman gained skills and insights which enable her to become an excellent teacher of young women. Thus, "she opens her mouth with wisdom, and the teaching of kindness is on her tongue" (vs. 26).

C. A CAPABLE TEACHER

> Tit. 2:3-5: "Older women likewise are to be reverent in their behavior, not malicious gossips, nor enslaved to much wine, teaching what is good, that they may encourage [teach to be sober--KJV] the young women to love their husbands, to love their children, to be sensible, pure, workers at home, kind, being subject to their own husbands, that the word of God may not be dishonored."

If a person doesn't know the meanings of the Bible words, it's impossible for him to understand what the various passages mean. Sometimes the simple English words which the translators chose hide the more complex or colorful Greek and Hebrew words of the original Bible. Often just defining key words with precise definitions makes the meanings of difficult passages more clear.

While some readers may find this tedious, other students working through difficult problems report that the definitions help them better understand and accept the meanings of the passages. As a result, studying the word definitions may well make the difference between a person's ability to bring about a permanent change in his life and just giving lip service to what is taught.

For these reasons, word definitions follow the passages used throughout this book. These definitions give the complete meanings of the selected words to demonstrate that no one manipulated the definitions or forced their meanings. This passage serves as a good example of how misunderstanding simple words often leads to a false interpretation of what the scriptures teach:

"Encourage" or "teach to be sober" *(sophronidosi)* means "to restore one to his senses, to moderate, control, curb, discipline, to hold one to his duty, admonish, to exhort earnestly" *(Thayer's Greek-English Lexicon of the New Testament,* p. 613). *Strong's Concordance* shows the intensity of this word by defining it as meaning "to breeze up, i.e. (by analogy) to agitate (into waves):--toss" (Strong, p. 63). It comes from a word which means "through the idea of sudden motion, to fling (properly with a quick toss) by qualification as if a load, to disperse:--cast (down, out), scatter abroad, throw" (Strong, p. 63).

Paul didn't say married women nor successfully married women nor even women with godly children. Instead, he said "older women." This verse includes *all older women* who meet certain qualifications of character regardless of their marital success or childbearing history. As a woman patterns her life after God's plan, advancing age frees her from the responsibilities of dependent children and transforms her into a readily available teacher of young women.

Unfortunately, many women find Paul's instructions to older women confusing because the King James Version uses the word "teach." The older women protest, "But I can't teach a public Bible class. This verse surely doesn't apply to me."

Young women assume, "This verse prohibits me from teaching women older than I am; so I can only teach little children."

The main problem stems from not knowing what the word "teach" means. First of all, "teach" is not the complete way the King James translators rendered the Greek word *sophronidosi*. They translated it "teach to be sober." Neither the Greek word *sophronidosi* nor its root word contain the idea of "public" teaching or admonishment. An older woman might choose to obey the verse by teaching a public class for young women, but "teach to be sober" doesn't demand "public" teaching.

In contrast, I Tim. 2:12, "But I do not allow a woman to teach or exercise authority over a man, but to remain quiet," uses the Greek word *didaskein* for teach. "Teach" in this passage means "a. to hold discourse with others in order to instruct them, deliver didactic discourses; b. to be a teacher; c. to discharge the office of teacher, conduct one's self as a teacher (used of Jesus and the apostles uttering in public what they wished their hearers to know and remember, etc." (Thayer, p. 144).

The difference between *sophronidosi* (what God commands the older women to do for young women) and *didaskein* (what God forbids all women to do with men) is the difference between informally sharing good news and making a speech. Yet I Tim. 2:12 doesn't prevent women from teaching men--it just regulates how they do it. God forbids women to *preside over* men in learning situations. On the other hand, the Bible encourages the *informal sharing of Bible knowledge* between men and women--an action in which women often excel (Acts 18:26; II Tim. 1:5; 3:15).

While many men will pick up this book and read it, I am not *"didaskein"* them. I exercise *no control* whatsoever over how much of it they read or if they do the exercises. Nevertheless, many men tell me how much they enjoy my books and profit from them. Preachers who have proofread these lessons have said, "Don't you dare label this book 'Ladies' Bible Class Material'!" And I haven't in subjection to their opinion on the matter.

On the other hand, when I teach a ladies' Bible class, I exercise authority over the women. I set the procedure for the class and give assignments which I expect the ladies to complete.

Instead of urging the older women to preside over public Bible classes for women, *sophronidosi*, focuses on more intimate forms of communication. Almost all women do especially well in female-to-female conversations regardless of whether or not they can stand before a group to deliver a lesson. God leaves *how* the older women communicate to the young women up to them. Whether they encourage the young women on an individual basis or in a classroom, the important thing is that they obey God. For God commands the older women to take the young women into their care as cherished daughters and to tell them God's plan for women.

A form of *sophronidosi* is translated "sensible" in both Tit. 2:2 and 6 in regard to the older and young men. "Teach to be sober" differs from "sensible" only in regard to who does the acting. "Sensible" refers to someone *making himself* think and act rationally while "teach to be sober" means to *show someone else* how to think intelligently and sanely.

God's command for the older women, instead of the preacher, to teach the young women how to act soberly shows God's special love for women. As the chapters on the stronger and weaker vessels show, men and women think differently. Many things which seem obvious to men aren't so self-evident to women, take for example "subjection." Women share similar fears, desires, discouragements, and feelings of fulfillment with each other. Thus, older women possess an ability to communicate with young women on a personal level that a preacher will never have, no matter how hard he tries.

Consequently, God holds the older women responsible for "teaching what is good" to the young women. Just living for forty, fifty, or sixty-plus years gives older women plenty of time and opportunities to master their own weaknesses through the use of God's word. This, in turn, helps them develop into wise and loving wives and mothers. As a result, they owe a debt to the young women to teach them how to love others, especially their husbands and children.

Sometimes young women think this passage prevents them from teaching other women their age or older. If true, of necessity this passages also excludes *everyone* who is not an "older woman" from teaching adult women *any* of the subjects mentioned. This would mean that preachers could not preach about the woman's role. Yet Paul told Titus to teach the older women their duties toward themselves and the young women (Tit. 2:1-4). Paul emphasized, "These things speak and exhort and reprove with all authority. Let no one disregard you" (Tit. 2:15). In other words, Paul told Titus to be persistent and blunt and not to listen to any excuses when teaching the older women their responsibilities to the young women.

If Tit. 2:3-4 limits who can teach women about their duties, it also prevents the elders from engaging in marriage counselling with women. However, an elder "must be one who manages his own household well, keeping his children under control with all dignity (but if a man does not know how to manage his own household, how will he take care of the church of God?)" (I Tim. 3:4-5). Thus, a *qualified* elder understands and practices God's rules for a happy, successful marriage and family. This enables him to wisely lead the flock of Christians which he oversees. A qualified elder serves as one of the best marriage counselors available to Christians--men or women. For these reasons, Tit. 2:3-5 cannot place restrictions on anyone other than the people named--the older women.

Even so, other passages limit the qualifications of teachers in general. For example, Gal. 6:1 says, "Brethren, even if a man is caught in any trespass; you who are spiritual, restore such a one in a spirit of gentleness; looking to yourself, lest you too be tempted." This passage admonishes *all spiritually-minded people,* whether male or female, young or old, to help bear the burdens of others including young women. Tit. 2:3-5 shows that *God holds the older women especially responsible for being spiritually minded and for keeping the young women mindful of their obligations to God.* God gives men and young women *a choice* about instructing the women; God gives older women *a command.*

Many older women argue, "But the young women don't want to learn! They don't ask for help with their problems. And it only makes them mad when I point out something they're doing wrong."

Strong's definition given earlier of "to toss or fling," etc. shows the force that God wants the older women to use in restoring the young women to their senses. No matter how the young women respond to correction, God still expects the older women to exhort them in much the same way that a mother disciplines her daughter when she misbehaves.

In reality, instead of rejecting instruction from the older women, many young women grieve when they can't find a qualified older woman to help them. So if the young women want instruction and the older women want to encourage them to be sober, then why can't the two of them get together?

The reason is simple. Many an older woman has collected a lot of wisdom and insight through the years. Often she draws on good basic worldly wisdom. So when a young woman comes to her with a problem, she tries to help her by saying, "I think..." or "My experience has been..." or "It looks to me like...might work." In effect, the older woman asks the young woman to place her faith in her instead of in God. Few women with problems, young or old, willingly trade their own opinions for another woman's opinions without a lot of argument. Thus, the young woman rejects what might be very sound advice simply because it's not Bible based.

To teach a young woman properly, an older woman must sit down with her and using the Bible say, "Here's what God says you should do for your husband..." or "God says you should do...for your children." Then the older woman can say, "My experience has been that when we do what God says, it makes our lives happier. I've seen other people obey God, and it's made their lives happier. For example,..." That's the place for an older woman's earthly wisdom--after she's taught the young woman God's will from the scriptures. Then by following up with her experiences, she encourages the young woman to obey and trust God rather than her opinion.

One young woman told about an older woman, "When I sat in her Bible classes as a young girl, I admired her so much. I thought she was such a wonderful person. But now that I'm an adult and am facing some marriage problems, I can't go to this woman. With the little bit I know about the male-female relationship, I realize how horrible this woman's marriage is. Her marriage is so full of problems, there's no way that she could begin to help me."

Invariably, these young women experience deep pain. They feel cheated, let down, and forsaken. They hurt deeply within their souls because the older women lack the qualifications to instruct them. Young women all over this country desperately want older women to teach them. But where are the older women?

One night after a class on the role of older women, two older women asked, "Do you really mean that *every older woman* has this responsibility?"

I answered, "Isn't that what Paul told Titus?"

They replied, "But we've been Christians for a long time, and we've never seen even one woman assume this responsibility."

Because of that sad state of affairs, many congregations suffer. Women, young and older alike, fail to rise to their full spiritual potential; and consequently, they can't spur their husbands or children on to greater service of God either. Certainly, some older women willingly fulfill their spiritual destiny. Often they're overworked, and sometimes discouraged as a result, but the young women usually sing their praises. While a few young women may not want instruction, the majority of them are searching, hungering, and thirsting for dependable information. The young women want to know how to make their husbands happy, how to raise well-balanced children, and how to enjoy their femininity. But who will show them the way?

Fortunately, these two older women, who dared to ask if Titus really meant "every woman," boldly took on the job of encouraging the young women. One quit her job and started teaching classes on marriage to small groups in her home. She told the women that she was on call for them because as she said, "The young women need me, and I think I owe it to them to be available to them." The other woman took an active role in the children's Bible classes and worked with the teachers, mothers, and children. In this capacity, she taught the young mothers how to teach the Bible to their children. While these two older women utilized different talents and developed different spiritual specialties, they both filled vital needs for the young women.

Ideally, God wants all young women to enter marriage knowing what to expect and how to enjoy a wonderful relationship as did the Shulammite maiden in the Song of Solomon. She confidently told the Shepherd, "I know we're going to enjoy a successful marriage for two reasons." Number one, their mothers began teaching them how to love as tiny babies when they nursed them. Number two, the Shulammite's mother spent time talking to her and instructing her about how to please a husband (Song of Sol. 8:1-2). So, with the legacy of love they both inherited from their parents, plus the Shulammite's knowledge of how to captivate a husband, she assured the Shepherd that married ecstasy awaited them.

In actuality though, mothers often neglect to teach their daughters these things. In many homes, the children seldom witness loving expressions between their mothers and fathers. Still victims of Victorian morals which considered it immoral for a husband and wife to kiss in front of their children, many people today grew up in homes deprived of physical affection.

As a result, these young women begin marriage without the most basic knowledge of how to love their husbands or care for their homes. Then children come along and compound the problems already there. They long for answers to the misery they experience and ache for someone to teach them what their mothers neglected to tell them. In many instances, young women with families lack both the time and the experiences of life to fully study and understand their role for themselves.

Thus, young women often need an older woman to adopt them, to bring them up to full maturity. Fortunately, when a woman's children leave home, it gives her time to devote to re-raising young women, to teach them how to cook, to show them how to discipline their children, and to help them conquer bitter and resentful feelings toward men in general and their husbands in particular.

Certainly, God loves all women! Through His wisdom and concern, He commands the older women to guide the young women into more perfect knowledge of His way. And when older women teach the young women, they see God's word working in the women's lives. This greatly increases the older women's confidence in God and their respect for Him. Finally, they reach a point where no matter what happens to them, their first reaction to problems is, "I wonder what God says?" Then they go to the Bible for the answer, because they've witnessed His word provide answers for so many problems.

God gives older women a tremendously important job. One reason the churches suffer so much today is because few older women qualify themselves for this

work. Churches desperately need older women who love
and care about the young women.

In the years to come, as Christians teach people
in the world, their neighbors, schoolmates, etc., they'll
teach people with the most horrible problems imaginable. Some will be lesbians and homosexuals; others
will openly practice fornication. Yet first-century
churches solved such repulsive problems (I Cor. 6:9-
11). Churches today can also successfully solve a
multitude of marriage problems if their older women
take up their Bibles and teach the young women as
God commands.

God holds the older women responsible for holding
the young women to their duties. *Every older woman*
has an obligation to qualify herself for this responsibility; the best time to begin is when she is a young
woman.

II. GOD'S PLAN FOR YOUNG WOMEN

The Bible clearly distinguishes between the duties
of older and young women. To determine if women are
young or older, the Bible looks at their childbearing
years and family responsibilities. During the time that
women care for children at home, the Bible speaks of
them as young women, young mothers, regardless of
their age. Once their children leave home, the Bible
views them as older women even though they might be
quite young. Then God gives the older women new responsibilities to replace the ones they've completed.

In the past, women stayed young longer than they
generally do today. In spite of commercials saying that
women look better with age, women are becoming older
earlier than ever before simply because they choose to
bear fewer children. So if a woman wants to put off
becoming an older woman for as long as possible, the
solution is simple: Keep bearing children and more
children and more children!

Technically, one woman might be a forty-year-old
young mother with a two-year-old toddler while another
woman is a thirty-eight-year-old older woman with a
grandchild. The difference? The first woman still has a
child at home who requires her care while the other
woman's children have all left. God designed special
work for the young woman with children in the home:

A. FAITHFUL DURING CHILDBEARING

I Tim. 2:15: "But she shall be saved through the bearing of children if the women continue in faith and love and sanctity with self restraint."

"Through" means "1. through; 2. throughout (during) which anything is done (a passing through space or time)" (Thayer, p. 132).

Many people regard this passage as extremely difficult. They wonder, "If a woman never gives birth to a child, does this verse mean she cannot go to heaven?" Yet understanding what the words mean takes away the mystery. The word "through" causes most of the difficulty. While a very simple word in the English language, the Greek word means "throughout (during) which anything is done, a passing through space or time." Thus, this passage says that a woman shall be saved during her childbearing years if she continues to serve God.

"If," a very important word, limits the woman's salvation. Rather than receiving unconditional salvation during her childbearing years, God expects young mothers to remain faithful to Him. For this reason, Paul says they will be saved *if* they continue in faith, in love, and in sanctity with self restraint.

This verse addresses a real danger that plagues all young mothers. During their childbearing years, young mothers serve God by teaching their children to love God and by molding them into stable mature adults. Yet many of them freely admit, "After I started having children, I started going downhill spiritually. I stopped hearing sermons because I couldn't concentrate with the children constantly wiggling or needing to be taken out. I stopped studying because I didn't have time, or I was too tired. Now that they're older, I'm having a hard time getting motivated to study again."

In His love, God warns young mothers about this danger. They'll be saved during this time when child-raising duties sometimes overwhelm them *if* they continue in faith, *if* they work at growing spiritually. While God emphasizes *teaching* for the older women, He emphasizes *learning* for young women.

Essentially, Paul says, "Young mothers, become Bible students. Study your Bibles and know what God wants you to do. Make a commitment to yourselves that you won't allow raising children to cause you to lose your souls. Make the effort to study."

Even with good intentions, many young mothers face real problems getting to listen to whole sermons and finding the time to study, because their children demand their constant attention. Yet other young mothers have solved this problem. The solution might be as simple as trading baby sitting with another mother in the same predicament.

Certainly, a young mother needs to teach her children very early to sit beside her during worship and not to talk to her or climb in her lap and squirm. Likewise, a mother should avoid holding her toddler over her shoulder. It's the adults who cause the problem. They can't resist looking at a cute little boy or girl and saying things or making faces. The child soon learns that even if mother won't play, the people sitting behind him will. Children learn that lesson a lot quicker than they learn to sit still. So it helps to sit the child down beside the mother facing forward to prevent him from distracting others who in turn distract him.

While a mother with a toddler sitting beside her can't listen as though she never had a child, she can learn more when she makes the effort. Rather than resenting her children during services, a young woman needs to find a way to solve the problem.

Then Paul tells young mothers to continue in love. Later chapters discuss the two Greek words for love in the New Testament. This word love comes from the Greek word *agapeo* which basically means "to make an intelligent estimate of another person's needs and to act in his best interest." In other words, young mothers must continue doing what is best for other people such as their husbands, children, friends, parents, and whoever they associate with. God wants young mothers to be known for their love and concern for others.

Next Paul tells them to continue in sanctity. "Sanctity" comes from the same root as "sanctify" and "holy" and means "to set apart." Young mothers who serve God with their whole heart and being become set apart or different from the other young mothers in the world. As the next chapter shows through a word study of sanctify, this means that they enjoy better marriages than their neighbors and friends who ignore God in their daily lives. They rise to a higher plain of accomplishment and fulfillment. If they don't, something is wrong. They need to go back to building their faith and studying their role as women.

Finally, Paul says that they must add self-restraint. This word is translated "sober" in Titus 2 where Paul instructs the older women to train the young women to be sober. While God expects the older women to teach the young women how to think rationally and sanely, the young women bear the same obligation to themselves. So if the older women refuse to teach them their duties, the young women must determine to learn their role for themselves. Thus, Paul warns young mothers, "Don't allow yourselves to deteriorate spiritually during your childbearing years. Be Bible students and know for yourselves what God expects of you."

B. A STUDENT OF MARRIAGE

Tit. 2:4-5: "...that they may encourage the young women to love their husbands, to love their children, to be sensible, pure, workers at home, kind, being subject to their own husbands, that the word of God may not be dishonored."

While God expects the older women to qualify themselves to teach the young women the secrets of enjoying a happy marriage, this requires that the young women be willing to learn. Thus, Paul lists the areas that he wants the women to pay particular attention to.

Just learning to love their husbands requires a lot of effort and study. The rest of this book and all of *Vol. II: Learning to Love* deal with this subject from various scriptures. The word for love comes from a different Greek word than explained previously. It comes from the word *phileo* and revolves around an emotional attachment to someone which leads to a physical display of affection. Chapters 7 and 8 develop the meaning in greater detail.

The Septuagint, a Greek translation of the Hebrew Old Testament, sheds some light on how the Jews used *phileo*. Since Jesus and the apostles generally quoted from The Septuagint when they referred to Old Testament passages, they approved of its use. *The Septuagint* uses this same form of love (*phileo*) in Prov. 5:19 which describes the older woman as an exciting lover. Thus, in marriage, this word encompasses *all of a woman's love* for her husband.

The Song of Solomon, likewise, shows that when young brides make proper preparation for marriage, they eagerly look forward to ravishing their husbands. For example, the Shulammite not only looked forward to lovemaking (2:6), but she also told the Shepherd that after they married she would freely give her love to him (7:12).

Young women also need all the help available from the older women to learn to love their children. No one claims that child-raising is easy or that it comes second nature to young mothers. "Love" comes from the same Greek word *phileo* and shows God's desire for mothers to build an emotional bond with their offspring. The hugging, patting, and kissing of loving mothers who openly admire and appreciate their children helps young children grow into emotionally stable and productive adults.

In a similar manner, being sensible and pure often requires study and effort, especially in the realm of being workers at home. "Workers at home" doesn't necessarily mean stayers at home, but refers to women who take proper care of their homes. And while being kind sounds easy, it often presents special problems for young mothers. Many times through trying to be kind to others, they allow their own lives to get out of balance. In over doing good deeds, they threaten the tranquility and stability of their own homes. A later chapter shows how to approach good deeds sensibly.

Even during the age when Paul wrote Titus, subjection was a dirty word. Many women view subjection as a horrible punishment inflicted upon innocent women. However, true Bible subjection blesses the lives of women. It causes their husbands to treat them better and to love them more than ever.

Many women who assume they know all about subjection in reality possess only a very shallow understanding of how it works. Subjection is a very meaty subject that plays an important part in the happiness of a marriage. Thus, young women especially need the older women to teach them the mechanics of subjection. If women practice it properly, it makes their lives happy. If they practice it improperly, it makes their lives miserable.

Since these subjects are so important to the well-being of women and to their happiness, young women can't afford to leave it up to older women to teach them. They must earnestly seek to learn about marriage on their own.

C. FAMILY ORIENTED

I Tim. 5:14-15: "Therefore, I want younger widows to get married, bear children, keep house, and give the enemy no occasion for reproach; for some have already turned aside to follow Satan."

While this verse refers specifically to younger widows, it shows God's plan for all young women. Ideally, God wants all young women to marry and to take care of a family--to be family oriented. Chapter 5 shows that God created women for this very purpose-- it is their destiny. However, God understands that all women cannot marry and He makes provisions for them which the next section discusses.

Chapter 5 also shows that God created both men and women to work--to be involved in productive activities. Without meaningful work, both men and women become miserable. In addition, they often become the source of many problems. So God warns young women against idleness which leads to unhappiness which makes them ripe for Satan's wiles. As shown later, women exert tremendous influence upon both their husbands and children. And Satan gleefully uses their power over others when women make it available to him.

Paul admonishes women to do the work that God assigns them--to stimulate and work with their husbands, to bear and enjoy their children, and to turn their homes into wonderful refuges of peace and love for all who enter. In this way, young women busy themselves doing God's work as family oriented women.

Basically, God instructs older women to teach the young women the necessary skills for caring for and enjoying their families. Then He tells young women to learn and practice these feminine talents. Later when their children leave home, they too will be qualified to teach the new generation of young women their duties. When women follow God's plan for them, the world enjoys a multitude of blessings that only women who dare to serve their Creator can give.

III. GOD'S PLAN FOR WIDOWS/SINGLE WOMEN

Many single women report that studying the husband-wife relationship increases their rapport with people at work, neighbors, fellow Christians, and their children if they were married before. This comes about simply because many of the guidelines for getting along with husbands appeal to their human qualities. Thus, conduct which enhances the husband-wife team also improves all relationships. So while this book speaks specifically about marriage, single women can apply it to themselves to strengthen their bonds with others.

While God designed for women to mate with men, sometimes circumstances beyond their control prevent them from marrying. Statistics alone show that women outnumber men. And as men and women age, the ratio of women to men increases. However, God desires that single women still commit themselves to serving Him. While many passages apply to all women, a few refer specifically to single women:

A. REPUTATION FOR GOOD WORKS

I Tim. 5:9-10: "Let a widow be put on the list only if she is not less than sixty years old, having been the wife of one man, having a reputation for good works; and if she has brought up children, if she has shown hospitality to strangers, if she has washed the saints' feet, if she has assisted

those in distress, and if she has devoted herself to every good work."

This verse talks about the church employing a certain class of widows to do certain work, most likely teaching the young women privately or publicly or both. The qualifications of these widows show that they share the expertise of the older women in Tit. 2:3-5. In addition, these women no longer have husbands who need their attention and love. This freedom enables these older widows to adopt young women who require more instruction than usual. Thus, their experience plus time on their hands makes these women very valuable workers.

The number-one feature of these women is their reputation for good works. They have spent sixty or more years living godly lives. This verse also shows that God considers raising children a good work in His service. Likewise, they readily did all that they could for others. They washed the saints' feet--they didn't consider any job too menial for them if it needed to be done. They also helped those in distress with meals, clothes, a kind word, or a hug--whatever they needed.

Furthermore, they showed hospitality to strangers. Hospitality involves many things such as fixing a meal or providing a bed overnight. But it also includes the ability to speak to strangers. Thus, over the years these women conquered what natural shyness they possessed to warmly welcome strangers in their midst. Obviously, God considers this quality an asset in women!

These single women didn't start out single, for they began adulthood as married women. Most married women today face the same fate--widowhood. In fact, it may well be that God created women with their longer life spans to give them a few extra years of intense activity in service to Him teaching the young women. In addition, God gave women the ability to survive the loss of a mate better than men generally do.[2]

[2]Jane Barr Stump, Ph.D., *What's the Difference? How Men and Women Compare* (New York: William Morrow and Company, Inc., 1985), p. 60.

However, when these few extra years come, will widows today be as prepared to serve God as these women? Will they enjoy a reputation for good works? Will they be valuable assets to the congregation and in demand for their teaching abilities?

God made plans for every woman, no matter what her age or marital situation. He has work to be done that only qualified women can do. But every woman decides for herself whether or not she trains for the position, or if she even applies for the job.

B. DEDICATED TO THE LORD

I Cor. 7:32: "But I want you to be free from concern. One who is unmarried is concerned about the things of the Lord, how he may please the Lord."

Vol. II: Learning to Love devotes the last chapter of the book to a verse-by-verse study of this section of I Corinthians 7. It explains in detail about the persecution that awaited the Corinthian Christians. To help them remain faithful during this time of trial, the apostle Paul wrote some special instructions to them. Mainly, he told them to remain true to God no matter what happened to them.

Paul explained that single people enjoy opportunities to serve the Lord that married couples don't have. God expects husbands and wives to always consider each other and to supply the other's needs. Of necessity, this limits the amount of time that married people can devote solely to God. Unfortunately, sometimes husbands and wives allow their duties of marriage to distract them from service to God.

On the other hand, the single life frees women to dedicate themselves wholly to God. For example, sometimes the job of raising children forces mothers to say, "No," to helping with certain projects for teaching others. Yet single women often say, "Yes," without fear of neglecting either husbands or children. Likewise, single women can easily schedule whole days to study God's word while mothers may need to find baby sitters for such spiritual treats.

Many single women make valuable contributions to the congregations where they worship by actively teaching in the class programs and making visual aids. In this way, they influence the children of others and help mold them into productive spiritual beings. They also encourage other workers and comfort the sick and the disheartened. As a result, they become loved and cherished members of their spiritual family.

C. HOLY IN BODY AND SPIRIT

> I Cor. 7:34: "...And the woman who is un-married, and the virgin, is concerned about the things of the Lord, that she may be holy both in body and spirit;..."

Paul says that when unmarried women concern themselves with pleasing the Lord, they become holy in both their bodies and minds. "Holy," a form of the word sanctify reviewed earlier, means "set apart." When single women study God's word and apply it to their lives, they become different from the people around them. They enjoy better and happier lives.

An older woman who taught a class on the special problems of single women interviewed as many women as possible from teenagers to widows. She asked each of them what kind of problems they faced and how they solved them. She learned that single women es-sentially confront the same problems as married women. For example, both married women and single women fight loneliness from time to time. Both struggle to meet financial obligations. Both sometimes suffer from sexual frustrations. Both occasionally experience depression.

This teacher also discovered something else: *The single women's attitudes toward serving God and toward serving others greatly affected their happiness.* The women with a woe-is-me attitude seldom did anything for others. Many attended services irregularly and could not be counted on to help with teaching pro-jects. Instead, they expected others to cater to them. These women often appeared depressed and demanded that others cheer them up.

On the other hand, the women who committed them-selves to Bible study and to taking an active role in their congregations, who invited people over for meals, and who assisted the needy and visited the sick lived fulfilling lives. Certainly, some of them missed the pleasures of married life, but they still encouraged and built others up rather than depending upon others to make them happy.

Purity plays an important role in the lives of single women just as it does in the lives of married women. Being pure in both thought and body is one of the best things women can do for themselves. It liberates them to be truly loving individuals--to really care about others. Chapter 8, "Honoring the Weaker Vessel," shows that the one word that should describe women is "loving."

Basically, the main difference between single women and married women is their opportunities to express love. Married women just have a few more people to love than single women do--their husbands and children. Yet single women who dare to love and serve God with both their bodies and their minds, indeed, rise to their full potentials as loving, caring feminine beings who make the world a better place for those they associate with.

IV. GOD'S PLAN FOR MEN

When I first began teaching this material, I left out the men's half. Two things happened as a result. First, some of the women started complaining, "It's not fair! We have to make all the sacrifices and our husbands just sit back and soak it up!"

Secondly, other women complained that their husbands picked up their printed class notes and read them. They didn't care except their husbands started criticizing them with, "Ah-hah! It's just as I suspected! You ought to be doing this and you're not!" And these women who were sincerely working at improving themselves began to resent their husbands for lording it over them.

Obviously, the class notes were actually making their marriages worse instead of better. So I added the men's half to protect my students from an unbalanced one-sided scrutiny of the woman's role on the part of either them or their husbands. The results were immediate. Contrary to what many of the women thought and complained about, the scriptures revealed that *God expects more sacrifices from husbands than He demands from wives.* Thus, including the men's half helped these women appreciate, love, respect, and admire their husbands more than ever. This in turn helped them work with, support, and balance their husbands.

The husbands still read the class notes, but they quit finding fault with their wives. Instead, many of them began talking to their wives about their joint-responsibilities in marriage. Thus, long-dormant lines of communication were opened once again for many of the couples.

God devised a very specific plan of conduct for men in marriage. However, this chapter just gives a general overview of the men's role to show how it blends harmoniously with the women's role. The first thing God requires of a men, many think is impossible:

A. UNDERSTAND THEIR WIVES

I Pet. 3:7: "You husbands likewise, live with your wives in an understanding way, as with a weaker vessel, since she is a woman; and grant her honor as a fellow-heir of the grace of life, so that your prayers may not be hindered."

In spite of many men exclaiming, "No one can understand a woman!" Peter tells husbands to live with their wives in an understanding way. Furthermore, if men refuse to make the effort to understand their wives, God won't hear their prayers. Men make their religion vain when they mistreat their wives.

The Bible abounds with female psychology. When husbands practice God's marriage instructions, they give supreme joy to their wives and bring out their better sides. At the same time, the husbands find satisfaction for their own needs.

While the emotional nature of women makes them appear complicated, in reality, they possess very simple desires: *They want to be appreciated and treated fairly.* As simple as this deep longing in women sounds, many husbands fail to satisfy it. Instead, they focus on their rights and mistakenly assume that they get to do everything their way and that their wives cannot object. This builds a barrier between husbands and wives because wives fear selfishness in their husbands more than anything else.

However, as the chapters on subjection and leadership show, God obligates husbands to manifest the attitude of always acting in the best interest of their wives. This means that the husbands may *never* get to do things their way. Thus, men who live with their wives according to knowledge overcome natural tendencies to think only of themselves. They treat their wives as team members who work *with them,* not as servants who work *for them.* This attitude balances the wives' subjection and turns it into a blessing for both husbands *and wives.*

Men may claim that they can't understand women, but they can. God commands that they apply their intelligence to discerning the marriage relationship and their wives. Just as God wants women to learn about marriage and to work at creating happy unions, He desires for men to do the same thing.

B. LEARN ABOUT SEXUAL LOVE

> **Prov. 5:1:** "My son, give attention to my wisdom, incline your ear to my understanding;..."

God, in His love for mankind, addresses three critical times in a man's sexual development. In each case, God shares the secrets for surviving these times as well as for reaping the most from the embrace of love.

For example, as young men begin to feel the first intense surges of sexual desire, God, through Solomon, warns them of the emptiness and the dangers of sexual intimacies based solely on techniques (Proverbs 7). Then God tells both men and women how to choose a lifelong sexual partner in the Song of Solomon.

> **Prov. 5:18-20:** "Let your fountain be blessed, and rejoice in the wife of your youth. As a loving hind and a graceful doe, let her breasts satisfy you at all times; be exhilarated always with her love. For why should you, my son, be exhilarated with an adulteress, and embrace the bosom of a foreigner?"

Finally, God alerts young men about another sexual danger awaiting them in middle age. He tells them to learn about it in their youth so that they can properly prepare to avoid it. Thus, in Proverbs 5, God teaches about the most dangerous time of all for husbands-- their middle years when their bodies start to slow down and they begin to look for youthful lovers to re- store their lost zest. God designed for middle-aged lovemaking to become the best sexual time of all for His people. But because of mankind's ignorance, many couples fail to reap all that God planned.

Over and over Solomon pleads with men to listen and to learn from his words rather than to sacrifice the happiness of their marriages for a few stolen, empty moments. Thus, Solomon strikes at the reluc- tance of men to learn about lovemaking and their ten- dency to leave the happiness of their love-lives up to chance or nature. Since God planned for husbands to be lovers all of their days, He provides the keys to sexual happiness in the Bible.

C. FAMILY ORIENTED

> Eccl. 9:9: "Enjoy life with the woman whom you love all the days of your fleeting life which He has given to you under the sun; for this is your reward in life, and in your toil in which you have labored under the sun."

The book of Ecclesiastes explores the various re- wards of life which men actively pursue on earth. It asks questions such as, "Does life consist of earning a lot of money or building an important name?" or "Is political power what makes life worthwhile?" or "Can the secret of happiness be in accumulating vast knowledge?" or "Does endless pleasure make life worth living?"

Over and over from various viewpoints, Solomon examines all of these questions. After personally ex- perimenting with each purpose for life, Solomon con- cludes that none of them give man any lasting happi- ness or sense of fulfillment. Instead, man's best re-

ward is to enjoy his ability to work and put food on
the table (Eccl. 5:18-19).

Then Solomon explains how men get so caught up
in their careers that they hardly notice their grandchildren. They even loose the capacity for enjoying the
simple pleasures of life. But God intends for men to
delight in their families--to be family oriented. In
fact, God created a wife to be a man's number-one reward in life. However, when men place their careers
ahead of their wives and children, then they turn their
backs on God's plan for them, and they fail to please
God.

V. GOD'S PLAN FOR MEN AND WOMEN

**Jer. 33:11: "...the voice of joy and the voice
of gladness, the voice of the bridegroom and
the voice of the bride, the voice of those
who say, 'Give thanks to the Lord of hosts,
for the Lord is good, for His lovingkindness
is everlasting'..."**

God choose the description of wedding joy and
gladness to explain to the Israelites how He would
bring blessings upon them once again. God wants husbands and wives to delight in each other and to live
together in harmony and love. To insure that they do,
He made plans for their lives. God in His wisdom designed a plan for older women, young women, and widows along with single women that gives them happiness. God's plan empowers them to use their influence
to bless everyone they come in contact with. Likewise,
God made plans for men. God wants men to learn how
to live with their wives and how to reap the most from
life.

God cares about husbands and wives and their
happiness. *God is family oriented, too.* In fact, God
loves His people so much that He gives the Bible for
everyone to study and to apply to their lives so that
they might find supreme marital love and joy. *The
question is, do God's people love themselves as much as
God loves them?* Do they love themselves enough to
study His word and to apply it to their lives so that
they might be truly happy? The question is, do you
love yourself as much as God loves you?

———

GENERAL INSTRUCTIONS FOR EXERCISES

Simply reading or listening to a lesson fails to supply the effort, sacrifice, and persistence that is necessary to implement God's word into one's life. Many people sit in classes and listen to lectures or read material such as this and give either mental assent or dissent. Yet mentally agreeing or disagreeing isn't the same as understanding. Opinions formed from merely listening to or reading material are often fuzzy and quickly forgotten.

On the other hand, stewing over questions and projects transforms cloudy concepts into concrete convictions. So to aid Bible students in reaping the most from these lessons and their marriages, thinking exercises are given at the end of each chapter for those students who are willing to toil for wisdom and happiness.

Not only do these projects help produce definite changes in the students' lives, but they also build self-confidence and self-respect. They assist the students in maintaining a positive outlook by focusing upon matters which they possess the power to change. This discourages the students from blaming their spouses for their marriages' shortcomings which is a major cause of depression. The more carefully the students perform these exercises, the greater the rewards they reap.

With the exception of the personal and goal-achieving exercises, all the homework should be turned in to the teachers. This helps teachers determine how effective their teaching is and encourages the students to do the assignments. This, in turn, crystallizes their thinking and develops better discernment and understanding. Doing the exercises may well make the difference between success or failure.

However, some of the less personal results of the personal and goal-achieving exercises can be discussed in class. Sharing ideas about how to apply the lessons to one's personal life motivates all the students to work harder.

This book is divided into four general solutions for solving problems. Then each solution is divided into four chapters. The study exercises for each solution are distributed among the chapters of that unit. The order of the exercises may vary between the four solutions. Each solution contains the following exercises:

Study Exercise: The students should answer these questions in their own words. Brief, concise answers should be the goal. However, sometimes students will want to elaborate on questions which have special meaning to them.

The last question gives the students a chance to disagree with anything taught in the chapter. The one stipulation, however, is that any disagreements must be based upon intelligent reasoning *instead of feelings.* So to insure that the reasons for disagreement are sound, the students are required to give scriptures to support their thinking.

Research Exercise: This drill enables the students to use the basic truths learned in the lesson to analyze the lives of Bible men and women. These exercises guide the students into a deeper study of various subjects and cover Biblical examples not discussed in the chapters of this book.

Personal Exercise: This activity aids the students in analyzing their own lives with the help of the scriptures. Since everyone has blind spots, this exercise helps the students be honest with themselves. The exercise also suggests ways the students can apply the principles taught to their individual lives.

Problem-Solving Exercise: This practice centers around newspaper articles to acquaint the students with real-life situations that they may encounter when trying to help others. Sometimes the articles are paraphrased to protect the original copyright, but the facts are true. This exercise develops the students' skills for using the Bible to solve common problems and for impressing upon their minds how practical a guide the Bible is for twentieth-century problems.

Goal-Achieving Exercise: This exercise helps the students implement the principles learned into everyday habits. The project is designed to focus the students' minds upon the changes that need to be made in their personal lives while making definite plans for achieving those goals. The goals should be measurable or something that can be seen so that the students will know when they attain them, and thus earn self-respect and esteem. Goals should also be realistic ones which the students have the ability to achieve.

By writing these goals down, thinking through different methods of accomplishing them, and then following a plan of action, the students enjoy maximum success in making lasting changes in their lives. If necessary, the students can also make a chart for each day with squares to check when they finish their projects. If they don't make a chart, they should at least look at their written goals and plans every day and pray about them.

Special Notebook: The students should keep a loose-leaf notebook for their projects and exercises so that they can refer to them from time to time.

———

STUDY EXERCISE

Answer all questions in your own words.

1. What is the difference between an older woman and a young woman?

2. Which older women does Tit. 2:3-5 apply to?

3. How important is it for the older women to teach the young women? Do you want to do this job when you become an older woman? Why?

4. What three things does God want older women to do? Give an example of each.

5. What three things does God want young women to do? Give an example of each.

6. What three things does God want widows and single women to do? Give an example of each.

7. What three things does God want men to do? Give an example of each.

8. How important do you think it is for men and women to follow God's plan for their lives? Explain in detail.

9. Do you disagree with anything in this lesson? If so, explain in detail giving scriptures for your reasons.

GOAL-ACHIEVING EXERCISE

Change the following points to fit your individual needs. Review this exercise as you study the next three chapters and make additions as necessary.

Purpose: To begin learning God's rules for marriage and to develop wisdom.

Goals:
1. To develop good study habits.
2. To be able to open the Bible and find basic scriptures relating to marriage.
3. To learn to pray effectively.

Priorities:
1. Forget hobbies for a few months to concentrate on goals.
2. Perhaps give up bowling or a club to have more time to study, etc.
3. Set aside some time each day to read the scriptures from your own Bible. Be sure to use a translation, not a paraphrase which gives someone's commentary instead of God's words.
4. Set aside some time each day to reflect on your attitudes and to be honest with yourself. Use this time to pray to God concerning your discoveries about yourself.

Plans:
1. Pray upon rising for strength to accomplish the goals that you have set for the day.
2. Use the children's nap time to look up all the scriptures discussed in class and to work on the work sheets.
3. Pray every night before going to bed.

CHAPTER 2

SOLVING ALL MARRIAGE PROBLEMS

The institution of marriage is one of the most widely criticized and shaky relationships in existence. Its reputation is so bad that many couples choose to live together without marriage. They fear that a legal, binding union will destroy their happiness. Of those getting married, many leave "until death do we part" out of their vows. The ever-increasing divorce rate, even among older couples, and the confusion about the male-female roles makes the future for marriage look bleak.

Many ask the question, "Is it possible to be married and happy at the same time?" Some women say, "No," and publish books on how to obtain a cheap divorce. They even print guidelines on how to prevent husbands from exploiting their wives. But God says, "Yes," and inspired a book to reveal the secrets of marital happiness--the Bible.

In fact, God provides a formula for *solving every marriage problem*. Now, that's not the same as saying a formula for *saving every marriage*. God doesn't guarantee that every marriage can be saved. For example, in Mt. 19:9 God allows divorce because of fornication. Thus, God acknowledges that some marriages *cannot* be saved in the case of adultery.

When someone, of his own free will, habitually walks in adultery, his intellect and feelings become so warped that he can no longer be reasoned with (Hos. 4:11; Prov. 5:20-22). For that reason, adultery presents the most difficult marriage problem of all to solve. In that case, the marriage problem *can be solved* by a scriptural divorce. Yet even in the case of adultery, some couples manage to save their marriages. As those couples determine what went wrong and make a new commitment to each other, they strengthen their bonds and the marriage becomes better than ever. *So while God doesn't guarantee that every marriage can be saved, He does guarantee that every marriage problem can be solved when His formula is followed.* All that remains is for God's people to learn the formula and to diligently apply it to their own lives.

I. GOD'S PLAN FOR MARRIAGE

I Tim. 4:1-3: "But the Spirit explicitly says that in later times some will fall away from the faith, paying attention to deceitful spirits and doctrines of demons, by means of the hypocrisy of liars seared in their own conscience as with a branding iron, men who forbid marriage and advocate abstaining from foods,..."

"Conscience" means "the soul as distinguished between what is morally good and bad, prompting to do the former and shun the latter, commending the one, condemning the other, conscience" (Thayer, p. 602).

"Forbid" means "(properly to cut off, cut short, hence) to hinder, prevent, forbid, to withhold a thing from any one, i.e. to deny or refuse one a thing" (Thayer, p. 366).

At the beginning of an important discussion about marriage, God, through the Holy Spirit, guided Paul to forewarn Christians that people would come teaching against the plain truths of the Bible. The teachings of these messengers of the devil would be so convincing that many would fall away from the faith or the word of God by believing deceitful lies about marriage. God cautions Christians not to believe the popular philosophies that degrade marriage because such teachings serve as a powerful tool of Satan.

In fact, false teaching concerning marriage can potentially do more harm than any other false teaching that Satan might devise. For example, Satan fills the world with false religions and doctrines that claim to be governed by the Bible. Yet in reality, they deny the wisdom of God by substituting man's opinions for God's divinely inspired words. In spite of this, many people study themselves out of the ignorance of false religions and grasp the true doctrinal teachings of the Bible.

But Satan owns another effective tool for destroying those who would trust God in spiritual matters-- marital discord and unhappiness. Marital misery saps the physical, mental, and spiritual energy of both men and women. Problems at home often hinder an individual's ability to think clearly. If Satan can just sow the seeds for marital disunity, it won't really matter if men and women believe the truth or a falsehood concerning baptism, the organization of the church, life after death, etc. Even when a person keeps himself doctrinally pure, if he pollutes his marriage with deceitful lies, he fails to please God. He cheats himself out of the marital blessings which God designed to reflect His wisdom. And he neglects to serve God with all his heart, mind, and body.

Indeed, many of the philosophies concerning marriage are deceitful because they claim to promote happiness while in reality they make it impossible for men and women to enjoy true marital bliss. Satan successfully uses marriage untruths and false practices to captivate people who try to practice and proclaim the whole counsel of God as revealed in the Bible.

Satan's messengers of discord lead others astray by the use of the hypocrisy of liars. "Hypocrite" originally referred to a play actor who pretended to be something he was not for the benefit of an audience. Paul warns Christians not to listen to people who pretend to be something they are not or who profess to know all the answers when their personal lives show otherwise.

Many people who teach untruths concerning marriage display a certain fulfillment and happiness. Often they don't even recognize their own hypocrisy because they are "seared in their own conscience as with a branding iron." In other words, the minds of these people no longer function properly to enable them to discern the full, complete truth in regard to marriage. Not only do they deceive others, but they are full of self-deceit.

Only a conscience educated with the truth concerning right and wrong serves as a proper guide. A person's conscience makes him feel good when he does what *he thinks is right* and makes him feel bad when he does what *he thinks is wrong.* So when a person fills his conscience with untruths and deceitful teachings, his conscience fails to warn him when he does evil. On the other hand, when a person continually fills his mind with the word of God, his conscience pricks him when he starts to stray from what he knows to be the truth.

Every time a person disregards what he knows to be right, he sears his conscience by developing scar tissue. This makes his thinking numb in that particular area. The next time he commits the same sin, his conscience causes him less pain than before. Thus, each time a person violates his conscience, he destroys part of his ability to think clearly and rationally. Eventually his conscience fails to function at all. Only when a person educates his conscience with the word of God and never violates it, does it become a safe guide for conduct.

A normal person wouldn't even consider listening to the advice of a person in an insane asylum who claims to possess the keys of life. Obviously, that's ridiculous! Yet to listen to the teachings and counsel of someone whose conscience is not based on God's law and who can no longer distinguish good from bad is just as foolish.

False teachings concerning marriage and the eating of certain foods began even before the apostles completed writing the New Testament in the form of Gnosticism. The gnostics believed in a separation of body and spirit and viewed the body as evil and the spirit as ultimately good. To them, anything that the body desired was evil. Thus, the gnostics slept on beds of spikes, avoided eating foods that they enjoyed, and turned their backs on certain aspects of marriage which satisfied their physical bodies.

A few centuries after the writing of the New Testament, these teachings emerged again through the church fathers of Roman Catholicism who forced "voluntary" celibacy on nuns and priests. They even denied married couples the right to use the sexual union as an expression of love by declaring it sinful, even in marriage. *Vol. II: Learning to Love* devotes chapter 2, "Mankind's Abuses of Sexual Love," to tracing this sad period of history and shows how it applies specifically to I Timothy 4. The next chapter, "The Victims of Victorian Morals," goes into detail about the harmful effects upon men, women, and children of these particular false teachings.

Unfortunately, these teachings aren't unique with either of these groups. Modern philosophers once again take a firm stand against marriage. Today, living with someone outside of marriage or raising children out of wedlock or ranting and raving publicly against the so-called evils of marriage is considered popular and smart.

Yet such teachings do not come from true intelligence, but are the doctrines of demons. Such dogmas serve Satan's purpose by ridiculing the wisdom of God. God created marriage and ordained the proper way for a man and woman to function together. God makes certain claims for marriage when mankind follows His counsel and rejects Satan's:

A. GRATEFULLY SHARE IN MARRIAGE

> **I Tim. 4:3: "...which God created to be gratefully shared in by those who believe and know the truth."**

"Believe" means "easily persuaded, believing, confiding, trusting" (Thayer, p. 514).

"Know" means "1. to become thoroughly acquainted with, to know thoroughly, to know accurately, know well; 2. universally to know; a. to recognize; c. to know i.e. to find out, ascertain; d. to know i.e. to understand" (Thayer, p. 237).

"Truth" means "verity, truth; 1. universally what is true in any matter under consideration (opposed to what is feigned, fictitious, false); 2. what is true in things appertaining to God and the duties of men" (Thayer, p. 26).

Anyone who wants to gratefully share in marriage and foods must do two things: First, *he must believe in God*. He must demonstrate his confidence in God, his Creator, by guiding his life by the word of God instead of allowing his own opinions or those of others to influence his thinking and actions. Belief is not a passive feeling of ignorance, but an intelligent, active submission of one's actions to God because of confident trust in His wisdom.

For example, a person may claim to have faith in his doctor. However, if he lets his doctor remove splinters from his fingers, but refuses to allow his doctor to do open heart surgery on him, he does not have complete faith in the skill and wisdom of his doctor.

The same holds true for a person who claims to believe God in doctrinal matters, but rejects some of God's teachings concerning men, women, marriage, or foods. He does not really have complete faith or confidence in the wisdom of God. He plays the part of a hypocrite--pretending to believe God when actually he only obeys God when he wants to and rejects God when God's will disagrees with his personal opinion. Just giving mental assent to God's teachings is not the same as believing in God. Obeying *all* of God's regulations out of allegiance to God is true belief in God.

Many a woman delights in God's commandment to the husband to love his wife as his own body by honoring, cherishing, and nourishing her. However, God's commandments for the wife test her faith in God. She must make a deliberate choice to either obey or disobey laws concerning her life. The way a husband or wife conducts his married life tells the world just how much he trusts and believes in God because most of God's teachings concerning marriage demand a change in the life of the average person.

The person who truly believes in God determines to do *everything* that God commands in *every area* of life, whether in the spiritual or the family realm. No amount of public claims of belief and confidence in the God of heaven undoes rejection of the same God in the home.

Second, a person who wants to gratefully share in marriage *must know the truth.* "Know" and "truth" involve precise concepts. Faith must rest upon accurate knowledge. God doesn't want anyone blindly following Him. Rather, He expects all of His people to choose for themselves to follow Him because of an intelligent examination of spiritual facts.

Heb. 11:1 says the same thing: "Now faith is the assurance of things hoped for, the conviction of things not seen." Faith is confidence or assurance that what one hopes for will come about. Rather than being a blind feeling, faith responds to a conviction of the intellect. "Conviction" means "a proof, that by which a thing is proved or tested, conviction" (Thayer, p. 202). Thus, faith results from an intelligent examination of the Bible.

In order for intelligence to lead to faith, a person must use accurate, precise information about the will of God to guide his life. Personal opinions, prejudices, and desires cannot be substituted. Many people falsely assume that following God multiplies problems, but it is the personal opinions, prejudices, and self-centered desires which others pass off as God's laws that cause misery and unhappiness.

People who *know God's will* and *who confidently trust His wisdom* gratefully share in marriage and in all foods. A woman who walks according to the revealed will of God can rejoice with her husband, enjoy her children, be a creative homemaker, and find fulfillment in her feminine nature. Likewise, living according to true knowledge frees a man to enjoy providing for his family, to love and protect his wife and children, and to find fulfillment in his masculinity.

B. ACCEPT GOD'S CREATION

I Tim. 4:4: "For everything [every creature— KJV] created by God is good,..."

"Everything" or "every creature" means "thing founded, created thing" (Thayer, p. 363).

"Good" means "beautiful, handsome, excellent, eminent, choice, surpassing, precious, useful, suitable, commendable, admirable, good, excellent in its nature and characteristics, and therefore well-adapted to its end, genuine, approved, precious" (Thayer, p. 322).

The King James Bible causes some confusion about this verse because it translates "everything" with "every creature." However, as the definition shows, the word simply means a "thing founded" or a "created thing" which applies equally to marriage and all types of food. Both marriage and food originated within the mind of God to supply special needs of men and women. Also, the context shows that Paul discusses *both* forbidding to marry and abstaining from foods.

"Good!" What a word to describe the marriage relationship! But only people who believe and know the truth about marriage can wholeheartedly support God's declaration. For example, how many times do people say publicly, "Marriage is great! My husband is wonderful! I sure enjoy my kids!"? Instead, many times older women chastise younger women with, "Why do you want to get married? Who needs men? You don't know how lucky you are to be single!" Such comments reveal the speaker's failure to gratefully sharing in a relationship that God created to be good. These women demonstrate a lack of faith in God and a refusal to obey the word of God.

Too many God-fearing people take their marriages lightly. They frequently give up instead of looking to God when they encounter marriage problems. When Christians, who claim to believe in God, allow their marriages to exist in a rundown state of ill feelings and mistreatment of their spouses and children, they curse the God of heaven just as much as if evil language poured from their lips because God ordained the marriage relationship and pronounced it "good."

The world hears these foul sermons. In fact, the world has listened to these vile speeches for so long that people in general think of marriage as a problem-filled institution with little happiness for the participants. Christians need to realize that others make judgments about God and the Bible by looking at the ones who claim to live according to the Bible. Frequently, outsiders don't bother to examine the Bible to see if the Christians are really guiding their lives by the word of God or by their personal opinions.

C. DON'T REJECT MARRIAGE

> I Tim. 4:4: "...and nothing is to be rejected, if it is received with gratitude:..."

"Rejected" means "to be thrown away, rejected, despised, abominated" (Thayer, p. 60).

Those who know the truth must not reject God's plan for men and women. Rather, God wants them to follow His instructions with gratitude or thankfulness in their hearts. Some people say they don't reject marriage, but neither do they receive it with gratefulness. They gripe and complain continually about marriage or their spouses. They have nothing good to say.

Some people find it hard to count their marital blessings because they fail to understand the mechanics of marriage. Blessings cannot be counted in any realm of life where the person doesn't know anything about the subject. In fact, a person can't even properly appreciate material possessions if he doesn't know how to use them or how to care for them.

An older woman told about a neighbor who many years ago received a silver teapot for a wedding gift. The neighbor did not know that silver turns black when exposed to the air or that tarnished silver can be restored to its original luster with polish. The neighbor let her teapot sit out until it turned coal black. Then, thinking that it was ruined, she threw the teapot away. Only after it was too late did she ask someone how to care for silver.

In a similar manner, a person does not enjoy doing something he cannot do well. For example, a woman who thoroughly enjoys sewing knows how to sew well. She eagerly takes classes and examines ready-made garments to learn new sewing methods. She talks about sewing with her friends and reads magazine articles to increase her knowledge. Then when her non-sewing friends look at the beautiful creations she makes, they marvel that a home seamstress turned out such professional looking garments.

Yet many another woman rarely uses her machine because sewing gives her little or no pleasure. When asked if she ever took a sewing class, she answers, "No." Obviously, this woman could learn to make quality garments and find personal gratification when she realizes that the problem is not with sewing, but with her lack of understanding and skill.

A woman who knows nothing about football doesn't enjoy watching the games with her husband. She may even resent the time he spends in front of the television and feel that he neglects her. However, her husband understands all the different plays and probably even played the game in school. People appreciate only the sports that they understand.

Likewise, when a man's new car fails to run properly, he doesn't take it to the junkyard. Since the car
comes with a guarantee, he takes it to an authorized
mechanic for repair. A man who is particular doesn't
wait for something to go wrong. Instead, he thoroughly
inspects his new car to find everything, no matter how
small, that needs repair. He doesn't hesitate to hound
the dealer until he fixes every item according to the
warranty. Then he follows the maintenance suggestions
to the letter to keep his new car in top running order.

Even feminists who hate housework know that the
woman who threw away her teapot because it turned
black made a bad mistake. Seamstresses know it's
ridiculous to discard a sewing machine as being no
good because a woman can't read a pattern. Sports
fans aren't impressed when a wife condemns the recre-
ational values of watching football because she
doesn't know the difference between a fumble and a
foul. Mechanics know that sane people don't drive a
car off a cliff just because a tire goes flat or the oil
needs changing.

Yet illogical thinking that sensible people reject in
every other realm of life is applied by otherwise
intelligent people to the most intimate and important
relationship on earth--that of husband and wife. Normally rational individuals, who would never even consider throwing away their sewing machines or cars because they did not know how to operate and maintain
them, are quick to blame the whole institution of marriage and throw away their marriages through divorce
or emotional withdrawal when they encounter problems.
Why?

Just as sewing machines and cars function according to definite laws of physics, chemistry, and
mathematics, marriages generate blessings from God
only when the spouses understand and practice divine
laws of marital harmony, productivity, and fulfillment.

Sadly, many people endure horrible problems simply
because they do not know the first principles of being
a wife or a husband. They don't have the foggiest idea
how to solve a problem so that it strengthens the
marriage instead of weakening it. They fail to acquaint
themselves with the daily actions and attitudes that
keep a chosen spouse deeply in love with them. As
the previous verse states, marriages can be gratefully

shared in *only by those who believe and know the truth* in regard to the marriage relationship.

II. GOD'S SANCTIFICATION OF MARRIAGE

I Tim. 4:5: "...for it is sanctified by means of the word of God and prayer."

"Sanctified" means "rendered or declared sacred or holy, consecrated; 1. rendered or acknowledged to be venerable, hallowed; 2. separated from things profane and dedicated to God, consecrated and so rendered inviolable" (Thayer, p. 6).

"Sanctify" basically means "to set apart from others for special use." Happy, sanctified marriages are set apart from broken and unhappy unions. As the divorce rate steadily increases, few of the people staying married really enjoy their marriage relationship. A recent announcement in the newspaper said that during the last three months more people in the city of Spokane filed a petition for divorce than got marriage licenses. Certainly, anyone who gratefully shares in marriage is set apart or obvious to all.

After declaring that God created marriages to be good, God gives the key for solving every marriage problem that arises. A marriage can be a success when all others are failures if a person follows this simple formula: (1) He must pattern his marriage after the word of God. (2) He must engage in frequent prayer.

A. THE WORD OF GOD SANCTIFIES

Too many Christians underestimate the power of the word of God. When problems arise, they buy popular marriage manuals and try one philosophy after another. Many look to the women's liberation movement to find the missing contentment in their lives. But the answers for which they desperately search are found in nearly every home--in the Bible.

God didn't inspire the Bible to provide a place for recording marriages, births, and deaths, but to guide Christians in their everyday lives. God created a flawless union for husbands and wives and designed a perfect environment for them to raise their children.

Then He wrote the Bible to reveal the secrets that keep homes functioning smoothly and happily.

When a man or a woman tries to make it on his own without thought or consideration for God, he practices the height of folly as recorded by David:

> **Ps. 33:11-15: "The counsel of the Lord stands forever, the plans of His heart from generation to generation. Blessed is the nation whose God is the Lord, the people whom He has chosen for His own inheritance. The Lord looks from heaven; He sees all the sons of men; from His dwelling-place He looks out on all the inhabitants of the earth, He who fashions the hearts of them all, He who understands all their works."**

"Fashions" means "(through the squeezing into shape), to mould into a form, especially as a potter, figuratively to determine (i.e. form a resolution)" (Strong, p. 51). Isa. 45:9 uses this same word to describe fashioning clay.

"Hearts" means "the heart, also used (figuratively) very widely for the feelings, the will and even the intellect, likewise for the *centre* of anything" (Strong, p. 58).

The nature of the human mind which God fashioned testifies to the marvelous wisdom of God. While men design electronic brains, computers cannot begin to compare with the brains which God places within men and women. In 1960 Maxwell Maltz recorded in his book *Psycho-Cybernetics* some of the functions of the brain as compared to computers of that day:

> Just how a mechanism as small as the human brain can store such a vast amount of information is still a mystery. British neurophysicist W. Grey Walter has said that at least ten billion electronic cells would be needed to build a facsimile of man's brain. These cells would occupy about a million and a half cubic feet, and several additional millions of cubic feet would be needed for the

'nerves' or wiring. Power required to operate it would be one billion watts....

Dr. Wiener has said that at no time in the foreseeable future will scientists be able to construct an electronic brain anywhere near comparable to the human brain. "I think that our gadget-conscience public has shown a lack of awareness of the special advantages and special disadvantages of electronic machinery, as compared with the human brain," he says. "The number of switching devices in the human brain vastly exceeds the number in any computing machine yet developed, or even thought of for design in the near future."

But even should such a machine be built, it would lack an "operator." A computer does not have a forebrain, nor an "I." It cannot pose problems to itself. It has no imagination and cannot set goals for itself. It cannot determine which goals are worthwhile and which are not. It has no emotions. It cannot "feel." It works only on new data fed to it by an operator, by feedback data it secures from its own "sense organs" and from information previously stored.[1]

More than twenty-seven years later, the brain's compact size and capabilities still remain a marvel of marvels. Even with today's technology and microchips, modern man still falls way short of duplicating God's ingenuous design. God knows more about the feelings, desires, needs, and intellect of men and women than the brightest philosopher would ever know if he lived and studied a thousand years. Not only does God know how minds function, but He also understands all the happenings on earth, whether good or bad, and what their effects will be on mankind. God, alone is the supreme expert on what men and women need to find happiness and fulfillment.

[1]Maxwell Maltz, *Psycho-Cybernetics* (New York: Pocket Books, 1960), pp. 22-24.

This divine ability gives God unrivaled qualifications to outline courses of action for men and women that will "stand forever." The Bible's rules for human interaction remain steadfast from generation to generation, from Adam and Eve to the twentieth century to the fortieth century. The same keys that sanctified the marriages of the great-great-great grandparents of today's couples still unlock the secrets of marital bliss.

No human being even begins to compete with the magnitude of God's insight and inherent ability to counsel men and women about their daily lives. Thus, Solomon sums it up:

Prov. 20:24: "Man's steps are ordained by the Lord, how then can man understand his way?"

"Steps" means "a step, figuratively companionship:--going, step" (Strong, p. 71). It comes from a root word which means "to pace, i.e. step regularly, (upward) to mount, (along) to march, (down and causing) to hurl" (Strong, p. 100).

"Understand" means "to separate mentally (or distinguish), i.e. (generally) understand" (Strong, p. 31).

A genius might choose to become an expert in any number of sciences that relate to human life. Yet the best he can ever do, regardless of how many degrees he accumulates or how many Nobel prizes he wins, seems but a superficial attempt at acquiring complete knowledge about his chosen field.

For example, medical scientists readily admit that they know very little about the chemistry and function of the human body. By chance doctors discovered aspirin from witch doctors in Africa who used it as a heart medicine. Aspirin is still a valuable tool for treating certain heart problems, but with all of man's modern research laboratories, doctors still do not know why aspirin works. Recently, doctors discovered that the common aspirin may cause birth defects when taken during the first two months of pregnancy. Who knows what scientists will learn about the aspirin's effects upon the mind and body in the future.

Today, farmers earn baccalaureate and doctorate degrees in agriculture; yet the ground they cultivate still remains largely a mystery to them. In recent years environmentalists became concerned about the effects of chemicals upon the soil, water, atmosphere, and animals and plants which provide food for humans. In addition, manufacturers often argue about what constitutes safe methods of food processing. Producing and packaging food is not a precise science in which all the answers are known.

Many people look to psychology for answers to their problems. In spite of so many college graduates doing research about the human mind, the experts are the first to admit that the mind still contains many puzzles for them.

For example, in her article "The Private Language of Marriage," Anne Roiphe expressed hope that some day counselors would fully understand the laws and ways of marriage. Roiphe lamented that with all of man's knowledge about the personality and the unconscious and conscious mind, man still did not really know the basic keys for saving marriages. She summed up modern marriage counselling as being not much better than "reading tea leaves or dancing to ward off evil spirits."[2]

Nor does a later statement by a leading Harvard psychiatrist, Robert Coles, promote confidence in the field of psychology. He admitted in an interview for *TIME* that the mental health experts cannot accurately determine whether or not a patient is sane or insane or even if they themselves are acting wisely or as fools "whistling in the dark."[3]

All this uncertainty stems from the fact that psychology continually changes with each generation as standards and beliefs change with the current morals and philosophies about life. For example, modern psychologists disagree about whether or not a healthy or a sick mind produces homosexuality. Likewise, psychologists debate about whether parents should spank their children or indulge them when they misbehave. Furthermore, the experts of the mind admit that they do not have concrete rules of conduct from

[2]Anne Roiphe, "The Private Language of Marriage," *Mc-Call's* (2/74).
[3]"Mental Health," *Time* (4/12/76), p. 24.

which to determine if someone is sensibly troubled or
utterly irrational,

Modern psychology grew up out of confusion from
the way Freud conducted his experiments. Freud laid
down many of the foundation principles still used today by randomly choosing and ignoring data:

> As Brill described Freud's procedure with
> patients, "He persuaded them to give up all
> conscious reflection, abandon themselves to
> calm concentration, follow their spontaneous
> mental occurrences, and impart everything to
> him. In this way he finally obtained those
> *free associations* which lead to the origin of
> the symptoms." The forgotten material, dredged
> up by the subject out of his unconscious, after
> perhaps months of psychoanalytical treatment,
> usually represents something painful, disagree-
> able, frightening, or otherwise obnoxious out of
> his past, matters he dislikes to remember con-
> sciously.
>
> Inevitably, in such a process, the rambling
> reminiscences produce a mass of diffuse,
> irrelevant, and apparently useless data. Every-
> thing, therefore, depends upon the ability of
> the physician to psychoanalyze this material,
> which, as various critics have pointed out, can
> be interpreted in an almost infinite number of
> ways. The intelligence and skill of the psy-
> choanalyst, therefore, are of basic signifi-
> cance.[4]

Freud formed his conclusions by choosing and
picking what *seemed important to him* and disregarding
what *seemed unimportant to him*. This is not an accurate nor scientific method of gathering data nor a reliable way of drawing conclusions. Biographers reveal
that Freud harbored prejudice against religion and
founded many of his psychological beliefs upon the
theory that mankind evolved from an animal:

[4]Robert B. Downs, *Books That Changed the World* (New
York: New American Library, 1956), p. 180.

That Freud thought little of religion in general and less of Christianity in particular is a historical fact. He called himself "a completely godless Jew" and a "hopeless pagan." When he was a child, some supposed Christians pushed his father around and muddied his clothes. The elder man did not retaliate. Freud was ashamed and thought his father should have fought back. He vowed that some day he would get even. In the eyes of some, psychoanalysis was the weapon he used.

Freud's *Moses and Monotheism, The Future of an Illusion*, and *Totem and Taboo* are books in which he gives religion a hard time. For him, Christianity was an illusion that had to be dispelled. Like all other religions, it was a sign of neurosis. Religion, he taught, was born out of the fear of the great untamed universe surrounding primitive man. At first there was no such thing as moral scruples. But since every man wanted to follow his own wishes (instinct), he clashed with others trying to do the same. In order to survive, men found it necessary to live and work together. Thus morality was the outcome of the growth of society, which could exist only by adopting codes of conduct. Conscience (the Superego) was built up because violations of the code were punished severely by the crowd. Eventually the code was said to be sanctioned by a god (or gods), thus raising the moral code in stature. Religion belongs to the infancy of the race. Man needs to grow up out of infancy, and that means out of religion. He calls the biblical accounts "fairy tales." Religion was invented he claimed, to fulfill man's needs. When one comes of age, he no longer needs religion. Before adopting Freudian principles, Christians should know these basic Freudian presuppositions which underlie all he wrote.[5]

---

[5]Jay E. Adams, *Competent to Counsel* (Grand Rapids, MI: Baker Book House, 1970), pp. 15-16.

While many modern psychologists and psychiatrists disown Freud, many of them still base their own concepts about human nature on a denial of the existence of God and a rejection of personal responsibility for sin. For instance, alcohol treatment centers usually frown on condemning the habit as a sin. Many use drugs to produce physically horrifying experiences when the patients drink alcohol. Supposedly, this helps motivate their patients to abhor drinking.

In addition, modern psychologists still do not have very accurate or rigidly controlled methods for testing a man's mind. Only time determines the effects of different environments upon several generations of humans. In contrast, physicists and chemists conduct their experiments with precise measurements of elements in a constant, well-defined set of tests. This enables them to either prove or disprove their theories beyond any shadow of doubt. Psychologists cannot do this.

In reality, psychology is a bewildering course of study for anyone to undertake. Many college professors simply present the different philosophies to their students and tell them to choose whichever viewpoint they like best. Some professors even encourage their students to disagree and argue with them because the classes are based upon assumptions rather than proven facts.

These wavering dogmas of the psychologists can cause a lot of damage to men and women because, more often than not, the errors in them are not discovered until a whole generation of people has been emotionally handicapped. A generation of neurotics is a high price to pay for the privilege of psychiatric research.

Therefore, the wise person compares the advice of a psychologist with the teachings of the Bible. Paul cautions Christians: "See to it that no one take you captive through philosophy and empty deception, according to the tradition of men, according to the elementary principles of the world, rather than according to Christ" (Col. 2:8). In other words, anytime what man says conflicts with what God says, the intelligent person rejects man's philosophies, traditions, and elementary principles as "empty deception."

For example, a woman went to a psychologist because she was on the verge of a nervous breakdown because of marital problems. The counselor told her to forget her husband and to think only of herself. As a result, the woman didn't have a nervous breakdown, but she became so selfish and so self-willed that for years she endured unbelievably terrible marriage problems. Finally, through Biblical teaching, the woman realized the sinfulness of her attitudes, and she began disciplining herself into becoming a more loving, understanding, and submissive wife. Within a short time, her marriage problems disappeared and she discovered what a wonderful, thoughtful, and loving husband she had. Even now, years later, she says, "I still have to fight some of the selfish attitudes that psychologist encouraged me to develop to protect my ego."

Man knows relatively little about himself or his mind even if he is an expert in his chosen field. The fact that many people disregard what God says in favor of a psychologist's opinion makes this principle important. *Even a renowned psychologist needs the guidance of his Creator!*

On the other hand, the works of *some* psychologists verify the reliability of God's commands to men and women for guiding their daily lives. Psychologists can also treat certain organic disorders of the mind just as medical doctors heal certain organic problems of the body. However, choosing an ill-qualified doctor may result only in the loss of one's life whereas choosing the wrong psychologist may result in the loss of one's soul.

When it comes to solving marriage problems, only the word of God provides a dependable source of information. Thus, the first part of the formula for solving all marriage problems is to go to the word of God to learn the truth about marriage. Paul says the next logical step is to go to God in prayer for help to practice the learned truth:

B. PRAYER SANCTIFIES A MARRIAGE

"Prayer" (*enteuxis*) means "a falling in with, meeting with, an interview, coming together, that for which an interview is held, a conference or conversation, a petition, supplication" (Thayer, p. 218).

Several different Greek words are translated "prayer" and each carries a different idea. I Tim. 2:1 presents an excellent example as it lists four different kinds of prayers that should be made on the behalf of all men. In this passage Paul urges that "entreaties" (*densis*) and "prayers" (*proseuche*), "petitions" (*enteuxis*) and "thanksgivings" (*eucharistias*) be made. Thayer gives a summary of these prayers and shows their differences:

> In I Tim. 2:1 to these two words is added *enteuxis,* which expresses confiding access to God; thus, in combination, *densis* [translated both prayer and entreaties--PRD] gives prominence to the expression of personal need, *proseuche* [translated prayer--PRD] to the element of devotion, *enteuxis* [translated prayer and petitions and used in I Tim. 4:5--PRD] to that of childlike confidence, by representing prayer as the heart's converse with God. (Thayer, p. 126)

A fourth kind of prayer, *eucharistias* (translated prayer and thanksgiving), means "the giving of thanks" (Thayer, p. 264).

The word translated "prayer" in I Tim. 4:5 (as part of the sanctification of marriage) and "petitions" in I Tim. 2:2, *enteuxis,* is not the usual word for prayer since it occurs as a noun in only these two passages. The word is used only six times as a verb in the New Testament. Studying the verb form of *enteuxis* helps shed light on exactly what this type of prayer involves:

Two examples use the verb form of *enteuxis* in situations where something bad is reported about someone else: "Elijah...*pleads* with God against Israel" (Rom. 11:2) and Festus told King Agrippa that "the Jews *appealed* to me, both at Jerusalem and here, loudly declaring that he [Paul--PRD] ought not to live any longer" (Acts 25:24).

The remaining passages translate the verb form of *enteuxis* with "intercede" and show how the the Holy Spirit and Jesus pray for Christians: "And in the same way the Spirit also helps our weakness; for we do not know how to pray [*proseuche*] as we should, but the

Spirit Himself *intercedes* for us with groanings too deep for words; and He who searches the hearts knows what the mind of the Spirit is, because He *intercedes* for the saints according to the will of God" (Rom. 8:26-27); "Christ Jesus is He who died, yes, rather who was raised, who is at the right hand of God, who also *intercedes* for us" (Rom. 8:34); and Heb. 7:25 says that Jesus makes *intercession* for Christians.

Each of the above examples show the "interview" quality of *enteuxis* or a coming face to face with another to discuss a problem. This can be seen the easiest in the verses discussing how the Holy Spirit and Jesus intercede or pray for Christians by representing them before God as they really are. As Paul says, a person often doesn't know how to pray as he should, so the Holy Spirit steps in and prays for those things that he needs "according to the will of God." The groanings of the Holy Spirit are too deep for human words, but God understands them. Jesus, at the right hand of God, also prays for what is best for Christians.

What a wonderful blessing that Christians enjoy-- two divine beings who understand them better than they understand themselves and who plead their cases before God. Just as parents lookout for the needs of their children and don't give them everything they desire, the Holy Spirit and Jesus lookout for the needs of Christians.

In a similar manner, God wants Christians to intercede with Him through this same type of prayer for all men including kings and all in authority, "in order that we may live a tranquil and quiet life in all godliness and dignity" (I Tim. 2:1-2). When a Christian sees someone else's need which that person doesn't necessarily recognize, he should intercede on that person's behalf by praying for him. For example, Christians might pray for the government to pass laws promoting capital punishment to help curtail crime, legislation which the politicians often oppose due to their lack of knowledge concerning God's demand for respect of life.

If a person wants to enjoy a sanctified marriage that is better than the marriages of the world, he must make this type of prayer in his own behalf. This prayer requires that he engage in a personal interview with God, laying himself open to God's cleansing power. It is not the kind of interview a person often has with a prospective employer where he tries to make himself look as good as possible by covering up his faults. Before this prayer becomes beneficial, it must be an *honest* inquiry into the attitudes and emotions which prevent a man or a woman from fully enjoying marriage.

As a person studies the word of God and finds areas in his life that fail to measure up to God's standards, he should earnestly ask for God's help to get rid of the sinful attitudes and feelings. But when he discovers a few negative feelings, he *must not* assume that he has succeeded in reforming himself and stop his search. This word for prayer *implies deep mental house cleaning which completely reveals a person as he really is with no feelings left unexamined.* Therefore, to succeed, a person must press onward and inward relentlessly until he exposes *every* hostile and irrational emotion and attitude that he harbors.

Often little bits of information that a person picked up during childhood haunt him during adulthood as they unconsciously influence his actions. For example, if a woman grew up in a home where her father frequently struck her mother, she may live in constant fear of her husband hitting her, even though the likelihood is remote. On the other hand, a man who grew up in the same type of home may think that a man should strike a woman occasionally. As they both learn the truth about how God wants a man to treat a woman, they must rid themselves of sinful responses to each other.

Deeply buried within the subconscious, false feelings and conceptions about marriage cause men and women to misinterpret everyday happenings. *Emotions founded upon untruths cause the majority of problems that men and women face in the marriage relationship.* Therefore, if a person did not grow up in a home patterned after the wisdom of God, he needs to do a lot of careful mental house cleaning.

Many Christians underestimate the power of prayer, but frequent interviews with God often mean the difference between liberating one's self to love others or remaining enslaved in self-love. *A person cleanses his subconscious of destructive influences by coming face-to-face with his emotions through soul-searching interviews with God.*

One woman's mother told her an untruth about how women became pregnant which caused her to be afraid of standing close to a man--any man. Her fear went to the point of preventing her from enjoying classes at school which male teachers taught. Even after she learned the truth about conception, she retained the fear of men. Obviously, learning the truth wasn't enough to rid this woman of her problem; she had to go to God for an interview to remove *the feeling* of fear when in the presence of any man.

Having an interview with God is extremely important because the reasons behind many feelings lie buried in the subconscious and influence a person's thinking and actions without him being aware of it. A personal examination with God enables a person to apply the truths he learned to himself so that he can successfully remove false feelings and attitudes.

Attitudes and feelings can do lasting harm only when hidden where they can't be dealt with and removed. Until a woman brings illogical feelings to the surface and logically removes them, she cannot understand her husband as he really is. Nor can a man understand his wife as she really is when he gives in to emotional judging. Even more serious, irrational attitudes prevent understanding of one's self.

The apostle John explains how a person should deal with himself when the word of God indicates that he needs to make changes:

> **I Jn. 3:19-21: "We shall know by this that we are of the truth, and shall assure our hearts before Him, in whatever our heart condemns us; for God is greater than our heart, and knows all things. Beloved, if our heart does not condemn us, we have confidence before God;..."**

"Assure" means "to persuade, i.e. to induce one by words to believe, to cause belief in a thing; c. to persuade unto i.e. move or induce one by persuasion to do something" (Thayer, p. 497).

"Condemn" means "to find fault with, blame" (Thayer, p. 330).

John's discussion on learning how to love others presents a perfect example of how *enteuxis* prayer changes a person. John says that when a person learns the truth about love, he should persuade his heart to change if it is not already filled with love for others. John warns that God knows what is in the heart of a person regardless of whether or not that person honestly examines himself. When a person thoroughly investigates his emotions and finds them to be in accordance with God's will, he can stand before God with confidence knowing that God approves of him.

On the other hand, if a man or a woman's heart is filled with hatred, bitterness, or resentment toward anyone, he must go to God in prayer and persuade his mind to accept the truth about love. This is what *enteuxis* prayer is all about--examining the mind in an honest manner to learn the truth about one's feelings and then persuading those feelings to change and conform to the will of God. Unless a person honestly examines his motives and feelings, not to make excuses for his actions, but to give his heart a chance to find fault with his attitudes in order to transform them, he has no hope of affecting permanent changes or of enjoying a marriage that is a taste of heaven.

A person who prays to God needs to carefully observe certain habits:

Eph. 6:18: "With all prayer and petition pray at all times in the Spirit, and with this in view, be on the alert with all perseverance and petition for all the saints,..."

"Alert" means "to be sleepless, keep awake, watch, to be circumspect, attentive, ready, absence of sleep, and, pointedly, the absence of it when due to nature, and thence a wakeful frame of mind as opposed to listlessness" (Thayer, p. 9).

When a person prays to God, he needs to pray with mental alertness so that he prays with all of his mind or with his spirit. To do this, he must make *specific* petitions or requests to God and avoid praying in a vague, general way like children who sometimes say, "Help me be good and forgive me for all my sins. Amen." A person needs to list his sins and make petitions concerning each individual one and ask for sincerity in discovering presently unknown sins.

One habit that frequently prevents people from praying with all their mind is waiting until they are in bed, tired, and ready for sleep before approaching God. Under these conditions, sleep easily overcomes the person in the middle of his prayer. This not only hinders the ability of the prayer to help a person conquer his faults because he is sleeping instead of praying about them, but it is also forbidden. Listless prayer can't substitute for alert prayer. Such prayer also shows a lack of respect for the one addressed--God.

To avoid this problem, some women make it a habit to pray before getting into bed. Others actually vocalize the words quietly to themselves. Of course, a person can also pray during the day and not wait for bedtime.

Some students set aside a certain time each day for their special interview with God. They find that their minds quickly adapt to the new schedule and start mentally preparing for their talk with God long before the actual interview begins. These students claim that this consistent meeting time actually enables them to make a more thorough mental housecleaning than a haphazard schedule permits.

One man's marriage problems seemed so severe that many people thought he was almost beyond help. But he made plans to spend thirty minutes every morning before going to work reading scriptures and praying for strength to live that day as he should. In just a few months, the whole congregation where he worshiped began remarking about the obvious changes in the man's disposition and in his ability to get along with others.

Only by deliberately examining himself and determining that he is going to live his life according to God's wisdom can a person grow and mature emotionally. If a person finds a particular commandment of God hard to obey, he should be honest with himself and examine his reasons for hesitating to submit to the will of God. Then he should throw out the excuses and replace them with God's truth. Only in this way can a person rid himself of deep-seated bitterness and frustration.

Every marriage problem can be solved by going to the word of God to find the truth of the matter and by then going to God in prayer for strength to apply that truth to one's life. Yet God does not guarantee that every marriage can be perfect, only that it can be "sanctified" or better than the marriages between people who do not obey God. Every normal marriage is composed of a man and a woman. If both of these individuals follow God's formula of (1) going to His word and (2) going to Him in prayer, then God guarantees them of having a taste of heaven in their marriage. But when one of the participants refuses to respect the word of God, God cannot make absolute promises. However, God assures the one who obeys Him that his marriage, while not being the best that it could be, will still be better than marriages in which no one serves God.

In I Cor. 7:14 God says, "For the unbelieving husband is *sanctified* thorough his wife, and the unbelieving wife is *sanctified* through her believing husband; for otherwise your children are unclean, but now they are *holy* [adjective form of sanctify--PRD]." Thus, marriages in which only one person strives to please God are sanctified or set apart and happier than the marriages of the world.

Nevertheless, God solves some marital problems by authorizing the breakup of marriages for two reasons: (1) adultery in Mt. 19:9 and (2) the refusal of an unbeliever to live with a Christian in I Cor. 7:15. Yet even in these instances, the breakups result from at least one of the partners refusing to obey God's marriage laws. The failure is not a reflection on God's wisdom, but the product of man's stubbornness and rejection of God's counsel. Even when the marriage must be dissolved, God's formula of (1) going to His word and (2) going to Him in prayer enables the innocent party to solve his particular marriage problem and to live peaceably with the final outcome.

However, at least ninety-five percent of all unhappy marriages can be turned into good ones. Many husbands who are real louses can become loving and considerate in response to the transformation of their wives. Domineering and temperamental women can become affectionate and thoughtful due to a change of action by their husbands.

While no one can dogmatically teach that all marriages can be saved no matter what the circumstances, it can be affirmed that marriage problems stem primarily from sin, either deliberate or thorough ignorance of the responsibilities of marriage. Until a person makes his life right with God and with his marriage partner, he does not know whether or not he could solve his problems or if his marriage could be supremely happy. Until he obeys God in every marital realm, considering divorce could just be one way of putting one more sin on top of other wrongs.

God teaches that a Christian should do everything possible to save his marriage and to make his spouse glad that they married each other. Then, if through no fault of his, his partner insists on pursuing a life of sexual immorality or refuses to live with a Christian, he must allow his spouse to depart. However, if the attitudes are godly, a Christian will grieve over the breakup instead of thinking "good riddance!"

III. GOD'S NOURISHMENT FOR MARRIAGE

I Tim. 4:6: "In pointing out these things to the brethren, you will be a good servant of Christ Jesus, constantly nourished on the words of the faith and of the sound doctrine which you have been following."

"Good" means "beautiful, applied by the Greeks to everything so distinguished in form, excellence, goodness, usefulness, as to be pleasing, hence handsome, eminent, choice, surpassing, precious, suitable, commendable, admirable; a. beautiful to look at, shapely, magnificent; b. good, excellent in its nature and characteristics, and therefore well-adapted to its ends, genuine, approved, superior to other kinds, competent, able, such as one ought to be, praiseworthy, morally good, noble; d. honorable, conferring honor; e. affecting the mind agreeably, comforting and confirming" (Thayer, p. 322).

"Nourish" means "to nourish in, a person in a thing, to educate, form the mind" (Thayer, p. 219).

God provides nourishment in the marriage realm in two important ways: (1) through His formula of allowing the words of the Bible to educate men and women about their proper relationship to each other and then going to Him in prayer to implement that truth and (2) by sharing the learned truth with the brethren, a person becomes a "good servant of Christ Jesus, constantly nourished on the words of faith."

When a woman's heart aches because of something her husband did or failed to do, she can soothe herself with the word of God. She finds peace and happiness by trusting God with her problem. She also learns how to bring out her husband's better side. The same holds true for a husband. When his wife lets him down and refuses to support him, he can go to the Bible and let its words form the right attitude in his heart so that he can encourage his wife's good side to surface.

As men and women mentally clean house and throw away all beliefs that contradict the word of God, their minds are nourished, transforming them into loving, beautiful people able to glorify their Maker.

After a woman makes her marriage pleasing in the sight of God, sharing the keys of happiness with others stimulates her thinking and keeps her goals fresh on her mind. The comments and questions of those she teaches makes her learn even more. As a result, her marriage continually improves and grows stronger. And while her brethren gain from her knowledge of God's word and experience in practicing it, she reaps the most benefits of all. Not only does she serve God with her teaching and become all that the word "good" implies as stated above, but she nourishes her own soul and marriage as well. The only thing better is when the husband and wife both work at nourishing their relationship with God and with each other. An unsolicited letter beautifully illustrates Paul's point about how a person finds nourishment:

Dear Patsy,

Four years ago someone recommended your book, *Marriage a Taste of Heaven, Vol. I.* I bought it and I began to read it. I loved it. The first few months I stayed in the first four chapters. Being a babe in Christ I needed to learn all I could on the subject of prayer. I began praying daily, asking for wisdom, that I might help create a godly marriage, that my children would have a godly example in my husband and I. Two months passed. My husband came home one night and said, "I'm leaving and divorcing you."

I believe with all my heart had I not been reading your book learning the power and strength we receive thru prayer, I would not be a Christian today. I had the strength and faith that God would see me through this and somewhere down the line some good would come of this. Five months later we were back together.

Since the people who knew us then and know us now are awed by the change in both of us, many couples and women in the church come to us or to me for help with their marriage problems. I love being able to help others because I knew of their pain that once was mine.

Just recently I was beginning to become very down and not much help to anyone, hearing and seeing so many Christian marriages in trouble. I'm teaching the young teenage girls on marriage and they (married couples) come up to me saying, "Tell them to hold off as long as they can"; "Try to talk them out of it"; "Don't forget to tell them how men *really* are"; etc. I was getting *NO* positive input on God's creation, marriage. I was beginning to feel guilty for having a happy marriage and forgetting how hard it has been getting here.

I've been reading your new book Vol. II. and once again being refreshed and encouraged to keep learning, growing, and teaching. Your positive attitude has reminded me that God does want His children to be happy and the only way we can is to apply His truth to our lives. Words cannot express how grateful I am for your knowledge, time, and love you have shared with so many. My life has changed.

With deep affection,
A student

If every married woman obeyed I Tim. 4:6 as this woman did by studying God's word to learn her role and then sharing that information with others, there would be more good servants serving Christ Jesus and there would be more older women teaching the young women how to love their husbands and children. And there would be a lot more sanctified marriages in this world.

STUDY EXERCISES

Answer all questions in your own words.

1. Where do teachings degrading marriage come from?

2. How do unhappy marriages between Christians cause people outside of Christ to disrespect the wisdom of God?

3. What does "sanctify" mean? What is a sanctified marriage?

4. How can learning the truth sanctify a marriage?

5. What kind of prayer sanctifies a marriage?

6. Who should a person believe if a psychologist contradicts something God says? Why?

7. Who should a person believe if her personal opinion contradicts something God says? Why?

8. What are the two ways a person becomes nourished?

9. Do you disagree with anything in this lesson? If so, explain in detail giving scriptures for your reasons.

RESEARCH EXERCISE

To reap marital happiness everyone needs a clear understanding of how to pray effectively. Five common types of prayer are listen below along with Thayer's definition and some of the prominent verses that use them. Look up each of the verses and write a brief definition in the margin of your Bible so that you will know what type of prayer is mentioned. When more than one kind of prayer is used, check the other definitions to find which other ones are cited.

Then write a paper discussing each type of prayer and how a Christian should engage in it. For example, Christians should make entreaties with joy (Phil. 1:4) and to help others (II Cor. 1:11). Prayers of thanksgiving should abound (II Cor. 4:15). In a concluding paragraph, discuss the value of prayer in marriage. The scriptures with an asterisk refer specifically to marriage.

1. "Entreaty" or "supplication" means "1. need, indigence; 2. a seeking, asking, entreating, entreaty" (Thayer, p. 126).

Rom. 10:1; II Cor. 1:11; Eph. 6:18; Phil. 1:4, 4:6-7; I Tim. 2:1, 5:5; I Pet. 3:12; Ja. 5:16.

2. "Prayer," a general term, includes many different kinds of prayers and means "prayer addressed to God" (Thayer, p. 545) and "prayer (worship)" (Strong, p. 61).

Mt. 5:44, 6:7-13; Acts 2:42, 6:4, 10:4, 31; Rom. 12:12; *I Cor. 7:5; Eph. 1:16, 6:18; Phil. 4:6-7; Col. 4:2; I Thes. 1:2, 5:17; I Tim. 2:1, 8, 5:5; *I Pet. 3:7, 4:7.

3. "Petitions" or "intercession" means "a falling in with, meeting with, an interview, a coming together, that for which an interview is held, a conference or conversation, a petition, supplication" (Thayer, p. 218).

Acts 25:24; Rom. 8:27, 34, 11:2; I Tim. 2:1, 4:5; Heb. 7:25.

4. "Thanksgiving" means "thankfulness; 2. the giving of thanks" (Thayer, p. 264).

II Cor. 4:15; Phil. 4:6-7; Col. 3:17, 4:2; I Thes. 1:2, 5:18; I Tim. 2:1, *4:5.

5. "Petitions" or "ask" means "to ask for one's self, request for one's self" (Thayer, p. 17).

Jn. 14:13-14; Phil. 4:6-7; Ja. 1:5-8; I Jn. 3:21-22, 5:14-15.

CHAPTER 3

THE PLIGHT OF SILLY OLD WOMEN

God wondrously gave women a sixth sense that He didn't give to men. Women possess the ability to "more accurately perceive 'subliminal' messages" than men. This empathy with the feelings of others (Webster) allows women to respond to the emotional needs and discomforts of others in a way that men cannot. God coupled this feminine intuition with a superior understanding and use of language. As a result, women not only more accurately sense problems with others, but they also possess the ability to give greater verbal comfort than men. These people-oriented skills and emotions make women more socially and family responsive than men.

Scientists have documented this sixth sense in the crib when baby girls respond to their mothers' facial expressions and words. In contrast, baby boys choose novel objects and their environment over words. Maturity brings these differences into play even more sharply.[1]

While God gave women this sixth sense to make them better suited for serving Him and others, God never intended for women to think with their emotions. The more sensitive nature of women simply serves as a means of gathering data for the brain--not as a substitute for logical reasoning. This unique ability of women to understand the feelings of others helps them

---

[1]Daniel Goleman, "Special Abilities of the Sexes: Do They Begin in the Brain?" Psychology Today (11/78), p. 59.

nurture their families and makes them specialists at bestowing love.

At the same time, women also possess a single-mindedness that prevents them from overlooking problems or burying them. The resulting stress and discomfort from relationships being out-of-sorts becomes an inner drive for peace. This, in turn, motivates women to relentlessly search for ready solutions and a means of emotional survival. In effect, this sixth sense stimulates women to make their homes and the world a better place for everyone.

Trouble enters the picture, however, when women cease to focus their emotional antenna on others. Instead, they turn their sensitivities inward to create and to magnify their own unhappiness as they allow their emotions to rule their intellect. The resulting inner turmoil demands a solution. Too often, that solution translates into misery and a warped existence for the very ones women exert the most influence over-- their husbands and children.

Because of this great influence over others and the peculiar ability of women to allow their emotions, rather than their intellect, to govern their actions, God issues two special warnings for all women: women can easily lose their feminine beauty and influence by grasping doctrines fit only for old women and by allowing themselves to become enslaved as weak or silly women:

I. FIT ONLY FOR OLD WOMEN

After giving the formula for solving all marriage problems (I Tim. 4:1-6), God sounds the alarm of approaching disaster. While the danger exists for men too, women are especially susceptible to this harm. So unless women take cover under the word of God, untold misery awaits to take over their lives:

A. AVOID WORLDLY FABLES

I Tim. 4:7: "But have nothing to do with worldly fables fit only for old women..."

"Worldly" means "1. accessible, lawful to be trodden; 2. profane (i.e. unhallowed, common)" (Thayer, p. 100).

"Fables" means "1. a speech, word, saying; 2. a narrative, story; a. a true narrative; b. a fiction, a fable" (Thayer, p. 419).

"Fit for old women" means "old womanish, anile" (Thayer, p. 122).

God cautions Christians to reject worldly fables as fit only for old women. While many different worldly fables have circulated throughout the centuries to entice men and women away from happy marriages, this warning is especially relevant today. The very foundation of the feminist movement in this country rests squarely upon worldly fables.

However, the term "feminist" should not be confused with the expression "feminine" which describes a woman whose actions, thoughts, desires, dress, and speech are distinctive to the female sex and who advocates maintaining the differences between men and women. According to Webster, "feminist" refers to a person, either male or female, who promotes "such legal and social changes as will establish political, economic, and social equality of the sexes." Feminist literature states:

> The goal of the women's liberation movement is nothing less than to eliminate sex-role stereotypes so thoroughly that one cannot tell from a factual description of a person's behavior whether the person is a female or a male....[2]

Incidentally, many feminists develop an immediate prejudice against the users of the expressions "lib women" and "libbers" because they regard these as derogatory and slanderous terms rather than logical arguments against their beliefs. It makes no sense to point out where the feminists use illogical worldly fables only to do the same with them by using inflammatory descriptions. Therefore, the word "feminist" will

[2]Jo-Ann Gardner, "Sexist Counselling Must Stop," quoting *Personnel and Guidance Journal*, Vol. 49, No. 9 (5/71), p. 706.

be used throughout this book. Teachers of this material are encouraged to do the same if they wish to influence young college girls who are considering the feminist way of life or members of the women's liberation movement.

Feminist literature abounds with worldly fables. The feminists delight in trying to prove their statements by telling stories about uncivilized natives, citing myths about Greek gods and goddesses, perpetuating false religious concepts of men, women, and children, and by pointing to the habits of different species of animals.

This favorite tactic became evident to the general public in the early 1970's as the feminist movement began to rise in power and influence. In feminist literature available only in their bookstores and special publications, the feminists shared feelings and views with each other too horrible to expose to the general public.

Several years later, the feminists realized that even the watered-down attitudes that they dared to express publicly cost them votes on the Equal Rights Amendment. As a result, Betty Friedan and other leaders of the movement urged their followers to tone down their rhetoric to appeal to more homemakers.[3] This attempt by the hard-core feminists to conceal their real views became so successful, that godly women ask, "Why do you keep the part about the feminists in your book? That's not an issue any more."

On the contrary, the only thing that changed was the feminists' *public* image. While the leaders muzzled their loud-mouthed abusive members, others quietly began changing text books in the schools and library books for young children. The editorial tone of many ladies' magazines began catering to the new woman. Feminists flocked to the laboratories to begin trying to prove that no physical or mental differences exist between men and women. Failing to find the evidence they desperately wanted, David Gelman reveals that the feminists resorted to suppressing scientific reports that

[3]"Feminist Leaders Seek Wider Appeal Following ERA Defeats," *The Spokesman-Review* (11/13/75), p. 33.

disagreed with their opinions. They were afraid of what the general public would do with the new information.[4]

In addition, the feminists began successful campaigns to elect congressmen and women who supported their issues. They made consciousness-raising classes on women's issues standard at nearly every college and university in the country. This format gives them excellent opportunities to influence young college girls who are trying to decide what to do with their lives. The 1970's saw the number of female law students triple over the 1960's, and the 1980's saw it double. While all of them are not feminists, many support the goals of the movement. Thus, the feminists placed themselves in position to directly change existing laws and to greatly influence the decisions of judges and legislators.

Obviously, the feminists' campaign to go underground subtly works its havoc on unhappy women and unsuspecting men who think the danger no longer exists. So while examples of how the feminists pay attention to worldly fables that are fit only for old women seems inapplicable to some women, other women, especially young women, steadily fall victim to the smooth tongue of deceit. Even the women, who don't care about the feminist movement, need to understand the logical outcome of a woman rejecting God's plan for her life while she allows her emotions to run rampant.

Una Stannard, Ph.D. gave up her position as Assistant Professor of English at the University of California at Berkeley to devote herself to research and writing. Her article "The Male Maternal Instinct" provides many typical examples of the feminists' love of worldly fables. She liberally uses the common types of worldly fables to show, not only that men would make better mothers than women do, but also that men secretly desire to become mothers:

> If the maternal instinct is defined as an innate tendency to want children, and to love, cherish, nurture and protect children, then

[4]David Gelman, "Just How the Sexes Differ," *Newsweek* (5/18/81), p. 72.

history reveals that men have had more of a maternal instinct than women.

For who, according to the Bible, was the first mother? It was a man--Adam. God put him to sleep and delivered a female from his rib cage. And, for that matter, wasn't a man, God the Father, the sole progenitor of Adam himself? He created Adam out of dust in His image, just as in Greek myth Prometheus created man out of earth, and he also acted as a midwife for Zeus, splitting his head open with an ax to facilitate the delivery of Athena. Zeus also had another baby. When Semele prematurely gave birth to Dionysus, Zeus snatched up the child and sewed him into his thigh and carried him there to term. Myths you say, but they are myths written by men and expressing the male's deep desire to be a mother.[5]

Chapter 5, "Woman, a Helper Meet for Man," shows whether or not God made man from dust because He wanted to be a mother, or if God took a woman from man's side because Adam wanted to be a mother. The feminists may be able to read the Bible, but as shown in I Tim. 4:3, reading is not enough. A person must *know* the truth. Since David said in Ps. 119:160 that "the sum of Thy word is truth," a person must combine all of God's teachings on a particular subject in order to know the full truth.

Anyone who doesn't respect God's word can twist and manipulate any scriptures he chooses. For example, someone may quote Ps. 14:1 as saying, "There is no God." But the context shows that "The fool has said in his heart, 'There is no God.'"

If someone doesn't want to know the truth, God gives him the privilege of being ignorant. Since the feminists reject God's wisdom, the Bible's creation account seems like just another story to be used, rather than studied and believed. God doesn't force anyone to accept Him or to enjoy His rich marital blessings. The feminists falsely accuse God of trying to stereotype

[5]Una Stannard, Ph.D., "The Male Maternal Instinct," (Pittsburgh, PA: Know, Inc., 1970), p. 1.

them. But He allows every woman to choose if she will be feminine or feminist.

Greek myths about Zeus and Hephaestus, etc. make interesting reading. However, trying to figure out the hidden meanings of an author who has been dead for centuries is not a very reliable basis for formulating a theory about whether or not men secretly desire to be mothers. Such human fabrications fail to really prove anything at all about men in general, even if men wrote them. Stories abound that women wrote about mothers enjoying their children, but no one uses them to affirm that all women instinctively look forward to motherhood.

In addition to using myths, the feminists also speculate about different native tribes in an attempt to prove their theories. Una Stannard tells about the customs and rituals of the Arapeshes of New Guinea, the Azandes of the Belgian Congo, the central tribes of Australia, the boys of the Arunta tribe, the boys in many East African tribes, and the Qatus of the New Hebrides which she believes demonstrate that men envy the role of women. She gives an interesting summary of her worldly fables:

> Without these feminizing initiation ceremonies it was thought, paradoxically, that boys could not achieve the status of men. Seemingly even more paradoxical, these "man-making" ceremonies were in many ways symbolic of rebirth. The initiation houses were often called wombs or birth enclosures and the exit door resembled a gaping vagina. After initiation, the adult males who were in charge treated the boys as if they had been newly born, giving them new names, milk to drink, not allowing them to speak and carrying them on their shoulders as if they couldn't walk. The boys were now born again as men. Since a boy could only thus become a man, it is as if the men were saying that though women give birth to boys, only men can give birth to men; and the boys having been ritually transformed into

women could in their turn give birth to the next generation of men.[6]

Now the feminists have it: proof that men would make better mothers than women make! Anyone who bases his life on a foundation of fables--true or otherwise--is bound to become enslaved. With worldwide information readily available on the news, in the newspapers, and in the *National Geographic,* anyone can easily find someone somewhere whose beliefs and actions demonstrate what he wants to believe and practice. For example, a random search of the *National Geographic* quickly produced the story of the Nambas on Malekula Island in the New Hebrides who illustrate exactly the opposite qualities:

"I'm a good wife, hard working and virtuous," proclaims the gaping smile of a Big Namba woman. At a special ceremony a tribesman knocked out two upper teeth, a sacrifice that established her status as a married woman. For the rite, her husband paid a toll in pigs.

Among the Small Nambas, women lose a single tooth during the agonizing ritual. Pounding a sharpened stick with a rock, a relative loosens an upper incisor of a young girl so that it can be removed with the fingers. Afterwards, a heated plant stem stops the blood as a tear trickles from her eye.[7]

If men undergoing a feminizing ritual proves that men really want to be mothers, what does a woman undergoing the pain of losing one or two of her front teeth to show her loyalty and devotion to her husband prove? Certainly, according to feminist logic, it must prove that women, deep down in their hearts, really want men to dominate them.

In like manner, what should the following example of a primitive woman prove to the feminists?

[6]Stannard, "The Male Maternal Instinct," p. 1.
[7]Kal Muller, "Taboos and Magic Rule Namba Lives," *National Geographic* (1/72), p. 64. Used by permission.

Still nursing at 3 years, a child clings to its mother, reflecting the affection that permeates all Tasaday life. Despite the ratio among adults of two men to each woman, wives are not shared. Both parents help with child-rearing and food-gathering chores.[8]

According to the feminists' standards, *the National Geographic* article proves that women really want to be mothers and nurse their children for three years. Yet for some reason the article hasn't appeared in their literature.

The feminists also find historical facts invaluable in propagating their philosophies about the roles of men and women. For example, Stannard uses history to support her theory:

Men, not women, have historically shown the most compassion for children. It was women chiefly who killed children, and not just illegitimate children...

Nor did the maternal instinct incline women to breast feed their babies. In Greek and Roman times among the upper classes, it was not fashionable to suckle one's own children; slaves were wet nurses. But it wasn't only the rich who were reluctant. It is estimated that in the eighteenth century in England 3 percent of children in towns were nursed by their own mothers; poor mothers regularly hired wet nurses because they were obligated to work...

It must be said in exoneration of these mothers and nurses that the love of children as we now understand it developed late in civilized societies. There was no special interest in methods of child rearing...[9]

---

[8]Kenneth MacLeish and John Launois, "Stone Age Cavemen of Mindanao, *National Geographic* (8/72), p. 245. Used by permission.
[9]Stannard, "The Male Maternal Instinct," p. 5.

Instead of proving the maternal instinct of men, the above examples of human behavior demonstrate the truth of God laid down in Tit. 2:4-5 that woman need to be taught how to love their children. Love is an attitude that must be learned. Instead of proving that women should reject God's role for them, such narratives show part of the consequences for disobeying God--people lose their ability to love. Paul teaches this principle in Rom. 1:28-31 which states that people who do not "see fit to acknowledge God any longer" become, among other things, "unloving."

The feminists also enjoy using another type of fable--stories about animals. But not all animals, only certain kinds of animals:

> ...Among the lampreys, a primitive fish, it is the male who builds the nest and prepares for the babies. In a higher order of primitive fish, the stickleback, it is the male who tends the young and even incubates the eggs.

> Men will object that they are not primitive fish or birds, and they object rightly. For when fertilization became internal, that is, when the female's body became the nest, parental solicitude passed to the female, and a built-in coded tape that programs child rearing does exist in lower forms of female animal life. But recent studies have shown that it is not innate in female primates. According to George Schaller, zoo apes who have never seen another female handling an infant ignore their own newborn babies or are afraid of them....[10]

Stannard concludes her argument based on animals with:

> Men seem to have always reduced woman to an animal, defining her by the purely biological function of reproduction.[11]

---

[10]Stannard, "The Male Maternal Instinct," p. 6.
[11]Stannard, "The Male Maternal Instinct," p. 7.

God sometimes uses examples of animals or insects to illustrate lessons about human nature. For example, in Prov. 6:6-11 God tells the sluggard to go to the ant to observe her ways and to be wise. Ants serve as perfect examples of industry, for they work hard all summer to prepare for the winter. A man can follow the example of hard work or he can choose the path of laziness and find himself in poverty and need. The example of the ant proves nothing about the nature of man or his need for honest labor. The ant just provides a model of hard work from which a man can learn to be diligent in all his endeavors.

Since animals don't possess the freewill choice to change the roles God created them to occupy, they serve as consistent examples for different types of behavior. For example, a loving puppy illustrates emotional warmth. But a puppy doesn't prove anything about people. He just provides an example of spontaneous affection. On the other hand, a cat's independence portrays aloofness. But a cat doesn't prove anything about people. He just shows how self-sufficiency acts. Of themselves, dogs and cats can't prove whether people should be affectionate or indifferent toward each other.

In a similar manner, the lamprey male serves as an example of a male who builds a nest and prepares for his babies. However, the lamprey male doesn't prove anything about the nature of human males. Any school child can easily compile a list of fish with the opposite traits where the female takes complete care of the young, while the male ignores his children and perhaps even tries to kill them. Rather than go all the way back to primitive fish to find an example, the school child need only look in the aquariums of his local pet shop. There the male guppy gobbles up his young as fast as the female gives birth if they don't hide from him.

On the other hand, perhaps a person shouldn't use the guppy as an example for a feminist because the female also eats the young. Consequently, a feminist might conclude that the guppy argument proves that neither men nor women really want children and everyone should remain childless. So what do stories about fish prove about men if the male guppies and lampreys can't agree on how to treat their babies?

Even if the example of the lampreys proves anything about human beings, it supports God's design for humans. The feminists' complaint that men often neglect their children is not a grievance against God. For in Eph. 6:4 God gives men the responsibility of looking after their children. Men who neglect their children violate the laws of God, not the preferences of the lampreys or the logic of the feminists. If the feminists want their husbands to assume their rightful position of helping raise their children, they should turn to God rather than digging up extreme examples in nature.

Likewise, the ape argument against motherhood also supports God's teachings concerning a woman's role with her children as taught in Tit. 2:4-5. If the feminists want to know the proper feminine attitude toward bearing children, they should listen to God instead of watching abnormal apes whose lifestyles have been damaged by captivity. Both men and women need God's word to learn how to become good parents.

Furthermore, *who* degrades men and women to a level equal with animals? The feminists claim that men degrade women, but when they say, "Look at those fish, birds, and apes! That proves men and women should reverse their roles!" they trample underfoot the dignity of both men *and women*. Indeed, such tales are fit only for old women.

Slander or placing disagreeable labels on different aspects of marriage serves as another standard argument of the feminists against God's design as Dana Densmore demonstrates:

> The distinction is often made in the female liberation movement between an "enemy" and an "oppressor." The real enemy, I think we all agree, is sexism and male supremacy; a set of attitudes held by men and women and institutionalized in our society (and by all societies throughout history).[12]

The feminists made the word "sexism" popular to equate the differences between men and women with "racism." The expression "male supremacy" serves the

[12]Dana Densmore, "Who is Saying Men are the Enemy?" (Pittsburgh, PA: KNOW, Inc.).

purposes of making men feel like tyrants if they function as the head of their homes, and it makes women
feel like inferior slaves if they choose the role of domestic queens.

If slander provides a valid and intelligent reason
for rejecting something, then a few changes in the
above quotation would help the mass-transit experts
prove the superiority of riding the bus over owning a
car. At the same time it would show the most logical
way to cure gasoline shortage and air pollution problems.

> The distinction is often made in the mass-
> transit movement between an enemy and an op-
> pressor. The real enemy, I think we all agree,
> is "carism" and big car supremacy; a set of
> attitudes held by car owners and insti-
> tutionalized by Detroit (and by all car manu-
> facturers).

Such slanderous slurs denounce owning a car in
favor of mass transit because of "carism" and "big car
supremacy." Carism equates cars with racism which everyone knows is bad; therefore, everyone should recognize that owning a car is nothing but pure prejudice
and close-mindedness. Likewise, big car supremacy
implies that small cars are inferior to big cars which
obviously means that small car owners should refuse
to give big cars the right of way under any circumstances.

Slander, whether against cars or men and women or
marriage, never proved anything about the subject under discussion. Nor does slander commend its author
as an open-minded or fair person. Slander, one of the
most potent forms of prejudice known to men and
women, is fit to be rejected as a worldly fable.

The most unbelievable of all the feminists' arguments against marriage is the one based on a plea to
ignorance. The very people who campaign for women to
use their brains condemn marriage because they don't
know very much about it. Densmore continues:

> The origin of these attitudes and institu-
> tions is immaterial. Whether they were insti-
> tuted by men acting out of fear of women or

by society as a whole for the survival of the
species is irrelevant. Whether it was some
kind of "plot" of "just the way things evolved"
need not concern us. All we care about are the
conditions right now, because it is right now
that we propose to change. If traditional attitudes are inappropriate or unjust today in our
experience, then they must be replaced.[13]

After casting aspersions on the governmental
organization of marriage by labeling it with sexism and
male supremacy, Densmore states that she doesn't care
where that system originated--that's "immaterial." She
lists several possible sources; none of which acknowledge a higher intelligence. She bases her conclusions
on "our experience" or the sermons about marriage that
the world preaches with its unsanctified marital
unions.

Essentially, she argues, "Marriage doesn't work. I
don't know why it doesn't work. Furthermore, I don't
care why it doesn't work. All I know is that I don't
like marriage so you shouldn't either." Again, if that is
a logical reason for condemning something, it is a
valid reason for disapproving of owning cars. The
mass-transit movement could assert, "Cars don't work.
We don't know why they don't work. Furthermore, we
don't care why they don't work. All we know is that
we don't like cars and you shouldn't either."

If the mass-transit leaders propagated such reasoning, the public would swamp them with letters and
telegrams pointing out their lack of logic. Using one's
own ignorance to denounce something as stupid, unworkable, and unpractical isn't rational, and doesn't
convince others of the equal intelligence of women
with men.

Yet many people accept such fabrications as fact
and allow them to influence their lives in the most
precious union they share with another--marriage. Why?
Surely, worldly fables cannot be all that deceiving. But
Paul started this section of verses with a warning that
many would be beguiled and led away from the truth
that makes marriages good and sanctified (I Tim. 4:1).

[13]Densmore, "Who is Saying Men are the Enemy?"

A woman who cannot see the good in the marriage relationship because she fails to acknowledge God's design for men and women is deceived. She is not liberated, no matter how many demonstrations she marches in. She is not her own master, no matter how many doors she opens for herself. She is not just like a man, no matter how many bras she burns. She is not her own boss, no matter how many companies she manages. *A deceived woman is not liberated, no matter how sincere she might be.*

The foundation of the women's liberation movement rests on such specimens of logic as quoted here. Fables don't prove anything because a good researcher can easily find a story to teach the opposite point of view. A woman who wants to be wise should listen to God who says shun or avoid worldly fables because they are fit only for old women.

B. DISCIPLINE FOR THE PURPOSE OF GODLINESS

I Tim. 4:7: "...On the other hand, discipline yourself for the purpose of godliness;..."

"Discipline" means "1. properly to exercise naked; 2. to exercise (vigorously, in any way, either the body or the mind)" (Thayer, p. 122).

"Godliness" means "reverence, respect, piety toward God, godliness" (Thayer, p. 262).

Instead of allowing worldly fables that are fit only for old women to lead her astray, a woman should discipline or exercise her mind for the purpose of godliness. But contrary to popular opinion, "godliness" doesn't mean "God-like." *Godliness is an attitude that causes a person to always strive to please God.* If a woman wants to please God, she must exercise by deliberately putting God's word into her mind so that God's will controls her actions.

"Discipline," which means "to exercise naked," carries the idea of not letting tight clothing hinder the activity. Heb. 12:1 demonstrates this: "Let us also lay aside every encumbrance, and the sin which so easily entangles us, and let us run with endurance the race that is set before us." In short, overcoming bad attitudes requires a vigorous workout. Many times a woman must literally force herself to do what she knows God wants since her *human* logic often rebels.

The strenuous exertion of exercising naked often produces some moans and groans and possibly some hesitation on the part of the participants. Inactive muscles, whether in the legs or in the head, ache when used for the first time. For example, a jogger, who starts a new training schedule, must fight the temptation to give up when his muscles and joints start complaining. In a similar manner, a person engaged in mental exercise must fight the temptation to quit studying and being honest with himself when he experiences mental anguish and regret over personal habits and past mistakes. The exerciser experiences full, unhampered use of his body and his mind only after long, diligent practice. Then the drills become second nature to him.

The older and the more bitter the marriage, the harder it becomes for a woman to face the mistakes of the past and to truly repent of them in order to do God's complete will. Generally speaking, a definite difference exists between newlyweds and older women studying about marriage. Ready to love and admire their husbands, young women eagerly search for answers to their problems. Sadly, the bitterness of many older women makes them demand constant reassurance that God's way really works before they chance obeying Him.

Just as physical exercise seems harder to out-of-shape oldsters than to youngsters who exercise regularly, individuals who haven't maintained a healthy spiritual physique find mental exercise more difficult. Thus, women who have allowed themselves to grow bitter need to realize that they must exert more effort than women whose basic attitudes more closely resemble God's plan. This doesn't mean that bitter women can't achieve a happy marriage relationship, only that they must work extra hard to overcome deeply ingrained bad thinking habits.

Afterwards, when the exercise becomes second nature, the reward is great mental delight in the previously thought impossible accomplishments. Describing this feeling, Solomon said, "Desire realized is sweet to the soul" (Prov. 13:19). Certainly, just as a runner experiences renewed self-esteem when he runs one to five miles without gasping for breath or falling down with a heart attack, an even greater sense of attainment and enjoyment results from the newly developed skills of communication and the ability to solve problems rather than suffering defeat by them.

God wants everyone to enjoy happy marriages because He created them to be good. And He did His part to ensure successful marital unions by inspiring the Bible. Thus, men and women don't need to experiment with one set of exercises for six months and then, if it doesn't work, try another set for six more months hoping to find the right exercises before they die of old age. God is the drillmaster for those who trust in Him; Christians need only to apply their intelligence and efforts to the exercises to reap the rewards of mental and spiritual fitness.

C. RECEIVE THE PROMISE OF HAPPINESS

I Tim. 4:8: "...for bodily discipline is only little profit, but godliness is profitable for all things, since it holds promise for the present life and also for the life to come."

"All things" means "1. any, every one; b. any and every, of every kind; 2. all the, the whole; 3. everything, (anything) whatsoever" (Thayer, pp. 491-493).

Many people excuse their conduct with, "I'm too old to change now." They prefer to keep enjoying their misery rather than to learn how to enjoy life.

A seventy year old woman, who didn't know how to solve her multitude of personal problems, asked, "Do you realize how old I am?" when I suggested that she needed to take these classes on marriage.   Yet age doesn't have anything to do with learning how to get along with others. Everyone has from now until the end of eternity to be a truly loving person. The   family unit gives humans a perfect opportunity to develop skills for getting along with others to prepare them for living with God, Christ, the Holy Spirit, and the angels. If a person refuses to learn how to dwell peaceably with the different individuals in his earthly family, a unit founded originally on love, then he will not be prepared to live with the heavenly family throughout eternity.

God could have made humans so that they didn't need to associate with other people as He did many animals and insects who live solitary lives until they need to reproduce. Then, after the fertilization process, they again separate to live independent lives. However, God placed humans in an environment that forces them to learn how to communicate and interact with others or be miserable.

The basic rules for getting along with a husband or a wife apply to every realm of human association. In fact, widows and single women taking the classes often remark about their improved relationships with neighbors and fellow employees. Many delight in better communication and fewer problems with teenage children as an added benefit. Marriage provides a unique opportunity to develop invaluable skills of communication that bless individuals in the present life and also help prepare them for the life to come.

The apostle Paul says that bodily exercise profits less when compared to the benefits of disciplining the mind for godliness. Furthermore, exercising unto godliness is profitable for "all things." What does "all things" leave out? Not one *necessary* ingredient of life! Not even married life! Striving to please God gives rich personal dividends.

At the same time, God doesn't promise to tell Christians everything they need to know to subdue the earth such as how to overhaul a car, send a rocket to the moon, sew, or can food. God challenges men and women to discover these secrets for themselves. On the other hand, God promises to tell His followers the most important secrets of life--everything they need to know to get along with others and how to prepare themselves to live with Him in heaven.

Thus, after giving the formula for solving all marriage problems, Paul warns God's people not to listen to those who degrade men, women, and marriage. They must not allow anyone to deceive them with worldly fables. Paul pleads with them to use their brains--to discipline their minds and to control their emotions. Only in this way can God's followers find true fulfillment and happiness on earth.

II. CAPTIVATING SILLY WOMEN

When women quit using their brains and begin thinking with their emotions, they leave themselves open to deception. In fact, deceivers find it easy to mislead weak or silly women. For that reason, God warns both men and women about the dangers of not searching for His truths. He pleads with His people to avoid those who prey on the emotions of others:

A. PEOPLE TO AVOID

II Tim. 3:1-5: "But realize this, that in the last days difficult times will come. For men will be lovers of self, lovers of money, boastful, arrogant, revilers, disobedient to parents, ungrateful, unholy, unloving, irreconcilable, malicious gossips, without self-control, brutal, haters of good, treacherous, reckless, conceited, lovers of pleasure rather than lovers of God; holding to a form of godliness, although they have denied its powers; and avoid such men as these."

"Last days" refers to the days of the New Testament church as revealed in Acts 2:16-17 when the church was established on the day of Pentecost after Jesus ascended back into heaven.

"Difficult" means "hard to do, to take, to approach, hard to bear, troublesome, dangerous, harsh, fierce, savage" (Thayer, p. 664).

Bible scholars translate several different Greek words with the English word "men." "Men" in this passage comes from the Greek word *anthropoi* which is related to the English word "anthropology," the study of mankind. "Men" means "1. universally, without distinction of sex, a human being, whether male or female; 2. someone; 3. people" (Thayer, p. 46).

Paul says, "But realize this," and proceeds to describe a danger that will come about during the last days--the time in which people now live. He warns that men and women with certain characteristics will try to deceive "silly women" and take advantage of them (verse 6). While the characteristics that Paul lists aren't limited to the women's liberation movement, these basic character faults run rampant within the feminist camp. And since the feminists preach their own brand of religion with enthusiasm, intelligent women need to be aware of the dangers. Therefore, this study examines these characteristics as they apply to the women's movement and the effect they wield over women. It is left up to each reader to make personal application of these qualities:

1. LOVERS OF SELF

"Lovers of self" means "too intent on one's own interests, selfish" (Thayer, p. 653).

The women's liberation movement rests upon a foundation of love of self, promotion of self, and protection of self at the expense of others. The feminists consider women's rights more important than the rights of others. Certainly, the following quotation from SCUM (Society for Cutting Up Men), a branch of the Women's Liberation Movement, is extreme; yet the attitude isn't an isolated one:

> If a large majority of women were SCUM, they would *acquire complete control of this country* within a few weeks simply by withdrawing from the labor force, thereby paralyzing the entire nation.[14]

> The few remaining men can exist out their puny days dropped out on drugs or strutting around in drag or passively watching the high-powered female in action, fulfilling themselves as spectators, vicarious livers or breeding in the cow pasture with the toadies, or they can go off to the nearest friendly neighborhood suicide center where they will be quietly, quickly and painlessly gassed to death.[15]

[14]Robin Morgan, editor, "Sisterhood is Powerful, an Anthology of Writing From the Women's Liberation Movement," *SCUM*, p. 516.
[15]Morgan, "Sisterhood is Powerful," p. 519.

2. LOVERS OF MONEY

"Lovers of money" means "loving money, avaricious" (Thayer, p. 653).

If the women's liberation movement was simply a plea for better jobs and equal pay for women, religious people could conscientiously join the cause. For Jesus said, "The laborer is worthy of his wages" (Lk. 10:7). However, the true feminists don't want just good jobs with good pay--they want the best jobs with the best pay. They willingly sacrifice their families as they seek promotions or run their own businesses.

Money doesn't appeal to the feminists because of the luxuries it buys. Rather, money gives them political power and independence from their husbands. It helps them shake off their feelings of inferiority and second-class status.[16] To the feminists, money is the difference between liberation and slavery. No wonder they love it!

3. BOASTFUL

"Boastful" means "braggart talk, insolent and empty assurance which trusts in its own power" (Thayer, p. 25).

This characteristic takes several forms. One is the common slogan "anything a man can do, a woman can do better." Another form utilizes bad language which Caroline Bird outlines in her book *Born Female,* which served as an important source book for the women's liberation movement in the early 1970's. Before listing some foul language the feminist want to make popular she boasts:

> Bad language is a way of proving you're not a lady, so liberated women may toss off...the four letter words from which men extract a sexual thrill.[17]

[16]Peter Jennings, "After the Sexual Revolution" (New York: ABC News Closeup Transcript (8/1/86), pp. 1-4.
[17]Caroline Bird, *Born Female: The High Cost of Keeping Women Down* (New York: David McKay Co., Inc., 1970), p. 206.

4. ARROGANT

"Arrogant" refers to "looking down on others and treating them with contempt" (Thayer, p. 641).

After describing taking care of little children as "inhuman work" for a woman, a feminist article by Vanauken cautions women not "to throw out the bath-water along with the baby." The article goes on to tell women that they should keep the womanly qualities of love, tenderness, and consideration while getting rid of child-rearing obligations.[18]

5. REVILERS

"Revilers" means "ones who use slander, detraction, speech injurious to another's good name" (Thayer, p. 102).

The feminists recognize religion as their greatest enemy and don't hesitate to attack it. Richard Gilman's article in *Life* magazine offers a good example:

> Eve was framed...Women have been the un-derdog since the Beginning--or at least according to those male authors of the Bible, since Eve. In fact, Eve was the first uppity woman. If she hadn't presumptuously gone after education, there would have been no future for death and the serpent Satan and the human race would still be sitting pretty in Paradise.[19]

6. DISOBEDIENT

"Disobedient" means "disobedience, obstinacy (to parents)" (Thayer, p. 55).

One way the feminists promote this attitude is by advocating "children's liberation" as Julie Loesch shows:

[18]Vanauken, "A Primer for the Last Revolution" (Pittsburgh, PA: KNOW, Inc., 1971), p. 4.
[19]Richard Gilman, "The 'Woman Problem'--Then and Now," *Life* (8/13/71), p. 41.

Kate Millett in *Sexual Politics* defines "politics" as that system of practices, attitudes, and beliefs which enables one group to maintain power over another. This definition should be applied to the politics of childhood, since children are the most universally lorded-over people in the world.[20]

Loesch pushes for the right of children to control where they go to school from kindergarten on up. She says that in addition to choosing where and with whom they will live, children should be given full access to food, clothing, shelter, peers, and the media.

Some years later a newspaper article took the attitude a step further by promoting children divorcing their parents:

The notion of children divorcing their parents and collecting alimony is not as far-fetched as it might seem, says lawyer Lori B. Andrews. In a magazine article on children's rights, the Chicago attorney says a Swedish lawyer and professor has already proposed such steps. Writing in the May issue of *Parents Magazine*, Andrews says contemporary legislation and current social attitudes put increasing weight on a child's decision-making ability--yet many parents cling to the tradition that says "my word is law."[21]

7. UNGRATEFUL

"Ungrateful" means "ungracious, unpleasing, unthankful" (Thayer, p. 90).

Generally, the feminists are very hard to please when someone tries to do something for them--especially if that someone happens to be a man! Graciousness is not a characteristic frequently associated with the feminists as Dana Densmore amply demonstrates:

[20]Julie Loesch, "Children's Liberation, The Politics of Childhood" (Pittsburgh, PA: KNOW, Inc.), p. 1.
[21]"Child Divorcing Parent 'Not So Far-Fetched,'" *Amarillo Globe-Times* (4/29/80), p. 9.

In less civilized ages and societies, if a woman got too uppity she was beaten up, or not thrown a piece of meat from the animal the man had killed, or she was raped. Here and now, men are usually more subtle, particularly in public with women over whom they have no legal rights.

Instead of it being necessary to beat her up to indicate his physical superiority, he finds he can make his point at least to his own satisfaction by opening a door for her, thus subtly indicating his superior strength and by implication her weakness and physical dependency. (This has the added advantage of tending to keep her weak in fact, due to lack of exercise.)[22]

8. UNHOLY

"Unholy" means "unholy, impious, wicked, (disloyal)" (Thayer, p. 49).

The feminists degrade God's purpose for creating women to work alongside the man in subduing the earth and filling it with people. Vanauken wrote "A Primer for the Last Revolution" for a group of college girls in Nashville to help them sort out their priorities:

The question for women--particularly college girls, girls who are not married or not so long married that the sexist pattern is set--is also simple. You've still got this feeling in your very bones that you've got to have a guy--and eventually home and kids--or die unfulfilled. You're much more focused on guys for fun than they are on girls, which is why you sometimes act like a groupie. But you know why you have this feeling in your bones and this dependence. Conditioning, brainwashing. Not just by your mother and father but by your friends and every book and film and picture on a cereal box. You know you should re-examine the

[22]Dana Densmore "Chivalry--The Iron Hand in the Velvet Glove" (Pittsburgh, PA: KNOW, Inc., 9/69), p. 1.

whole thing. Now here's the question: Do you
keep your integrity and your womanhood (your
human status)--or do you cop out? Have you
got the sheer courage (the virtue on which all
the rest hang) to say to some beautiful guy: "I
love you, but I'm not copping out. I don't have
to have home and kids--or even you--for a
good life: not if it costs my womanhood."[23]

9. UNLOVING

"Unloving" means "without natural affection (used
here and in Rom. 1:31 only)" (Thayer, p. 82).

When the women's liberation movement first began
in earnest, the feminists kept their association with
lesbianism under wraps. However, when Karen DeCrow
ran for re-election as president of NOW in 1975, she
declared in her keynote address to the national conference, "Our failure has been in not seeing the connec-
tion between sexual stereotyping and fear of gay people." She went on to say, "NOW also makes a public
apology to gay men and women."[24]

Four years later homosexual rights became a formal
part of NOW resolutions:

> Delegates to the 12th annual convention of
> the National Organization for Women closed a
> three-day meeting after adopting resolutions
> supporting homosexual rights and the rights of
> women to have abortions.

> "We are going to launch the broadest repro-
> ductive rights campaign that we can," NOW
> President Eleanor Smeal told the 848 delegates
> Sunday after being elected to a second two-
> year term. "And lesbian rights will be right up
> front."[25]

[23]Vanauken, "A Primer for the Last Revolution"
(Pittsburgh, PA: KNOW, Inc., 1971), p. 12.
[24]"NOW President Defends Way of Life," *Spokesman-Review* (10/26/75), p. A18.
[25]"Now Supports Abortion, Lesbian Rights," *Amarillo
Globe-Times* (10/10/79), p. 13.

10. IRRECONCILABLE

"Irreconcilable" means "1. without a treaty or covenant; (of things not mutually agreed upon, e.g. abstinence from hostilities); 2. that cannot be persuaded to enter into a covenant" (Thayer, p. 81).

One special program of the feminist movement is their campaign against "sexist" books. "Sexist" doesn't refer to books about sexual intercourse, but books portraying women as wives, mothers, and homemakers. The feminists want books to portray women as the breadwinner while the father stays home with the children. "A Child's Right to Equal Reading" offers guidelines for groups to rid public libraries of all books which promote sex-role stereotyping.[26]

11. MALICIOUS GOSSIPS

"Malicious gossips" means "prone to slander, slanderous, accusing falsely" (Thayer, p. 135).

Feminists frequently accuse the homemaker of acting like a high type of prostitute who sells her body for food, clothing, and shelter as the following article shows:

> She has traded "sex, services and society" and a good deal more, for a modicum of security in the form of economic support...[27]

Vol. II: Learning to Love contains quotation after quotation in chapter 4, "Victorian Morals and Feminists," to show that this is a big issue with the feminists.

12. WITHOUT SELF-CONTROL

"Without self-control" means "without self-control, intemperate" (Thayer, p. 23).

[26]Verne Moberg, "A Child's Right to Equal Reading" (Washington, D.C.: National Education Association).
[27]"Marriage and Divorce as Political Institutions: A Working Paper from Women in Transition, Inc.," (Philadelphia: Women in Transition, Inc.), p. 6.

The feminists determinedly fight for their own rights regardless of what others want or who they hurt. Their attitudes toward preserving the marriage relationship and sexual purity illustrate their intemperate practices. Kate Millett advocates in her book *Sexual Politics* that women use fornication as a means of attaining their goals:

> A sexual revolution would require, perhaps first of all, an end of traditional sexual inhibitions and taboos, particularly those that most threaten patriarchal monogamous marriage: homosexuality, "illegitimacy," adolescent, pre- and extra-marital sexuality. The negative aura with which sexual activity has generally been surrounded would necessarily be eliminated, together with the double standard and prostitution. The goal of revolution would be a permissive single standard of sexual freedom, and one uncorrupted by the crass and exploitative economic bases of traditional sexual alliances.[28]

13. BRUTAL

"Brutal" means "not tame, savage, fierce" (Thayer, p. 45).

A newspaper article highlighted this characteristic when it described what happened in New York when the legislators tried to pass a law in favor of abortion in 1972. The Right to Life proponents sent each of the congressmen slick pictures of "gory aborted fetuses" and a bottled fetus was displayed in the Assembly. The effort so shocked the legislators that they refused to pass the bill. However, the feminists reacted with promise of even greater horrors than pictures of aborted fetuses:

> Pro-abortion leaders like Dr. Alan Guttmacher of Planned Parenthood and Gloria Steinem of the Feminist Coalition have spoken of the pos-

[28]Kate Millett, *Sexual Politics*, (New York: The Hearst Corp., 1970), p. 92. Used by permission of Doubleday and Company.

sibility of matching the anti-abortionists by bringing battered unwanted babies or women mutilated by illegal abortions to Albany.[29]

In other words, the feminists threatened, "If you don't let us kill our babies before birth, we'll harm or kill them after birth." How more brutal can a person become?

14. HATERS OF GOOD

"Haters of good" means "opposed to goodness and good men" (Thayer, p. 89).

The feminists show their distaste for good by teaching that homemakers are stupid. In "No More Fun and Games," Jayne West gave her view of marriage:

> The private home as it now exists will appear a torture chamber to post-revolutionary people...If you don't want to be property, you must give up the protection and honor of the man's name, too.[30]

Betty Friedan agrees:

> But is her house in reality a comfortable concentration camp? Have not women who live in the image of the feminine mystique trapped themselves within narrow walls of their homes? They have learned to "adjust" to their biological role. They have become dependent, passive, childlike; they have given up their adult frame of reference to live at the lower human level of food and things. The work they do does not require adult capabilities; it is endless, monotonous, unrewarding.[31]

[29]Anthony Astrachan, "New York's Abortion Law Faces Serious Political Test," *The Spokesman-Review* (1/14/73), p. F7.
[30]Jayne West, "No More Fun and Games" (Pittsburgh, PA: KNOW, Inc.).
[31]Betty Friedan, *The Feminine Mystique,* (New York: Norton, 1963), p. 298.

15. TREACHEROUS

"Treacherous" means "a betrayer, traitor" (Thayer, p. 538).

The feminists demonstrate treacherous behavior in several ways. One obvious way is how they betray the companion of their youth and recommend divorce to others. Perhaps not so obvious is their betrayal of their country as reported by Ti-Grace Atkinson, the first president of New York City's NOW:

> Feminists must learn to accept the risks and the seriousness of revolution. The only way to get someplace is to live outside the law, against the government. Like the Mafiosi.[32]

16. RECKLESS

"Reckless" means "1. falling forward, headlong, sloping, precipitous; 2. precipitate, rash, reckless" (Thayer, p. 541).

After worrying so much about what they get, the feminists show little concern about the consequences to others of their actions. Germaine Greer explains, "What will happen is that providing jobs for these women will create a squeeze at the bottom. Those who suffer most will be working men, who, under the present system, have enormous family responsibilities and who will be pushed out of work. That, unfortunately, will be the result of abolishing discrimination against females."[33]

17. CONCEITED

"Conceited" means "1. to make proud, puff up with pride, render insolent, to be puffed up with haughtiness or pride; 2. to blind with pride or conceit, to render foolish or stupid, beclouded, besotted" (Thayer, p. 633).

[32]Ti-Grace Atkinson, (St. Paul, MN: *Dispatch*), (8/21/74).
[33]"Who Are the Proponents of ERA?" (San Antonio, TX: Committee to Restore Women's Rights), p. 3.

The feminists show their pride in such silly things as trying to change everyday words such as "manicure" to "womanicure," and establishment of the "First Bank of Women." However, their actions are as sexist to the opposite extreme as they claim men's are.

18. LOVERS OF PLEASURE

"Lovers of pleasure" means "loving pleasure" (Thayer, p. 654).

The whole society is geared toward love of pleasure and in seeking the easy way. The feminists are no different. Their promotion of the attitude that women should use sexual relationships just like men do demonstrates this attitude. They think that if men can "love 'em and leave 'em" they should do the same thing.[34]

19. DO NOT LOVE GOD

The feminists show a lack of love for God by rejecting His word concerning women. They address God in prayer as "Mother" and "She."[35] Likewise, they try to teach that the Holy Spirit is a woman. They even ridicule God's creation of the man and woman:

The story of Adam and Eve has been described as the hoax of the millennia. So also now the idea of the God-Man (God-Male, on the imaginative level)--the dogma of the hypostatic union--is beginning to be perceived by some women as a kind of cosmic joke.[36]

Determined to have their way, not only with earthly men and women, the feminists also want to take over the Creator of the universe. Such boldness, one cannot imagine!

[34]Millett, *Sexual Politics*, 92.
[35]Gloria Steinem, "Sisterhood," as quoted in *The First Ms. Reader*, (New York: Warner Books Inc., 1973), p. 5.
[36]Mary Daly, "A Call for the Castration of Sexist Religion" (Pittsburgh, PA: KNOW, Inc., 1972), p. 34.

20. HOLD TO A FORM OF GODLINESS

"Godliness" means "reverence, respect, piety toward God, godliness" (Thayer, p. 262).

While the feminists appear to work toward an honorable goal of equal opportunities for women, in reality their actions deny the power of godliness. They impiously turn their backs on God's design and purpose for a woman. Instead of taking control of their minds and emotions and exercising to put on godliness so that they might really improve their lives, they follow after their own whims.

Ironically, their philosophies give off such an illusion of godliness that politicians and school administrators eagerly join the bandwagon. All around their influence steadily changes the way America thinks, talks, and acts.

21. DENIED THE POWER OF GODLINESS

"Power" means "strength, ability, power, inherent power, power residing in a thing by virtue of its nature" (Thayer, p. 159). It comes from the Greek word *dunamin* which the English word "dynamite" comes from. It refers to the power of an army or host.

Through trying to solve their own problems in their own way, the feminists, in effect, deny the power of true godliness. True godliness solves problems in a way that benefits *all* of the participants. Godliness makes a woman happy, fulfilled, and content.

In renouncing God's plan for women, the feminists boldly embrace the doctrines of evolution and humanism. Through the use of the instincts of animals, studies of primitive tribes, and explanations of how man has evolved since the days when he hunted for his food, they hope to disprove the value and necessity of male-female differences. Modern articles continually cite examples of anthropology and biology that contradict the norm. The feminists think man is ready to involve into his next stage of development where men and women share *all* abilities and responsibilities.

Tragically, in their rejection of God's wisdom, the feminists and their supporters turn their attention to the creatures for their standard of conduct rather than to the Creator. Even though the feminists don't fall down

before wooden or golden statutes of animals, Paul describes this attitude as idolatry in Rom. 1:25: "For
they exchanged the truth of God for a lie, and worshiped *and served the creature rather than the Creator,*
who is blessed forever. Amen." The feminists couldn't
deny the power of godliness anymore than if they
tried.

True godliness allows women to rise to their full
potential as human beings, to use their intelligence
and energy to the fullest, and to rise to the greatest
challenges possible. However, enslavers creep into the
houses of the unsuspecting:

B. CREEP INTO HOUSES

II Tim. 3:6: "For among them are those who
enter [creep--KJV] into households..."

Women may think they're secure in their homes
and safe from being enslaved. But the enslavers pretend to befriend women and creep into their households
in many ways--through magazines, television, newspapers, neighbors, children, etc. God warns that certain
women are particularly susceptible to enslavers:

C. CAPTIVATE SILLY WOMEN

II Tim. 3:6: "...and captivate weak [silly--
KJV] women weighed down with sins, led
on by various impulses,..."

"Captivate" means "to lead away captive, to subjugate, bring under control, to take captive one's mind,
captivate" (Thayer, p. 123).
"Silly women" means "a little woman, silly woman"
(Thayer, p. 123).
The Bible uses the expression "silly women" only
one time--in this passage. Even if the word itself
doesn't adequately explain what makes a woman silly,
the apostle Paul does. Only a certain kind of woman is
silly and prone to exploitation: the woman who thinks
with her emotions instead of her brain quickly becomes
a silly woman.
God didn't give the woman her emotions to think
with, but to make her sensitive to the needs of others

so that she can truly love her husband and children and make their home a refuge from the world. However, a woman gets into trouble when she starts to think with her emotions. This happens when she gets emotionally involved in something. Then because she feels so strongly about it, she assumes her feelings must be true and dependable. Yet feelings are the most undependable things around.

The more emotionally involved a woman gets in something, the less clearly she thinks about it, and the more she becomes a silly woman. Led on by her divers lusts, she's always drawing conclusions, but never really knowing the full truth.

The apostle Paul gives an example of this type of action in Acts 26:9-11. Paul says he killed Christians because he was "furiously enraged at them." Paul's emotional involvement in the problem convinced him that he was doing right. Thus, he did everything in all good conscience (Acts 23:1). But even though Paul felt good about his actions, they were still wrong--still sin. Sin makes up an important part of the character of silly women:

1. WEIGHED DOWN WITH SINS

"Weighed down" means "to heap together, to heap up, to overwhelm one with a heap of anything" (Thayer, p. 612).

Instead of correcting their sins and making their lives right with God, silly women simply allow their sins to mount up until they become weighed down with them. As a result, the women lose their ability to think clearly and rationally. Jesus explained this principle in Mt. 7:3-5. He asked, "And why do you look at the speck in your brother's eye, but do not notice the log that is in your own eye? Or how can you say to your brother, 'Let me take the speck out of your eye,' and behold the log is in your own eye?" Jesus continued, "You hypocrite, first take the log out of your own eye; and then *you will see clearly enough* to take the speck out of your brother's eye." Until a person takes care of his own sins, he can't see clearly the other person's sin.

Thus, if a woman allows disrespect for God's word to reign in her life by acting contentiously toward her husband, wishing she'd never had children, and despising her own femininity, then she is weighed down with sins. She can't see! She can't think! She's incapacitated! She's a silly woman!

2. LED BY VARIOUS IMPULSES

"Various" means "of divers colors, variegated, of divers sorts" (Thayer, p. 527).

"Impulses" means "desire, craving, longing" (Thayer, p. 238).

When a woman can't think clearly because of her sins, something must lead her. God certainly isn't her guide. All that's left is her emotions--her various impulses. Anything that appeals to her fancy, she pursues wholeheartedly.

One preacher said, "You can't reason someone out of something he didn't reason himself into." Sad indeed is the plight of silly women who give in to their emotions and allow them to take over their lives. For while they search for answers to their misery, their basic attitudes toward God's authority and word prevent them from discovering the truth:

3. ALWAYS LEARNING

II Tim. 3:7: "...always learning and never able to come to the knowledge of the truth."

"Liberate" means to release from restraint or bondage; to free" (Webster).

"Learning" means "a. to increase one's knowledge; b. i.q. to hear, be informed; c. to learn by use and practice" (Thayer, pp. 388-389).

"Knowledge" means "precise and correct knowledge" (Thayer, p. 237).

"Truth" means "verity, truth, what is true in any matter under consideration" (Thayer, p. 26).

The role God created for women requires all the intelligence, imagination, creativeness, and strength which they possess. However, God gives women the choice of either obeying Him and rising to their full potential as human beings or of disobeying Him and living a shallow unfulfilling life.

In this passage, through inspiration, Paul tells how both men and women become enslaved. They seek after knowledge, but they settle for worldly wisdom and fables. On the other hand, true liberation involves precise thoughts and actions. For "knowledge" includes correct information, and "truth" represents what is true in any matter under consideration.

A woman liberates herself by repenting of living her life according to her various impulses and by turning to God's word for guidance. When she comes to her senses by learning the truth, she escapes from the doctrines of demons and the enslavers. If she is liberated or enslaved depends upon no one but herself and whether she thinks with her brain or if she allows her emotions free reign.

III. THE WOMAN'S CHOICE

The feminists openly blame men for the lot of women, but every woman, whether feminist, career woman, or homemaker, must make a choice for herself. That choice depends solely upon her and not men--not even her husband. Every woman chooses for herself if she puts on the beauty of femininity or if she suffers as a silly old woman.

A. THE WISE CHOICE

Prov. 14:1: "The wise woman builds her house,..."

The woman who guides her life through wisdom, according to the plan of her Creator, builds her house and improves the quality of life for everyone. Of course, her house consists of much more than four walls to *keep out* the cold. Her house surrounds a heart that *keeps in* the warmth.

Many women don't like to acknowledge it, but the truth remains that what the home becomes depends largely upon the woman and how she accepts her responsibilities and challenges. Women aren't second-class citizens without purpose or intelligence. The next section, "Solution II: Male & Female vs. Feminism & Unisex," shows that God designed a great plan for *every woman*. But before a woman can rise to her true greatness, she must become a woman of intelligence--of wisdom.

A woman cannot succeed in the home in spite of herself--she must deliberately act and think wisely. A woman cannot properly love her husband by yielding to the dictates of nature--she must follow the path of wisdom. A woman cannot raise obedient children by listening to popular philosophies--she must reach toward wisdom. A woman cannot serve God in the church by assuming that her husband serves for her too--she must put on wisdom. A woman cannot even be a good housekeeper by just doing menial tasks--she must give her whole being to the pursuit of true wisdom.

I.Q. scores fail to accurately measure wisdom. Instead, success achieved in the home and in solving personal problems indicates true wisdom. It takes intelligence to earn a college degree, but it takes *true wisdom* to raise a family successfully. A woman might work as a business executive, doctor, teacher, engineer, or lawyer and still fail in the home.

If a woman wants a happy marriage, she must work for it by studying the word of God and going to God in prayer to change her attitudes and feelings. Subjective thinking and honesty are the most difficult parts of changing one's self, thus Paul's admonition to exercise naked. Once a woman puts false feelings out of the way, new truthful reactions toward men begin to grow. Therefore, if a woman wants to build a taste of heaven into her marriage, she must deliberately make the choice to be wise instead of a silly old woman:

B. THE FOOLISH CHOICE

> Prov. 14:1: "...But the foolish tears it down with her own hands."

God created marriage to be just as good for women as for men. God's regulations don't make a marriage turn sour. But acceptance of the doctrines of the philosophers, who are seared in their own consciences, makes a woman unable to think clearly or intelligently. Feminists clamor for men and women to base their relationships upon truth, which God advocated from the very beginning of time. Unfortunately, many women who

claim to want the truth, instead choose to ignore it by
letting their emotions guide them.

For example, one woman became furious at her
husband over an incident that she thought showed a
lack of consideration for her. When she vented her
anger to another woman, the friend kept asking her,
"Why are you really mad? None of your reasons seem
to justify your rage." The woman finally admitted that
she didn't trust men in general.

When the friend asked her why she didn't trust
men, the woman replied, "I know that men carry on
with their secretaries!"

It was a rather amusing reason because the
woman's husband didn't have any female employees.
He was such a homebody that his wife had to encourage him to take the family out to dinner. But the
woman's distorted view of *all men* made it impossible
for her to see her husband as he really was. Her irrational view that all men cheat on their wives cheated
her out of appreciating and enjoying her husband. She
used this erroneous analysis of men to read unkind-
ness into her husband's every action.

Such false concepts destroy homes. Many women
simply don't realize the power they hold in their
hands--the power to either build up their homes or to
destroy them. A woman can destroy her home without
any help whatsoever from her husband or children. She
can do it all by herself. And she doesn't even need to
use her brains to do it. Such power is frightening!

Because the woman holds a mighty power, she
needs all the help she can get. She can't afford to
turn her back upon the only reliable source of information available to her, the word of God. When a
woman takes the keys of happiness God provides for
her and applies them to her marriage, she unlocks
doors of fulfillment and contentment that she never
dreamed possible. No matter what hardships life might
hold for her, the mental rewards far outweigh them.

When a woman chooses to make her home a refuge
for her husband and children, she becomes the kind of
woman God created her to be. She frees herself from
the powers of Satan. She becomes free to enjoy her
husband, free to relish taking care of her children,
free to enjoy her femininity, free to think and use her
brain, free to be a real person, and free to bring love

to others. She frees herself to reap the greatest ful-fillment a woman can ever achieve as she becomes liberated in the fullest sense.

Not just any woman can turn a house into a home. God said the *wise woman* builds her home. Being a real woman involves much thought, imagination, dedication, love, patience, and plain old hard work. A woman can choose to become wise by putting on truth, love, sober-mindedness, purity, and the love of God, or she can choose to become foolish by basing her life on fables, lies, half-truth, hatred, envy, and sexual im-morality.

Every woman owes it to herself to make the right choice--to know the truth and to obey it. Only then can a woman gratefully share in marriage and praise God for designing the most wonderful relationship two people ever enjoy on earth--wedded bliss. But the choice belongs to the woman alone. She can give up the beauty and the splendor of her femininity in all its glory and choose instead to wither away as a silly old woman.

STUDY EXERCISE

Answer all questions in your own words.

1. What is a worldly fable? Is it wise to base one's life on worldly fables? Why?

2. What does it mean to exercise naked? Give an example of how a person might do this.

3. Why must a person discipline himself to get rid of marriage problems?

4. Do you think the feminist movement is a danger to women today? Why?

5. What makes a woman become like an "old woman"?

6. What makes a woman become like a "silly woman"?

7. How does a person's attitude toward learning what he is doing wrong make him be either wise or foolish?

8. What was the most important thing that you learned from this chapter?

9. Do you disagree with anything in this lesson? If so, explain in detail giving scriptures for your reasons.

PROBLEM-SOLVING EXERCISE

The Problem: The following excerpts are selected from "Unwed Motherhood by Choice--Another Lifestyle Gaining Popularity," *Spokane Daily Chronicle* (1/6/76).

> When Steven, now 6, asks about his father, Miss E says she tells him: "He doesn't live here. We cared enough for each other to make a baby but not to live together. Fortunately, more than half of Steven's class have single-parent families."
>
> It has not been easy these last years. Ms. E and her son are both in psychological therapy. She says she is quite sure she never wants to marry. She says she is a lesbian.
>
> Ms. E is studying for a degree in psychology and is on welfare. "That (being on welfare) bothers me but I know I'm not abusing it," she said. "I wanted to go to school and prepare myself for a positive function in society. Having Steven made me realize that I would have to pay a lot more attention to where I was going in life."
>
> "But I'm so proud of myself. Steven has given me deep satisfaction, and I'm making use of all the positive feelings he has generated. I'm much more interested in myself and the world."

The Exercise: Discuss the above article in detail telling whether you believe the woman is guiding her life according to wisdom or folly. Use scriptures for your reasons.

CHAPTER 4

THE SECRET OF TRUE HAPPINESS

Nowadays, nearly every magazine contains articles directed toward the "new woman" who does and has it all. They quote doctors, lawyers, psychologists, sexologists, judges, congressmen and women, corporate executives, home economists, feminists, and others with impressive titles to prove their points. But the publications often cause more bewilderment than enlightenment. These reports teach nearly every available position from helping women become efficient homemakers to teaching them how to start their own businesses.

In this ocean of mass confusion, finding the truth and wisdom seems nearly impossible. When a woman fails to find her special place in society, she usually takes a big guilt-trip. If she stays home with the kids, the articles and her friends make her wonder, "What's wrong with me? I ought to be accomplishing more with my life. I know I have time to bake cookies and read stories to my toddlers, but what will I have when they go to school or leave home? What if I end up a forty-five-year-old divorcee with no skills? But I feel like my place is at home."

And if she works outside the home, her conscience torments her about the mildewing pile of laundry and the mending that never gets done before her children outgrow the clothes. Her conscience agonizes, "Would my son do better in school if I stayed home more? Would I not yell so much at the kids if I didn't feel under pressure all the time? Would my husband show more affection for me if I didn't nag him continually to help with the housework? Will I be sorry later that I gave up these years at home to buy a second car? But I feel like I have to work."

With all the conflicting messages that today's woman hears, can she possibly find inner peace and contentment? Or is she doomed to be tossed to and fro as public opinion changes from generation to generation about the role of the woman? Where are the answers that a woman can depend upon for herself and teach to her daughter who will teach them again to her granddaughter. Is that too much to ask for--solid, dependable answers?

"No," says Solomon:

I. THE PURPOSE OF WISDOM

Prov. 1:1-2: "The proverbs of Solomon the son of David, king of Israel: To know wisdom,..."

"Wisdom" means "to be wise (in mind, word, or act)" (Strong, p. 39).

Wisdom, a quality of the mind, language, and actions, can be learned when one understands the purpose of wisdom. Fortunately, the wise man Solomon, through inspiration, reveals in the book of Proverbs the secret of wisdom and how it solves the profound problems of life.

Many people mistakenly think that wisdom results from accumulating facts, but a college education or the memorization of a multitude of Bible verses won't make a person wise. Wisdom involves the ability to apply facts or truths to one's life to both correct and avoid mistakes.

For example, a person with a high I.Q. might easily be a fool if he doesn't know how to apply his education to solving his personal problems. On the other hand, a person with a low I.Q. might display more wisdom than the person who went to college. Why? Because he uses what knowledge he has as a guide for proper conduct, and thus he enjoys a more tranquil life than inherently smarter individuals.

Solomon begins the book of Proverbs by showing how true wisdom enables a person to solve conflicts:

A. RECOGNIZES PROBLEMS

Prov. 1:2: "...To know wisdom and instruction,..."

"Instruction" means "properly chastisement, figuratively reproof, warning or instruction, also restraint:-- bond, check, correction, discipline, doctrine, instruction, rebuke" (Strong, p. 63).

According to Solomon, wisdom involves "instruction" or learning where one is wrong and then making the necessary corrections. Wisdom includes self-discipline, self-rebuke, and self-chastisement. Wisdom demands that one restrain and check his own behavior when tempted by foolishness rather than truth. *Thus, wisdom cannot exist without the ability to recognize that one has a problem.*

Some argue, "That's ridiculous! Everyone knows when they have a problem!" Sadly, that's not always true. For example, sometimes hunters lose their way in the woods, but don't realize it until it's too dark to find their way out. Likewise, many married couples ignore their problems until one of them asks for a divorce.

More than one woman has said, "I have a friend who really needs these lessons. But when I invited her to come to class with me, she got mad. She said that she didn't have any problems and didn't want to waste her time. And the more I tried to get her to come, the madder she got."

Sometimes, when a preacher or a Christian tries to help another person involved in sin or just obnoxious behavior, he must work really hard to persuade that person that he, indeed, has a problem and that his life is not in harmony with divine wisdom. Often even specific examples fail to convince him. Pride allows a person to hear sermon after sermon, which would solve his particular problem, to go away saying, "That was a good lesson for the other members. They sure needed it!"

Proud individuals seldom manifest real wisdom. However, open-minded students of God's word who acknowledge that they don't know all the answers usually display great understanding. The person who seeks after wisdom must desire to know the truth at all costs, which requires humility and the ability to admit that he is wrong at times. A person who refuses to accept responsibility for his mistakes may save his face, but he loses his reasoning abilities in the process. Willful ignorance is a terrible price to pay for pride.

It is better to be right by admitting that one is wrong, than to be wrong by claiming that one is right. Unfortunately, the majority of the people disagree. Many even stoop to telling lies to protect their allusions of never making mistakes. In a store the other day, a mother told her daughter, "Don't you know all grandmothers tell little lies." They both chuckled as if that were an accepted fact of life. Honesty with one's self and with others seems to be a rare trait. Perhaps that is one reason why true wisdom is also a rare quality.

B. FINDS SOLUTIONS

Prov. 1:2: "...To discern the sayings of understanding,..."

"Discern" and "understanding," both forms of the same Hebrew word, share the same basic meaning: "to separate mentally (or distinguish), i.e. (generally) understand" (Strong, p. 20).

Translating this verse with the definitions of the words makes it read: "to separate mentally and to distinguish the sayings of understanding." In other words, when a person recognizes that he has a problem, the next step is *to propose a solution for the problem that will work.* Unfortunately, many people who know that they have a problem don't have the slightest idea of how to solve it. And many who try to solve their problems propose solutions that actually make the problems worse instead of better.

Many men try to solve their problems by ignoring them and hoping they will go away. This seldom works because few problems get better when left to themselves; most become only worse. On the other hand, women usually find it hard to disregard their unhappiness, so they frequently turn to self-pity as a way of coping with a bad situation. However, this, too, only makes their lives more miserable instead of happier.

Some individuals try to solve their problems by distracting their minds with time-consuming hobbies, sports, or extra employment which helps them stop caring. Again, this only makes the problem worse as it allows their emotions to become calloused.

Other people try to solve their problems with psychiatric treatment. As shown in chapter 2, unless they obtain help from a counselor who is well versed in the scriptures, they risk placing their confidence in harmful advice. For example, a magazine article told about a couple who went to a marriage counselor. He advised them to get their feelings out into the open by fighting more vigorously. The couple soon discovered an ugliness in each other that horrified them; and as a result, they got a divorce.

Some men and women turn to alcohol, drugs, or affairs to solve their marital difficulties. Yet Hos. 4:11 says, "Harlotry, wine, and new wine take away the understanding." "Understanding" or "heart" (KJV), a different Hebrew word than the one defined previously, is used "very widely for the feelings, the will and even the intellect" (Strong, p. 58). In other words, the person who turns to either mind stimulating or numbing methods for solving his problems loses his ability to discern true wisdom or to think clearly.

Still other people try to solve irritations by conducting their lives according to their feelings. An emotional response constitutes one of the most unreliable methods of dealing with perplexing situations. Such people act a certain way not only because they *feel* as if that is what they should do, but also because of what they *assume* the other individual feels.

First of all, accurately second guessing someone's feelings is an impossibility because in I Cor. 2:11 Paul says, "For who among men knows the thoughts of a man except the spirit of the man, which is in him?" In the second place, trying to figure out what someone else feels is a sin for which Paul rebuked the Corinthians in I Cor. 4:5 by saying, "Therefore do not go on passing judgment before the time, but wait until the Lord comes who will both bring to light the things hidden in the darkness and disclose the motives of men's hearts; and then each man's praise will come to him from God." Paul makes it clear that even assigning *good motives* to others is reserved for God, not human beings.

Judging motives probably creates and magnifies problems more than any other single factor. More than likely, if one partner judges motives, the other does too. Husbands and wives help each other overcome this sin by pointing it out when it occurs.   For example, in the heat of an argument, a husband might say, "You don't care what I think! You just always do things your own way!"

The wife retaliates with, "You never have really loved me! You always blame me for everything!" One partner (who determined ahead of time to stop judging motives and who prayed to God for strength to stay calm and rational during an argument) needs to apologize to the other for judging his motives. The wife could say in a normal tone of voice, "I'm sorry I said, 'You never have really loved me. You always blame me for everything.' I don't know what your thoughts are until you tell me. Will you please forgive me?" After he forgives her, she can continue, "Our judging of each other's motives is destroying our marriage. Every time you accuse me of thinking something I really don't think, I think you're unreasonable. And the fight just gets worse. I'm not going to judge your motives in the future and I won't accept you judging my motives. I'll point it out every time that you don't know my motives. And if I slip and judge your motives, I want you to point it out to me and I will apologize. I'm serious about this. I want us to have a good relationship."

The husband might counter, "Does that mean you can do whatever you want and I can't say anything about it? I don't buy that!"

The wife can reply, "No, you have a right to know why I do certain things. But you need to ask me why I did something rather than assuming you know why I did it. Then when I tell you, if my motives were wrong, you can chew me out for what I *really thought and did* rather than for what you assumed I thought. And when you do something that tempts me to think you don't love me, I'm going to ask you why you did such and such. But I won't accuse you of not loving me. If I have doubts I'll ask you if your actions mean you don't love me? I'll listen to what you say."

Only in this way can a couple deal with the real issues that cause strife between them instead of fighting straw men and women all the time. However, just understanding the problem of judging motives and determining to stop won't solve the problem overnight. It may take months of constantly reminding themselves not to judge motives before they break the habit. Not only should they not judge motives of each other verbally, but neither should they give into it with their thoughts. Judging motives causes much more damage to the one who does it than to the one who hears it.

Judging motives for *good* causes just as many problems as assigning evil motives to someone. For example, many a wife works at thinking up excuses for her husband's behavior so that it won't bother her. She may get away with this habit for several years. But the day will come when she's too tired or too agitated to think up a good excuse for questionable behavior. Then all of those good excuses that she made up will come flooding to the surface to blow the present irritation all out of proportion. Invariably, unless a woman asked her husband why he did each thing and heard from his mouth his reasons, her subconscious knows that she just made the excuses up, and it reserves the right to change its mind at a later date.

So instead of assuming that her husband came home late for dinner because he got so busy he forgot, she should ask him. She can ask pleasantly during supper, "What happened tonight, I expected you at 6:00?" Then when he tells her about the accident on the freeway she can sympathize with his problem. Or if he says he stopped by the computer store on the way home and lost track of time, she'll understand. But if it *bothers her* that he came home late and *she doesn't ask* him about it, one day when he comes home late, she'll explode, "You don't care how I work and slave to fix meals for you! You just take me for granted! You're *always* late for supper!" and on and on it goes.

The modern feminist movement presents a classic example of proposing a solution for a legitimate problem without verifying that it will work. Betty Friedan, who wrote *The Feminine Mystique* which launched the new feminist movement in 1963, began to realize her mistake eighteen years later. In an article for *Woman's Day* in 1981 Friedan acknowledged that in spite of the gains in job opportunities for women, "something went wrong."

The young women who answered the call of the feminists and who gave up enjoying their husbands and children to compete with men in the marketplace felt cheated and disillusioned. As these young college women approached middle age, they discovered that sacrificing the fulfillment of motherhood for a career "denied life's realities" for them.

Regardless of the unhappiness of career women, Friedan said, "There is no going back" to being home-makers. She explained that the first stage of the feminist movement was over--women had changed themselves. It was time for the second stage--time to change the men. She advocated that the feminists should no longer *fight against men,* but that they should *work with them.*

However, her way of working with men differs drastically from God's plan for women to assist men. Friedan now proposes that women *insist* that their husbands take over more of the responsibilities at home and with the children. Role swapping would be nice. But nothing less than the chores split fifty-fifty will do. This way she thinks women can enjoy an exciting career and the fulfillment of a family at the same time without having to perform as "superwomen."[1]

Such audacity! After nearly twenty years of experimenting with other women's lives, Friedan discovered that *masculinizing women* only frustrated the women. Now she wants women to trust her for another twenty years and work at *feminizing the men.* Since she failed in her attempts to help women find fulfillment, why does she think she'll suddenly succeed with the men? Besides, men thought they were happy before she came along! And now she wants to restructure their lives, too. She may not even live long enough to see the full fruits of that project. Is the world ready to place its confidence in the unproven theories of an unproven woman and accept the consequences?

George Gilder warns in his book *Men and Marriage* that feminizing men results in dire consequences for society. He cites Margaret Mead's work with three

---

[1]Betty Friedan, "Being 'Superwoman' is *Not* the Way to Go," *Woman's Day* (10/13/81), pp. 53, 58.

primitive New Guinea tribes in the late 1940's as examples. He says that the liberals like to use these anthropology studies to promote abolishing the differences between the sexes. Una Stannard did this when she referred to these same tribes in her article "The Male Maternal Instinct" discussed in the previous chapter. Because these native men went through feminizing rituals, she concluded that men secretly want to be mothers.

However, Gilder quickly points out that the liberals ignore what eventually happened to these tribes. At the time of Mead's study, *they were all on their way to extinction.* The more feminized the men, the more they lost their natural aggression and ceased to hunt for food or to protect their families from hostile tribes. So while the men "nurtured" their children, their children died for lack of food. And while the women became more aggressive in response to the more passive nature of the men, the women failed to successful replace the men in providing for the family or in protecting it from outside harm. Gilder states that history does not record one example of a nation where its men and women switched roles or even shared roles fifty-fifty and it survived for long.[2] Thus, Friedan boldly proposes a solution for the lack of maternal fulfillment in career women, but she fails miserably to verify that it will work without causing lasting damage to society. Dare anyone blindly follow her lead?

A person might select any one of the above as a solution to a real problem, but the wise person diligently examines the matter to make sure that the chosen remedy *will really solve the problem instead of making it worse.* Many people experience marriage problems because they neglect to choose wise solutions; they simply react to their irritations. When a person thinks through a problem and chooses a solution which he verifies will work, wisdom results:

[2]George Gilder, *Men and Marriage* (Gretna, LO: Pelican Publishing Co., Inc., 1986), pp. 41-43.

C. SOLVES PROBLEMS

> **Prov. 1:3:** "...To receive instruction in wise behavior, righteousness, justice, and equity;..."

"Instruction," the same word defined earlier, basically means to receive reproof, correction, and warnings.

"Wise behavior" means "to be (cause, make or act), circumspect and hence intelligent" (Strong, p. 116).

When the ability to recognize problems is coupled with the ability to find a workable solution, the final step in acquiring wisdom *is to put into practice the discovered truth*. Then wise behavior or success in all endeavors results. If a person fails to act with righteousness, justice, and equity, he has not yet discovered wisdom. He needs to seek to uncover his real problems and to propose genuine solutions before he acts. While closely related, righteousness, justice, and equity each show a different aspect of wise behavior:

Righteousness involves always doing what is right regardless of what others do or do not do. For this reason, a person must accurately analyze problem situations to separate what is right from what is wrong. Many people think that children automatically receive this ability when they reach a certain age. However, the Hebrew writer says that a person must learn the skill to distinguish right from wrong: "For every one who partakes of milk is not accustomed to the word of righteousness, for he is a babe. But solid food is for the mature, who because of practice have their senses trained to discern good and evil" (Heb. 5:13-14).

The attitude, "Make him straighten up and then I will!" hinders many people from practicing righteousness. In effect, they want to "do unto others as they did unto them." But Jesus said, "Whatever you want others to do for you, do so for them." People who worry more about how others treat them rather than worrying about how they treat others magnify their problems instead of solving them.

Justice, another part of wise behavior, describes the ability to make wise decisions in regard to the affairs of others. Many people who think they are judiciously wise are really troublesome meddlers (I Pet.

4:15). Human nature often enjoys pronouncing sentences on others, but justice reigns only when the person makes verdicts according to divine laws rather than personal whims and prejudice.   God calls upon His people to make judgments upon others in many disciplinary circumstances such as in Mt. 18:15-17; I Cor. 5:11-13; Gal. 6:1; and II Thess. 3:6. Without wisdom and a determination to be fair, Christians cannot exercise these responsibilities properly.

Instead of exercising discipline as God outlined in the Bible, some people try to take their own vengeance. Paul warns, "Never take your own revenge, beloved, but leave room for the wrath of God, for it is written, 'Vengeance is Mine, I will repay, says the Lord. But if your enemy is hungry, feed him, and if he is thirsty, give him a drink; for in so doing you will heap burning coals upon his head.' Do not be overcome by evil, but overcome evil with good" (Rom. 12:19-21).

Many people practice the very thing Paul warns against: they try to overcome evil with evil. The opposite of justice, this actually usurps God's authority. In addition, taking one's own vengeance perpetuates marriage problems. For example, many husband and wives withhold their love in retaliation to something the other did. However, the wise person obeys God's marriage laws regardless of what the other partner does or does not do. God nowhere in the Bible gives husbands and wives the right to punish their spouses for failure.

Invariably, when husbands and wives take vengeance into their own hands, they overreact. Justice demands that they treat the other right and leave the vengeance up to God, the only one who *executea it completely fair and without respect of persons (I Pet. 1:17).

Equity, the last quality of wise behavior that Solomon mentions, refers to the ability to treat others equally and fairly, without prejudice. Paul emphasizes the equity of Christians in Gal. 3:28 by saying, "There is neither Jew nor Greek, there is neither slave nor free man, there is neither male nor female; for you are all one in Christ Jesus."

Equity honors the human dignity of other people. For example, a wise person refuses to talk down to others or to maintain an "I'm better than you" self-righteous attitude. Equity also respects the God-ordained authority and rank of everyone. Men of wisdom show respect for women and honor them as God commands. Intelligent women avoid slandering men and live with them in the harmonious manner designed by God.

The Jews' attitude toward Jesus and John the Baptist presents a perfect example of the lack of equity in Mt. 11:18-19: "For John came *neither eating nor drinking*, and they say, 'He has a demon!' The Son of man came *eating and drinking*, and they say, 'Behold, a gluttonous man and a drunkard, a friend of tax-gatherers and sinners!' Yet wisdom is vindicated by her deeds." Jesus' reply to the Jews that "wisdom is vindicated by her deeds" mocked the hypocritical two-facedness that they used to find fault with both Jesus and John the Baptist in opposite circumstances.

When a person puts the word of God into his mind and allows it to govern his actions, he exemplifies the qualities of wise behavior: righteousness, justice, and equity. Whenever a person experiences difficulty in deciding if he chooses a good course or not, he should ask himself the following questions: (1) "Am I doing what is right regardless of what other people are doing? Or am I treating others as they treat me?" (2) "Am I practicing justice? Or am I trying to take my own vengeance?" and (3) "Am I practicing equity by being fair? Or am I prejudiced and one-sided?"

Without the qualities of righteousness, justice, and equity, or acting properly toward others, it is impossible to engage in wise behavior. All the college courses on psychology and all the books which attempt to teach wisdom in specialized fields of human behavior show that many people want to practice wisdom. Fortunately, without the benefit of a college education or a vast library, every person with a functioning brain can learn how to act wisely as Solomon affirms:

II. THE NEED FOR WISDOM

Amazingly, many people feel satisfied with themselves and don't think that they need to change anything. However, Solomon takes care of this deceitful attitude of pride by emphatically affirming that *everyone* needs to learn about their mistakes. Both the naive and the wise have room for personal growth and need for self-chastisement:

A. THE NAIVE NEED WISDOM

Prov. 1:4: "...To give prudence to the naive, to the youth knowledge and discretion,..."

"Prudence" means "discretion:--guile, prudence, subtlety, wilily, wisdom" (Strong, p. 92).

"Naive" means "silly (i.e. seductible):--foolish, simple (icity, one) easily misled or persuaded" (Strong, p. 97).

This verse offers a lot of encouragement, for even the most foolish, silly, and easily misled person can develop keen judgment and perception that enables him to make wise decisions on his own. In fact, Solomon wrote Proverbs for the purpose of giving prudence, knowledge, and discretion to the naive and the youth by teaching basic truths about human nature and giving rules for conduct.

When men and women learn the book of Proverbs from their youth up, they experience fewer marriage problems, employment difficulties, child-raising failures, quarrels with in-laws, or contentions with neighbors. Studying God's word turns innocent naivete into wisdom that blesses a person throughout his entire life.

B. THE WISE NEED WISDOM

Prov. 1:5-6: "...A wise man will hear and increase in learning, and a man of understanding will acquire wise counsel, to understand a proverb and a figure, the words of the wise and their riddles."

"Hear" means "to hear intelligently (often with implication of attention, obedience, etc.)" (Strong, p. 118).

"Acquire" means "to procure, especially by purchase (causing to sell), by implication to own" (Strong, p. 104).

Scholars say that "words of the wise" refers to the book of Proverbs and includes the sayings of all the wise men such as Agur (Prov. 30:1) and King Lemuel (Prov. 31:1). Some scholars even think that perhaps David wrote some of the proverbs. At any rate, Solomon presents the book as an excellent source of wise counsel and discernment or understanding.

In fact, God packed the whole Bible full of information on how to live every day of one's life. Paul says, *"All scripture* is inspired by God and profitable for teaching, for reproof, for correction, for training in righteousness; that the man of God may be adequate, equipped for every good work" (II Tim. 3:16-17).

The words of the wise men, who wrote Proverbs, come in three closely related yet different forms:

A true "proverb" gives a basic rule of conduct as found in Prov. 15:28: "The heart of the righteous ponders how to answer, but the mouth of the wicked pours out evil things."

"A "figure" ridicules misconduct. The same Hebrew word is used in Hab. 2:6 which says, "Will not all of these take up a taunt-song [figure--Strong] against him, even mockery and insinuations against him,..." Prov. 22:13 contains an example of this type of wise saying which mocks the lazy person: "The sluggard says, 'There is a lion outside; I shall be slain in the streets!'"

A "riddle" differs from the other two maxims by using an obscure allegory or comparing two unlike objects to each other. Prov. 26:11 does this by saying, "Like a dog that returns to its vomit is a fool who repeats his folly."

Even wise men need to listen intelligently or with careful consideration to the words of God. In this way, they learn even more and become even wiser. A wise man tries to discover all of his errors by seeking out those who disagree with him rather than asking for advice from only those who congratulate him. A wise man is not content to be right most of the time; he continues to search for true answers to his problems so that he can always be right all the time.

C. MEN NEED WISDOM

Many a man leaves the happiness of his home up to his wife and to chance. Then when things go bad, he feels helpless to do anything about the situation.

But a happy home is not the result of chance nor at the mercy of just one spouse. A happy home is within the reach of everyone who willingly does the mental work necessary to achieve true wisdom. Men as well as women need the ability to recognize problems, to propose workable solutions, and to implement them into their everyday lives.

1. OLDER MEN

> **Tit. 3:1-2: "But as for you, speak the things which are fitting for sound doctrine. Older men are to be temperate, dignified, sensible, sound in faith, in love, in perseverance."**

"Dignified" means "august, venerable, reverend, to be venerated for character, honorable" (Thayer, p. 573).

"Sensible" means "of sound mind, i.e. a. in one's right mind; b. to exercise self-control, think of one's self soberly" (Thayer, pp. 612-613).

Other scriptures use "sensible" to show the opposite of being insane or crazy: Mk. 5:15 says, "And they came to Jesus and observed the man who had been demon-possessed sitting down, clothed and in his *right mind,* the very man who had the 'legion;' and they became frightened." Likewise, II Cor. 5:13 says, "For if we are beside ourselves, it is for God; if we are of *sound mind,* it is for you." Thus, the Bible uses "sensible" to refer to someone who has recovered from being demon-possessed or as the opposite of being beside one's self. Basically, "sensible" means to think clearly.

Therefore, when Paul instructs Titus to teach "sound doctrine," he wants him to urge the older men to be, among other things, "sensible" or to take the necessary steps to think clearly and rationally. This requires that men put some effort and study into learning about their roles as husbands, fathers, and leaders in the church. In fact, a man cannot become an elder if he is not sensible at home (I Tim. 3:4-5).

When a man guides his life according to wisdom he becomes "dignified," or highly respected. Thus, God wants older men to provide role models for young men to imitate. As Solomon said, "A gray head is a crown of glory; it is found in the way of righteousness"

(Prov. 16:31). Truly, wisdom creates a crown of splendor when exhibited in the life of older men.

2. YOUNG MEN

Tit. 3:6-8: "Likewise urge the young men to be sensible; in all things show yourself to be an example of good deeds, with purity in doctrine, dignified, sound in speech which is beyond reproach, in order that the opponent may be put to shame, having nothing bad to say about us."

"Sensible" and "dignified" come from the same words as above. Just as God wants the lives of older men to reflect these qualities, He also wants the young men to set examples of wise behavior. In fact, Paul says that young men should conduct themselves so that "the opponent may be put to shame, having nothing bad to say about us."

This places quite a responsibility upon the shoulders of young men--to act in such a way that no one can make a bad charge against them stick. Of necessity, such young men conduct themselves wisely in the marriage realm. No one sees them mistreat or neglect their wives--not even their wives. Through wisdom and proper examples in the home, men become effective teachers of the lost.

However, if a man does not know the truth about women and marriage, he will misinterpret everyday events and react to them in a harmful way. For example, a man grew up in a home with a father who viewed women as somewhere below an "army dog" and a "navy ship." Since the man's father considered women lazy sponges upon society, the son grew up with a modified version of the same attitude which he projected onto his wife. Nearly everything she did irritated him because of his underlying belief that women are mentally inferior to men. Everyday happenings easily furnished him with more ammunition for disapproving of his wife's activities. Thus, his lack of respect for women brought great heartache to his marriage.

Men need wisdom so that they can fully appreciate and enjoy their marriages. The more knowledge men

have of their marital roles, the more they free themselves to delight in their wives and in their own masculinity.

D. WOMEN NEED WISDOM

God assigns different jobs to women based on their
age and family responsibilities. Wisdom plays a vital
role in the ability of women to fulfill their individual
jobs:

1. OLDER WOMEN

**Tit. 2:3: "Older women likewise are to be
reverent in their behavior, not malicious
gossips, nor enslaved to much wine, teaching what is good, that they may encourage
[teach to be sober--KJV] the young
women..."**

"Reverent" means "befitting men, places, actions or
things sacred to God, reverent" (Thayer, p. 299).

God wants all older women to work toward the goal
of encouraging the young women. However, age alone
does not qualify a woman for this important job. She
must develop certain attitudes along the way. Most important, she is reverent in her behavior. This simply
means that she keeps men, places, and things in
proper perspective. She fully understands the male-female relationship in every realm--in the home, in the
church, and in the community. Wherever she is, she
understands God's universal law of authority. Without
this wisdom of where women fit into God's plan, an
older woman can't begin to teach the young women
how to love their husbands being submissive to them,
etc.

In addition, the older woman who governs her life
according to wisdom refuses to spread malicious gos-
sip. She respects the privacy of others and the confidence of young women who seek her advice. She protects her ability to think clearly at all times by not
becoming enslaved to much wine. Through her example
and her words, she teaches what is good to all who
know her.

Without these outward signs of sensible thinking, older women cannot teach that which is good. Thus, older women need God's wisdom in their lives. However, regardless of how the older women fulfill their duties toward the young women, God gives young women the personal obligation to study and to apply wisdom to their own lives:

2. YOUNG WOMEN

I Tim. 2:15: "But she shall be preserved through the bearing of children if the women continue in faith and love and sanctity with self-restraint."

"Self-restraint" comes from the same root word as "sensible" and has the same meaning.

Properly training and loving children is an important work in service to God. Thus, during a woman's childbearing years when caring for her children rightfully consumes her time, God wants young mothers to devote themselves to their families. In this way, they serve God best by teaching their little ones about His love. So God excuses young mothers from the duties of the older women whose families have grown and left their homes. The older women often have time on their hands while the young mothers wonder where their time went.

But while God does not expect the young mothers to devote themselves to teaching others to the same degree as the older women, He still requires them to grow spiritually and to think soberly. If anyone needs wisdom, young mothers do. During this time of pressure and responsibility, it's easy to become distracted from growing mentally. Yet mistakes in judgment can destroy their marriages or leave emotional scars on their children.

With the pressing need for wisdom, young mothers can't afford to neglect their own mental welfare if the older women fail to teach them. Thus, God gives the young women the responsibility of learning for themselves how to think properly.

In summary, these passages affirm that everyone, whether male or female, whether young or older, has a personal responsibility to apply God's instructions to himself in order to think wisely. In an age of bankrupt marriages, mentally-crippled children, and ungodly men and women, thinking sensibly requires much deliberate effort through the guidance only God can give.

III. THE MECHANICS OF WISDOM

After seeing the purpose of wisdom for recognizing and solving problems, and that everyone needs wisdom, all that remains is for each person to put on wisdom. Wisdom begins with a person's attitude toward God:

A. FEAR GOD

> **Prov. 1:7: "The fear of the Lord is the be-ginning of knowledge; fools despise wisdom and instruction."**

"Fear" means "1. the emotion of fear; 2. the intellectual anticipation of evil without emphasis upon the emotional reaction; 3. reverence or awe; 4. righteous behaviour or piety; and 5. formal religious worship."[3]

"Despise" means "to disrespect:--condemn, despise" (Strong, p. 19). The Hebrew word "appears only twenty-four times in the Old Testament, almost entirely in wisdom and poetic material. It serves as an antonym for reverence and regard."[4]

"Knowledge," "wisdom," and "instruction" are the same words studied previously. They refer to a person's expertise for recognizing problems and choosing workable solutions.

Surely, everyone wants the ability to make life more profitable and enjoyable. But many lack even the beginning of wisdom--the fear of the Lord or a wholesome dread of displeasing God. They prefer to trust their own intelligence by ignoring God's rules for living found in the Bible. This amounts to despising true wisdom and instruction.

Many people excuse their conduct by saying, "You can't teach an old dog new tricks" or "What was good

---

[3]R. Laird Harris, Gleason L. Archer, Jr. Bruce K. Waltke, *Theological Wordbook of the Old Testament,* (Chicago, IL: Moody Press, 1980), p. 907.
[4]Harris, *Theological Wordbook,* p. 213.

enough for my parents is good enough for me" or "I've always done it this way and always will." Too lazy to learn, some don't even bother to offer excuses.

Sometimes people complain, "The Bible just doesn't cover my problems. It's old-fashioned!" Not true, for God gives Christians everything they need to know in order to live peacefully and happily with others. A person may not like God's answer. He may refuse to take the time to search out God's solution. Likewise, he may not know the Bible well enough to find the remedy for his problem. But that does not mean that the Bible doesn't contain the answer. Rather, it means that he needs to spend more time studying the Bible to find the solution.

Solomon warns that the witless reasoning of fools often leads them to commit murder (vs. 11) and to acquire excessive wealth and fancy homes (vs. 13). Solomon says in verse 16 that "it is useless to spread the net in the eyes of any bird" because the bird will see the trap and avoid being caught. Yet even the common sense of dumb animals escapes fools, for Solomon states, "But they lie in wait for their own blood; they ambush their own lives." The foolish not only set their own traps, but they also waltz boldly into them.

Thus, Solomon pleads, "How long, O naive ones, will you love simplicity? And scoffers delight themselves in scoffing, and fools hate knowledge?" (Prov. 1:22). Tragically, one consequence of a lack of wisdom is that it usually accompanies the inability to even recognize that a problem exists. The false advice readily available in books and magazines easily satisfies the thirst for guidance in many individuals who look no further for answers. Their fancy cars, elaborate homes, and challenging jobs make them think that they already hold the keys to success.

They resemble the hunter who wanders in circles in the forest enjoying the trees and the wild life and thinking only of the deer he wants to shoot. He fails to realize that he is lost or that the temperature will be near freezing that night. Unless someone wiser than he sends out a search party that know the ways of the woods and how to guide him safely out, he will die in the beautiful forest and maybe no one will ever find his body.

In much the same way, God sends out a search party for those who do not know that they are lost in the world, walking in circles while enjoying the fruits of this life and thinking only of momentary pleasures. They do not know that while life seems good, they are not on the path of true happiness. Since happiness pulsates with varying degrees of intensity, many people assume that they enjoy life to the fullest, but they reap only a shallow, vanishing form of pleasure. God sends out His search party to guide everyone to true contentment, but He cannot lead anyone to safety who refuses to study and obey His word.

For a marriage like God designed in the garden of Eden when He pronounced His creation "good," a person must place his confidence in the word of God, not in this writer, not in any other book on marriage, not in any other person, and not in his own logic; but in the divinely inspired word of the God of heaven who reveals the many secrets of sanctified marital bliss. While those who reject God's precious gift of wisdom pay the price of misery, God freely gives wisdom to those who fear Him. Thus, true wisdom and happiness begins with a determination to obey God regardless of the consequences one *thinks* he might be called upon to pay.

For example, probably more than any other part of God's word, women fear subjection. If their husbands mistreat them now, they fear that they'll abuse them just that much more. But when a woman fears God more than she fears her husband and determines to obey God no matter what the cost, then she begins the journey toward wisdom. She discovers firsthand how God's laws bring out the best in both her husband and herself. She enjoys the blessings of practicing true subjection and avoids the curse of other women's misdirected submission or outright contention.

Then the next time God asks her to do something that she doesn't understand, she'll feel more confident and will obey Him readily. She's on her way to complete wisdom when she stops arguing with God and starts trusting His judgment. When problems arise she'll say, "I wonder what the Bible says about this situation. I'm going to find out before I do anything." Now she's really growing and the joy of wise living has just begun:

B. TAKE TIME TO GROW

Prov. 4:18-19: "But the path of the righteous is like the light of dawn, that shines brighter and brighter until the full day. The way of the wicked is like darkness; they do not know over what they stumble."

"The path of the righteous is like the light of dawn" means that turning to God for help is like seeing the sun slowly come up in the morning after a long dark night. Finally, after many hours the sun shines brightly overhead at full noon. In the same way, as a person studies and applies the Bible's teachings to his life, the light of truth and wisdom "shines brighter and brighter until the full day." The more he studies God's word, the clearer it becomes until he fully understands how to walk to please God and how to reap the most from life.

True wisdom liberates its followers from the sinful influence of others (Prov. 2:12), warns against sexual sins and misery (Prov. 2:16-17), gives length of days along with peace (Prov. 3:2), produces favor and influence with others (Prov. 3:4), promotes healing for the body (Prov. 3:8), teaches the proper attitude toward worldly possessions (Prov. 3:9-10), gives happiness (Prov. 3:18), enables one to walk securely without stumbling (Prov. 3:23), and gives pleasant sleep (Prov. 3:24). Those who reject the wisdom of God lose the benefit of these principles for getting along with others. As Solomon warns "They do not know over what they stumble."

When a person becomes a Christian, he often doesn't know anything other than what to do to be saved. As he continues to study God's word, he learns of sins that he commits through ignorance. In his determination to obey God, he eliminates these sins as quickly as he discovers them. The more he learns, the more mistakes he discovers in his life. The more he corrects his faults, the deeper his understanding becomes and the more he puts on true wisdom. Then as he continues to live by the standard of knowledge to which he has attained or learned, God reveals through

His word more areas that need correcting (Phil. 3:15–16; II Pet. 1:19).

While always correcting one's life sounds unpleasant, just the opposite occurs, actually. Once a person gets on the path of knowledge, he often becomes so excited about the happiness flooding into his life that he eagerly searches for ways to improve and to reap even greater blessings from God. His desire to know the truth and live according to it spurs him on to greater Bible study and causes him to glorify God. Truly, the rewards of wisdom are great when a person takes time to grow and to see the sunrise.

C. LOOK FOR ANSWERS IN SMALL PLACES

> **Ps. 119:160: "The sum of Thy word is truth, and every one of Thy righteous ordinances is everlasting."**

Psalms says that the *sum* of God's word is truth. A "sum" is not a piece of something but the total amount of *all* the pieces. Thus, it takes all of God's teachings about the marriage relationship to fully understand and practice God's truth. Picking and choosing won't produce the benefits of wisdom.

For example, an older woman started her young women's Bible class by saying, "The Bible doesn't say very much about being a woman, so I'm going to rely on some outside material. And I hope you'll always remember that *I told you these things.*" To make matters worse, she didn't believe God's teachings concerning subjection, so she left that topic out of her classes on marriage. Her students never once heard her mention the word "subjection." Nor did she practice subjection at home because she didn't think her husband deserved her submission. Just because she left out *one ingredient* in her life, this woman endured an unhappy and miserable marriage as did her husband.

Unfortunately, two of her students were new converts and unfamiliar with the Bible. All they knew about the Bible's teaching on marriage was the little bit they learned in her class. Since the teacher left subjection completely out of her instructions, being submissive to their husbands never occurred to them. Their marriages began to deteriorate rapidly until an-

other student in the class explained Bible subjection
to them privately. After they began to practice *the sum*
of God's word, their marriages began to improve. These
two women now encourage other wives to obey and
practice *all* of the word of God so that they too, can
delight in a wonderful marriage relationship.

Many times when a woman feels overwhelmed by
marriage problems, she wants one solution that will
make things one hundred percent right. However, since
it takes the sum of many parts to make God's truth,
solutions seldom come in single pieces. As a woman
studies and practices what she learns, she adds one
thing upon another, until she reaches the sum. Often-
times, it's the little pieces of truth that make all the
differences in her marriage.

For instance, a woman experiencing serious marriage problems may start off by just increasing her
self-esteem. She does this by learning why God created her and about the tremendous challenges that
await her. Her new feelings of self-worth perk up her
moods. And her family responds to her more cheerful
nature.

Nonetheless, she has only fitted one small piece
of the puzzle into place. Her marriage still lacks
something, so she keeps searching. She studies the
Song of Solomon and learns not to withhold her affection. Her husband becomes warmer, but that sparkle
between them still isn't there. Now she's ready to
tackle subjection. She agonizes and prays earnestly to
God about His will. Little by little, she begins to
yield her stubborn will to her husband. Each time she
conquers a part of her will, he becomes less demanding.

Things are definitely getting better, but still
missing a piece or two are missing in the puzzle. She
can't quite see the whole picture. And so she keeps
working, determined not to give up. She turns her attention to learning more about loving her husband. Her
study shows her that a husband requires reverence that
comes from his wife's heart. So she prays to God for
help and guidance. As true reverence begins to flood
her being, she truly delights in her husband. Best of
all, when he looks at her, love glows in his eyes. At
last, the puzzle fits perfectly together to bring happiness and contentment to them both. Now she can see

the full picture that shows her God's love for men and women.

And so she determines to look for solutions to future problems in little pieces instead of big chunks. By practicing each piece of truth as she discovers it and searching for the next piece, she's confident that with God's help, that together they can face the challenges of life.

———

STUDY EXERCISE

Answer all questions in your own words.

1. How does a person's attitude toward learning what he is doing wrong make him either wise or foolish?

2. Who should a person believe if her personal opinion contradicts something God says? Why?

3. How can practicing righteousness, justice, and equity solve marriage problems? Give an example of each.

4. Can a naive person develop wisdom? How?

5. How does judging motives either for good or bad magnify marriage problems?

6. Is the Bible a realistic source of information on how to have a happy marriage? Why?

7. Is man's wisdom a realistic source of information on how to enjoy a happy marriage? Why?

8. What are some of the rewards of finding true wisdom?

9. Do you disagree with anything in this lesson? If so, explain in detail giving scriptures for your reasons.

SPECIAL PROBLEM-SOLVING EXERCISE

This exercise is designed to help you develop your abilities to teach the young women when it becomes time for you to assume that responsibility. Select a newspaper, magazine article, or a current book on some aspect of the marriage relationship and give a report on it at the last class. Use scriptures to either verify or disprove the views presented. Your report should be about five minutes long. If you do not feel that you can give an oral report, prepare a written one to turn in. Begin to look for your article now.

PERSONAL EXERCISE

This exercise will also help you develop your abilities to teach the young women: Get a notebook, an expanding file, or a filing cabinet for collecting newspaper and magazine articles that deal with marriage and raising children. Be sure to date your clippings and put the source on them. As you read the articles, highlight significant parts and write notes and scriptures in the margins. Later when you want to use these clippings, your notes and highlights will enable you to find what you need quickly. These articles will stimulate your thinking both now and in the future when you want to use them as examples when you discuss these topics with others either in private or as a teacher.

SOLUTION II:

MALE & FEMALE

vs.

FEMINISM & UNISEX

(How to Balance Masculinity with Femininity)

"And the man said, 'This is now bone of my bones, and flesh of my flesh; she shall be called woman, because she was taken out of man. For this cause a man shall leave his father and his mother, and shall cleave to his wife; and they shall become one flesh.'"

(Gen. 2:23–24)

CHAPTER 5

WOMAN, A HELPER MEET FOR MAN

People everywhere want to know the purpose and design of a woman. However, the uncertainty of where women fit into the scheme of life is not new, but centuries old. For example, Thomas Aquinas, who mixed together the writings of Plato, Constantine, and Jesus and then wrote them down to form the first written Catholic creed, promoted a very low view of women. Not understanding conception and birth, he thought that defective males turned into women in the womb as a result of some flaw in the father's reproductive powers or because an external factor, like the south wind, which is damp, interfered with the life-creating processes.[1]

A woman might say, "What a ridiculous belief! Certainly, no one believes that sort of thing today!"

Unfortunately, many women, while rejecting such ignorance for themselves, believe that God and the Bible view women in a similar derogatory way. For example, a Roman Catholic nun, who taught at a local college, began a meeting to promote feminism by saying, "I'm going to give you an idea of how God views women." Then she proceeded to read quotations from the apocryphal books about how women are devils and the worst of all evils who always cause the downfall of innocent men, etc.

Sadly, no one in her audience seemed aware of the fact that the apocryphal books contradict much of the accepted Bible or that scholars generally recognize

[1]Richard Gilman, "Where Did It All Go Wrong?" *Life* (8/13/71), p. 52.

them as being uninspired. Thus, her quotations showed only what uninspired men thought about women--not how the God of heaven views women. But the women at the meeting left thinking that God held a low view of femininity!

Literature written by the leaders of the feminist movement shows that many women have been exposed to this type of negative teaching regarding women through the Roman Catholic church. Because of this, many women blame God for any mistreatment they suffer today without investigating for themselves what God really thinks about women.

Likewise, Protestants, who reject the apocryphal books, often promote their own brand of misinformation about the role of women. Many resent anything that the apostle Paul says about women. They circulate stories that he was jilted in love, and it soured him on women and marriage. "That's why," they claim, "he wrote all those horrible things about women and subjection." Many do not consider any of Paul's teachings binding on women today.

As a result, the religious teachings of the world leave many women in the lurch as they desperately search for the answers to such questions as: "Is the woman an intelligent creation or just a biological accident? Is the woman a toy for her husband to use at his pleasure? Is a woman to function as her husband's personal slave, ready at his beck and call to say, 'Yes, sir' and jump right to it? Is a woman socially a second-rate citizen without rights or privileges? Do any differences really exist between male and female?"

The feminists shout, "No!" to each of these questions and work at drowning out the ignorance of the past and the present. But intelligent women still want to know if the feminists teach the full truth or if they only replace one set of misconceptions with a more modern version of half-truths. They also want to know God's purpose for their lives to increase their self-respect.

The women's unrest even affects the men. They, too, question why they were created. "What is their role in life? Are they only pawns to serve the fancies of women? Are they just to provide a living and to forget their own needs and longings in the process? Can a woman really do anything a man can and better?"

The answers to the perplexing questions, "Why were men and women created?" and "Are men and women really different?" cannot be found by going to the apocryphal books or to the assumptions of those who reject Paul's teachings or to the personal opinions of men and women. True answers can be found only by going to God's inspired word. God begins the Bible with the story of creation and the beginning of the man and woman's relationship to each other:

I. GOD'S CREATION

Gen. 1:26-27: "Then God said, 'Let us make man in our image, according to our likeness, and let them rule over the fish of the sea and over the birds of the sky and over the cattle and over all the earth, and over every creeping thing that creeps on the earth.' And God created man in His own image, in the image of God He created him; male and female He created them."

"Image" means "to shade, a phantom, i.e. (figuratively) illusion, resemblance, hence a representative figure" (Strong, p. 99).

"Likeness" means "resemblance, model, shape, like" (Strong, p. 31).

Through inspiration, Moses begins the book of Genesis with a day-by-day account of the creation of the earth and everything that lives upon it. On the sixth day, Moses records that after God made the animals, He created man in the form of a male and a female in the likeness of His own image. Thus, mankind originated within the mind of God and both men and women reflect the image of God.

After finishing the general account of how God created the world in six days and rested on the seventh, Moses gives a more minute description of the special creation of the male and the female. He deals with each separately and shows how God made them inherently different from each other from the very beginning. First, God made man:

A. FORMED MAN FROM THE GROUND

> **Gen. 2:7: "Then the Lord God formed man of dust from the ground, and breathed into his nostrils the breath of life; and man became a living being."**

"Formed" means "(through the squeezing into shape), moulded into a form, especially as a potter, figuratively, determined" (Strong, p. 51).

Man did not just happen to evolve from sea slime as some modernists claim. Rather, God deliberately designed and created the man just as a potter deliberately fashions a vase to reflect his skill and intelligence. But the questions still remain, "Why did God make man?" and "Why did God make man from dust?"

1. TO FILL THE EARTH WITH PEOPLE

> **Gen. 1:28: "And God blessed them; and God said to them 'Be fruitful and multiply, and fill the earth,...."**

After God made mankind "male" and "female," He commanded them, "Be fruitful and multiply, and replenish the earth." To insure that man would obey this command, God created a strong sexual drive in both men and women. Unfortunately, many abuse this tool that enables mankind to serve God by engaging in sexual immorality and by refusing to care for their children.

The fulfillment of the command to "be fruitful and multiply, and fill the earth" doesn't stop with the sexual act which creates a new life, but begins with procreation. God gives parents the responsibility of raising their children to adulthood, and for helping their children rise to their full potential as human beings. Just as God created man in His image, God desires for man to fill the earth with like beings--children in the image of God.

In the ideal home environment, little children serve as the crowning act of God's creation. Innocent little toddlers and pre-schoolers possess many qualities that reflect the image of God. Consider for instance, their happiness, honesty, devotion to their parents, unfeigned love, genuine sorrow for the afflictions of others, humility, trust, and purity. Jesus said, "Unless you are converted and become like children, you shall not enter the kingdom of heaven" (Mt. 18:1-6). Sadly, somewhere along the line, most little children grow up only to lose many of their God-like qualities. Then as Christians, they must learn how to put them on again. In addition to telling man to be fruitful and to multiply, God gave man another important job:

2. TO SUBDUE THE EARTH

Gen. 1:28: "And God blessed them; and God said to them, 'Be fruitful and multiply, and fill the earth, and subdue it; and rule over the fish of the sea and over the birds of the sky, and over every living thing that moves on the earth.'"

"Subdue" means "to tread down, to conquer, subjugate, violate:--bring into bondage, force, keep under, subdue, bring into subjection" (Strong, p. 54).

"Earth" means "the earth (at large), or partitively a land):--common, country, earth, field, ground, land, nations" (Strong, p. 17).

"Rule" means "to tread down, i.e. subjugate; specially to crumble off:--(come to, make to) have dominion, prevail against, reign, (bear, make to) rule, (-r, over), take" (Strong, p. 107).

By explaining the meaning of "to tread down," the *Theological Wordbook* gives insight into how God wants men to subdue the earth:

> In the OT it means "to make to serve, by force if necessary."...It assumes that the party being subdued is hostile to the subduer, necessitating some sort of coercion if the subduing is to take place. Thus the word connotes "rape" in Est. 7:8, or the conquest of the Canaanites in Num. 32:22, 29; Josh. 18:1; I Chr. 22:18. In II Chr. 28:10; Neh. 5:5; Jer. 34:11, 16 it refers to forced servitude.
>
> Therefore "subdue" in Gen. 1:28 implies that creation will not do man's bidding gladly or easily and that man must now bring creation

into submission by main strength. It is not to rule man....[2]

God's command to Adam and Eve to subdue the earth shows that He intended for them to work and use the earth and its products along with the animals to make a living for themselves and their family. God's choice of the word "subdue" shows that from the very beginning God expected man to *work hard* for his food, clothing, and shelter.

Farmers recognize the hostility of the earth to their efforts. They must clear their fields of rocks, boulders, and trees before they can plant their crops. Yet having done that, if the farmers allow their fields to lie idle for a period of time, trees and vines soon take it over. If enough time passes, all evidence of the farm disappears and the new farmer must begin all over again.

Likewise, when men build roads, they must clear the vegetation and blast their way through rocks--the land does not yield submissively to their desires and plans. And after the construction crews finish their new freeways, the asphalt freezes and forces them to patch the pot holes. Or a flood may wash the road completely away.

No matter what scientific data a man might use to determine the weather, the weather doesn't always cooperate. Thus, wind, rain, and snow often foil the best of man's plans. Also, the beasts of the field don't always cooperate with man's efforts to breed certain characteristics into their offspring. In like manner, man has only begun to discover how some of his efforts to subdue the earth have actually harmed his environment and threatened his future existence. And on and on go the examples of how man must use his strength and ingenuity to subdue a hostile earth in order to survive.

God not only told Adam and Eve that He wanted them to work and to use the earth to provide for themselves, but God also acted as the first employer and gave Adam a specific job. In this way, God further emphasized man's purpose in life by placing him in the Garden of Eden to work:

[2]Harris, *Theological Wordbook*, p. 430.

Gen. 2:15: "Then the Lord God took the man and put him into the garden of Eden to cultivate [dress--KJV] it and keep it."

"Cultivate" or "dress" means "to work (in any sense) enslave, etc:--keep in bondage, be bondmen, bond-service, compel, do, dress" (Strong, p. 84).

"Keep" means "to hedge about (as with thorns), i.e. guard, generally to protect, attend to, etc:--beware, be circumspect, take heed, keep, preserve, watch (-man)" (Strong, p. 118).

Mistakenly, some people visualize Adam lying under the fig trees picking fruit when hungry, getting a drink when thirsty, sleeping when tired, and playing with the animals when bored--just soaking up all the beauty of a wonderful paradise without a single care or responsibility in the world. To the contrary, God did not design man to be lazy and unproductive--God ordained that man should provide for himself and his family through hard work.

From the very beginning, God created Adam for this purpose as He instructed him to cultivate and keep the Garden of Eden. Cultivating the garden, Adam prevented his garden plots from turning back into a jungle of overgrowth. Adam also began the Oriental custom of fencing his land with hedges of thorns to protect it from animals who might eat his crops or trample the young plants. Even though Adam lived in a luxurious, wonderful world, he still labored to put food on his table each day.

Solomon wrote in Eccl. 5:12, "The sleep of the working man is pleasant, whether he eats little or much. But the full stomach of the rich man does not allow him to sleep." God not only gave man a job to do, but God also created within man *a need to work.* When a man satisfies this desire, his life takes on meaning and pleasure for him. On the other hand, when a man neglects his need to work, boredom sets in and even sleep fails to satisfy him. The angry people on welfare testify to man's compelling inner drive for meaningful work. Working on the earth as a human being, Jesus set the example for men to follow:

Jn. 5:17: "But He answered them, 'My Father is working until now, and I Myself am working.'"

One way that man reflects God's image is by working. God worked during the creation of the world and continues to work even now. At the same time, *Jesus the Savior works.* A man who refuses to work does not share anything in common with God and Jesus who created man in Their image. As a result, God doesn't manifest any sympathy for the hunger of men who avoid working for their food. In like manner, work is so important to God's plan for man that God commands His followers not to pamper those who refuse to work:

II Thess. 3:10: "For even when we were with you, we used to give you this order: If anyone will not work, neither let him eat."

God said in Gen. 3:19, "By the sweat of your face you shall eat bread." No sweat--no bread. God did not create man to be an idle loafer but an active bread winner.

A woman's husband lost his job, and even though he was highly educated and many work possibilities existed for him, she encouraged him to apply for welfare. He refused and said that he would rather support his family himself. However, one day while her husband was job-hunting, the wife secretly signed them up for welfare. Her actions completely changed the nature of her husband's attempts to get a job. He became extremely critical of all job offers and turned down good-paying jobs because "It required too much of his time and he couldn't travel" or "He might get too dirty" or "He didn't feel like working at that job." When he did get a job, he soon became too "sick" to work steadily and he was laid off. Each time, his wife quickly enrolled them back on welfare.

Meanwhile, as the family's standard of living decreased, the wife became an expert at manipulating others to do things for her that her husband should do and at covering up her husband's unwillingness to work at an honest job. In the beginning, the other members of the congregation where they worshiped gladly helped this family which seemed to be down on their luck. However, this woman never tried to do anything for herself if she could get someone else to do it. She asked other people to mail her letters for her rather than walk a block to mail them herself. She asked people to spend an hour driving to her house and then to the school and back to take something to one of her children that the child had forgotten instead of allowing the child to learn to be responsible. She always called at the last minute and never planned grocery shopping trips in advance. She expected others to drop whatever they were doing, jump in their cars, drive to her house, and take her wherever she wanted to go. Usually half-way to her house, the person would think, "Wait a minute! Is this a legitimate need or is this something she should be doing for herself? Would I ask someone to do this for me?" Often the answer was, "No." When other women helped her clean her house, she made no effort to keep it clean. Instead, she made it clear that she now expected them to come each week.

If anyone asked how her husband was coming along on his job or if he was even looking for work, she often said, "He's sick."

Finally, one person asked her, "But do *you* really believe he's sick?"

She replied, "No, I think he's pretending."

Usually, when a congregation became aware of the husband's unwillingness to work and the wife's willingness to cover up for him at the expense of others, this family moved to a new congregation. Over a period of several years, this woman and her family *literally* wore out whole congregations who wanted to do right by them.

This wife's bad attitude toward a man's purpose for being on the earth led to a lot of misery for her family as well as for numerous other families who wanted to help. Likewise, her lack of respect for a man's need to work helped destroy the productivity of her husband who willingly looked for work in the beginning.

A man who now owns a lumberyard his father started over fifty years ago said, "Wives going to work ruin more good carpenters than anything else. Most of our unpaid accounts are with men who used to be dependable and responsible. But when their wives went to work to help out, they didn't feel as dependent upon their income as before and they started becoming very choosy about the jobs they'd do. Now they spend a lot more time in the bars drinking while waiting for the perfect job to come their way."

Through inspiration the apostle Paul expounds on the seriousness of a man not providing for his family:

I Tim. 5:8: "But if any one does not provide for his own, and especially for those of his household, he has denied the faith, and is worse than an unbeliever."

"Provide" means "forethought, provident care, to make provision for" (Thayer, p. 540).

God does not say in this passage, "If any one does not *work,*" but rather He says, "If any one does not *provide for his own."* Sometimes men do not know the difference between working and providing for their families. These men may go from job to job ever seeking something better but never being employed for long. Other men chase impractical dreams in search of making an easy buck or of becoming wealthy. In any case, their families suffer from insecurities as the bills pile up and they wonder where their next meal is coming from.

God says that such a man "has denied the faith, and is worse than an unbeliever." When a man neglects his responsibilities to his family by failing to provide for them, he turns his back on the very purpose for which God created him. This is especially tragic when a man, who claims to follow God, rejects God's plan for him--*even unbelievers* accept this basic quality of manhood by providing for their families.

So if a woman's husband works hard and steady, and if he takes his responsibilities toward his family seriously, she should hug his neck and tell him how lucky she is to be married to such a manly man as him. Whatever faults she thinks he has, her husband fulfills an important part of his destiny as a man which God ordained in the very beginning when He told the man to subdue the earth.

Even if a woman's husband doesn't profess to serve God with his life, she can still admire his determination to work hard and to provide for his family. Her unbelieving husband *still* presents a picture of *an important part of the image of God* to his children. He sets an example of honest and fruitful labor which they can imitate and be proud of. However, God desires for His people to serve Him with all of their hearts, souls, and minds:

3. TO GLORIFY GOD

Isa. 43:7: "Everyone who is called by My name, and whom I have created for My glory, whom I have formed even whom I have made."

God not only created men and women to bear children and to work, but God also created mankind to glorify Him. Glorify basically means to cause someone to be well spoken of by others. By their lives on earth, men and women either cause God to be well spoken of or to be blasphemed. Jesus said that men and women glorify God when they bear spiritual fruit or do the things that God commands through His word:

Jn. 15:8: "By this is My Father glorified, that you bear much fruit, and so prove to be My disciples."

Many people ask, "Why did God make men and women so that they could sin? Why didn't God just make everyone so that they couldn't sin no matter how hard they tried? God could have molded each individual into a sinless being who was never tempted to say a wrong word or do a wrong deed, and who always automatically sang praises to God all day long. Wouldn't that be better?"

Yet if God had designed men and women without the ability to sin, renounce Him, reject His word, or to refuse to obey Him, no one would be able to glorify Him. For example, when a woman turns on a vacuum cleaner, it sucks up dirt. When she turns it off, it doesn't suck up dirt. But that vacuum cleaner doesn't give the woman any personal glory just because it works for her. Any other woman can turn on that same vacuum cleaner and it'll suck up dirt for her, too. In fact, that vacuum cleaner will even suck up dirt for a feminist who hates housework and who thinks her husband ought to be running it! A vacuum cleaner isn't partial at all!

If men and women were incapable of disobeying God, God would not be glorified when they obeyed Him. Without a choice about obedience, glory cannot result. When men and women express love for God when they could just as easily denounce Him, they glorify God because they serve Him of their own free will. Jesus glorified God in the same manner:

Jn. 17:4: "I glorified Thee on the earth, having accomplished the work which Thou hast given Me to do."

Jesus taught mankind how to glorify God by doing God's will of His own free choice. Service to God glorifies God only when done cheerfully out of love rather than necessity.

B. MAN SERVES THE GROUND

Gen. 3:23: "...therefore the Lord God sent him out from the garden of Eden to cultivate the ground from which he was taken."

Man's origin shows what his work centers around-- subduing the earth. *Man was taken from the ground to serve the ground.* A man who refuses to work denies the very purpose for which his Creator made him and frustrates his inherent need for fulfilling accomplishment.

II. MAN'S PROBLEM

Gen. 2:18: "Then the Lord God said, 'It is not good for the man to be alone; I will make him a helper suitable for him.'"

It is probably impossible to comprehend fully how beautifully serene and restful the garden of Eden was. Man's first home was yet unmarred by man as the natural wonders are today. No papers or bottles spoiled the beauty. No motorcycle riders on the trails frightened the animals or broke the tranquility. No murderers or thieves made Adam afraid to stroll through the garden at night. Along with the perfected beauty of nature, Adam enjoyed plenty of good food and fresh water. Yet in this unique paradise that God created for man to enjoy and work in, man had a problem.

A. NOT GOOD TO BE ALONE

"Alone" means "properly separation, by implication, *a part* of the body, *branch* of a tree, apart, only, besides:--alone, by self." It comes from a word which means "to divide, i.e. be solitary:--alone" (Strong, p. 19).

Most women find it humanly impossible to totally comprehend the depth of man's loneliness in the garden of Eden. More than a problem of boredom, man suffered from *a gigantic problem!*

Many times a woman wails, "My husband doesn't need me!" But every man possesses needs that he cannot satisfy for himself. Due to pride, many a man puts on airs of self-sufficiency when his wife, in ignorance, fails to satisfy his longings. No matter how much a man denies his need for companionship, God said, "It is not good for the man to be alone."

When a woman complains that her husband doesn't need her, she is probably right. He doesn't need her the way she treats him now! If a woman satisfies her husband's inherent requirements for a wife, he cannot get along without her.

Several years ago Paul Harvey quoted in one of his columns from George Gilder's book *Naked Nomads* to show that statistically men need wives. Gilder believed that a man who remained single "courted disaster," for "a man with no roots, no one to worry about him, to look after him, is lost."

As proof, Gilder offered the following indisputable facts: single men commit ninety percent of all crimes of violence, earn less than their married peers, are five times more likely to be hospitalized for emotional distress, have the highest suicide rate, are four times more likely to be killed in a car crash and generally--from all causes--die younger, and are six times more likely than married men to die of accidental falls. Gilder theorized that perhaps this phenomenon occurred because single men had no one to nag, "Be careful!" Gilder gave women the credit for making both their children and husbands creative and emotionally stable. He concluded his case for marriage by describing the single man as statistically "poor, neurotic, disposed to alcohol, drugs and violence, accident-prone, and less resistant to disease."

Of course, statistics don't apply to everyone and some single men don't possess these qualities. However, these facts and figures show that the average man endures *gigantic personal problems* without a wife to encourage him, beg him to be careful, worry about him eating right and getting enough rest, and to soothe his nerves as only a loving wife knows how.

Statistics further show that when men loose their wives through death, their own death rate increases significantly. However, when they remarry, they return to the much "healthier married record"![3] Thus, modern statistics prove the validity of God's declaration that it was not good for the man to be alone!

B. NEEDED A HELPER

"Help" means "to surround, i.e. protect or aid:-- help, succor" (Strong, p. 87). "Help" also refers to "one who functions so as to change for the better, furnishes what is needed to accomplish work." The translators' choice of the word "help" differs from its synonyms "aid" and "assistant" in that "help has a strong impli- cation of advance toward a goal" (Webster).

Ahead of man lay the important jobs of subduing the earth and filling it with people as he glorified God. Yet with all the physical strength and mental in- genuity that God endowed man with, man was incapable of rising to his full potential by himself. Man needed someone to help him; but he didn't need a baby sitter, nor an overseer, nor even someone to boss around while he played. Man needed *a true helper*--someone to work by his side--because God gave him a hard as- signment. Thus, man desperately needed someone *to*

---

[3]Jane Barr Stump, Ph.D., *What's the Difference? How Men and Women Compare* (New York: William Morrow & Co., Inc., 1985), p. 60.

help him reach the goals God placed before him and thereby glorify God.

C. A HELPER MEET FOR HIM

"Meet" means "fit, in harmony of mood and spirit, suitable, suited to one's needs" (Webster).

Some people misread the King James Version and claim that God created the woman to be a "helpmeet" or "helpmate" for man. To the contrary, the King James translation says, "And the Lord God said, It is not good that the man should be alone; I will make him an help *meet for him.*" "Help" and "meet," two separate words with independent meanings, form different grammar functions.

For example, the phrase "meet for him" modifies "help" and tells what kind of a helper man needed to solve his problem. The New American Standard translation says, "A helper suitable for him." Man needed a helper who was in harmony with his mood and spirit; a helper who could work and get along with him; a helper who could supply all of his needs. Since man was alone with an enormous job ahead of him, he needed the best help possible, not just any kind of help, but specialized help.

Unlike many employers whom the government often compels to hire employees, not on the basis of their ability to do a particular job, but on the basis of their race, sex, or labor union memberships, God selected man's helper on the basis of qualifications. Man needed a special, highly-talented helper. God alone determined the qualifications of man's helper, and He did not yield to any pressure to place a substandard assistant by man's side.

First, however, God allowed man to experience his deep loneliness and great need as he attempted to solve his own problem without God's help:

D. THE ANIMALS NOT MEET FOR MAN

Gen. 2:20: "And the man gave names to all the cattle, and to the birds of the sky, and to every beast of the field, but for Adam there was not found a helper suitable for him."

As man named the animals, he examined each one of them to find a helper that was meet for him. Not a single animal measured up to Adam's needs or completely harmonized with his mood and spirit. Even man's best friend, the dog, failed to qualify for satisfying man's overwhelming problem.

Yet many a woman encourages her husband to go to his dog to solve his problem of loneliness. Sometimes emotionally bankrupt husbands and wives even lavish love and attention on separate pets. But God didn't create the woman to solve some animal's problem--God created her to solve *her husband's problem.*

Adam recognized that none of the animals possessed the inherent qualities needed to solve his problem even though many magnificent animals existed then which are now extinct. None could fill the void in man's life. Thus, before God intervened with the perfect solution to man's problem of being alone, God allowed man to experience for himself his great need and emptiness. Yet in spite of Adam's understanding of his problem *few women fully comprehend how terrible it is for a man to be alone.* Surely, a man whose wife sends him to the family pet to find a counterfeit of the answer to his problem is, indeed, deserving of pity.

III. THE WOMAN

Gen. 2:21-22: "So the Lord God caused a deep sleep to fall upon the man, and he slept; then He took one of his ribs, and closed up the flesh at that place. And the Lord God fashioned into a woman the rib which He had taken from the man, and brought her to the man."

"Made" means "to build (literally and figuratively)" (Strong, p. 22).

God made the woman from a different substance than He made the man. Even the word used to describe her creation, "made," differs from the word used to describe the man's creation, "formed." Obviously, only God knows the difference in technique for forming a man out of dust or making a woman from a rib.

Nonetheless, the Genesis account shows that the woman was not an accident, but a deliberate creation by God to fill a specific need in man's life which could not be satisfied in any other way. Therefore, assuming that a husband doesn't need his wife or that she's not vital to his existence shows supreme ignorance of God's word. *Every normal man needs a woman of his own.*

A. MADE WHILE MAN SLEPT

Both men and women seldom appreciate presents they don't need. Thus, to help Adam treasure the priceless gift He was about to give him, God created a helper for man *only after Adam recognized his great need for a companion.* Then instead of asking Adam what kind of a mate he wanted, God put Adam to sleep and solved man's problem *without any assistance or interference from the man.* In so doing, God created the woman according to His own infinite wisdom rather than designing her to conform to the opinions of man who often doesn't know what is best for himself.

Suppose God had given Adam a say in what the woman would be like. Surely, Adam would have asked for someone strong enough to plow the fields and carry away the boulders to relieve him--not for a woman with delicate strength who needed him to open pickle jars and carry heavy boxes for her. Adam would have asked for someone with an analytical mind to help him design bridges and buildings--not for a woman who cried easily and who got emotionally involved in matters. And Adam certainly would have asked for someone tough enough to work out in the harsh elements on the evening swing-shift while he slept--not for a soft, tenderly formed woman who wanted to pat, hug, squeeze, and kiss him all the time.

God said, however, that Adam didn't need just any kind of helper--man needed a helper who harmonized with his mood and spirit. God designed the woman to fulfill man's needs without the advice of either man or woman.

Many times, neither a husband nor a wife gives God credit for knowing what man needed. Instead, they deny the woman's weaknesses, which chapter 8, "Honoring the Weaker Vessel," shows to be the very strengths which equip a woman to solve the man's problems of loneliness and incompleteness. Being the weaker vessel gives a woman honor and makes her precious in the sight of her husband and God (I Pet. 3:7).

Unfortunately, many men try to solve their problem of loneliness in ways that God did not design such as devotion to a hobby, attention to a pet, total absorption in a job, or addiction to television, while others turn to alcohol and illicit sexual contacts. These unhappy men share the same problem that Adam experienced and demonstrate modern man's lack of ability to solve his own problem of loneliness.

B. MADE FROM MAN'S SIDE

Beginning with the Jews through modern times, many people have devised silly reasons why God made the woman from man's rib instead of some other body part. For example, some say that she came from man's side instead of his head to prevent her from lording it over her husband. At the same time, she didn't come from man's feet so he wouldn't walk all over her, etc. Others speculate that the woman's origin proves her inferiority to man while some claim it shows her superiority to man. The latter assume that flesh is better than dirt; therefore obviously, a woman must be superior to a man!

In spite of these sayings, the question still remains, "Why did God create the woman from the man's side?" and "Does the woman's origin have any significance?" Paul eliminates the need for guesswork by explaining why God created a woman from man's flesh rather than from the ground like the man:

> I Cor. 11:7-12: "For a man ought not to have his head covered, since he is the image and glory of God; but the woman is the glory of man. For man does not originate from woman, but woman from man; for indeed man was not created for the woman's sake, but woman for the man's sake. Therefore the woman ought to have a symbol of authority on her head, because of the angels. However, in the Lord, neither is woman in-

**dependent of man, nor is man independent
of woman. For as the woman originates from
the man, so also the man has his birth
through the woman; and all things originate
from God."**

While many controversies rage in regard to some
of the teachings in I Corinthians 11, a discussion of
those various beliefs is beyond the scope of this
chapter. At the same time, however, *basic undisputed
principles* of I Corinthians 11 shed light on the creation of the woman. Namely, God created the woman as
the glory of man. Because God took her from the man
and designed her for the man's benefit, God wants the
woman to adapt herself to the man and serve him.

The woman's origin, man's side or man's flesh,
shows her relationship to man. *The woman was taken
from the man to serve the man, just as the man was
taken from the ground to serve the ground.* The woman's
origin, like the man's, simply shows *what* her work
centers around.

After showing that the woman owes a debt of
subjection to her husband, Paul points out that inferiority and superiority have nothing to do with a man
and woman's relationship to each other. Men and
women who are "in the Lord," or who understand God's
plan for them and who strive to serve Him, realize
that men and women depend on each other and that
each possesses needs that only the other can satisfy.

The woman is not independent or separate from the
man, nor is the man independent or sufficient without
the woman. Even though God created the woman from
the man for his benefit, the man has his birth through
the woman. No doubt, men and women cannot reproduce
themselves without each other. This simple biological
fact serves to remind even the most independent men
and women of their need for each other.

Nevertheless, while the man and the woman enjoy
a different, but dependent, relationship to each other,
they both share the same relationship to God from
whom they both originated. God made the man to serve
the ground *in order to serve Him;* God made the woman
to serve the man *in order to serve Him.* Equal in importance in the eyes of God and His true followers,
men and women possess inherent differences in their

capabilities and responsibilities which enable them to serve their Creator.

Man was taken from the ground to serve the ground.
Woman was taken from the man to serve the man.
Both man and woman are from God to serve God.

After creating the woman from the man's rib to solve man's problem, God presented the woman to the man that she might never doubt her function:

C. BROUGHT TO THE MAN

Many a man searches a lifetime, going from job to job, trying to find a worthwhile cause to invest his life in. But a woman doesn't need to wander aimlessly through life wondering about her purpose. God made her role clear in the very beginning by personally presenting her to the man. Thus, the First and Eternal Father gave the first bride away and ordained the institution of marriage.

From that first marriage ceremony to the present day, God has always shown concern for the success of the marriage relationship. For example, Mal. 2:14 records, "The Lord has been a witness between you and the wife of your youth, against whom you have dealt treacherously, though she is your companion and your wife by covenant." Again, in Mt. 19:6 Jesus states, "Consequently they are no more two, but one flesh. What therefore God has joined together, let no man separate."

Vitally interested in the marriage union, God listens to the pledges of love and devotion of modern husbands and wives just as He watched the wedding vows of Adam and Eve. Since God participates in the joining together of every husband and wife, men and women must not take their marriages lightly.

Then after experiencing his great need for a wife and seeing God's solution to his problem, Adam rejoiced in the oneness that he would now enjoy with Eve:

D. NAMED "WOMAN"

> **Gen. 2:23: "And the man said, 'This is now bone of my bones, and flesh of my flesh; she shall be called Woman, because she was taken out of Man.'"**

Recognizing the significance of the material that God used to make the woman, Adam logically named her "woman" or "womb-man." Thus, the woman's name, a derivative of the man's name, reflects her function-- that God took her out of the man to serve the man.

The woman's name also reveals her essential difference from the man--her womb. A woman's unique function differs from the man's by centering around her ability to bear and nurture children. A woman who rejects her childbearing abilities denies the basic difference between men and women and essentially spurns her femininity.

However, an inability to bear children doesn't render a woman unfeminine. *A woman's attitude* toward the bearing of children, not the number of children she bears, reflects either her acceptance or rejection of herself as a woman in contrast to being a man. Interestingly, the feminists not only denounce many of the differences between men and women, but they also campaign heartily for abortion reform and day care centers. A recent newspaper article stated that over half of the women in France wished they were men.

Such women find it very hard to enjoy their wombs and taking care of little children. Some of these women so despise their female organs that they advocate both artificial insemination and placing their fertilized eggs into the body of another woman for the gestation process. This way they can avoid what they view as the inconveniences of pregnancy. Yet other women thrill to these same developmental processes that go on inside their bodies. Unbelievable! These women go to any length to reject themselves as women!

However, a woman who gladly serves God accepts the name "woman" and cherishes all the implications that go along with it. She views the title "woman" as one of dignity and respect without any inferiority at all. Along with the man, God created the woman in His image making her personal worth equal to the man's value. Her name "woman" signifies only that God created her for a different purpose than the man--to serve the man instead of the ground.

Just as Adam named her "woman," God also gave her a name to wear--the man's:

> **Gen. 5:2: "He created them male and female, and He blessed them and named them Man [Adam--KJV and NAS footnote] in the day when they were created."**

The feminists staunchly objected to using the generic term "man" to refer to a woman in the early 1970's and began a serious movement to change that custom. Time shows that they succeeded at reaching this goal in many areas of public communication. Children growing up today hardly seem aware that the word "man" can refer to both men and women.

Yet God originated the practice of using "man" to refer to both men and women as a reflection of His wisdom. Thus, the woman who proudly wears her husband's name reflects God's wisdom, for she shows all the world that she desires to function as a helper meet for her husband. But the woman who complains about being called "man" generically and who refuses to wear her husband's name demonstrates that she refuses to function as God designed. However, if she chooses to wear her father's name, she *still* wears a man's name. If she wants to wear her mother's maiden name, she only substitutes her maternal grandfather's name for her husband's and she *still* wears a man's name. The name a married woman wears shows whom she serves--her husband or herself--God or Satan.

Then, after stating that God made the woman for the man's benefit, Adam declared man's need for a wife:

E. BECOME ONE FLESH

> **Gen. 2:24: "For this cause a man shall leave his father and mother, and shall cleave to his wife; and they shall become one flesh."**

"Cleave" means "glue together, cement, join or fasten firmly together, join oneself to, cleave to, give oneself steadfastly to, labor for" (Thayer, p. 353).

Upon seeing the woman, Adam immediately knew that she would bring him the comfort that only a loving woman knows how to give a man. Thus, he prophesied that throughout the centuries of time men would gladly leave their fathers and mothers and cleave to their wives. Adam recognized marriage as the most wonderful relationship possible for human beings to enjoy. Even the affection of a child for his parents pales beside the devotion and love that only husbands and wives share.

Adam demonstrated some understanding of female psychology when God presented Eve to him. For he immediately declared that she was the answer to his problem--he desperately needed her. And when his modern sons follow his example by taking the time to tell their wives how much they cannot get along without them, then they reap many benefits.

The more a husband makes his wife feel needed, the more she loves him and the more she wants to do for him. Many a wife aches because her husband doesn't make her feel wanted. When a man fails to spend time with his wife, she begins to feel like only a housekeeper, cook, and baby sitter. Of course, the husband knows that she is much more than just domestic help to him, but a woman judges life according to her feelings more than on the basis of facts. A woman wants to *feel* needed more than she wants to *know* that she is needed.

Then as a husband and wife begin their life together, they become "one flesh"--a finely tuned unit for accomplishing the work God gave them to do of raising children, subduing the earth, and glorifying God. Much more than just the sexual act, the one-flesh union involves the personalities and capabilities of both the man and woman blending together in total harmony. The beauty and mystery of this relationship between a husband and wife is so profound that *Vol. II: Learning to Love* devotes a whole chapter to explaining "The Secret of Becoming One Flesh."

F. ABSENCE OF SHAME

Gen. 2:25: "And the man and his wife were both naked and were not ashamed."

After their marriage, Adam and Eve remained in the original state of nakedness in which they were created, and they were not embarrassed. Admittedly, this passage presents some difficulties since the next chapter of Genesis reveals Adam and Eve becoming ashamed of their nakedness after eating of the tree of knowledge of good and evil which God had commanded them not to eat.

However, Isa. 7:15-16 sheds some light on the quality of innocence that probably existed in the garden at that time. Isaiah, talking about the Messiah as a young child, said, "He will eat curds and honey at the time He knows enough to refuse evil and choose good. For before the boy will know enough to refuse evil and choose good,..." All small children go through a stage of development when they do not have the ability to refuse evil and choose good. Such young children are not embarrassed to streak naked through a room full of people. They don't have any evil intentions nor are they conscious of sinful thoughts which they might provoke in others.

Adam and Eve appear to have had this same concept of nudity that little children manifest. Even the first commandment God gave them resembles the first rules parents enforce with their children: Do not touch or eat specified things. Little children are not capable of understanding the why's or even deciding for themselves what they should or should not touch. In a similar manner, Adam and Eve do not appear spiritually mature enough to refuse evil and choose good for themselves; thus, God gave them one simple law to obey which the next chapter discusses in detail.

IV. THE "VERY GOOD"

Gen. 1:31: "And God saw all that He had made, and behold, it was very good."

"Behold" serves as "an interjection demanding attention, 'look!' 'see!' It is mainly used to emphasize the information which follows it" (*Theological Word-book*, p. 220).

"Very" means "properly vehemence, i.e. by implication wholly, speedily, etc. (often with other words as an intensive or superlative:--diligently, especially, exceedingly, good, greatly" (Strong, p. 60).

"Good" means "good in the widest sense:--beautiful, best, better, bountiful, cheerful, at ease" (Strong, p. 45).

Since modern writings so greatly overwork both of the words "very" and "good," they often lose much of their force for the readers. Yet, instead of being insignificant expressions, both words contain a wealth of information. "Very" intensifies and magnifies "good" through the idea of vehemence. "Vehemence," in turn, refers to "vigorous or forceful expression or intense emotion." At the same time, "behold" increases the magnification of the whole phrase "very good."

Obviously then, the expression "and behold, it was very good" shows great emotion and delight at the wonder of God's creation of the earth and the man and woman. In other words, "Look! See God's wonderful, magnificent creation! Isn't it great!" The apostle Paul says that the glory of the creation testifies to God's eternal power and divine nature and to His wisdom and love for mankind. As a result, everyone who turns his back on belief in God is without excuse (Rom. 1:20).

Then Adam and Eve began a life together in happiness with total innocence and purity. Such shared happiness has always been part of God's plan for husbands and wives:

A. A GOOD GIFT TO MAN

Prov. 18:22: "He who finds a wife finds a good thing, and obtains favor from the Lord."

In all likelihood, any feminist who reads this verse will exclaim, "A woman is not a THING! This is just another example of how God and men degrade women by regarding them as objects to be used rather than persons to be valued!" However, Jesus, a divine being filled with miraculous powers, referred to Himself as a "thing" in Mt. 12:6 when He compared Himself to an inanimate object, the temple in Jerusalem.

Referring to a person as a "thing" doesn't necessarily reveal a derogatory attitude toward that person. Instead, it contrasts the person with something physical to show the greater value of the person. Thus, Solomon shows that when a man finds a wife who patterns her life after God's marriage regulations, he finds an extremely precious companion to help him build a sanctified marriage.

The expression "favor" describes a special gift that wasn't earned. Logically then, God created the woman as His favor or charitable gift to the man for solving the worst problem any man ever faced--loneliness. Yet, few women realize just how much the average man cherishes a happy home life. Sadly, they give in to self-pity by wailing, "I'm not needed!" Instead, they should endeavor to put the sparkle back into their marital unions. Women need to recognize that not just any women is a "good thing," but the woman who strives to learn and practice God's divine truths of love and marriage becomes the most priceless treasure a man ever possesses as Solomon again affirms:

B. THE MOST VALUABLE GIFT

> **Prov. 19:14: "House and wealth are an inheritance from fathers, but a prudent wife is from the Lord."**

"Prudent" means "to be (make or act) circumspect and hence intelligent" (Strong, p. 116).

Men often equate their success in life by the amount of money they collect and save to pass on to the next generation. However, a godly wife far exceeds the most fabulous fortune a man might inherit from his father. On the other hand, just any wife doesn't necessarily bless a man's life, for God emphatically states that she must also make an intelligent use of her brain in her day-to-day life. Only then does a wife offer a man more happiness than all the mansions and Swiss bank accounts to be had. In this way, a truly good wife comes from God as she guides her life with His word and rises to her full potential as a woman.

One woman complained that her husband did not need her. She resented his continual bragging about how independent he was and his pressure for her to get a job to make herself useful. But after she began satisfying his needs, she found that his boasting had simply covered up his hurt feelings. To her delight, her husband began to defend her desire to stay home and praised her homemaking talents to their friends. Her husband didn't need her when she neglected his needs, but when she began serving him as God designed, her husband couldn't get along without her.

An executive told the wives of a group of salesmen, "Every successful business man has a supporting woman standing behind him. Unfortunately, that woman often isn't the man's wife!"

Adam, *a perfect creation of God,* needed a helping wife, and modern man, a descendant of Adam, still feels that same longing deep within his being. Any woman who thinks that her husband doesn't need her probably fails to be a helper *meet* for her husband. But the woman who adapts her mood and spirit to her husband rapidly becomes the most valuable gift he could ever receive.

In spite of God's wonderful creation and design of the man and woman, many a modern man fails to reap the most from this life because he hasn't found a woman who believes in him, sees the greatness in him, or gives him self-confidence. In his book, *Magic in Marriage*, James H. Jauncey observed, "The genius of many a man has been lost to the world because he could not exercise it alone and there was nobody to help him."[4]

Likewise, many a woman rejects the very purpose for which God created her. Every house on every block doesn't contain a helper who is meet for her husband. In fact, one can look and search and hunt and still not find a woman who functions as God created women to be. Not a single secular job offers the potential for fulfillment, the rewards for service, or requires the talent to accomplish the work that the job of being a loving wife offers a woman. Truly, God offers a woman the greatest honor and challenge on earth--that of being the answer to man's problem. A woman needs only to reach forward to her destiny and purpose for creation to find true inner peace and happiness.

[4]James H. Jauncey, *Magic in Marriage*, (Grand Rapids, MI: Zondervan, 1966), p. 71.

STUDY EXERCISE

Answer all questions in your own words.

1. What is the significance of the material that the man was made from?

2. What is the significance of the material that the woman was made from?

3. Why were the animals not suitable to be Adam's helper? What about man's best friend, the dog?

4. What does it mean for a wife to be meet for her husband?

5. How can a person glorify God? Give an illustration.

6. What is the significance of the woman being made while the man slept?

7. Name the three reasons God created men and women.

8. How can a man deny the purpose of his creation?

9. Do you disagree with anything in this lesson? If so, explain in detail giving scriptures for your reasons.

GOAL-ACHIEVING EXERCISE

Change the following suggestions to fit your individual needs. Review this exercise as you study the next three chapters and make additions as necessary.

Purpose: To be a helper who is meet for your husband.

Goals:

1. To fully understand and appreciate the role of a woman.

2. To fully understand and support the role of your husband.

3. To hear your husband express appreciation for you being his wife.

Priorities:

1. Learn what the Bible says about how a husband and wife function together as one flesh while each finds fulfillment and satisfaction in separate roles.

2. Give Bible study priority over personal ambitions, hobbies, home decorating, etc.

Plans:

1. Look for something to appreciate in your husband everyday.

2. Look for something to appreciate in your children everyday.

3. Look for something to appreciate in yourself everyday. You have complete control over whether or not you do something worthwhile everyday.

4. Continue to set aside a time every day for Bible study and prayer. Look for something to thank God for in your husband and children. Thank God frequently for giving you His word to guide you and ask Him to help you have an attitude of learning rather than one of argument.

CHAPTER 6

THE "VERY GOOD" LOST AND FOUND

Misconceptions abound about what happened to Adam and Eve in the garden of Eden. Many women resent subjection claiming, "It's not fair! God created Adam and Eve equal in authority! God just gave the law of subjection to punish Eve for her sin!"

The feminists contend, "Eve just wanted an education! But God and men conspired to keep women ignorant and subservient!"

Still others assert, "The creation story is just a myth invented by men to help them dominate women. It really doesn't have any bearing at all on women today."

These and similar misunderstandings about what happened long ago in the garden of Eden foster anger and frustration in many women. They fuel a general lack of respect for womanhood on the part of both men and women. On the other hand, understanding how Eve contributed to the fall of mankind helps many women avoid the same mistake that Eve made and enables them to rise to all the glory and beauty of their own femininity and destiny. Thus, a study of Eve's sin fills a vital need for establishing how men and women should relate to each other.

I. THE FALL

After God created Adam and Eve and united them in marriage, He pronounced His creation "very good." Unfortunately, danger lurked around the corner waiting to steal the very good from the first husband and wife.

This devastating crisis occurred when Eve confronted the choice of either obeying God or Satan.

Even though in the beginning God designed for Adam and Eve to live forever, God did not let them wander aimlessly through life trying one lifestyle after another while searching for the keys to success. God told them exactly what He expected of them: He instructed them to bear children and to subdue the earth. Specifically, He told them that He created the green plants and the fruit of the trees for their food (Gen. 1:28-30).

While God lovingly provided everything that Adam and Eve needed for survival and their happiness, God withheld one thing from them. God warned, "From any tree of the garden you may eat freely; but from the tree of the knowledge of good and evil you shall not eat, for in the day that you eat from it you shall surely die" (Gen. 2:16-17). Following God's laws produces happiness, security, and enjoyment of life to the fullest. But Eve made the wrong choice and gave up the very good:

A. THE FIRST LIE

> **Gen. 3:1-5: "Now the serpent was more crafty than any beast of the field which the Lord God had made. And he said to the woman, 'Indeed, has God said, "You shall not eat from any tree of the garden"?' And the woman said to the serpent, 'From the fruit of the trees of the garden we may eat; but from the fruit of the tree which is in the middle of the garden, God has said, "You shall not eat from it or touch it, lest you die."' And the Serpent said to the woman, 'You surely shall not die! For God knows that in the day you eat from it your eyes will be opened, and you will be like God, knowing good and evil.'"**

Satan promised Eve that eating the forbidden fruit would make her equal to God. In this way, he slandered God's motives while Eve listened. How difficult would Eve's choice have been if Satan had told her the truth--that disobeying God would cause the death of every baby ever born, would get them kicked out of the garden, would cause them to have to work extremely hard for a living, and would bring about great pain in childbirth for all women? But sin seldom reveals its consequences until it's too late. Promising happiness and liberation, sin traps its luckless victims.

Satan craftily made Eve choose between obeying God or him in an unfamiliar area since she didn't know firsthand the results of eating from the forbidden tree. The question to Eve seemed to be, "Should I listen to the serpent or should I obey my Creator who the serpent says is holding me back and mentally oppressing me?"

In reality, Satan tricked Eve by impugning her intelligence. Many people today still use this same argument to manipulate women. For example, when the feminist movement began its campaign for women's rights in earnest in the early 1970's, the cover of *Life* magazine reproduced a picture supposedly of Eve accepting the forbidden fruit from the serpent alongside a modern woman holding a sign which said, "Eve Was Framed." The accompanying article called the woman the "underdog" from the beginning. It explained that Eve had simply gone after an "education." Quoting historical writings, the article tried to show that the only real problem between men and women exists when women insist upon developing their brains. Thus, the author claimed that man's fear of intelligent women intimidates men into mistreating women.[1]

Likewise, when a disagreement occurs in the home, many a husband ridicules his wife's intelligence. But instead of making his wife give in, such accusations accelerate the fight, often to the bewilderment of the husband. Even if the wife yields to her husband's demands, she deeply resents his lack of respect for her inherent intelligence. The wife's pain may smolder for years as it destroys her respect and regard for her husband.

Satan, along with many people today, ignored the fact that God created the woman as an intelligent being. In truth, the job God gave the woman of being a helper meet for her husband *requires tremendous*

[1]Richard Gilman, "The 'Woman Problem,'" pp. 40–55.

intelligence. Yet from the beginning of time, just calling the quality of a woman's brains into question riles many women and makes them ready to fight to prove their intelligence. Degrading a woman's mentality attacks one of her most vulnerable spots to make her feel inferior and serves as one of the easiest ways of coercing her into doing something foolish. No different than many of her modern daughters, Eve based her choice *on her feelings rather than her intellect* and committed the first sin:

B. THE FIRST SIN

> **Gen. 3:6: "When the woman saw that the tree was good for food, and that it was a delight to the eyes, and that the tree was desirable to make one wise, she took from its fruit and ate; and she gave also to her husband with her, and he ate."**

Eve's motives revealed that she gave in to *every* impulse in the world which resulted in sin as recorded in I Jn. 2:16 which says, "For all that is in the world, the lust of the flesh and the lust of the eyes and the boastful pride of life, is not from the Father, but is from the world." Eve picked the fruit and ate it because, first of all, she saw that the tree was good for food. In other words, the fruit appealed to the lust of her flesh, for it would satisfy her fleshly appetite of hunger. Secondly, Eve saw that the fruit was a delight to the eyes which amounted to giving in to the lust of the eyes by partaking of something that gave pleasure to her mind. Thirdly, Eve wanted the fruit because it would make her wise, the equivalent of the boastful pride of life or a desire to be able to confidently trust in her own wisdom.

Obviously, Eve allowed her desire for the forbidden fruit to completely overcome her. Without exercising any self-control whatsoever, she surrendered to her urges and disregarded God's warning not to eat from the tree of knowledge of good and evil. Even though Eve sincerely thought she was acting intelligently, she really gave in to the deceitfulness of sin.

Afterwards, Eve took the initiative and gave some of the fruit to Adam. The passage says she gave to her husband "with" her. God does not tell what Adam's attitude or motives were or even if he knew that the fruit came from the forbidden tree. No one knows if Adam overheard the discussion between Eve and the serpent, or if Eve simply picked the fruit and brought it to him for a snack.

Certainly, Eve did all the talking, all the thinking, and all the acting. Eve listened to Satan when she should have listened to God. Then Eve gave to Adam when she should have asked Adam for his opinion in the matter. Adam listened to Eve when he should have listened to God. Thus, Eve led Adam in the way of sin when she should have followed in the way of righteousness. In the end, she paid a big price just to make one decision without advice from anyone. True to God's word, Adam and Eve immediately faced the first consequences of their sin--guilt:

C. THE OPENING OF THEIR EYES

> **Gen. 3:7-10: "Then the eyes of both of them were opened, and they knew that they were naked; and they sewed fig leaves together and made themselves loin coverings. And they heard the sound of the Lord God walking in the garden in the cool of the day, and the man and his wife hid themselves from the presence of the Lord God among the trees of the garden. Then the Lord God called to the man, and said to him, 'Where are you?' And he said, 'I heard the sound of Thee in the garden, and I was afraid because I was naked; so I hid myself.'"**

"Opened" means "opened (the senses, especially the eyes), figuratively observant" (Strong, p. 96).

After eating the fruit from the tree of knowledge of good and evil, Adam and Eve's eyes were opened. The word "opened" doesn't mean that their eyesight improved. Rather "opened" refers to their increased ability to *understand* something, to *perceive* it, and to *mentally separate* issues such as found in true wisdom. In this way, Adam and Eve instantly matured mentally and gained a clearer understanding of what went on around them including their relationship and responsibilities toward other people.

Essentially, Adam and Eve lost the innocence of their creation and grew up overnight. They became more responsible for their behavior. As a result, they quickly became aware of the virtue commonly called "modesty" and made loin coverings for themselves from fig leaves. However, when God came to the garden, they still felt unpresentable to Him, and they hid themselves, for Adam said, "I was naked."

One of the hardest features of modesty to teach others is the aspect of considering the viewpoint of those who see a person. Practicing modesty is not so much for one's own benefit as for the well-being of others. Many naive people excuse improper dress by claiming, "You just have a dirty mind!" Normally, however, someone with a dirty mind doesn't criticize others for dressing immodestly--he enjoys it! He's the last one to raise an objection! However, Adam and Eve, who had just eaten from the tree of knowledge of good and evil, made an effort to keep their bodies covered even in the sight of God, the One who created their bodies and in whom no evil thoughts existed.

II. THE PUNISHMENT

> **Gen. 3:11-13: "And He said, 'Who told, you that you were naked? Have you eaten from the tree of which I commanded you not to eat?' And the man said, 'The woman whom Thou gavest to be with me, she gave me from the tree, and I ate.' Then the Lord God said to the women, 'What is this you have done?' And the woman said, 'The serpent deceived me, and I ate.'"**

God's reaction to Adam and Eve's sin instituted a pattern of dealing with mankind that God follows all the way through the Bible. Understanding the way God approaches sin helps His people face their own sins properly, shows them how to discipline their children, and aids them in restoring other people who sin.

God began by asking Adam and Eve three important questions: *"Who told you* that you were naked?" *"Have you eaten* from the tree of which I commanded you not to eat?" and *"What is this* you have done?" By the standards of modern psychology, God conspicuously left out one question. God never asked Adam and Eve, *"Why* did you do this?" Although the Bible *tells us* Eve's motives, God did not explore *with Adam and Eve* their motives for their sin. Instead *He emphasized their actions.*

Some may counter, "But God knows the thoughts of every man's heart. He didn't need to ask them 'Why?'"

Even so, God asked them, "Who told you?" "Have you eaten?" and "What is this?" Yet God knew the answers to all of those questions, too. Through His infinite wisdom, God asked *all of the questions necessary* to deal properly with Adam and Eve's sin by bringing their actions into the open for both His and their consideration. Then God punished them on the basis of the facts. *All the way through the Bible, God expects everyone to accept responsibility for their own actions without making excuses.*

Unfortunately, modern psychology ignores God's wisdom and emphasizes judging motives. For example, child psychologists tell parents to find out "why" their children do certain things and then to punish them on the basis of the reason. This gives children the impression that if they have a good enough reason, they might not suffer the consequences of their actions.

One young couple with a three-year-old boy fell under the influence of this modern child psychology. One Saturday morning the couple woke up to discover that their son had awakened much earlier and had totally destroyed his bedroom. So the mother and father began to ask him, "Why did you tear up your room?"

The little boy replied, "I don't know. Spank me."

They asked him again, "Why did you tear up your room?"

And again he replied, "I don't know. Spank me." This cycle went on several times until the parents and the little boy became totally frustrated with each other.

So the parents went to another couple with six well-behaved children and asked their advice. The couple with six children advised them to discipline their son for *what he did wrong* rather than worrying about why he did it.

The very next Saturday, the little three-year-old boy got up before his parents and totally demolished his room again. When the parents saw what their son had done, they didn't ask him, "Why?" Instead, the father gave him a spanking, and then he told him, "Now you cleanup your room."

In a little while when the parents heard their son crying frantically, they went to check on him. In the process of tearing up his room, he had pulled out all his drawers of clothes and dumped them on the floor. Not knowing how to fold his clothes, he had stuffed them back into the drawers, and now they wouldn't close. But he had learned his lesson that he'd better mind his mother and father when they told him to do something, and he was afraid he couldn't obey them. That was the last Saturday that he tore up his room.

God deals with His people in this same way. He doesn't ask them, "Why?" but "What?" Then He expects them to accept the responsibility and the consequences of their actions. Even after sinners repent of their sins, God still expects them to face the consequences--that's part of being a responsible person.

Sadly, the Bible contains no record of Adam and Eve or the Serpent repenting of their sins. They each just passed the blame on to the other. Adam blamed Eve and Eve blamed the serpent. Thus, God's punishment may have been harsher than it would have been had they repented and asked for His forgiveness and His strength to remain strong in the face of temptation:

A. THE SERPENT'S PUNISHMENT

Gen. 3:14-15: "And the Lord God said to the serpent, 'Because you have done this, cursed are you more than all cattle, and more than every beast of the field; on your belly shall you go, and dust shall you eat all the days of your life; and I will put enmity between you and the woman, and between your seed and her seed; he shall bruise you on the head, and you shall bruise him on the heel.'"

Beginning with the serpent, who sinned first, God gave an appropriate punishment for everyone involved. The serpent paid the penalty of becoming despised more than all cattle through a lifetime spent crawling upon his belly eating the dust of the ground. Through his false attempt to help the woman elevate herself, the serpent lowered himself to the depths of degradation--a fitting reward, indeed! No longer would the serpent be able to "befriend" the woman because God would create enmity between them. To this day, women generally fear snakes and try to stay as far away as possible from them.

Just because the sin originated with the serpent, he wasn't the only one who suffered punishment. God held all of the participants responsible for their individual actions and didn't allow any of them to escape the consequences:

B. THE WOMAN'S PUNISHMENT

Gen. 3:16: "To the woman He said, 'I will greatly multiply your pain in childbirth, in pain you shall bring forth children;...'"

God punished Eve by increasing her pain in childbirth. Women today still experience this consequence of Eve's sin in one form or another from monthly cramps and emotional disturbances to morning nausea in pregnancy to complicated childbirths. Only in this one area do animals seem to possess an advantage over humans.

Interestingly, since perhaps the beginning of time, many people refer to a woman's menstrual functions as the "curse." Yet God nowhere told Eve that He *cursed her* in this manner. On the other hand, God told the serpent, *"Cursed are you* more than all cattle," and He told Adam, *"Cursed is the ground* because of you." God didn't punish the woman by causing her to menstruate, but by increasing her pain in conception and childbirth. Labeling a woman's reproductive functions as a curse ignores the facts, for God cursed only the serpent and the ground.

The woman's pain centers around her unique differ-ence from the man--her womb--her ability to bear and nurture children. Thus, a woman's menstrual functions serve as a constant monthly reminder that she is different from a man and focuses her attention on the bearing of children. In fact, this time of the month is the most likely time for a woman to become depressed over an inability to conceive readily as it reminds her of her motherly role.

Few people argue about the first part of God's conversation with Eve, but the second part poses some problems:

Gen. 3:16: "...Yet your desire shall be for your husband, and he shall rule over you."

"Desire" means "in the original sense of stretching out after, a longing:--desire" (Strong, p. 126). It comes from a root word which means "to run after or over, i.e. overflow:--overflow water" (Strong, p. 114).

"Rule" means "to rule:--(have, make to have) dominion, governor" (Strong, p. 74).

Many people think that this verse institutes subjection as part of Eve's punishment--that as a result of her sin women will desire to be submissive to their husbands. People holding this position assume that God created men and women completely equal in function, and that subjection had no place in God's original plan for women. They lament that if Eve had never eaten of the forbidden fruit, men and women would still be equal today in all realms of activity and authority.

Such a view of this verse ignores the meaning of "desire" and its use in other passages. The definition of "desire" does not mention a single aspect of subjection, but instead describes a longing for someone or something. Also, this same Hebrew word is used in only two other passages in the Bible, neither of which even hint at subjection. The first example, in Gen. 4:7, quotes God telling Cain, "...and if you do not do well, sin is crouching at the door; and its *desire* is for you, but you must master it." Here the word "desire" refers to sin longing for or running after Cain. The Song of Solomon uses the only other example of the word to describe the sexual longing of the Shepherd for the Shulammite (7:10).

Consequently, the word "desire" never refers to subjection, but expresses desire for another person, sexually or otherwise. The only conclusion seems to be that God consoles Eve by promising that her punishment will not be more than she can bear, nor will it interfere with her sexual love for her husband. Thus, God comforts Eve with the words, "Yet [in spite of your punishment] your desire shall be for your husband [No matter how bad the birth experience might be, it will not be bad enough to cause you to stop desiring sexual relations with your husband. You may not want to have any more children, but you will continue to feel sexual desires for your husband.], and He shall rule over you."

As a general rule, women do not desire or run after their husbands for the purpose of being submissive. The desire to be submissive must be learned, either from one's mother, the Bible, friends, or from the examples of others. On the other hand, the desire for physical lovemaking throbs much stronger in most women than the desire to be submissive. Ironically, women, who dislike the sexual union due to Victorian upbringing, usually detest subjection even more. While many women must be convinced that they should be submissive, most women eagerly look forward to learning how to enjoy the sexual relationship more while giving their husbands greater pleasure. Even the feminists, who openly turn their backs on everything that vaguely hints of subjection, write great volumes of material to help women gain the most from the sexual act.

In short, God punished Eve with increased pain in conception and childbirth, but He also comforted her with the promise that the pain would not be bad enough to take away her pleasure in the embrace of love with her husband. Then God told Eve, "And he shall rule over you," thereby summing up His admonition with a reminder to be submissive.

In Gen. 1:16-18 the Hebrew word "rule" refers to how the sun governs the day while the moon and the stars watch over the night. Throughout the Old Testament it describes how kings, governors, Christ, and God exercise dominion over others. In like manner, when God tells Eve that Adam will rule over her, He doesn't describe a fifty-fifty relationship, but one where Adam will completely control their life together.

Rather than subjection becoming a punishment for sin, Eve violated the law of subjection that originated with the creation of man and woman. God never designed the woman to lead, but to serve as a helper to work alongside the man and to assist him in subduing the earth, filling it with people, and glorifying God. Instead of helping, Eve took the initiative to lead.

The mechanics of subjection are a deep and complicated subject which chapters 13-16 treat in minute detail. However, Paul outlines three reasons for a wife to practice subjection which prove that it was very much a part of God's plan for women before the serpent ever lied to Eve:

1. THE ORDER OF CREATION

I Tim. 2:12-13: "But I do not allow a woman to teach or exercise authority over a man, but to remain quiet. For it was Adam who was first created, and then Eve."

In the Old Testament the first-born or the first one created always enjoyed an undisputed right of leadership over all the others. For instance, the first-born son received a double inheritance and became the family leader when the father died. In a similar manner, the Bible speaks of Jesus as the first-born from the dead to show His authority over all the dead.

This same principle holds true in the man-woman relationship. *Eve owed subjection to Adam from the very moment God created her simply because God created Adam first*. Not an afterthought, God planned subjection from the very beginning. Priority of creation does not show superiority, but relationship, that women are to show subjection to men by deferring to their leadership.

2. THE SOURCE OF CREATION

I Cor. 11:7-10: "For a man ought not to have his head covered, since he is the image and glory of God; but the woman is the glory of man. For man does not originate from woman, but woman from man; for indeed

man was not created for the woman's sake, but woman for the man's sake. Therefore the woman ought to have a symbol of authority on her head, because of the angels."

Paul gives two reasons to show how the woman reflects the glory of the man and that a woman "ought" (owes a debt) to have a "symbol of authority" (a sign of subjection) on her head: (1) Because the woman was taken from the man and (2) she was designed for the man's benefit. For these two reasons, God wants the woman to adapt herself to the man and serve him.

Thus, the very material that God chose to make the woman from--Adam's rib--shows that God intended for women to submit to their husbands' leadership. Such deliberate action on God's part denies the theory that God ordained subjection as an punishment for the woman.

3. THE PURPOSE OF CREATION

I Cor. 11:9: "...for indeed man was not created for the woman's sake, but the woman for the man's sake."

The final reason Paul gives to prove that a woman owes subjection to her husband comes from the purpose of creation. God didn't create the man just for the woman's sake, but He principally created the woman for the man's sake because it was not good for the man to be alone.

In fact, the woman's job description of being a helper meet for her husband implies this aspect of subjection since she was to adapt her mood and spirit to his mood and spirit. Only in this way can a woman make herself suitable for her husband's needs. Undoubtedly, without the man's overwhelming need for a helping companion, the woman has no purpose for being created in the first place. Just as God created the man for the specific reasons of subduing the earth, filling it with people, and glorifying God; God also designed the woman to fulfill a special purpose--that of assisting the man.

These three reasons: (1) the order of creation, (2) the source of creation, and (3) the purpose of creation, all demand that *the law of subjection existed before sin entered the garden of Eden.* Likewise, these same three reasons deny the assumption that God gave the law of subjection to punish the woman for her disobedience.

For example, suppose a woman's daughter washed the dishes every night as part of her normal family responsibilities. Then the mother would not tell her daughter to wash the dishes every night to punish her for some disobedience. That would be ridiculous on the mother's part, and the daughter would go away thinking she had not been punished at all since nothing had changed. On the other hand, if the mother told the daughter to add cleaning the bathroom to her list of duties, the daughter would know that she was being punished.

This same logic also applies to understanding God's relationship with His children. Since God intended for the woman to be submissive to her husband when He created her, God could not logically give the law of subjection to punish the woman when she disobeyed Him. If that had been the case, the woman would not have felt punished at all. Paul affirms that *Eve's sin did not establish subjection, but simply reinforced it:*

4. THE VALUE OF SUBJECTION

I Tim. 2:14: "And it was not Adam who was deceived, but the woman being quite deceived, fell into transgression."

In this New Testament account of the fall, Paul, through the verbal inspiration of God, said that Adam was not "deceived" by the serpent, but the woman was "quite deceived." Both "deceived" and "quite deceived" come from the same Greek root word, but differ in intensity. "Quite deceived" carries the Greek prefix *"ex"* in front of "deceive" which strengthens the force of the simple verb "deceive" (Thayer, p. 221).

The same Greek word for "quite deceived" is used in a corresponding passage in II Cor. 11:3 which says, "But I am afraid, lest as the serpent *deceived* Eve by

his craftiness, your minds should be led astray from
the simplicity and purity of devotion to Christ."

For further emphasis, this passage contains an
ellipsis--a "not-but" construction to show a
relationship. While, in reality, Adam was deceived
when he ate the forbidden fruit, in comparison to how
much Eve was deceived, he was not deceived at all.
The ellipsis acknowledges the deceiving of both Adam
and Eve, but places the emphasis on how much more
Eve was deceived than Adam--she was "quite
deceived."

Paul's basic point? Eve went the limit by being
"quite deceived." For instance, Eve yielded to all three
types of sin in the world--the lust of the flesh, the
lust of the eye, and the pride of life. Instead of
submitting to God's leadership, Eve wanted to be "like
God"--not like man. Eve listened directly to Satan
while Adam listened to her. Eve sinned before Adam.
Eve led in sin; Adam followed. While Adam sinned, he
did not sin in the same manner as Eve. For all time,
Eve demonstrated the wisdom of subjection and the
logic of not trusting in one's own wisdom.

Paul uses Eve's sin to impress upon modern
women, who might argue with the rules of subjection,
that subjection is, indeed, a logical way for a woman
to act. In short, Paul begins his case for subjection
by giving the ground rules--that a woman is not to
teach or exercise authority over a man.

Next, instead of just saying that a woman must be
submissive because God said so, Paul gives a basic
reason for subjection--that God created the man first.
Then, because the reason is often not enough for
women inclined to be contentious, Paul uses a familiar
historical account to illustrate the reasonableness of
subjection. If the first woman, a perfect creation of
God, couldn't take matters into her own hands without
getting herself and all of humanity into trouble, how
can a modern woman think that she can tamper with
God's law of subjection without paying the
consequences?

Finally, as all good teachers anticipate objections
to their teaching, Paul answers two common arguments
many women use against subjection, "But what can a
woman do if she cannot teach or exercise authority
over men?" and "But men get to do everything and

women don't get to do anything in the church!" Paul briefly states the responsibilities of a woman--that a woman can serve God within her realm of bearing children *if* she continues in faith, love, and sanctity with self restraint." God considers the job of properly raising children so important that He exempts mothers from many spiritual duties while they devote themselves to their families. Yet God wants all women to continue to study His word and grow spiritually, to love others, and to live in such a manner that God's wisdom shines forth for all the world to see.

Surely, whatever "Yet your desire shall be for your husband, and he shall rule over you" means, it cannot possibly be an enactment of subjection as a punishment. The law of subjection didn't originate with Eve's sin. Eve simply reinforced the wisdom behind subjection.

As a result, God reminded Eve of her place, that He didn't create her to be the leader, but the man to rule over her. It is as if God were saying to Eve, "Alright, Eve, you've seen what happens when you aren't submissive. Now, put on subjection and don't let something like this happen again."

This same type of situation comes up in modern life. While federal regulations require seat belts in all new cars, and most states issue fines to people caught not wearing their seat belts, many people still refuse to wear them. Suppose that a woman was badly hurt in a car accident all because she neglected to wear her seat belt. Even though the seat belt was available to the woman, it was useless to protect her because she refused to wear it.

In such a situation, the average husband would probably tell his wife, "I don't want you to ever ride in a car again without buckling your seat belt! I don't want you to get hurt again!" However, the woman's accident didn't cause the car manufacturers to invent seat belts, they already had seat belts. Her accident just reinforced the wisdom behind the safety legislation that requires the wearing of seat belts.

In a similar manner, the example of Eve proves that *subjection works only when used.* When a woman wears subjection around her heart, she protects herself from all kinds of mental, physical, and often spiritual harm. William Hendriksen said it best:

> ...let a woman not enter a sphere of
> activity for which by dint of her very creation
> she is not suited. Let not a bird try to dwell
> under water. Let not a fish try to live on land.
> Let not a woman yearn to exercise authority
> over a man...[2]

Subjection reflects the wisdom of God, not the punishment of woman. When a woman practices subjection right, it makes her life happy and secure. But when she fails to use it properly, it makes her life miserable and bitter as Eve discovered.

In fact, God's statement, "Yet your desire shall be for your husband, and he shall rule over you" is used to catalog every scripture concerning the woman's relationship with her husband in the research exercise at the end of this chapter. That God wants a wife to love her husband and to be submissive to him summaries the whole of a woman's duties. Few verses concerning the woman's half of marriage would not come under either love or subjection.

God's conversation with Eve ended with Him clearly stating the woman's function as a wife in such a way that women cannot logically deny its truth or force. But countless women attempt to. From the beginning of time, many women have devised various gimmicks to try to nullify God's teachings concerning the creation and the subjection of women. One of the most common tools for discrediting subjection is slander--to label the teacher as prejudiced in favor of subjection.

For example, women often accuse the apostle Paul of hating women because of his teachings on subjection. Some even concoct stories about how he was jilted in love and even invent names for the supposed women. However, even if Paul hated women as the result of an unhappy love affair, that does not void a single scripture. *All scriptures* come from God-- not the wisdom of men (I Cor. 2.10-16).

Undoubtedly, if people slander a man, who wrote by the inspiration of God about subjection, any woman

[2]William Hendriksen, *New Testament Commentary, I-II Timothy-Titus*, p. 109.

who teaches about Bible subjection can expect others to question her motives and character. A woman who dares to mention the hated word "subjection," let alone teach the mechanics of it, may even find that the detractors also slander her husband as a "male chauvinist" or a woman hater. Or they may go to the other extreme and claim that the teacher's husband is so kind and thoughtful that she doesn't know what she's talking about.

Indeed, slandering a teacher represents one of the most illogical objections against subjection that exists. Even if *every woman* who teaches and tries to practice subjection is one of the most dominated, hypocritical, two-faced women who ever tried to read and understand God's word, the errors in her personal life do not destroy a single passage of scripture. All scriptures about women came directly from God who designed the feminine body and mind in the first place. None of them depend upon any woman for ratification.

Some women even attempt to slander God by claiming that He doesn't like women, but degrades them. However, a careful study of *all scriptures* pertaining to women and marriage reveals that many of the so-called degrading passages actually contain laws designed to protect women from being mistreated by their husbands. Other passages show that God will not permit men who mistreat their wives to enter heaven. Studying the truth of the scriptures exposes slander as folly.

Likewise, other women attempt to slander the scriptures themselves by claiming that they are only myths written by men and not to be accepted by women. Such an attitude shows a lack of respect for the wisdom of God and for the verbal (word-for-word) inspiration of the Bible.

Still other women attack the creation account itself in an effort to scripturally discredit subjection. *The Woman's Bible*, written by several early feminists and edited by Elizabeth Cady Stanton, serves as a good example of this tactic. Ellen Battelle Dietrick wrote the section on the creation account:

The most important thing for a woman to note, in reading Genesis, is that that portion which is now divided into "the first three chapters" (there was no such division until about five centuries ago), contains two entirely separate, and very contradictory, stories of creation, written by two different, but equally anonymous, authors...

It is now generally conceded that someone (nobody pretends to know who) at some time (nobody pretends to know exactly when), copied two creation myths on the same leather roll, one immediately following the other...

Now as it is manifest that both of these stories cannot be true; intelligent women, who feel bound to give the preference to either, may decide according to their own judgment of which is more worthy of an intelligent woman's acceptance. Paul's rule is a good one in this dilemma. "Prove all things: hold fast to that which is good." My own opinion is that the second story was manipulated by some Jew, in an endeavor to give "heavenly authority" for requiring a woman to obey the man she married...[3]

Thus, Dietrick claims that Genesis contains two contradicting creation accounts: the first one where God created the woman completely equal with the man while the second record teaches the subjection of women to men. Her main argument for this theory asserts that two different men *had to write* the two accounts because the two narratives use different words from each other. Dietrick concludes that since two entirely different sets of vocabulary are displayed, two different men must of necessity be the authors.

However, Gen. 1:26-30 follows a consistent chronology beginning with the creation of the world to describe the order of the earth, sun, moon, stars, plants, animals, and man and woman. The second account, on the other hand, leaves the time pattern and goes into more depth by giving a detailed record

[3]Ellen Battelle Dietrick, *The Woman's Bible*, (Originally published New York: European Publishing Co., 1895, reprinted Seattle, WA: Seattle Coalition Task Force on Women and Religion, 1974), pp. 15-18.

of the creation of Adam and Eve. Instead of emphasizing the time, the second account focuses upon Adam and Eve's relationship to each other. Quite understandably, God gives more details about the creation of the man and woman since they are the only beings He created in His own image.

Since the two accounts reveal different aspects of the creation, they obviously require different words to give different facts. For example, some of the lessons in this book contain special vocabularies not used in other chapters because they deal with specific subjects. Yet only one woman wrote this book.

If God left out the second creation account, men and women would still know that He made them. However, the details of the second account reveal many facts which answer the ageless questions of men and women, "Why am I here?" "Why was I created?" and "Are men and women really different?"

Since God inspired *all* the words of the Bible, women don't have a choice about which creation account to believe. Instead, they must combine the two in order to fully understand all that can be learned from the creation.

To bolster their view of two separate creation accounts, modern feminists use another gimmick to ridicule the creation of man and woman--They perpetuate a Jewish fable about a demon named Lilith who originated from Babylonian and Assyrian myths. History records that when the Jews came out of captivity from these two nations, they brought Lilith with them and tried to give her a basis in scripture. Lilith remained relatively unknown in this country until the 1970's when the feminists decided to use her to illustrate their dogmas.

The feminists maintain that God created Lilith as the first woman in Gen. 1:26-30. They also credit her with being the first feminist as she insisted on equality with Adam. According to the legend, Lilith abandoned Adam so that she could have her own way. Then God provided Adam with a more subservient woman named Eve. Unfortunately, as the story goes, Eve climbed a tree and saw Lilith standing free outside the wall which was the beginning of Adam and Eve's problems.

As ridiculous as this story, undoubtedly, sounds to Christians, many feminists take it seriously and teach it as truth in their literature. For this reason, Christians need to know enough facts concerning the origin of Lilith to show the absurdity of holding her up as a mascot for feminism. Hayyim Schauss exposes the folly of belief in Lilith in his book *The Lifetime of a Jew*:

> The Lilith myth is not of Jewish origin, but originated in ancient Babylonia. Long before Lilith entered the realm of Jewish folk-belief, she played a prominent role among the demons of Babylonia and Assyria...The religion of ancient Babylonia developed into triads of gods, and Lilith also became one of a triad of demons...It is certain that the belief in Lilith came down to the Jews from the ancient Babylonians....
>
> Among the ancient nations of the East, Lilith played the role counterpart to Ishtar...The ancient Babylonians and many other peoples of the ancient East originally had two goddesses in their mythology, who counteracted one another--one good and benign, and the other evil and malicious. The good goddess was Ishtar and the malicious and destructive goddess was Lilith, who in time was degraded to a demon. Ishtar was the goddess of love and fertility and, in the belief of the people, she protected and assisted women in labor and childbed. Lilith, on the contrary, sought to kill the mothers and their new-born babes. In the mythology of the Ancient East, Ishtar, the Great Mother, the Queen of heaven, represented the good woman, who is a good wife and a good mother. Lilith typified the neurotic woman, without a husband, who detests men and hates the offspring of human wedlock....
>
> In medieval Jewish lore the Lilith myth spread far and wide. It was interwoven with the Biblical tale of Adam and Eve, and Lilith became, in the fantastic folklore, the demoniac first wife of Adam. She was called the First

Eve, a name which she still retains on the
amulets of the present day....[4]

One of the most interesting facts about the Lilith
myth is that she is the counterpart of Ishtar who
represented the good wife and mother. Women who
want to base their beliefs on superstitions and myths
could just as easily choose Ishtar for their mascot as
Lilith. But since Lilith represents the basic philosophy
of the feminist movement--"detestment of men and hate
for the offspring of human wedlock"--she makes the
perfect choice. Lilith presents an excellent example of
how the foundation of the feminist movement rests
upon peculiar myths and legends. Her use constitutes
nothing more than blind prejudice and fails to convey
an image of intelligence for the women who promote
her life story.

In addition, the feminists overlook the obvious fact
that if God created two women, He could just as
easily have created two men, too. The Bible says as
much about two men as it says about two women. If
feminist thinking reasons two women because the Bible
contains two creation accounts, but ignores the
possibility of two men, that isn't logic. That's biased,
prejudiced antagonism toward men!

If inventing stories is their game, the feminists
could easily assume that the first man was a male
chauvinist while the second man was a gentle, consider, affectionate man who valued the talents of
womanhood. Indeed, Adam said that he appreciated the
woman and that a man would leave his father and
mother just to cleave to his wife.

However, such a view of the creation doesn't
agree with what the feminists want to believe about
God, men, or women. So they pick and distort the
scriptures until they find a version that tickles their
ears. Rejection of the creation accounts and
acceptance of Lilith isn't logical. Yet countless
women, who complain that society denies women the
right to use their brains, readily grasp the teachings
about Lilith. Furthermore, not a single man forces such

[4]Hayyim Schauss, *The Lifetime of a Jew* (New York:
Union of American Hebrew Congregations, 1950), pp.
68-73.

ignorance upon women. Many willfully choose it for themselves!

Throughout the history of mankind, Eve's sin and punishment have sparked many debates about the implications for women. Even many of the women who want to serve God resent the teachings of the creation account. However, Eve demonstrated for all time how a woman loses the "very good" in her marriage--by forsaking her role of subjection. God simply told Eve and her modern daughters how to find it once again by loving their husbands and submitting to their rule. All the argument in the world won't change the truth recorded in Genesis. Even though God told Eve to submit to Adam, He held Adam equally responsible for his sin:

C. THE MAN'S PUNISHMENT

> **Gen. 3:17-19:** "Then to Adam He said, 'Because you have listened to the voice of your wife, and have eaten from the tree about which I commanded you, saying, "You shall not eat from it," cursed is the ground because of you; in toil you shall eat of it all the days of your life. Both thorns and thistles it shall grow for you; and you shall eat the plants of the field; by the sweat of your face you shall eat bread, till you return to the ground, because from it you were taken; for you are dust, and to dust you shall return.'"

"Listened" means "to hear intelligently (often with implication of attention, obedience, etc. causing to tell, etc.)" (Thayer, p. 118). "Listened" is often translated "obeyed" throughout the Bible (Gen. 22:18 and 26:5).

God punished Adam because he obeyed Eve and ate the forbidden fruit. While a man cannot always control his wife's behavior, God expects him to control his own conduct. If his wife tries to rule him, he must not quietly relinquish the authority over his own body.

This doesn't authorize a man to force subjection upon his wife because God nowhere gives man that authority. God gave all the commands to be submissive to the wife--even after Eve sinned. For this reason, God didn't punished Adam for letting Eve get out of control, but for not controlling himself. Every man assumes responsibility for himself regardless of what his wife might do or not do.

Man's punishment centers around his job of subduing the earth. As a penalty, he must now work harder than ever at tilling the ground--He must sweat in order to learn a living. Even today with college degrees in agriculture and modern machinery, man still has not conquered the curse of weeds and insects or tamed the weather.

Man's punishment serves as a constant reminder of what happened when Adam let Eve boss him around. As a man labors to provide for his family, it reminds him to take his responsibilities seriously and to not let someone else take them over for him. Perhaps this is one reason why God gave the man such a strong determination to function as the leader--to help protect both him and the woman from what happened in the garden of Eden.   And so God punished Adam and Eve individually in such ways which would remind them of their relationship to each other. However, more punishment awaited them:

D. THE PUNISHMENT OF BOTH

Gen. 3:21-24: "And the Lord God made garments of skin for Adam and his wife, and clothed them. Then the Lord God said, 'Behold, the man has become like one of Us, knowing good and evil; and now, lest he stretch out his hand, and take also from the tree of life, and eat, and live forever'-- therefore the Lord God sent him out from the garden of Eden, to cultivate the ground from which he was taken. So He drove the man out; and at the east of the garden of Eden He stationed the cherubim, and the flaming sword which turned every direction, to guard the way to the tree of life."

Adam and Eve's individual punishments centered around their unique jobs of subduing the earth and filling it with people, but their combined punishment of banishment from the garden centered around their relationship to God. They lost the privilege of walking with Him in the garden and the pleasures of that free association. No longer given access to the tree of life, they faced certain physical death. As a direct result of Adam and Eve's sin, all of mankind must die.

Eve got her own way when Adam gave in to the woman he cherished and loved. But all of mankind knows that the price she paid in destroying their beautiful home and in taking away their close fellowship with God wasn't worth it. As a result of the sin and death that she brought into the world, her modern daughters must work harder than ever to find the "very good" for their own marriages. Yet God's love shines forth for women, the special ones He designed to be the answer to the man's problem. God placed the keys for happiness and true marital bliss in the Bible for each woman to use.

However, like Mother Eve, each woman must make her own choice to serve God or to listen to Satan's cunning lies. Since women now despise snakes, Satan won't ever take that form again to tempt a woman. But he's still out there saying, "Use your brains! God doesn't want you to be smart! Don't let God and men take away your rights!" And yes, some of Eve's daughters are still listening and reaching for the forbidden fruit. Some are even offering the fruit to their husbands who cherish and love them. Eve learned her lesson. Will her daughters learn it, too, before it's too late?

———

STUDY EXERCISE

Answer all questions in your own words.

1. List the three reasons the Bible gives for why Eve sinned.

2. Do women fall victim to these same temptation today? Explain.

3. What happened when Adam and Eve's eyes were opened? Explain in detail.

4. What was Eve's punishment and what did it center around?

5. What did God mean when He said Eve's desire would be for her husband?

6. Did God punish Eve by saying that from now on she would have to be submissive to her husband? How do you know?

7. What was Adam's punishment and what did it center around?

8. What punishment did Adam and Eve share? How did their actions affect all of mankind?

9. Do you disagree with anything in this lesson? If so, explain in detail giving scriptures for your reasons.

RESEARCH EXERCISE

This exercise is designed to help women form a clear mental picture of the role of a wife as revealed in the Bible. A successful marriage is not due to chance or falling in love with the right person. Success comes from worthwhile values, clear workable goals, responsibility for one's own actions, and mature emotions based upon rational thinking. Having the scriptures clearly in the mind and understanding their relationship to each other helps the student achieve success. Without clarity of thought, true success is impossible because ignorance invites fuzzy conceptions, unrealistic goals, irresponsible behavior, and irrational emotions--the companions of failure.

On a sheet of paper make five columns for listing the scriptures which teach the role of a wife. As the basis, use God's summary of Eve's responsibilities in Gen. 3:16: "Yet your desire shall be for your husband, and he shall rule over you." Head the first column "Love," the second "Subjection," the third "Miscellaneous," the fourth "Rewards," and the fifth "Penalties." The rewards and penalties should contain examples of Bible women.

As you go through the lessons, write out the scriptures which belong under the respective columns. This exercise is due at the end of lesson sixteen. At that time you will need to write a paper summarizing the role of a woman and stating what you have learned. If you wait until that time to do this project, you will overlook many scriptures, and you will not learn as much as you could. Ideally, this project should also be carried out through the study of *Vol. II: Learning to Love.*

This is not busy-work. This is one of the first projects I did for my own use when I first began studying this material. I benefited so much from it that I want others to profit, too. This exercise will help impress upon your mind the consistency of the Bible as it reveals the woman's role. Also, it will give you a complete catalog of scriptures for helping others. You can personalize this project by putting a check mark by the scriptures which describe you. Then you can work toward placing a check mark by every one of the positive scriptures.

As an option, you might also do the man's half of marriage. The main difference would be column two which should be titled "Leadership." This part of the project should not be undertaken for the purpose of exposing a particular husband's fault. Time spent trying to change your mate is wasted and usually detrimental to the marriage. On the other hand, ruthless examination of yourself along with a determination to achieve the goals God outlines for you produces lasting result. *Every woman is guaranteed personal success when she changes herself for better.*

The main value in a woman studying and understanding the man's half of marriage comes from her increased ability to support her husband instead of usurping his authority and role. With this attitude, studying the man's half helps a woman accomplish her own particular work and impresses upon her how consistently God assigns work respectively to men and woman.

CHAPTER 7

APPRECIATING THE STRONGER VESSEL

With the passing of the Equal Pay Act in 1963 and a feminist march in August 1970, the equal rights movement began in earnest. The feminists promoted not only equal pay for men and women, but also equal job opportunities. The movement leaders claimed that any apparent differences between the abilities of men and women resulted from conditioning in the homes and schools. They denied that any inborn male-female differences existed at all.

The next fifteen years saw great reforms in employment laws that guaranteed women the right to pursue any career they desired. Welcoming this new freedom, masses of women left their homes and flocked to the marketplaces to take hold of new career opportunities. However, statistics show that women still lag far behind men in their climb up the corporate ladder in spite of their determination to succeed.

A recent television special lamented that modern men still resent women's abilities and that they still deny women their lawful right to earn large paychecks. But does male hostility toward women really keep women on a lower pay scale than men? Can women really do anything a man can and better? Or could the problem possibly be that men and women *really are different* after all? When the facts are all in, is the man's masculinity really worthy of respect?

The feminists stand firm in their refusal to acknowledge any significant mental and physical male-female differences which help prepare men for business careers. Yet while searching for proof of the similarities between men and women, modern scientists discovered instead greater differences than ever before. The stronger vessel really does exist in the form of a man:

I. THE STRONGER VESSEL

I Pet. 3:7: "You husbands likewise, live with your wives in an understanding way, as with a weaker vessel, since she is a woman; and grant her honor as a fellow-heir of the grace of life, so that your prayers may not be hindered."

"Weaker" means "weak, infirm, feeble" (Thayer, p. 80). "Weaker" also means "literally strengthless (see impotent), is translated 'weak'; (a) of physical weakness, I Pet. 3:7 (comparative degree)."[1]

"Since she is a woman" means "of or belonging to a woman, feminine, female" (Thayer, p. 123).

"Since she is a woman" modifies "as a weaker vessel" and explains why the husband must treat his wife as a weaker vessel: not because she is inferior, but because she is feminine and possesses the characteristics and attributes of a woman. Some of the other translations show "as a weaker vessel" modifying "since she is a woman." This does not change the meaning of the verse because which ever phrase comes first, the "weaker vessel" and the "woman" remain synonymous.

Through the guidance of the Holy Spirit Peter emphasizes the inherent differences in men and women in this verse. Thus, a man must treat his wife as a feminine being and not a masculine one. When compared to each other, the man, in the normal situation, is stronger than the woman. Saying that a man is "stronger" than a woman is not the same as saying that a man is "superior" to a woman. It simply says that a man and a woman possess inherent differences.

For example, if a squirrel challenged a man to a race to see who could climb a tree faster, who would win? If they both started off at the same time and the

[1] W. E. Vine, *Expository Dictionary of New Testament Words* (Westwood, NJ: Fleming H. Revell Company, 1950), p. 204)

same place, it wouldn't be a contest. The squirrel would shoot up to the top of the tree before the man even got his cleats on. Even so, the squirrel couldn't look down at that feeble man and laugh, "Ha! Ha! I'm already at the top! You haven't even gotten started? Squirrels are superior to men because I beat you up the tree!"

Obviously, such a boastful squirrel would be ignoring the fact that God made squirrels to climb trees. He gave them four feet, claws, and small bodies. Squirrels can do about anything they want to on a tree from playing tag around the trunk and through the branches with each other to leaping from tree to tree. Squirrels can even walk the power lines without falling to get from tree to tree. Everyone knows that men and squirrels possess completely different capabilities. God gave squirrels the characteristics they need to climb trees. While a man can climb a tree when the need arises, God didn't create the man primarily to live in trees. Instead, God incorporated within the man the qualities he needs to exercise dominion over the earth and the animals, including the squirrels.

By the same reasoning, the man can't brag to the woman, "I'm stronger than you are so that means I'm superior to you!" The only logical conclusion is that the man and the woman are different from each other. God gave them the different qualities they each need to carry out their individual responsibilities.

While the Bible points out the differences between men and women, the Bible nowhere authorizes sexual bias against either men or women. Since these differences originated within the mind of God, they reflect His wisdom. Displaying partiality on the basis of sex shows ignorance and a lack of appreciation for God's way. For example, Peter told husbands to honor their wives for their differences (I Pet. 3:7). Likewise, the apostle Paul rebuked the Jews who proudly yielded to racial, economical, and sexual prejudice by telling them that all were equal in the sight of God (Gal. 3:28).

Scientists now recognize that sex hormones play an important part in the way male and female fetuses develop. If the baby is to be a male, at about six weeks the Y chromosome causes the testes to develop and to begin to produce the male hormone testosterone.

This hormone affects every part of the developing fetus from his brain to his physical structure. On the other hand, at about the twelfth week, female babies begin producing the hormones estrogen and progesterone which create special feminine characteristics.[2] *Human Physiology* with updates from Jane Barr Stump's book *What's the Difference? How Men and Women Compare* (WTD) lists a few of those differences which no one disputes:

MAN

Larger corporal development [the average man's chest measures 38 3/4 inches while his waist measures 31 3/4 inches--WTD]

Higher stature [the average man is five feet nine inches tall and weighs 162 pounds--WTD]

Rudimentary mammary glands

Narrow pelvis

Greatest transverse diameter at shoulders [encloses larger heart and lungs and a higher center of gravity which affects balance--WTD]

Less subcutaneous fat [about 15 percent fat which makes men less sensitive to heat and more sensitive to cold--WTD]

Thick, rough skin

Beard, mustache, tendency to baldness

Hair on pubis extending toward the umbilicus and the anus (lozenge shape)

Abundant body hair, especially on chest and limbs

Well developed larynx [evident by the Adam's apple--WTD] and low-toned voice

Higher basal metabolic rate [burns seventeen to twenty calories per pound of body weight (about 2700 calories per day)--WTD]

Higher erythrocyte count [20 percent more red blood cells--WTD]

Smaller adrenals and thyroids

Male character of hypophysis [pituitary body or gland--PRD]

---

[2]Stump, *What's the Difference?* p. 79.

Male psychic character and response, initiative, aggressiveness, abstract thinking, idealism, interest in social problems [from higher levels of the hormone testosterone-- WTD].

WOMAN

Smaller corporal development [the average woman's bust measures 35 1/2 inches, her waist measures 29 1/4 inches, and her hips measure 38 inches--WTD]

Lower stature [the average woman is five feet three inches tall and weighs 135 pounds-- WTD]

Well-developed mammary glands

Broad pelvis

Greatest transverse diameter at hips [larger liver, kidneys, and appendix and a lower center of gravity which affects balance-- WTD]

More subcutaneous fat [about 27 percent fat which makes women more sensitive to heat and less sensitive to cold--WTD]

Thin, soft skin

No beard or mustache, hair on head longer and without tendency to baldness

Hair on pubis limited by horizontal line (triangular shape)

Body hair fine and scarce

Less developed larynx and high-toned voice

Lower basal metabolic rate [burns ten to fifteen calories per pound of body weight (about 2000 calories per day)--WTD]

Lower erythrocyte count

Larger adrenals and thyroids, which respond more readily to stimulation

Female character of hypophysis [pituitary body or gland--PRD]

Female psychic character and response, more highly developed emotivity and affections, maternal and family sentiment, practical outlook [from higher levels of the hormone estrogen--WTD].

It is absurd to discuss the superiority of one sex over the other; each one has its own characteristics, which compliment those of the other.[3]

The Bible points out two specific ways men demonstrate more strength than women:

A. BIOLOGICALLY STRONGER

Prov. 20:29: "The glory of young men is their strength,..."

Men, especially young men, excel in pure brute strength. Jane Stump, Ph.D. who listed all the recorded differences between men and women that she could find in her book *What's the Difference? How Men and Women Compare* states that when men and women are equally trained, the woman possesses only about two thirds of the overall strength of the man. Yet the woman displays only about one third of the man's strength in her upper body. The man's massive bones, larger joints, and longer arms and leg segments all work together to give him greater leverage and power. The woman utilizes about two thirds of the man's strength in her legs. Only a woman's stomach muscles contain as much strength as a man's.[4]

Another source of a man's strength comes from his large muscle mass which results from the action of the hormone testosterone. During the man's adolescence testosterone builds his muscles by adding bulk and fiber. Likewise, a man's muscle cells increase in size until he turns forty. But a woman's muscle cells stop growing by the time she is ten or eleven. Men possess about 50 percent more muscles than women.[5]

In contrast, the female hormone estrogen creates a greater fat storage in the woman, 27 percent to the man's 15 percent, to make her soft and lovely in appearance. Weight and height charts easily demonstrate

[3]*Human Physiology* (New York: McGraw-Hill Book Co., Inc., 1951), pp. 613-614 with inserts from Stump, *What's the Difference?*
[4]Stump, *What's the Difference?* pp. 135 and 191.
[5]Stump, *What's the Difference?* p, 134.

this as men always weigh more than women of the same height and bone structure. The extra amount of fat in the female body plus her lack of comparative muscle fibers significantly lowers her physical strength. The man exhibits greater physical strength than the woman simply because his body contains more lean muscles with which to lift objects and work. While a man develops powerful muscles without effort on his part, a woman develops strength in her muscles *only through vigorous exercise* to overcome the action of her hormones. Even then she only achieves 60 to 70 percent of the strength of a man.[6] Thus, a man who never exercises, but who simply lies on the divan all day long watching television still has more brute strength than a woman who exercises to her maximum limit. To do better, a woman must take anabolic steroids--artificial male hormones to stimulate muscle growth. Then she risks considerable health problems.[7]

A man's larger lungs also affect his physical strength by supplying him with about two quarts more air than a woman's always do. He also has a larger heart and 20 percent more red blood cells to transport the oxygen to his cells. This gives a man more quick energy than a woman normally utilizes and explains why a woman is more prone to faint. Of course, when a man fails to exercise his body and lungs properly, he may get out of breath quicker than a woman who maintains excellent physical condition. However, in the normal situation a man enjoys a greater capacity for doing strenuous work then a woman.[8]

At the same time, a woman's extra fat gives her an advantage over a man in the realm of endurance. Since fat burns slowly, the woman's extra fuel storage keeps supplying her with energy long after the man's reservoir runs dry. Only sports such as English Channel swimming and long-distance running which take advantage of a woman's extra fat give the woman an edge over the man. Yet even with this advantage, women athletes run only about 90 percent as fast as

[6]Stump, *What's the Difference?* pp. 134-135.
[7]Eric Gelman, "In Sports, 'Lions Vs. Tigers,'" *Newsweek* (5/18/81), p. 75.
[8]Stump, *What's the Difference?* pp. 35, 72, 120.

the men.[9] The longer the distance, the better their chance of catching the man and passing him. Thus, saying that women manifest as much strength as men denies simple biological facts.

As Solomon says, young men delight in their *natural* strength and ability to perform hard tasks. Unfortunately, many wives fail to realize just how much young husbands love to glory in their strength--older husbands too, for that matter. Invariably, wives exclaim, "Not my husband! I ask him to empty the trash and he gripes all the way out to the garbage barrel and back!"

The problem often lies in a habit many wives proudly display--the ability to do many things for themselves without assistance. Many husbands, who their wives accuse of not wanting to empty the trash, often offer to do some small job for their wives only to be ignored or refused because they were not needed. Yet these same husbands frequently help other women who know how to allow men to glory in their strength. Usually, the fault is not with the husband, but with the wife's attitude toward assistance.

A wife either encourages or discourages chivalry by her response to her husband's offers of help. If a wife allows her husband to do the jobs *he offers to do,* she will be surprised at just how much he wants to do for her. Then when she *really needs his help*, he doesn't resent giving it. The secret? A wife should learn how to accept favors from her husband before asking for them: *If at all possible, she should never refuse her husband's offers to do something for her even if she thinks she can do it all by herself."*

Many women complain, "But isn't that hypocritical to accept help when you really don't need it?" Certainly, it's hypocritical if the woman *pretends* to not be able to do the job when she really can. However, when a man offers to carry out the trash, he knows that the woman can carry it out, too. Likewise, when a man holds the door open, he knows that the woman can open it all by herself. Or when a man takes a heavy box from a woman's arms, he sees that she can carry it. Most men offer to do many things which they

[9]K. F. Dyer with Bob Wischnia, "Why Men Run Faster than Women," *Runner's World* (11/83) p. 108.

know the women can do for themselves, so where does pretending to be helpless need to come in?

A woman lets the man glory in his strength, not by saying, "Oh, you big hunk of a man, I never could have opened that door by my little ole self!" but by smiling pleasantly and saying, "Thank you, kind sir." Hypocrisy or artificial flattery doesn't let a man glory in his strength. *Sincere appreciation does.* The woman shows appreciation for the offer of help first by accepting it if at all possible and second by expressing thankfulness.

One student remarked that she always complained to her husband about his lack of consideration because he seldom offered to open a door for her. She lamented, "And that is so important to me! But do you know that I have never thanked my husband once for opening a door for me because I expected him to do it." As a result, she gave her husband absolutely zero motivation for ever doing a single kind deed for her because she didn't think he deserved a simple, "thank you."

Just as women want to feel needed and appreciated, so do men. Yet God created men and women with different sources of self-esteem with the man's strength playing an important part in his:

Prov. 11:16: "A gracious woman attains honor, and violent [strong--KJV] men attain riches."

"Attain" means "grasp, lay hold of, hold fast, support with the basic idea of grasping securely" (*Theological Wordbook of the Old Testament*, p. 973).

"Violent" or "strong" means "fearful, i.e. powerful or tyrannical, mighty, oppressor, in great power, strong, terrible, violent" (Strong, p. 92). The word also means "mighty and awe-inspiring" and describes God's power for protecting His people as that of a "dread champion" in Jer. 20:11.

Two schools of thought exist concerning what "strong" means. Some say that the passage describes evil strength and riches attained as the reward for wickedness. However, other scholars claim that the verse contrasts a successful woman with a successful man. As such, the verse portrays a man as a tremendous source of energy and power. When a man applies the personal resources God gave him, he more than adequately subdues a resisting earth and attains the means for providing for his family.

This second view corresponds with the different goals and talents inherent within men and women. These differences also lead to the man and woman's own special avenues for achieving self-respect. Matthew Henry points out the special praise a strong man achieves when providing for his family:

> It is allowed that *strong men retain riches*, that those who bustle in the world, who are men of spirit and interest, and are able to make their part good against all who stand in their way, are likely to keep what they have and to get more, while those who are weak are preyed upon by all about them.
>
> It is taken for granted that *a gracious woman* is as solicitous to preserve her reputation for wisdom and modesty, humility and courtesy, and all those other graces that are the true ornaments of her sex, as strong men are to secure their estates; and those women who are truly gracious will, in like manner, effectually secure their honour by their prudence and good conduct. *A gracious woman* is as honourable as a valiant man and her honour is as sure.[10]

Much of a man's sense of accomplishment rests in his strength as he uses it to earn a living for his family. Yet few wives take time to praise that expenditure of energy. Instead, they often make their husbands feel like a paycheck on Fridays and in the way the rest of the time.

Appreciated or not, when a man marries he becomes duty-bound to actively pursue food, clothing, and shelter for his family for the rest of his life. The relentless responsibility many men feel causes their wives great consternation when they cannot get their

[10]Matthew Henry, *Matthew Henry's Commentary on the Whole Bible*, Vol. III (New York: Fleming H. Revell Co., 1710), p. 852.

husbands to go to the doctor, stay home when they have the flu, or take a vacation. Yet a mature man knows that he must provide for his family even if his tooth throbs endlessly or if his joints complain if he bends too much or if the economy struggles under a depression or when he doesn't like his boss or if computers and robots threaten to replace the skills he mastered through years of on-the-job training. Family obligations weigh hard on responsible men.

On the other hand, when a woman wakes up tired and full of aches, she often can do a minimum amount of work that day and curl up on the divan with an interesting book. The next day or the next week, whenever she feels energetic again, she can catch up on all the housework in just one day of hard labor. But a man's relaxation comes only after work-hours. If he doesn't work, he won't get paid. His job and his boss show little sympathy for his personal whims or problems.

For example, one man came down with such a severe case of the flu that he couldn't eat or get out of bed at a time when his company had scheduled an out-of-town business trip for him. During his illness, his boss told his wife that the only excuse the company would accept for him not going on the trip was a signed report from a doctor saying it was physically impossible for him to go.

A man needs all the physical strength he can muster to be a good provider and protector for his family. To make his job a little easier, God instilled another strength within the man:

B. PSYCHOLOGICALLY STRONGER

Prov. 20:29: "...And the honor of old men is their gray hair."

People everywhere associate gray hair with wisdom. Some even joke about each gray hair resulting from a lesson learned the hard way. As a man's body ages and the production of the hormone testosterone slows down, he loses some of his ability for strenuous work that he enjoyed in his younger days. At the same time, however, if he lived his life wisely, his mental abilities greatly increased over the years. Now his primary source of honor comes from his wisdom that developed through years of squarely facing the challenges of life.

While a godly woman, likewise, develops wisdom as she ages and solves the daily problems of life (Prov. 31:26) men and women think differently from the time of their birth. Thus, their mental abilities and realms of wisdom differ.

Thanks to medical breakthroughs and the catalyst of feminists disputing that any mental differences exist between men and women, scientists understand the functions of the brain better than ever before. While many questions still lack answers, modern research continually unmasks previously unknown wonders of the male and female brains. David Gelman's excellent article, "Just How the Sexes Differ," discusses some of the more recent findings. He explains how the sex hormones hold the "key to the difference" by "masculinizing" or "femininizing" fetal brains in the womb. These hormones affect the way the male and female brains develop which greatly influences their mental abilities and temperaments.[11]

For example, the two sides of the male's brain work independently of each other instead of together as the woman's brain does. This gives the man an edge over the woman in mathematics, especially higher mathematics such as geometry and trigonometry.[12] This also provides the male with visual-spatial abilities that women often lack. Thus, many mechanical tasks prove much easier for men than women because of their greater perception of space and depth.[13]

Likewise, the man's specialized brain enables him to home in on the root of particular problems once he has all the facts and to solve them better than women generally can.[14] This gives the man the potential of becoming an excellent leader at work, in the home, and in the church when he develops this skill.

Furthermore, the design of the man's brain helps him concentrate on two thinking projects at the same time such as running a computer program while watch-

[11]Gelman, "Just How the Sexes Differ," p. 83.

[12]Stump, *What's the Difference?* p. 127.

[13]Stump, *What's the Difference?* pp. 38 and 128.

[14]Gelman, "Just How the Sexes Differ," p. 81.

ing the news on television.[15] This ability makes the man more suited than the woman for worrying about financial problems and responsibilities. He can worry and fulfill his obligations at the same time. While many women exhibit financial resourcefulness, personal problems can so occupy their thinking that it incapacitates them and prevents them from successfully doing their work. Yet, as the next chapter explains, the woman's single-mindedness becomes an asset when she applies herself to her God-given role.

The man's sex hormones also affect his temperament by promoting aggression. Women, on the other hand, must learn aggressive behavior. Little boys demonstrate this aggression in their rough and tumble play and competition with other boys. Most violent crimes are committed by young men at an age when their testosterone levels are the highest.[16] While women speak with familiarity when seated next to each other, men display aggression when sitting close to other men with wise-cracking, fun-poking, etc.[17]

A recent newspaper article said that the Russians discovered that if they sent a woman into space with a man, the cosmonauts endured the flight with much less stress than when they sent only men. The woman's more passive emotional makeup counteracted the man's more aggressive nature. The article added that NASA has observed the same calming effect of women on their flights and also prefers to send mixed crews of astronauts. Obviously, it is not good for man to be alone, even in outer space!

While valuable in the close quarters of a space capsule, this lack of natural aggression inherent within women probably contributes to the small number of women succeeding as corporation heads. Sylvia Porter reported in 1982 that women made up only six percent of the corporate managers in the United States.[18] The televised ABC News report "After the Sexual Revolution" stated that fewer women served as corporate execu-

---

[15]Goleman, "Special Abilities of the Sexes," p. 54.
[16]Stump, *What's the Difference?* pp. 15-16.
[17]Stump, *What's the Difference?* p. 152.
[18]Sylvia Porter, "You and Your Money: The Truth about Equal Pay," *Ladies' Home Journal* (8/82), p. 22.

tives in 1985 than in 1982. The program asserted that "male hostility and suspicion" created the problem.[19]

On the contrary, rather than men denying women their constitutional right to succeed in the commercial world, the women's own lack of a driving aggressive nature holds many women back from competing effectively. Even when women work their way up through numerous promotions, their different mental outlooks continue to affect their work performance.

For example, women generally make more sacrifices with their families for their jobs and appear more career-oriented than most men. Yet women commonly negate this work advantage by failing to efficiently utilize their authority and by bringing a nurturing quality to the office. They make themselves more accessible to other employees by leaving their office doors open twice as much as men. They walk among their employees to make sure everything is "okay" and encourage interruptions both on the job and at home. In contrast, men more often expect their employees to work on their own, and they depend upon their secretaries to protect them from interruptions and unimportant matters. Essentially, men conduct themselves in a more independent and businesslike manner than women generally do.[20]

Consequently, if women want to compete more equally with men for higher-level corporate jobs, they might do well to take testosterone to increase their level of aggressiveness. At the same time, however, they should prepare to shave their faces daily have their voices change as they develop an Adam's apple, and try to avoid flexing their new muscles.   A better solution might be to accept the differences between men and women along with the different roles God created for them to occupy:

II. THE MAN'S ROLE

When a man takes a wife, he assumes many God-given responsibilities that take advantage of his differing physical and mental capabilities. Paul lists the husband's primary obligations toward his wife in Eph.

[19]Jennings, "After the Sexual Revolution," p. 5.
[20]Stump, *What's the Difference?* pp. 12, 116, and 123.

5:23-33 and shows how God wants him to pattern himself after Christ:

A. LEADS HIS FAMILY

> **Eph. 5:23-24: "For the husband is the head of the wife, as Christ also is the head of the church, He Himself being the Savior of the body. But as the church is subject to Christ, so also the wives ought to be to their husbands in everything."**

The husband is the head of the wife as Christ also is the head of the church. As Christ considers the needs of the church and guides her wisely, a husband has the responsibility of leading his wife in all matters. God not only placed a big responsibility on the man's shoulders, but He expects him to perform it to the best of his ability.

Many a wife, who spends hours trying to persuade her husband to her way of thinking, fails to realize that God made her husband think differently from her to help him be a better leader. As the next chapter shows, a woman possesses a far greater ability than a man to focus on emotions. While this quality makes the woman superior to the man for performing her God-given jobs, it easily gets in the way of wise leadership. A man's masculine viewpoint enables him to make wise decisions as he leads, protects, and provides for his family.

Likewise, the ability to disregard his emotions equips a man to better love his wife and to act in her best interest. For instance, after the heat of intense emotions dies down, many problems take on completely different perspectives. While emotions require consideration, the wisest decision possible demands that the leader act according to the facts rather than his feelings. Many a wife can look back on her husband's decisions which she viewed as unsound at the time and say, "He was right. I was wrong." The reason? She allowed her emotions to influence her decision; he didn't.

Because a wife wants what is best for the family just as the husband does, she is tempted to meddle in her husband's affairs. When a woman takes over the man's role, she says by her actions that God made a mistake when He created the man as the head of his wife. God didn't make a mistake when He created men differently from women. Yet God gives men the right to make mistakes. Solomon said that the glory of "old" men is their gray hair. Older men benefit from years of experience and mistakes that young men don't have. Consequently, a wife must allow her husband the right to make mistakes during his young years so that she can confidently trust his wisdom during his later years. *A wise person is not someone who never makes mistakes, but someone who corrects his mistakes when he makes them and learns from them.*

A man who refuses to exercise his God-given duty to lead as a young husband, denies himself the valuable learning experience of making mistakes. The consequences of mistakes stimulate a man's thinking and help him become just that much wiser as he matures. In fact, a person often profits more from doing something wrong than if he did it right in the first place.

With her husband's permission, one wife assumed the role of leadership during their early years of marriage. Later when she learned that her actions displeased God, she tried to give her husband back his authority. To her dismay, he didn't know how to guide his family. Suddenly being handed full financial responsibility along with a house full of rebellious children and other problems horrified him.

Allowing the man the privilege of learning how to control his children during the "terrible two's" helps him gain self-confidence and a greater ability to help them through the adjustments of the teen-age period. In a similar way, a man needs to learn how to handle money in the early days of the marriage when financial obligations are usually smaller. If a wife worries about balancing the checkbook and writes letters to the creditors when they get behind in their payments, she steals her husband's motivation for dealing with financial burdens. Expecting her husband to speak to the creditors himself allows him to experience the consequences of his spending habits firsthand. This gives him an opportunity to develop principles of spending and saving when the penalty for his mistakes is usually not as great as later in life. A forty or fifty-year-old man who still doesn't know the ABC's of financial management is pitiful. To make matters worse, his wife probably played an important part in his deficiency.

God also gives the man the responsibility of guiding his children wisely:

Eph. 6:4: "And, fathers, do not provoke your children to anger; but bring them up in the discipline and instruction of the Lord."

"Discipline" means "the whole training and education (which relates to the cultivation of mind and morals, and employs for this purpose now commands and admonitions, now reproof and punishment)" (Thayer, p. 473).

"Instruction" means "to admonish, warn, exhort" (Thayer, p. 429).

Good News for Modern Man, a paraphrase or one-man's opinion of the scriptures, says, "And *parents* do not provoke your children to anger." However, God did not make a mistake and leave the mothers out of this passage. While God designed a very important role for mothers to fulfill with their children, this passage addresses the father's responsibility.

God gives fathers the special job of overseeing the complete education of their children. Even though many people consider this the woman's job, God places the primary responsibility on the man's shoulders. As the next chapter shows, the woman helps the man in this area, but God gives the position of leadership in training the children to the man.

The man's leadership involves "discipline." God wants fathers to oversee every bit of their children's training in the home, the public school system, and in the Bible classes. This doesn't mean that he teaches everything himself, but that he stays abreast of the child's development and makes sure that these needs are supplied. "Instruction" makes up an important part of the father's responsibilities. He gives his children verbal instruction to admonish them and to warn them about the dangers of life. Obviously, God gives the man a tremendous responsibility to lead his wife and children. Yet God expects more of him:

B. PROTECTS HIS FAMILY

> **Eph. 5:23: "For the husband is the head of the wife, as Christ is the head of the church, He Himself being the Savior of the body."**

"Savior" means "savior, deliverer, preserver (the name was given by the ancients to deities, especially tutelary deities, to princes, kings, and in general to men who had conferred signal benefits upon their country)" (Thayer, p. 612).

While the word "savior" carries a lot of religious connotation to modern people, it did not to the Jews. They viewed their kings and leaders as saviors--men who protected them from all financial, political, and physical harm.

Christ, the ultimate Savior, protects His followers from their sins and from physical and mental harm through obedience to His word. The husband portrays this same image of a deliverer and preserver on a lesser scale in the family realm as he protects his wife from mental and bodily harm. A husband cannot save his wife from her sins as Christ does, but he can foresee hazardous situations and avoid them. When necessary, he physically defends his wife. This job demands that a man stay constantly alert for hidden dangers, both physical and mental. In like manner, God expects the man to protect his children:

> **I Tim. 3:4-5: "He must be one who manages his own household well, keeping his children under control with all dignity (but if a man does not know how to manage his own household, how will he take care of the church of God?);..."**

> **I Tim. 3:12: "Let deacons be husbands of only one wife, and good managers of their children and their own households."**

"Manage" means "1. set or place before, set over; 2. a. be over, superintend, preside over; b. be a protector or guardian, give aid; c. care for, give attention to" (Thayer, p. 539).

Both elders and deacons serve as models for a congregation to imitate. But before a man can serve as an elder or a deacon, he must know how to manage his own house, which includes protection of his family. In this troubled world, being responsible for the actions of one's wife and children isn't always easy or pleasant. Nevertheless, God assigns the job of protecting his family to the man.

Several hundred years ago, a man more easily recognize his enemies. If a bear growled outside, the man knew that he needed to get his gun and shoot him. If his children came running in screaming, "There's a snake in the woodpile!" the man knew what to do. In addition, the man spent the summer preparing for the winter gathering wood and storing food.

Now many single women and single mothers claim that a man in the house just hinders their lives. They think that since few bears and snakes roam the earth terrorizing women and children, and since equal pay along with many social benefits and welfare programs help families in need, the man should be phased out of his position of leader and protector. "Who really needs a husband?" they ask.

What a disastrous attitude for society! Women need a strong man more than ever because modern dangers are cleverly camouflaged. Often people fail to recognize them until after the harm is done to innocent minds and bodies. In many ways, it would be easier for a man to fight bears than drug pushers, or to kill snakes than to refute the teachings of evolution in the public schools. A man could easily see if he had chopped enough wood to get his family through the winter, but does he foresee how sexual immorality on television warps and destroys his children before its too late?

Wives still need protection, too. Modern society makes it easy for a woman to over-extend herself so that she harms both her health and her emotional reserve. God expects a husband to lookout for his wife's best interest and to help her say, "No," to the children, the neighbors, the school, and even sometimes to jobs within the church.

One husband said that many times when he came home from work, his wife acted angry toward him without cause. Other times she acted glad to see him. He

CHAPTER 7: APPRECIATING THE STRONGER VESSEL   227

finally discovered that she watched a favorite soap opera each day. If the men treated her heroine right that day--the wife received her own husband with open arms. But if her heroine suffered mistreatment from some man in the show--the wife's irritation toward him came out in the way she treated her husband that evening. The husband finally forbade his wife to watch the program anymore because of the damage it did to their marriage.

Whatever subtle dangers society holds for a modern family, God still expects the husband to provide adequate protection for them. Part of that protection includes providing the necessities of life:

C. PROVIDES FOR HIS FAMILY

> **Eph. 5:28-30: "So husbands ought also to love their own wives as their own bodies. He who loves his own wife loves himself; for no one ever hated his own flesh, but nourishes and cherishes it, just as Christ also does the church, because we are members of His body."**

As Christ nourished and cherished the church, God holds the husband accountable for providing his wife with food, clothing, and shelter. In so doing, the husband must follow the standard of the "nourishment" he provides for his own body. If he feels cold, he turns up the heat, or he buys himself a new jacket, or he eats something to warm his body internally by raising his blood sugar.

In this day of easy welfare and a lack of shame for lazy and unproductive men, a good provider and manager of the budget is rarer than ever. Especially so, since many men who work steadily waste their incomes before they furnish the necessities of life.

Today men exercise less control over their ability to work than the average man did a hundred years ago when the majority of men worked in a family-owned business. Now many jobs are boring busy-work and don't require much imagination. Frequently, men must work for someone who doesn't fully appreciate their efforts which gives them little motivation to excel. Thus, too many times all a man receives for eight hours a day, five days a week, is a paycheck which is soon spent. Yet a man's aggressive temperament and ability to leave his emotions out enables him to keep working after the glamour disappears.

Providing for a family is not equal to turning a paycheck over to a wife for her to worry about stretching it to meet all the bills. When a man provides for those under his care, *he makes sure that his income covers all their necessities*. Whether he writes the checks or she does isn't important. What matters is that the husband knows firsthand the financial condition of the family and controls the situation. The man's financial obligations also extend to his children as the verses about the elders and deacons demonstrate (I Tim. 3:4-5,12).

The word "manage" in these same verses includes another qualification that a man must fulfill before he can become an elder or deacon. The Bible nowhere tells a man that he must provide a high standard of living for his family, but it cautions everyone not to place their hopes in physical luxuries. As part of his leadership over his family, the man determines what their standard of living should be and maintains it.

Most husbands, whether or not they acknowledge God in their daily lives, want to lead, protect, and provide for their families. Yet God wants every husband to balance these natural desires with a genuine love and concern for his wife. Loving his wife as himself serves as a safety regulation to prevent the man from misusing his authority:

D. CONTROLS HIS ACTIONS WITH LOVE

> **Eph. 5:28-29: "So husbands ought also to love their own wives as their own bodies. He who loves his own wife loves himself; for no one ever hated his own flesh, but nourishes and cherishes it, just as Christ also does the church,..."**

"Love" comes from the Greek word *agapeo* and means "to have a preference for, wish well to, regard the welfare of" (Thayer, p. 3).

Infatuation, commonly called love-at-first-sight, incites intense physical feelings in response to what the love-object says, does, or looks like. This type of love often first attracts a man to a certain woman, but it fails to sustain a marriage. A shallow form of love, it lasts only as long as the physical attraction throbs excitedly or until someone more desirable, who creates sharper sensations, comes along. Invariably, such love vanishes only to leave the mystified lover wondering why.

In contrast, God commands a husband to love his wife with a permanent love that withstands the ups and downs of marriage. *Infatuation lacks a personal commitment to always "regard the welfare" of the object loved.* Thus, true love doesn't focus on what the loved one can do for the lover, but on what the lover can do to make life happier and more successful for the loved one.

Jesus, the perfect example of this kind of love, loved the church to the point of giving up His own life because it was the best thing He could do for His bride. Jesus' strong commitment to the church caused Him to make the supreme sacrifice. Jesus did this even though those who later become Christians rebelled against His authority to the limit by killing Him. That is commitment to acting in the best interest of the object loved! (Acts 2:22-41.)

Essentially, this love balances the man's oversight of his family and prevents him from letting his God-given power go to his head by becoming a selfish, egotistical tyrant. The command to love his wife as his own body strikes at the weakest point in the man's exercise of his authority. Many husbands demonstrate this fact by gloating, "I'm the leader and I get to do anything I want! And you have to like it!" *Thus, God commands the man to control his dominion with love.* With authority goes the responsibility to use it righteously and with justice and equity.

A leadership position contains no room for selfishness. Instead, it demands that considerate love control every decision and action of the one in charge. This type of love promotes trust--even when opinions differ. But when selfishness reigns, the home often deteriorates into a jungle where every man, woman, and child fights for his own rights with the strongest one winning.

Feminists complain bitterly about selfishness on the part of husbands. But their solution of removing the man from the head of the family only makes matters worse. Even with the better educated and self-sufficient women of today, the man is still the best inherently qualified one to serve as the leader. Obviously, the solution is to remove the selfishness, not the man.

E. THE GUARDIAN OF AUTHORITY

"Guardian" means "one who guards, keeps safe, or secures, a custodian" (Webster).

As a man goes about subduing the earth and filling it with people, God gives him the responsibility of guarding authority in the home, the world, and the spiritual realm. A man exercises this duty in the family realm as he leads, protects, and provides for his wife and children. Then as he keeps respect for authority safe as the head of the family, he prepares himself to keep God's authority secure in the spiritual realm as he leads as an elder or serves as a deacon (I Tim. 3:1-13).

> I Cor. 11:3: "But I want you to understand that Christ is the head of every man, and the man is the head of a woman, and God is the head of Christ."

The universal law of authority places the man over the woman in a position of leadership. While God designed the man as the custodian of authority, the woman serves as the man's helper. Her efforts aid in preserving authority as she works alongside the man and shows respect for his leadership.

> I Cor. 11:7: "For a man ought not to have his head covered, since he is the image and glory of God; but the woman is the glory of man."

This section of scripture reveals a special function of the man that the woman doesn't share--the role of reflecting the image and glory of God in the realm of authority as verse three demonstrates by stating the universal law of authority. Thus, God gave the man a position of authority which He never intended for the woman to occupy. When a man fulfills his God-given position of leadership and responsibility, he glorifies God who created him differently from a woman.

Before any marriage becomes a taste of heaven and reaps the blessings of God, mutual respect for the role of each marriage partner must exist. The man must respect both his own role and the woman's. The woman, likewise, must show respect for the man's position and her relationship to him. Where no respect presides for the spouse or the divine office which he or she holds, pure love fails to thrive.

The man also serves as the guardian of authority for his children:

> **Heb. 12:7-9: "It is for discipline that you endure; God deals with you as with sons; for what son is there whom his father does not discipline? But if you are without discipline, of which all have become partakers, then you are illegitimate children and not sons. Furthermore, we had earthly fathers to discipline us, and we respected them; shall we not much rather be subject to the Father of spirits, and live?"**

As a man functions as a father, he portrays the image of God, the Father. As a result, a father who doesn't back-up his word teaches his children disrespect for what God says. God created the man as the stronger vessel, both biologically and psychologically, so that he could be a wise guardian of authority as he leads, provides for, and protects his children.

III. MASCULINITY AND FEMININITY

Even though sex hormones begin surging through a fetus' body soon after conception to shape and mold both his physical and mental characteristics which distinguish men from women, the environment also plays a key role in the development of those differences. The hormones lay down a "genetic blueprint" in the growing fetus' brain for his potential as a productive human being. Yet the brain was meant to "experience," and thus it matures according to "the growing child's experiences." Treating boys and girls differently from each other helps stimulate these hormone-produced brain differences.

Take for example the male's superior visual-spatial skills which facilitate calculating math problems, reading maps, building bridges, or designing computers. Outdoor activities along with rough-and-tumble play help develop this characteristic to its fullest while constant television watching inhibits it. As a result, the primitive lifestyle of Eskimo women helps them develop better visual-spatial abilities than many city-bred men have. But when compared to Eskimo men, the men maintain their edge. However, when comparing city-bred men and women to each other, a greater gap exists between the abilities of the men and women. This results from the action of the hormones without adequate stimulation from the environment for either the men or the women. Thus, a woman might well show greater ability over a man in a certain area because she exercised her brain to its limit in a certain area during childhood while he failed to stimulate and fully develop his.[21]

In truth, while the feminists advocate bringing up boys and girls exactly alike, their individual sex hormones will cause them to continue to react differently to the same environment. Sadly, however, failure to honor the differences between boys and girls weakens their special genetic potentials. For example, boys fail to fully develop their visual-spatial talents when denied masculine play. As a result, in future years men may lack the intellectual abilities for solving the increasing energy crisis in the world, and advancing electronic technology may be jeopardized by the lack of male genius. Likewise, the resulting greater aggression and visual-spatial skills in women won't make up for their lack of well-developed sensitivity to the needs of others. Without the feminine input and touch of love to balance the masculine nature, imagine what might become of the world.

[21] Goleman, "Special Abilities of the Sexes," pp. 54, 59.

A. GOD CREATED THE DIFFERENCE

Gen. 1:27: "And God created man in His own image, in the image of God He created him; male and female He created them."

The creation itself shows that the male-female differences originated within the mind of God. God made the man for a different reason, from different material, and with different hormones and abilities than He made the woman in order to qualify him for his special jobs. God also designed the female and equipped her to be a specialist at giving comfort and sustenance to the man.

Since the male and female reflect God's wisdom, they each share a responsibility to be what they were created to be--males and females--not its. In spite of what the feminists say, physical and mental biological differences exist. The unisex and feminist movements which seek to nullify all differences between men and women conflict with nature, common sense, and the God of heaven.

The man or woman who acts as if he or she were no different from the opposite sex preaches that God made a mistake when He created them male and female instead of "its." Which is worse: to teach that man's existence came by evolution or to preach that God did not know what He was doing when He created them male and female? Either doctrine denies God's creation.

To help men and women achieve the goals of personal fulfillment and individuality, God commanded His followers to act differently from each other and to maintain their uniqueness:

B. OLD TESTAMENT TAUGHT THE DIFFERENCE

Lev. 12:2-5: "Speak to the sons of Israel, saying, 'When a woman gives birth and bears a male child, then she shall be unclean for seven days, as in the days of her menstruation she shall be unclean. And on the eighth day the flesh of his foreskin shall be circumcised. Then she shall remain in the blood of her purification for thirty-three days; she shall not touch any conse-

crated thing, nor enter the sanctuary, until the days of her purification are completed. But if she bears a female child, then she shall be unclean for two weeks, as in her menstruation; and she shall remain in the blood of her purification for sixty-six days."

Many feminists enjoy using this verse in an attempt to show that God degrades women. But the verse actually proves the opposite—that God loves and protects women. God told the Jews to wait forty-one days before resuming intercourse for a boy and eighty days for a girl. Modern doctors give their patients this same advice by telling them to wait four to six weeks before engaging in intercourse. This gives the woman's body a chance to heal and prevents harmful bacteria from entering the womb through lacerations. At the same time, the woman avoids a painful sexual encounter with her husband due to soreness, etc.

Feminists gasp at calling women "unclean." But actually, the law protected the Jewish women in a more effective way than doctors protect their patients today. While doctors advise their patients to wait several weeks, many give in to their sexual desires. By calling new mothers unclean, God made the Jewish husbands afraid to insist upon sexual relations before their wives recovered from the birth experience.

A similar passage to this one, Lev. 15:19-33 instructs the children of Israel concerning a woman's menstrual impurity. The feminists often, likewise, quote it in an attempt to show that God is prejudiced against women. However, just as the regulations concerning childbirth protected women, modern science supplies several reasons how these restrictions also benefit women instead of degrading them.

For example, women who are prone to cramps often find that intercourse during their monthly periods increases the intensity of the pain. At this time of the month, sexual relations seem like an act of selfishness instead of an expression of love to many women. Thus, by calling the women unclean during menstruation, God protected them from any unreasonableness on the part of their husbands during that time.

Medical doctors now know that a woman's cervix, the opening to the womb, normally contains a mucous plug in it to prevent sperm and bacteria from entering the womb at all times except for the woman's few fertile days and during her menstrual time when the blood must escape. Thus, intercourse during menstruation could easily inject harmful bacteria into the woman's reproductive organs.

Dr. S. I. McMillen in his fascinating book, *None of These Diseases*, states that Jewish and Indian Moslem women enjoy the lowest rate of cervical cancer of any other group of women. Doctors attribute this to the hygiene practices of both the men and women who still follow the cleanliness rules of the Old Testament.[22]

After menstruation ceased, the women counted off seven more days and remained unclean for that additional period (verse 28). As a result, when marital relations resumed, the women usually found themselves at the height of their fertility period. Since God wanted the Jews to multiply, and the Jewish men and women were eager to do this, this command carried a special blessing for them--children.

Interestingly, the verses preceding the regulations concerning the women give similar laws governing the man's conduct. For example, a man with a discharge was also considered unclean. Therefore, if calling women unclean degrades them, men were equally degraded because the same term applied to them.

Instead, such laws give evidence of God's love and concern for women rather than showing degradation. God protected women from sexual abuse from their husbands during painful and medically harmful times. Indeed, God loves His women!

This law of uncleanliness not only protected women, but it also created respect for the differences between men and women by designating a longer unclean period for girls. Thus, from the moment of a Jewish baby's birth, God's law encouraged the parents to sex-stereotype the child as either a male or a female. Verse eight makes it evident that God didn't consider the female babies inferior to the males, just different: God told the parents to give the priest *exactly the same offering* for both boys and girls.

[22]S. I. McMillen, M.D., *None of These Diseases* (Old Tappen, NJ: Revell, 1967), pp. 18-19.

Many feminists complain about parents sex-stereotyping baby boys and girls. Some researchers proved this happens by showing slides of a week-old infant named Sandy to college students to test their reactions. When the students thought the baby was a girl, they described her as "littler," "weaker," or "cuddlier." But when they thought the baby was a boy, the same people noticed a whole set of manly qualities instead.

Rather than teaching the harm of knowing a baby's sex as the feminists think, the test actually proves God's wisdom in ordaining this law for the Jews. By insisting that His people honor male-female differences beginning with their birth, God assured Jewish boys and girls of a chance to fully develop their genetic blueprints.

God gave the Jews still another command to help guarantee the separation of the sexes and to provide for complete development of their inherent mental capabilities and temperaments as valuable human beings:

Deut. 22:5: "A woman shall not wear man's clothing, nor shall man put on a woman's clothing; for whoever does these things is an abomination to the Lord your God."

Under the law of Moses (which is not binding on Christians, but is preserved for their example) God demanded that the Jews respect basic male-female differences throughout their lives. *Pulpit Commentary* explains:

The divinely instituted distinction between the sexes was to be sacredly observed, and, in order to do this, the dress and other things appropriate to the one were not to be used by the other. That which pertaineth unto a man; literally, the apparatus of a man, including not dress merely, but implements, tools, weapons, and utensils. This is an ethical regulation in the interest of morality. There is no reference, as some have supposed, to the wearing of masks for the purpose of disguise, or to the practice of the priests at heathen festivals of wearing masks of their gods. Whatever tends to obliterate the distinction between the sexes tends to licentiousness; and that the one sex should assume the dress of the other has always been regarded as unnatural and indecent...Such a change of vesture is here declared to be an abomination to the Lord, because of its tendency to immorality.[23]

A newspaper article, describing the practice of men wearing women's clothing, told about a new store serving this type of man. The article said that "in a discreet location, a newly opened boutique sells women's shoes in size 14, oversized silk corsets and black, wet-look lingerie to male customers." The manager of the store bragged that he catered to transvestites who came out of society's closet to dress in women's clothes in the evening. He claimed to wear women's lingerie himself.[24]

The manager excused the conduct of himself and his customers with the statement, "Transvestites usually are not homosexuals, but most people don't understand that. Homosexuals have become more acceptable in public than transvestites." However, God doesn't excuse their conduct, but says that "whoever does these things is an abomination to the Lord your God."

Even if a person disagrees that Deut. 22:5 refers primarily to transvestites, it certainly includes them. God didn't want men and women acting alike--He wanted the differences between the sexes recognized and maintained. Since the creation of male and female, God has consistently wanted His people to respect His wisdom by living as males and females--not its. When men and women cease to appreciate masculinity and femininity, they easily become immoral and lose all reverence for God's design for human life. As the unisex movement becomes more popular, immorality in all forms grows more open as the clothing store announcement shows.

If men and women fail to heed the Bible's admonition, God expects them to exhibit a certain amount of common sense in regard to themselves:

[23]*Pulpit Commentary, Vol. III* (Grand Rapids, MI: Wm. B. Eerdmans Publishing Co., 1950), p. 355.
[24]"Shop Is Stocked for Transvestites," *The Spokesman-Review* (3/5/76), p. 19.

C. NATURE TEACHES THE DIFFERENCE

I Cor. 11:14-15: "Does not even nature itself teach you that if a man has long hair, it is a dishonor to him, but if a woman has long hair, it is a glory to her? For her hair is given to her for a covering."

"Nature" means "1. to make natural, to cause a thing to pass into nature; 2. the nature of things, the force, laws, order, of nature, nature, i.e. natural sense, native conviction or knowledge (as opposed to what is learned by instruction and accomplished by training or prescribed by law), the sum of innate properties and powers by which one person differs from others" (Thayer, pp. 660-661).

The Greek word for "long hair" differs from the word "hair" used in the second sentence. The word "long hair" means "to let the hair grow, have long hair" (Thayer, p. 354). However, the word which describes the woman's hair as a covering means "hair, head of hair; it differs from *thrix* (the anatomical or physical term) by designating the hair as an ornament (the notion of length being only secondary and suggested)" (Thayer, p. 354). I Pet. 3:3 uses the anatomical term, *thrix*, to discuss braiding the hair.

"Dishonor" means "dishonor, ignominy, disgrace (in a state of disgrace, used of the unseemliness and offensiveness of a dead body" (Thayer, p. 83).

Science is only now proving what mankind has resisted believing--that a certain amount of inborn "common sense" really exists in men and women. Yet scientists readily admit that they have only scratched the surface. Most of God's ingenuity in designing the human brain still awaits discovery.

Nonetheless, over two thousand years ago, Paul, through inspiration, declared that God held mankind accountable for using that common sense. God expects the common sense of a normal person to teach him that men and women are basically different and should act and look different. Paul gives the example of hair to prove his point. A man who wears his hair in a manner that makes him undistinguishable from a woman incurs shame equal to the unseemliness and offensiveness of a dead body. On the other hand, when a woman wears her hair long enough to make her femininity obvious to everyone, she receives glory. Why? Because she shows all the world that she gladly embraces the role of a woman.

More than any other bodily feature, the hair possesses the ability to reveal masculinity and femininity beyond any shadow of a doubt. For instance, some women sport boyishly slim figures which hide their femininity. However, even a woman with a super-slender figure makes her femininity absolutely clear to others by the way she wears her hair. Likewise, a man who resembles a ninety-pound weakling without rippling muscles makes his masculinity obvious by wearing his hair shorter than the normal woman. Unfortunately, sometimes people fail to take advantage of this natural distinction between men and women and only whiskers or feminine curves establish their sexual identity.

The apostle John used the natural differences between men and women to describe certain beasts in Rev. 9:8 whose "faces were like the faces of of men" and who had "hair like the hair of women." Without John's description of the creatures' other body features such as bodies of horses and wings of locusts, a person might wonder if such beasts roamed the earth today.

To make matters worse, in the early 1970's prominent French fashion designers predicted that masculine and feminine appearance will go out of style in the twenty-first century. Andre Courreges, Emmanuelle Khanh, and Paco Rabanne declared that dress will be: "unisex, seasonless, and totally synthetic." Garments will consist of "a one-piece unisex jumpsuit with built-in heating and air-conditioning to maintain a comfortable body temperature all year round. The transparent, phosphorescent garment is worn over skin-tone bikini underwear. Topping it, is a helmet equipped with transistor radio and telephone.

Designer Christiane Bailly added that the jumpsuit model for women would contain a special feature: "an electric beam which at different currents will alternately attract or repel male suitors." When people can't tell what "It" is that walks down the street, then women's jumpsuits will need something in them to let

men know that they're females. The designer went on
say that shaven heads would become the rage.

One college girl engaged in a running discussion
with her friend about who "It" was. One day they
thought It surely must be a girl, but the next day they
decided It must, indeed, be a boy. The following day,
however, they were not sure what It was. By the end
of the semester they still didn't know what It was.
Was It glorifying God who created It either a male or
a female?

To hear men and women talk, God did not know
what He was doing in the garden of Eden when He designed a woman as the answer to Adam's problems. All
men needed was another being like himself to go 50-
50 on the work load--not someone with completely
different abilities and responsibilities. In effect, the
feminists and unisex people say that man didn't have
a problem at all. Who is worthy of belief: the creatures or the Creator?

Sometimes people object, "But what if a little
boy's mother makes him wear his hair long from his
birth and he never knows any different? Surely he cannot have any common sense about hair styles!" Maybe
not, but ignorance doesn't keep such a child from suffering harm from his mother's neglect:

**Jude 10: "But these men revile the things
which they do not understand; and the
things which they know by instinct, like
unreasoning animals, by these things they
are destroyed."**

"Instinct" comes from the same word as "nature" in
I Cor. 11:14.

In a discussion about sexual immorality, Jude reveals that certain men slander things they don't understand, but things that their common sense should tell
them. Nonetheless, their ignorance will not save them,
for they will be destroyed by the very things they
deny.

In like manner, men and women may deny their
natural instincts about male-female differences, but
their rejection of facts will not void a single one. God
designed for His creation of the male and female to
last throughout all time. Anyone can intellectualize

away the natural differences between men and women, but they cannot physically destroy them.

If a person's common sense fails to make the differences between the sexes clear, God gives a plain command to Christians:

D. NEW TESTAMENT TEACHES THE DIFFERENCE

> **I Pet. 3:7: "You husbands likewise, live with your wives in an understanding way, as with a weaker vessel, since she is a woman; and grant her honor as a fellow-heir of the grace of life, so that your prayers may not be hindered."**

If someone becomes a Christian without prior knowledge of the differences between men and women, God commands him to learn. God expects men to act like stronger vessels and to treat woman as weaker vessels, not in a degrading manner, but with honor as joint-heirs of the grace of life.

For a man to treat a woman differently from himself, the woman must cooperate by acting differently from a man and by allowing the man to honor her in this area. For example, God stopped treating the Babylonians as "tender and delicate" because they quit acting that way (Isa. 47:1-5). Unfortunately, many women refuse to be treated as women. A man can't force femininity on a woman anymore than a woman can force masculinity on a man. A woman must enjoy being a woman and being treated as a woman for her femininity to honor her and to appear precious to her husband.

Failure to respect masculinity and femininity is a serious offense, for God refuses to hear the prayers of such men. Likewise, men who cease to appreciate their own masculinity and who try to function as females in a degrading sexual way incur separation from God:

> **I Cor. 6:9-10: "Or do you not know that the unrighteous shall not inherit the kingdom of God? Do not be deceived; neither fornicators, nor idolaters, nor adulterers, nor effeminate, nor homosexuals, nor thieves, nor covetous,**

nor drunkards, nor revilers, nor swindlers, shall inherit the kingdom of God."

"Effeminate" means "soft, soft to the touch, effeminate (of a catamite [boys kept for homosexual purposes--Webster], a male who submits his body to unnatural lewdness)" (Thayer, p. 387).

The list contains two classes of people who exhibit sinful attitudes toward male-female differences: God refuses to allow homosexuals, who do not honor the differences between men and women in the sexual act, to enter heaven. In addition, God rejects effeminate men, for they despise their own sexual nature and attributes. Both of these sins stem from a disrespect for the differences between men and women.

While these sins represent examples of extreme denial of male-female differences, even rejection of the differences on a smaller scale isn't without penalty. Mental disregard for these differences often creates insurmountable gulfs between husbands and wives. For as Jesus told His disciples, God designed for a truly wondrous relationship to result when the differences of a male and female join in marriage:

E. MARRIAGE REQUIRES THE DIFFERENCE

Mt. 19:4-5: "And He answered and said, 'Have you not read, that He who created them from the beginning made them male and female, and said, "For this cause a man shall leave his father and mother, and shall cleave to his wife; and the two shall become one flesh"?'"

Jesus emphatically stated that because they are "male and female," the man will leave his father and mother and cleave to his wife. A normal male doesn't get excited about leaving his parents to cleave to another male. From the very beginning, God designed males and females to fit perfectly together both mentally and physically in marriage. *Vol. II: Learning to Love* devotes a whole chapter to explaining the importance of accepting these male-female differences. Only in this way can a truly wonderful one-flesh relationship with a glorious sexual life result.

With acceptance of the male-female differences and appreciation for the wisdom of God in so creating them, a husband and wife can fulfill the prophecy that Adam made in the beginning concerning marriage: "And the two shall become one flesh." God gave women different brains, intellects, and temperaments from men because it isn't good for man to be alone. Man needs a special being to help him achieve the jobs of subduing the earth, filling it with people, and glorifying God.

Fortunately, while mankind's wisdom frequently fails to see the importance, God makes the most of the individual characteristics of men and women. In God's plan of uniting the male and the female, the female *must* retain her distinct personality and attributes in order to be effective. Likewise, the male *must* keep his unique traits and mental characteristics in order to accomplish his God-given responsibilities.

While the world seeks personal fulfillment and individuality, often the very methods chosen to achieve these goals actually make their attainment impossible. The more women try to assume the male's traditional and God-given role, the less they appreciate men and the more they lose their own unique characteristics of femininity. In the same manner, the more men envy the traditional rights of women and relinquish their responsibilities, the less they will appear to be strong men.

God gave men and women a certain uniqueness from each other and this individuality must be retained if they are to accomplish the work He assigned them. The teachings of God don't destroy personalities, but rather enhance them. On the other hand, the philosophies of feminism and unisexism which promote the abolition of all distinctions between men and women erase personalities and personal worth in the process.

STUDY EXERCISE

Answer all questions in your own words.

1. Give two examples of how being the stronger vessel qualifies the man to be a good leader.

2. Give two examples of how being the stronger vessel qualifies the man to be the protector.

3. Give two examples of how being the stronger vessel qualifies the man to be provider.

4. What do people's actions say when they dress and act unisex?

5. Why should mankind show respect for masculinity and femininity?

6. What two things cause masculine behavior in a man?

7. What do young men glory in? Give two examples of your husband's strength in this area.

8. What do older men take pride in? Give two examples of how your husband is developing this strength.

9. Do you disagree with anything in this lesson? If so, explain in detail giving scriptures for your reasons.

PROBLEM-SOLVING EXERCISE

The Problem: The following letters to the editor come from a college newspaper, *The Daily Evergreen* (10/12/72 and 10/17/72), in Pullman, WA:

Fragile Female Days Numbered

Dear Editor:

If you ever had to depend on the "superior male sex" to open your classroom doors, the chances are you never made it to class. Too frequent are the times we've been nearly blended into the concrete by an enthusiastic male eagerly rushing to or from a class.

Today it is the exception rather than the rule for a man to hold a chair or a door for a woman. Maybe this is to the advantage for that rare breed we shall label the "considerate male."

It is indeed a fact that a woman will look twice (from shock if nothing else) at the man who shows his masculinity by holding those two-ton doors open for her. She can't help but admire these virile traits.

The days of the fragile female may be numbered, but they haven't yet disappeared. Unless you males favor an Amazon for a companion perhaps you should think about preventing the over-development of the female biceps.

2 fragile females

The response:

Bound in 1902 Tradition

Editor:

This is in reply to the two "Fragile Females." You fluff heads are beyond belief--theoretically this university is supposed to set the progressive trend for the rest of society. However, you two are obviously very determined to remain bound up and closeted in 1902 chauvinistic tradition.

What are you even doing at an institution of higher learning? I think it's all too obvious that your heads (or rather, minds) are nonexistent if you would even consider skipping classes because you feel your biceps would enlarge to the extent of "nonfemininity"; by opening doors yourself. You are women with minds as well as bodies. Your purpose for being on this university is supposed to be to enrich your mind--not to prove your femininity.

2 different females

The Exercise: Write a letter to the editor in response to these two letters telling which group of women you believe is thinking wisely. Use scriptures for your reasons.

CHAPTER 8

HONORING THE WEAKER VESSEL

What a wonderful age for a woman! Throwing off much of the ignorance and superstition of the past about the woman's second-class status, society reaches toward greater understanding of the feminine nature. Intense studies on how the environment shapes attitudes and abilities become more commonplace. Along with them, new technology continually explores the human body and mind in search of a physical basis for a more meaningful relationship between the sexes.

Ironically, many researchers admit to conducting biased experiments in hopes of dispelling the idea that male-female differences really exist. More open-minded scientists express fear of publishing their results because of the hostile reaction of feminists.[1] Still others refuse to accept the logical conclusions of their experiments with such hedges as, "We don't know this"; "We have no evidence for that"; "Our experiments are inconclusive"; "Our knowledge is limited"; "We just don't know"; or "We have very conflicting data on that point. We need more research."[2] Yet in spite of these drawbacks, a tremendous body of evidence surfaced during the last fifteen years to prove beyond all doubt God's wisdom in creating them male *and female*.

Thus, it's a wonderful time to be a woman! A woman can hold her head up high and glory in her differences--her special abilities and potential for contribution as a unique helper meet for man. In her

[1]Gelman, "Just How the Sexes Differ," p. 72.
[2]Gilder, *Men and Marriage*, p. 19.

heart, she can confidently know that she makes an intelligent choice when she reaches out to grasp all that femininity offers her. She can use her powerful influence over her husband and children wisely. She can enjoy a healthy self-image. The words of the Bible have always made it great to be a woman after God's own wisdom. And now modern science must bow its knee before a loving Creator who wondrously designed the woman as the weaker vessel.

I. THE WEAKER VESSEL

I Pet. 3:7: "You husbands likewise, live with your wives in an understanding way, as with a weaker vessel, since she is a woman; and grant her honor as a fellow-heir of the grace of life, so that your prayers may not be hindered."

"Vessel" means "1. a vessel (the female sex, as being weaker than the male, is likened to a *skeuce asthenesteron*, in order to commend to husbands the obligation of kindness towards their wives for the weaker the vessels, the greater must be the care lest they be broken); 2. an implement, household utensils, domestic gear" (Thayer, p. 577).

"Grant" means "(to dispense a portion, to distribute) to assign, portion out" (Thayer p. 66).

"Honor" means "1. a valuing by which the price is fixed, hence the price itself, (contextually with emphasis) at a great price, thing prized; 2. honor which belongs or is shown to one, the honor of one who outranks others, pre-eminence, the honor which one has by reason of the rank and state of the office which he holds, veneration, deference, reverence, preciousness" (Thayer p. 624).

God made it clear in the garden of Eden that man didn't need just any kind of a helper. He required a specialist who could supply what he lacked. God *deliberately* made the woman as the weaker vessel so that she could become the answer to man's problem. Being a weaker vessel qualifies a woman to do the special jobs God gave her--giving love in all realms. A man lacks the ability to do the work of a woman simply because he is the stronger vessel.

Understanding the significance of the word "vessel" makes the marriage relationship much clearer. God designed the male and female bodies as "tools" which work together to serve Him. Just because the male tool is stronger than the female tool doesn't make it superior.

For example, some men organized a work party to paint a building. They brought all kinds and sizes of paint brushes. Some of them brought big six-inch thick brushes for slapping the paint on the walls. Others brought small two-inch thin brushes for painting the trim around the doors and windows.

Obviously, the two-inch brushes become the weaker vessels or tools when compared to the six-inch brushes. However, no superiority or inferiority exists between the two sizes of brushes. If a man tried to paint a wall with a two-inch brush, it would wear him out. He could do it, though. But his arm would get tired before he finished because it would take him three or four more brush strokes to do the job. A two-inch brush was never designed for painting walls.

On the other hand, suppose that after a man finished painting the walls with his big six-inch brush, he decided to paint the trim. Instead of switching to a two-inch brush, he says, "Well, I've already got this brush dirty, no point in messing up another one." Then he goes ahead and paints the trim with his big brush, and he gets the job done in a hurry. Yet everyone knows that he didn't use the right size brush. They see where the paint slopped over onto the walls.

Brush manufacturers never designed six-inch brushes to paint trim on a door or a window--they're too big to do a good job. But a two-inch brush paints trim very neatly. At the same time, both brushes can substitute for the other when necessary. However, they fail to perform with the same excellence as when they do their own jobs.

That's the way with men and women. God designed men to perform specific tasks. Obviously, men can replace women in their roles at times. Even so, men lack the natural expertise that women possess for nurturing their families. Likewise, while women can carry out the men's jobs at times, they lack their special skillfulness for earning a living. God designed both the male and the female tools for different, but equally important, work.

Humans design their tools for specific jobs the same way. Then when they use their tools, they choose the one which will do the best job. Sometimes they substitute one tool for another because they don't have the right one. But they recognize the problems that making-do with the wrong tool often causes. That's what God did when He created men and women. He designed the female tool for a certain job; He designed the male tool for a different job. Absolutely no superiority or inferiority exists! Just different abilities and duties.

Thus, a woman's strength lies in her weaknesses; her ability to be a good gift to man lies in her weaknesses. When a woman properly uses her weaknesses, she glorifies God. For this reason, God commands the husband to honor his wife because of her weaknesses. In other words, God wants a husband to *deliberately assign great value* to his wife because of her weaknesses. The very qualities that create problems when his wife tries to take over his job, cause her to outrank him in her own role.

Likewise, when a woman denies her weaknesses, she rejects her remarkable abilities and the purpose for which God created her--to help man. The man's strength needs the woman's weaknesses and vice versa:

A. BIOLOGICALLY WEAKER

Jer. 51:30: "The mighty men of Babylon have ceased fighting, they stay in the strongholds; their strength is exhausted, they are becoming like women;..."

Understanding that women possess only one half of the muscles and only one third of the upper-body strength of men shows the accuracy of God's comparison of exhausted men to women. Also, as every dieter knows, the man's metabolism operates at a faster pace than the woman's; thus, he consumes a much larger amount of calories which enables him to work longer and harder than the woman. God simply designed a man's body for more strenuous work than He designed a woman's body for.

The design of the woman's body shows the efficiently of God's creation. For instance, many animals possess unique characteristics that make them especially adapted to their environments. The polar bear benefits from built-in sunglasses that other bears don't have or need. A duck's feathers contain natural waterproofing which other birds wouldn't use because they don't swim.

In a similar manner, the man's muscles and fast metabolism would be just as wasted on a woman as sunglasses are on a grizzly bear and waterproofing is on a chicken. For example, taking care of children and the home rarely requires the same strength and energy from a woman that plowing a field or doing construction work demands of a man. Powerful, gripping muscles don't help a woman teach and love her children, wash dishes, run the vacuum cleaner, or make the beds.

A woman's work involves industry--all the strength and energy of a woman--but not the robust output of a man. God gave the woman what she needs to successfully accomplish her work, not the man's. In fact, the woman's weaknesses bless both the man and woman:

Song of Sol. 2:14: "O my dove, in the clefts of the rock, in the secret place of the steep pathway, let me see your form, let me hear your voice; for your voice is sweet, and your form is lovely."

The Shepherd longed to be near the Shulammite maiden, whom he considered his "dove"--a continual source of peace and comfort to him. He wanted to see her lovely form, for God designed a woman's body, not to do a man's work, but to comfort the man after a day of hard labor.

A woman's voice sounds differently from a man's because her smaller larynx and shorter vocal cords give her a higher pitch. Her range of five tones to the man's three also produces a softer voice.[3] In addition, she enjoys a way with words that few men rival. From

[3]Stump, "What's the Difference?" p. 214.

the moment of birth, while baby boys ignore voices to busily observe novel objects and their surroundings, baby girls respond less to objects and more to what they hear. And so it will be for the rest of their lives.[4]

Researchers think this excellent verbal ability is connected to the woman's "superior tactile sensitivity." For the most part, a woman's physical senses, such as touch, taste, and hearing are more sensitive than a man's. Bright lights, repetitive sounds, and loud noises often found in earning a living and freeway driving distress women more quickly than men. Yet these sensitivities translate into the feminine "affinity for precision and detail." As a result, women usually make better typists, bookkeepers, needleworkers, and neurosurgeons than men. This devotion to detail helps girls talk faster than boys, carry a better tune, and remember conversations longer than men. On the other hand, boys are more likely to stutter, spell worse, and suffer more learning disabilities.[5]

A woman uses her voice tones and verbal specialties as either a blessing or a weapon. For example, a woman's soft, sweet voice soothes her husband into rest when he needs it the most; cheers him up when he suffers discouragement; and expresses soft, tender, affectionate love when he feels alone. On the other hand, many a man suffers a nervous breakdown because the tension at home compounds the frustrations at work. A wife who acts like a hawk instead of a dove can easily destroy a man, even a strong man.

Unfortunately, many a woman fails to realize how much her strength lies in her weaknesses. Instead of taking advantage of them, she tries to cover up the qualities which make her precious to her husband. God made a woman's body different from the man's for a reason. A man can work hard all day with little personal recognition or credit and come home to his dove and find fulfillment. He can go to work again, day after day, year after year, when he comes home to peace and tranquility.

---

[4]Annie Gottlieb, "Men and Women: What Differences Do the Differences Really Make?" *Mademoiselle* (7/81), p. 80.

[5]Gelman, "Just How the Sexes Differ," p. 73.

While biologically weaker, a woman possesses all the strength she needs to do her work. Plus, she enjoys a body which provides physical pleasure for both her husband and herself. Thus, her weaknesses become an even greater strength in lovemaking:

Prov. 5:18-19: "Let your fountain be blessed, and rejoice in the wife of your youth. As a loving hind and a graceful doe, let her breasts satisfy you at all times; be exhilarated always with her love."

As Chapter 1 explains the expression "wife of your youth" refers to an older husband who still lives with the bride he married in his youth. They have grown old together. *Vol. II: Learning to Love* discusses this whole chapter of Proverbs in detail and shows how an older wife satisfies her husband's physical needs better than a different woman every night can. The chapter deals with the special charms an older wife holds for her husband as she becomes an exciting lover.

Many people consider the honeymoon the highlight of marriage. They assume that the physical attraction naturally grows colder over the years. Not true! When a husband and wife conduct their marriage according to the standards of God, the honeymoon becomes a low point of the marriage. The couple who spends a lifetime loving and living together knows how to enjoy each other much better than the newlywed couple.

Adam and Eve provide an example of an older husband finding what he needed in his older wife. When Adam was 130 years old, Eve bore him a son named Seth. Then Adam lived eight hundred more years and had other sons and daughters through Eve (Gen. 4:25; 5:3-5). While the Bible doesn't tell how long Eve lived, God obviously gave her the qualities necessary to keep Adam interested in her for at least 130 years, plus many more.

Since few women today live more than 130 years, a woman doesn't need to worry about being able to satisfy her husband until "death do they part." No matter how much a husband and wife age, an elderly wife continues to possess the qualities necessary to solve her husband's problem of loneliness if she lives according to God's wisdom.

Solomon lists several qualities that a godly woman uses to keep her husband's interest throughout the years. Just as softness combined with free, spontaneous love causes men to cherish affectionate animals, these same qualities enhance a wife's appeal. God personally designed the soft and delightful nature of a woman's body to captivate her husband. That extra ten percent *tela cutanea* or fat doesn't help open pickle jars, but it certainly satisfies a husband's physical needs. Then as a wife gives herself freely in love to her husband, her skin texture and form become beautiful to him.

A woman's thin skin also contributes to her soft and fragile nature:

> Women really are thinner skinned and more fragile than men, says Dr. John Bliznak of Hendrick Memorial Hospital here. In research with Tom W. Staple of St. Louis Radiological Institute, Bliznak found the average woman's skin was 20 to 25 per cent thinner than the average man's.[6]

Just as God designed the woman's skin to help her express love to her husband, the man's skin comes equipped with special features to help him work in all kinds of weather. For instance, when allowed to grow, whiskers protect a man's face from mosquitoes in warm climates and from ice and snow in cold ones. Also, a man's thicker skin withstands the rays of the sun and the harshness of the wind better than a woman's which helps him provide for his family year-round.

Thus, in His wisdom and love for mankind, God designed both the man and the woman with unique physical characteristics to enable them to expertly perform their individual jobs. In like manner, the woman's emotional nature differs from the man's to help her master the important jobs awaiting her:

[6]"Women More Thin-Skinned," *Spokane Daily Chronicle* (11/20/75).

B. PSYCHOLOGICALLY WEAKER

Prov. 11:16: "A gracious woman attains honor, and violent [strong--KJV] men attain riches."

"Gracious" means "graciousness, i.e. subjective (kindness, favor) or objective (beauty):--favour, grace (-ious), pleasant, precious, (well) favoured" (Strong, p. 41).

"Honor" means "splendor or copiousness:--glorious (-ly), glory, honour (able)" (Strong, p. 54).

Men quickly recognize graciousness in women. Gladly, they honor such women who create home environments of comfort and splendor. Likewise, men understand that the graciousness of women balances their own aggression. While strong men require aggressive natures to subdue a resisting earth, they especially enjoy the pleasant kindness and favor of gracious women.

One minister's wife said, "When my husband comes home from preaching a meeting, he knows that I'm interested in the women he met. He frequently comments, 'I met a woman you'd enjoy knowing. She was certainly a gracious woman! I really enjoyed being in her home. I hope you get to meet her sometime because she was such a gracious woman.'"

While men tend to measure their success by the size of their paychecks and bonuses, woman often evaluate themselves according to the happiness of their homes. Thus, a woman's primary source of self-esteem comes from how she gets along with others. One reason so many homemakers feel depressed is because their husbands and children are unhappy, making them feel like failures. One woman cried, "When no one in your family likes you, it's hard to like yourself."

Many a wife who rates herself as a failure in the home suffers from ignorance of both her role and her special talents for fulfilling it. For example, the way God created the woman's brain especially equips her for graciousness. As the previous chapter on the stronger vessel shows, a man possesses a specialized brain. He uses the two sides of his brain independently which helps him solve problems and become a wise leader.

However, while no measurable difference in intelligence exists between men and women, a woman's brain works much differently than the man's. The two halves of her brain are more closely connected and work together. Also, a woman possesses a larger *corpus callosum*, or bridge between the two brain halves, than a man. Scientists theorize that this gives the woman "more room for neural pathways" and better inner brain communication.[7]

This ability to transmit information back and forth more rapidly than the man produces the female intuition--the woman's ability to interpret facial expressions, bodily movements, voice tone, etc. Rather than being specialized like the man's brain, the two sides of the woman's brain work together on problems. This generalized way of looking at things makes the woman more perceptive to her emotional environment than the man is.[8]

Scientists first discovered these differences in the male and female brains when they studied stroke patients. A woman who suffers a stroke can usually train the undamaged side of her brain to take over for the damaged half. Unfortunately, when a man suffers a stroke, the damage is more permanent since the two sides of his brain work independently of each other.[9]

In addition, women excel in analogies.[10] This involves a woman's skill for drawing logical inferences based on the assumption that if two things are known to be alike in some respects, then they must also be alike in other respects (Webster). For example, a woman might observe her child do something which causes her great concern because of her ability to compare it with his earlier actions. Thus, she recognizes a pattern of conduct as it begins to develop before it actually becomes entrenched. This enables her to tell her husband, "I'm really worried about our son. He's done...which reminds me of what he did last summer. I'm afraid it will lead to...." Giving the hus-

[7]Stump, *What's the Difference?*, pp. 54-55.
[8]Stump, *What's the Difference?*, pp. 106-107.
[9]Stump, *What's the Difference?*, p. 38.
[10]Stump, *What's the Difference?*, p. 22.

band this information helps him make a wise decision about what to do. In this way, her keen perception combines with the husband's excellent solution-finding abilities to protect the children.

However, a woman's analogy-drawing abilities can get her into trouble. If she remembers everything that her husband ever did wrong over the many years of marriage and never gives him the right to make mistakes and learn from them, then she usually views their problems as being much worse than they really are. Heeding God's regulations of forgiving and forgetting along with not judging motives prevents a woman from abusing her mental gift from God. A woman's intuition is not a righteous substitute for the principles of wisdom found in the Bible.

Likewise, a woman's single-mindedness serves as either a weakness or as an advantage in her role in the home. For example, while many a wife accuses her husband of not caring, the way her brain works helps her recognize problems *long before her husband does*. The man's ability to concentrate on two things at once enables him to work to earn a living in spite of the emotional atmosphere of the home. This is an asset for him.

Just the opposite, the woman's brain combines her quick perception of problems with a single-mindedness which refuses to allow her to forget them. So as a woman tries to read stories to her children or work as a secretary, her problems greatly affect her performance. Her preoccupation with her problems brings on irritableness or depression which *drives her to find a solution*. If she seeks solutions after God's wisdom, her single-mindedness becomes a blessing which benefits her husband and children. She soon becomes an expert and valued problem-solver who keeps a warm, happy emotional tone in her home. This brings out the best in her husband and children.

On the other hand, a woman courts disaster when she ignores the needs of her family and turns her perceptions inward to feel sorry for herself. Chapter 3, "The Plight of Silly Old Women," shows the logical conclusion when a woman starts thinking with her emotions rather than gathering data with them: She becomes totally selfish in all her thinking and activities.

In this way, the woman's thinking abilities become a great weakness for both her and her family.

The problem of self-centeredness frequently stems from a woman measuring the *amount of love received* instead of the *amount of love given.* A woman cannot enjoy success as a gracious woman until she makes an intelligent commitment to satisfy the emotional needs of her husband and children to the best of her ability.

Many a man hungers for love and acceptance as much as his wife does, but he lacks the inborn know-how, the intuition, and the emotional depth that a woman possesses. When properly used, a wife's emotional makeup helps her apply God's instructions to the saving of her marriage. Many an unhappy husband desperately awaits a gracious woman to come along as the answer to his problem of loneliness. When such a woman accepts the challenge of filling her home with love and understanding, the grateful husband usually responds gladly. If more women radiated graciousness, more men would project strength.

II. THE WOMAN'S ROLE

Tit. 2:4-5: "...that they may encourage the young women to love their husbands, to love their children, to be sensible, pure, workers at home, kind, being subject to their own husbands, that the word of God may not be dishonored."

This passage summarizes a woman's responsibilities toward God, her husband, her children, herself, and others. Since chapter 15, "Avoiding the Curse of Subjection," explores the various aspects of this verse in detail, this chapter just notices the overall quality of her duties--her love:

A. LOVES HER HUSBAND

"Love" comes from the Greek word *phileo* attached to the word for husband and means "1. to love, to be friendly to one, to love, i.e. delight in, long for; 2. to kiss" (Thayer, p. 653). Wigram's lexicon defines this word as meaning "to manifest some act or token of kindness or affection, to kiss, to love, regard with affection, have affection for, to like, be fond of, delight in a thing, to cherish inordinately, set store by."[11]

The love *(philo)* that God wants a wife to learn to feel for her husband and children differs from the love *(agape)* that God commands a husband to manifest toward his wife in Eph. 5:22-33. Thayer describes the differences between *philo* and *agape:*

> As to the distinction between *agapan* and *philein:* the former, by virtue of its connection with *agamai,* properly denotes a love founded in admiration, veneration, esteem, like the Lt. *diligere,* to be kindly disposed to one, wish one well; but *philein* denotes an inclination prompted by sense and emotion. (Thayer, p. 653)

Philo expresses an affectionate, emotional, and physical love which a woman manifests by patting, hugging, squeezing, and kissing her loved one. Mt. 26:48 demonstrates this by using a form of *philo* for the word "kiss" when Judas betrayed Jesus. On the other hand, *agape* results from love based primarily upon an intellectual estimation of the needs of the loved one.

Peter gives an example of the differences between *philo* and *agape* by using them together in I Pet. 1:22: "Since you have in obedience to the truth purified your souls for a sincere love of the brethren, [*philadelphian*--combination of *philo* and brother] fervently love [*agapesate*--form of *agape*] one another from the heart." Again, Peter uses these two root words together in I Pet. 5:14: "Greet one another with a kiss [*philemati*--form of *philo*] of love [*agape*]."

The Jews had a tradition that demonstrates the affection of *philo.* They considered weaving a woman's work, and unmanly for a man. For this reason, they looked down upon an unskilled man who could only weave for a living. However, if the man's wife proudly

---

[11]Wigram, *Analytical Greek Lexicon of the New Testament* (Wilmington, DL: Associates Publishers and Authors Inc., n.d.), p. 426.

sat on the rooftop with him in the cool of the evening and visited with the neighbors as they passed by, the Jews said that the man married a wonderful wife who really loved him.

Philo includes this type of admiring love. Regardless of what the husband does for a living, a wife's true emotional attachment to him makes her beam with pride. She considers him to be the greatest husband that she could ever want. This kind of love comes easy during courtship. When a young girl dates a boy, onlookers often ask, "What does she see in him? How can she care anything about him?" These skeptics recognize that courting love is blind. In addition, men and women seldom marry without this type of love. Men seek it in their wives, and women insist on feeling it for their husbands.

Unfortunately, this type of love often disappears after marriage as a husband and wife begin to notice irritating habits in the other. Then love gives way to bitterness in the hearts of both the husband and wife. Married love isn't so blind. Observing that many a man suffers from a loveless marriage in spite of marrying a woman whom he thought truly admired him, the husband of the woman of great price declared, "Charm is deceitful," (Prov. 31:30). Then he praised his own wife for her continual esteem and love throughout the many years of their marriage.

Consequently, after marriage most wives must learn once again to feel the excitement and devotion of their courtship days. Thus, God tells young women *to learn* how to restore that same innocent kind of love and how to keep it alive in their hearts. By a wife learning how to look at her husband in a very positive way and continuing to view him as the greatest husband for her brings out his best side. It also gives a husband a desire to succeed fully and to successfully provide for and protect his family. *The woman's tender love balances the man's aggressive nature and channels it toward productivity. This type of love also brings the wife great personal happiness and fulfillment as it answers her own deep emotional needs.*

God did not make a mistake and accidentally leave out part of the woman's metabolism or lean muscles when He created Eve. God made a woman exactly like He wanted her to be--a wonderful giver of physical and emotional comfort to her family. A woman's emotional and sensitive nature becomes a marvelous trait when she uses it to love others. Some male authors suggest enviously that women seem to possess a greater ability for giving and enjoying love than men. When women accept their weaknesses and their femininity, they become all that God wants them to be.

Sadly, many a woman moans, "I would give anything if my husband would just come up to me when I'm washing dishes and put his arms around me and hug me, just some little something like that." Due to Victorian morals, many a modern woman still views men as active givers of love while women passively receive their attention. Such a woman enters marriage expecting to just sit back and soak up all her husband's love. However, the Bible teaches exactly the opposite! *The Bible portrays the woman as the giver of love and as the one to initiate affection.* If anyone sits back and soaks up love, it should be the husband.

A man, who teaches salesmen how to succeed, said, "The more manly a man is, the more restrained he is at displaying affection publicly. But such husbands love for their wives to openly express affection. A wife pays her husband a high compliment by publicly patting him on the knee, rubbing his back, or even kissing him."

One wife told about when she and her husband visited another couple. She said, "I decided to practice showing affection like we talked about in class, so I reached over and patted my husband on the knee. I was really shocked when the other woman's husband immediately spoke up and said, 'Boy, I wish my wife would do that! I wish my wife would pat me on the knee! But she never does.'"

The differences between their roles makes it necessary for the man and woman to pay particular attention to different forms of love. For instance, many a man enjoys expressing physical love for his wife, but physical attraction alone doesn't help him preside over her with wisdom and justice. So God focuses on the husband's weaknesses and commands him to develop the type of love *(agape)* which prevents him from misusing his authority. *Agape* balances the man's leadership over his wife by eliminating selfishness. Thus, *agape* requires a husband to make an intelligent estimate of his wife's needs and to act in her best interest in preference to his own desires.

Just as God shows His love for women by commanding husbands to intellectually love their wives as their own bodies, God shows the same compassion for men by commanding wives to learn how to openly love their husbands. Many women naturally enjoy expressing tenderness to their husbands, but many more fall into the trap of wanting to receive affection before they willingly give physical love.

Basically, affectionate love that pleases God comes from a deliberate commitment to satisfy the emotional needs of the object loved rather than a selfish desire to soak up all the tenderness possible. Many love-starved women suffer simply because they focus their attention upon receiving love rather than giving love. Women who complain that their husbands don't greet them affectionately often don't themselves display any joy at their husbands' homecoming.

This is one of the greatest lessons women as a whole need to learn--to place the emphasis on giving love instead of receiving love. A woman's tender emotional nature often causes her to turn her feelings inward to feel sorry for herself instead of outward to love her husband. Thus, God's command to the wife strikes at her greatest danger for misusing love.

After studying the first edition of this book, Ocie Lue Snodgrass wrote a poem to highlight the rewards of freely bestowed love:

Marriage Account

MARRIAGE...
Is like a savings account;
We must put something in
Before we can take something out.
The amount we deposit
Day by day
Is doing kind deeds
And kneeling to pray.
Love and sweet words
Will make our account grow:
With loads of hugs and kisses
We are millionaires
Next thing we know.

It almost seems humanly impossible for wives to fully understand just how much their husbands depend upon their love, given freely and without thought of reciprocation. A man without a wife affectionately and obviously loving him still endures deep loneliness, and he still searches for the answer to his problem.

B. LOVES HER CHILDREN

When a woman truly cherishes her husband, she naturally treasures the fruit of their union, their children. God wants mothers to express the same kind of emotional tenderness for their children as they exhibit for their husbands--*philo*. Little children soak up this display of warmth like dry sponges and thrive on it.

A mother's nurturing nature helps her create a wholesome environment in the home for her children. She may not possess the man's muscles or aggressive nature, but her soft voice and calm spirit provide exactly what her children need. One woman observed, "My children misbehave the most when I'm tense and nervous."

Another mother said, "My children show more affection to both my husband and me when I have a calm day and take the time to visit and play with them. But when I keep a rigid schedule that doesn't allow for any interruptions, they pout and withhold their kisses."

A loving mother thinks her children are the best she could have even if they are homely and failed the first grade three times. She readily pats, hugs, squeezes, and kisses her children. She surrounds them with warm love to give them the self-confidence necessary to mature into stable adults. Her commitment of emotional involvement with her children continually finds ways of expression regardless of what the world thinks of them.

After hearing this description of a mother's love, one woman said, "I really appreciate the example of a mother loving her child even if he's failed the first grade three times, because my little boy *really* has failed three times in school. Not only that, but he has a bladder problem, and he's always wetting his pants. It's smelly and bothersome. I've really had a bad problem with my attitude and resenting him. Now I realize that I need to love him in spite of his problems because to me, his mother, he should be the most wonderful little boy I could have."

Irving Wallace's book *The Two*, about the original Siamese twins, provides a beautiful study of this type of love. It tells the true story of a mother in Siam who gave birth to twin boys joined at the breast. The sight of the boys so horrified the midwife that she could not finish assisting with the birth or clean up the twins afterwards. So the mother finished the birth and cleaned up her two sons without any help. The story describes the mother's extraordinary devotion to her sons and the way she molded their personality and character. In spite of their deformity, the Siamese twins grew up with healthy self-images, simply because of the way their mother loved them, taught them, and took care of them.[12]

While *philo* for one's children comes naturally to some women, such as the Siamese twins' mother, many young mothers need help in mastering it. Mothers who feel trapped and worthless often label the toddler years as the "terrible two's." Other mothers abandon their children to day care centers to build defenses against neglect, indifference, and emotional coldness. In the eyes of many, caring for little children no longer holds any prestige for a woman, but instead leans toward public scandal.

One mother said that she couldn't wait until her child was old enough to put in a nursery so she could get back to more "human" work. What is so inhuman about loving a child? What is so degrading about enjoying playing with a child and teaching him how to live? Where is the dishonor in raising a child to be a happy and loving adult? A woman who works outside the home receives only a paycheck for her labors, but a woman who works with her children produces beautiful adults and grandchildren for her efforts.

One husband said, "I used to think my job of providing for my family was more important than my wife's job of caring for the home and our children. One day I realized that if my wife neglected our children

[12]Irving Wallace, *The Two* (New York: Simon and Schuster, 1978).

and they grew up mentally deficient, then all my work to provide for them would be spent in vain. Now I consider my job as only a necessary means of enabling my wife to do life's most important job--properly caring for our children."

God gives the woman very important work to do. Neither her husband nor her children survive very well without her devotion to her duties. They need her weaknesses as they delight and feel secure in her love.

C. CARES FOR THE HOME

"Workers at home" doesn't mean "*stayers* at home, but *keepers* or *guardians* of the household."[13]

Many people falsely equate being a woman with being a housekeeper. *Instead, being a woman equals being a giver of love and comfort.* But part of bestowing love on others involves taking care of the home and transforming it into a refuge and place of peace for those the woman loves.

Unfortunately, many times a woman reverses her jobs and takes care of her husband because he messes up her house. A man needs a loving wife more than he needs a housekeeper. Never should the home become more important than the family who lives in it. A woman is not to ignore her husband and children in order to be a spotless housekeeper. Neither should she go to the other extreme and embrace sloppy housekeeping, for this prevents the home from becoming a relaxed sanctuary.

The way a woman keeps or fails to keep her home reflects the love she feels for her husband and children. If she indulges in hobbies, clubs, visiting, watching television, or reading to the neglect of her home, then she loves herself more than her family. A woman's attention to her home tells much about her character and how seriously she takes her responsibilities.

If a woman wants a happy marriage, she must learn the art of relaxing and enjoying her femininity. In this way, she puts her whole family at ease when

[13]Marvin R. Vincent, *Word Studies in the New Testament* (Grand Rapids, MI: Eerdmans, 1887), p. 342).

they step through the front door into her domain. If a woman does everything else right that God teaches about marriage--becomes a wonderful mother, an efficient homemaker, a marvelous cook, an exciting lover, and an adoring wife--but fails to make her home a palace of luxurious emotional comfort and relaxation, she fails to achieve the success she and her family desire.

A wife who quit her job told her husband that she felt more relaxed than when she worked outside the home. Her husband quickly replied, "I feel more relaxed, too." While only the woman changed, she set the mood for the entire house.

One young bride said, "After my wedding shower, my grandmother asked, 'Now that you've gotten most of your wedding gifts, what do you need? I want to get you something that you really need.' Before I could name some of the appliances that I really wanted, my husband spoke up and said, 'What we really need is some pictures on the wall, some knick-knacks and things that will make it a home.' So my grandmother bought us some pictures, but I wanted to choose those things myself."

A lot of times women discount little womanly touches to their homes such as throw pillows, flowers, and pictures. Yet men notice these things and miss them when absent. They may not say anything about it, but a woman's touch in the home creates an atmosphere that they like and appreciate.

D. CONTROLS HER ACTIONS WITH SUBJECTION

The controlling factor for a woman's role is her subjection to her husband. The phrase "being subject to their own husbands" modifies all of the items about it: loving her husband, loving her children, and being a keeper at home, along with being sensible, pure, and kind. (Chapter 15 discusses each of these areas in detail.) For now, subjection basically means *to work with someone* which is what a helper does. Subjection makes a woman meet for her husband in each of the areas discussed above.

A woman loves her husband being subject to him or adapting herself to his particular needs. Every man is different and each wife must seek to satisfy her *own* husband's emotional desires, not the needs of the average male. For example, a man who owns his own business may crave more affection than the man who simply punches a time clock because he is under more pressure during the day.

One wife loved to baby and pamper her husband, and to talk baby talk to him. But it offended her husband who grew up as the youngest in a family with a number of girls in it. He felt demeaned by the way his older sisters delighted in talking to him with baby talk. He told his wife, "I'm a man! I don't want to be treated that way!" So while this wife wanted to shower her husband with syrupy love, it alienated him instead of creating warmth. Yet other men thrive on this type of love. So a submissive wife looks at her husband and determines to satisfy his needs instead of looking to herself and seeing what she wants.

While God created the man to reflect His image and glory in the realm of authority, God created the woman to reflect the glory of the man (I Cor. 11:7). Just as the man glorifies God when he serves him of his own free will, the woman glorifies her husband when she obeys him of her own free will. Without a free choice, the woman lacks the ability to glorify her husband.

For example, with modern technology, men know how to build female robots with skin that feels as delightfully supple and soft as feminine flesh. They can construct the individual robots to meet the specifications that each man likes best, such as height, hair and eye colors, general body proportions, facial features, etc. Microprocessors enable scientists to program the robots with buttons that make them say, "Honey, I love you!" and "Boy! You're the greatest!" in the softest, sweetest voices imaginable. The designers can easily add features such as scratching the man's back, rubbing her fingers through his hair, or popping frozen T.V. dinners into the microwave oven.

Why doesn't someone start assembling female robots and make a fortune? Certainly, such a robot would be an ideal companion since she would always do what the man wanted and never argue back. Yet even with all the modern technology for creating the perfect woman, men know that there is no money in manufacturing robots to take the place of wives. Why?

Because when some other man pushes her buttons, she still says, "Boy! You're the greatest!" and "Honey, I love you!" or scratches his back and fixes his dinner. A man receives absolutely no glory when a robot bestows all these acts of love on him because the robot has no other choice.

Instead of a gorgeous robot, a man would rather marry a woman who isn't too pretty and who has all kinds of physical ailments because she can say, "You slob, I hate you! I don't want to live with you any more! I don't want to bear your children! And I don't want to keep your house clean or fix your meals!" A man prefers to marry an ugly woman who can say all kinds of hurtful words because when she says, "Honey, I love you!" she says it of her own free will and it means something. Thus, she glorifies him. When a woman glorifies her husband, she also glorifies God because she does what He created her to do.

Subjection also controls the way a woman loves her children. She works with their father and doesn't go behind his back in matters of discipline. Children need a father as well as a mother. By her love for their father, a mother teaches her children how to love. Only when a mother totally loves their father do children grow up feeling secure and freely loved.

God gave the woman tremendous power for creating an atmosphere of love within the home. Instead of using it, many women complain, "My husband doesn't show much interest in the children." However, many times the fault lies with the wife, not with the husband. For example, many children hesitate to show affection to their fathers like they should. When a father comes home from work with a five o'clock shadow, his cheeks don't feel too good when he hugs his little daughter. Thus, little girls and boys aren't too eager to be cozy with their father. In those cases, a mother should talk to her children and tell them, "God gave Daddy his whiskers to make him strong so that he can go out and work. Because Daddy works hard, we have a nice home and good food to eat. And, God created women to love, and it's our job to love Daddy. He loves us and he needs our love." In this way, mothers help their children become Father-centered and create an environment of love that both their children and husbands readily respond to. That's part of a woman's challenge.

One student said, "I always blamed my husband for not showing much interest in our little girl, but it never occurred to me that it might be my fault. When he would come home, she always acted like she didn't care because she was busy playing in the back yard. So I decided to get her ready and to prepare her for his coming home. As I gave her a bath, I kept telling her, 'Daddy is coming home! And let's get all dressed up and put on a pretty dress for Daddy! Won't it be fun when Daddy comes home! I'm excited! Aren't you? Won't that be fun?'"

She continued by telling what happened that evening, "We watched out the window for my husband to drive up. When he did, we ran out the front door and greeted him when he got out of the car. He sat his briefcase down right beside the car and picked up our little girl. He was so excited to see her, and she was so excited to see him! And just think, all that time I blamed my husband and didn't realize that I had a responsibility to create an atmosphere of love within the home."

Many times it's not the man. It's the woman, because it's her job to create an atmosphere of love in the home. God gave the woman her tender emotions to enhance the loving natures of her husband and children. And she does this by adapting herself to her husband's needs.

Likewise, God wants a woman to keep her house to please her husband. Some wives must clean their homes spotlessly to make their husbands feel comfortable. Some husbands love leftovers; others hate them. And on and on the differences go. Who can find two men who are exactly alike? Men appreciate *the attitude of always trying.* Then if a wife slips occasionally, her husband hardly seems to notice because he knows she wants to please him.

Subjection goes hand-in-hand with love and makes it effective. Only by respecting the man's God-given right of leadership can a woman experience uninhibited emotional love for her husband and children. When respect is lacking, resentment soon fills the void. God created the woman to fulfill a wonderful role of love:

E. THE GUARDIAN OF LOVE

Certainly, love should be as much a way of life for a masculine man as for a feminine woman, for God commands the man to love his wife as his own body and to nourish and cherish her. Women thrive on this love from their husbands. By protecting a wife from the need to earn a living, God placed her in a sheltered environment where she can devote her total energies to preserving love in her family. Anyone who thinks that giving love isn't a full time job hasn't read the Bible's job description of a gracious woman.

Secular fields utilize many specialists such as doctors, nurses, scientists, electricians, mechanics, farmers, policemen, teachers, nutritionists, computer scientists, accountants, and on and on goes an endless list of professions. But serving as an administrator of love is not an unskilled or low-paying vocation. It requires a profound education, unwavering dedication, and unlimited endurance along with complete selflessness.

Unfortunately, many women fail to even understand their divine challenge, let alone become successful as guardians or protectors of love. Victorian concepts about love deceive women into thinking that the man is the guardian of love and that they are merely its recipients. On the contrary, the Bible, over and over again portrays the woman as the chief initiator of love within the family.

This theme surfaces many times in the remaining chapters. It's impossible to adequately study the woman's role in the Bible without appreciating the importance of the feminine expression of love. The following verses give just a brief hint of how the woman functions as the guardian of love:

Song of Sol. 4:10: "How beautiful is your love, my sister, my bride! How much better is your love than wine,...'"

A woman's outpouring of love is one of the most beautiful features about her. The Shepherd spoke of the value of the Shulammite's love for him, for he prized her love above all else. He had no need to numb his senses with alcohol because she smoothed over the

rough spots of life and made the happy times just that
much more pleasant. She knew how to listen to his
triumphs and how to encourage him when he felt de-
feated.

Wiser than many wives today, the Shulammite
promised the Shepherd that when they married, she
would freely give her love to him (Song of Sol. 7:12).
Likewise, she openly longed to unite with him in the
embrace of love (2:6; 8:3). Everything about the Shulammite conveyed her love to the Shepherd: the way
she looked (4:9), the way she talked (4:11), the way
she acted (8:2), and the way she thought (5:10-16).
Being a woman is synonymous with giving love.

The Shepherd valued the Shulammite's open, free
love, and he begged her to never hide her affection
from him:

> **Song of Sol. 8:6-7: "Put me like a seal over
> your heart, like a seal on your arm. For love
> is as strong as death, jealousy is as severe
> as Sheol; its flashes are flashes of fire, the
> very flame of the Lord. Many waters cannot
> quench love, nor will rivers overflow it; if a
> man were to give all the riches of his
> house for love, it would be utterly despised."**

The Shepherd pleaded with the Shulammite to keep
her love for him as obvious as a seal on her arm and
only for him. He didn't want her telling some other
man that she loved him or that she thought he was
great. The Shepherd wanted her to glorify him by freely
giving her love to him and *only* him.

Floods of water cannot quench true love because
honest affection results from a commitment of concern
and emotional responsibility. A woman who functions
as a helper meet for her husband continually gives him
her love no matter what trials they face. Even when
she is a 101 years old, a woman should be a picture
of love to everyone she comes in contact with.

Statistics prove that married men, as a group, live
longer than bachelors, and happily married men live
longer than men with unhappy marriages. A man needs
his strength to labor day after day, but he needs the
weaknesses of his wife to survive the strain. *A man's
physical strength protects his wife from physical harm*

while a woman's tender loving care protects her husband from mental harm.

Thus, while a man desperately needs the love of a wife, he cannot buy love from a woman. Tenderness must go forth as a free gift without thought of reciprocation to benefit the receiver. For this reason, if a woman refuses to bestow her love freely upon her husband, he cannot demand that she love him, for her affection will be utterly despised as duty instead of welcomed as love.

God uses a woman who voluntarily serves Him as a giver of love as a shining example of His love for mankind:

> **Isa. 66:13: "As one whom his mother comforts, so I will comfort you; and you shall be comforted in Jerusalem."**

A loving mother who delights in bearing children and in caring for them provides an earthly example of God's love and concern for Israel. A woman's tender, loving emotions make her the perfect guardian of love for her husband and children. Her family should be loving individuals, but the woman can easily inhibit their love or bring it to the surface.

God honored the woman by creating her with the necessary qualities to be the perfect helper for man and to teach the world about God's love. God even made a woman's arms to cradle naturally around her babies. When a man stands erect with his arms hanging down to his side with elbows still and palms facing forward, his arms are straight. But when a woman stands in the same position, her arms curve outward from the elbow. Thus, a man throws a ball straighter and easier than a woman, but a woman cradles her baby in a nursing position easier than a man.[14]

Two college students observed this same phenomena of the differences in the arms by the way other students carried their books. While wondering how she could tell the boys and girls apart, one of the students said, "And suddenly, I noticed there was one thing, and that was the way they carried their books."

[14]*Gray's Anatomy* (Philadelphia: W. B. Saunder's Co., 1973), p. 204.

She observed that almost all female students wrapped one or both of their arms around their books and either rested the books on their hips or clasped them against their chests. Just the opposite, male students almost invariably carried their books in one hand at the side of their bodies. During a year's travel to many different universities, the student and her husband found the book-carrying habit held true everywhere.

The two students speculated that morphological differences seemed to cause the distinct methods of book carrying. The most important was the fact that "in most females, the carrying arm was unable to hang vertically but angled downward." Their study showed that most girls carried their books in "boy fashion" until grade school, when they switched to typical "female carrying behavior."[15]

Women may not like it, but the fact remains, unless a woman is unusual or goes in for special surgery, a woman's arm *is not* like a man's. The woman's arm demonstrates God's ingenuity in giving men and women the qualities they need in order to do their respective jobs.

Not every woman is a guardian of love, for some women display scorn for men and children alike. Only women who dare to live their lives according to God's wisdom portray God's love for the world through their love for their husbands, children, and other people. A woman honors herself by letting God's love shine forth from her life. Such a woman blesses herself and everyone whose life she touches.

III. THE ONE-FLESH RELATIONSHIP

Gen. 2:24: "For this cause a man shall leave his father and his mother, and shall cleave to his wife; and they shall become one flesh."

"Cleave" means "properly to impinge, i.e. cling or adhere, figuratively to catch by pursuit:--abide fast, cleave (fast together), follow close (hard after), be joined (together), keep (fast), overtake, pursue hard, stick, take" (Strong, p. 29).

---

[15]*Spokesman-Review*, (12/17/76), p. 27.

Even though a man depends upon his parents while he grows up, his mother and father cannot fulfill his needs when he is grown. It takes a wife to answer a man's call for help. Since God designed the women specifically to help the man, the natural conclusion is that a man will leave his parents and seek a wife. However, if a husband stays tied to his parents, he causes many marriage problems.

In the same way, God designed a wife to help her husband, *not her parents*. When a wife refuses to place her allegiance with her husband, she fails to render the aid to her husband which he so desperately needs.

In the marriage union, the woman supplies what the man lacks in order to make a complete unit. As a result, the man and woman work together as "one flesh" for the benefit of both. The following discussion briefly shows the ways that the male and female join together harmoniously for mutual support:

A. ONE FLESH SEXUALLY

> **I Cor. 7:3-4: "Let the husband fulfill his duty to his wife, and likewise also the wife to her husband. The wife does not have authority over her own body, but the husband does; and likewise also the husband does not have authority over his own body, but the wife does."**

A man doesn't have power over his own body. In other words, a man can't satisfy his own physical needs. It takes a wife to satisfy a man's God-given sexual desires. Likewise, a woman doesn't have power over her own body, but her husband does. It takes a husband to satisfy a woman's God-given sexual desires. So obviously, one flesh *includes* sexual love.

To assure happiness in this area, God gives a very simple law of compatibility. He commands both the husband and wife to give unselfishly of themselves for the satisfaction of the other. Since the sexual union originated in the mind of God, it becomes a righteous act when performed according to the principles laid down in the Bible.

Furthermore, when both the husband and wife work together as God directs, they satisfy the needs of the other. God designed the bodies of the male and female to fit perfectly together to give pleasure to both of them.

Man satisfies the woman.
Woman satisfies the man.
God blesses the union.

B. ONE FLESH REPRODUCTIVELY

Gen. 4:1: "Now the man had relations with his wife Eve, and she conceived and gave birth to Cain, and she said, 'I have gotten a manchild with the help of the Lord.'"

Reproducing the human race requires both a man and woman. God gives the husband the job of fertilizing the egg within the woman. The wife then carries the child to maturity and gives birth. Neither a man nor a woman can reproduce another human being without the assistance of a member of the opposite sex.

Adam and Eve recognized God's hand in the act of reproduction and considered Him the source of life. The bodies of the husband and wife fit perfectly together not only to give both of them pleasure, but also to create another life with the help of God (Eccl. 12:7).

Man plants the seed.
Woman bears the child.
God gives the spirit.

C. ONE FLESH PARENTALLY

Eph. 6:4: "And, fathers, do not provoke your children to anger; but bring them up in the discipline and instruction of the Lord."

After the birth of the children, the husband and wife work together to raise the fruit of their union-- their children. However, God assigns the father different parental duties than He gives the mother. Thus, Paul directs this passage toward the father, not the mother, giving the man the job of setting the discipline standards for his children. As a man serves as the guardian of authority, he teaches his children proper respect for authority and how to be in subjection.

On the other hand, God gives the mother a different parental responsibility:

Tit. 2:4-5: "...that they may encourage the young women to love their husbands, to love their children,...being subject to their own husbands, that the word of God may not be dishonored."

The woman's tender loving nature makes her emotionally suited to make her children feel loved and to give them self-confidence. As the guardian of love, she creates an atmosphere of warmth and tenderness to which both her husband and children respond as she teaches them how to love.

Rather than the father whipping the children while the mother loves them, *both parents work together as God directs*. In this way, the mother follows the discipline standards set by her husband and teaches the children subjection by her example. Likewise, the father expresses love for his children and works with the mother to bring them up to maturity as stable adults who know how to give love unselfishly to others.

Since God equips the mother and father with their own areas of special ability, both must work together to achieve full success. Their different psychological natures fit perfectly together to give their children what they need most--love balanced with discipline.

> *Man sets the discipline standards.*
> *Woman sets the love standards.*
> *God balances discipline with love.*

D. ONE FLESH DOMESTICALLY

Ps. 128:2-4: "When you shall eat of the fruit of your hands, you will be happy and it will be well with you. Your wife shall be like a fruitful vine, within your house, your chil-

dren like olive plants around your table. Behold, for thus shall the man be blessed who fears the Lord."

God told man that by the sweat of his face and by tilling the ground he would earn his bread in Gen. 3:17-19. Thus, through hard labor, a husband accepts the job of providing the physical necessities for his wife and children. The writer of Psalms says that doing the work God created him to do gives a husband happiness. Life goes well for a productive man.

A husband, who assumes his rightful role and worries about the money and paying the bills, frees his wife to devote herself to her own job:

I Tim. 5:14: "Therefore, I want younger widows to get married, bear children, keep house, and give the enemy no occasion for reproach;..."

The wife's job involves caring for the children and keeping the home running smoothly. Her duties include preparing the meals, mending the clothes, sweeping the floor, and making the home a livable refuge for her family.

It takes both a husband and wife working together to subdue a hostile earth. God gave the man the necessary biological and psychological qualities for earning a living for his family. Likewise, God created inherent attributes within the woman which make her especially suited to making a house a home. Men and women must work together as God designed to subdue the earth in obedience to their Creator.

> *Man is the bread winner.*
> *Woman is the bread warmer.*
> *God is the bread provider.*

E. ONE FLESH PSYCHOLOGICALLY

Eph. 5:33: "Nevertheless let each individual among you also love his own wife even as himself; and let the wife see to it that she respect [reverence--KJV] her husband."

Probably the greatest needs of both men and women are psychological. A man fails to thrive either physically or emotionally without someone to build him up and to admire him. His wife's emotional attachment to him makes her perfectly suited for restoring his self-confidence when the world beats him down.

A woman, on the other hand, needs the security of unselfish love before she can give herself without restraint to the happiness of her husband. Thus, God commands the husband to supply this psychological desire of his wife. As a husband loves his wife as his own body, he frees her to confidently lean on him for leadership and security. In return, the wife protects her husband's happiness by encouraging him, believing in him, and cheering him on to success.

Fortunately for mankind, God regulates these needs. God doesn't leave it up to the husband and wife to discover through trial and error what the other requires for full emotional health. Through His love for both men and women, God commands wives to reverence their husbands and husbands to love their wives. Thus, through obedience to God, both husbands and wives supply the deepest emotional needs of each other.

Man is woman's hero.
Woman is man's cheerleader.
God is the coach.

F. ONE FLESH GOVERNMENTALLY

Eph. 5:23-24: "For the husband is the head of the wife, as Christ also is the head of the church, He himself being the Savior of the body. But as the church is subject to Christ, so also the wives ought to be to their husbands in everything."

When an organization exists without some type of government, confusion, turbulence, and disorder take over in the vacuum. Competent leadership and willing obedience bring success to just about any organization. Yet the home provides an even better opportunity for perfect government because all relationships revolve around love. This emotional bond seldom exists in civil governments, the schools, or the marketplace.

God, in His divine wisdom, appointed the husband to lead as the head of the family unit. However, the wife shares responsibility in leadership. For government cannot operate effectively without cooperation from the ones governed. Thus, when a wife refuses to follow as her husband's body, her rebellion and the resulting insurrection destroy the home.

Without a government of some type, the husband and wife function as a spastic body--limited in their ability to do everyday jobs. As a result, the husband and wife fail to work together and to glorify God. Through His love for mankind, God designed the work and natures of the man and woman to fit perfectly together to efficiently subdue the earth and to fill it with people.

> *Man leads as the woman's head.*
> *Woman follows as the man's body.*
> *God makes them become one flesh.*

G. ONE FLESH SPIRITUALLY

Eph. 5:23-24: "For the husband is the head of the wife, as Christ also is the head of the church, He himself being the Savior of the body. But as the church is subject to Christ, so also the wives ought to be to their husbands in everything."

God created man in the image of Christ in the realm of authority and leadership. In this way, the man presents a picture of Christ in the religious realm as he leads his wife and takes the oversight in the church. On the other hand, the woman presents a picture of the beautiful bride of Christ, the church, as she serves her husband and follows in the church. Both the man and the woman work together to present a picture to the world of Christ and His bride, the church. In spite of their different spiritual roles, God counts the woman as important as the man:

I Pet. 3:7: "You husbands likewise,...grant her honor as a fellow-heir of the grace of life, so that your prayers may not be hindered."

God refuses to hear the prayers of any man who fails to honor his wife as a joint-heir of the grace of life. The woman's tender, loving emotions make her well suited for doing good works and serving others. The man's leadership skills in the family realm enable him to lead the church wisely. The church desperately needs both men and women who have mastered their own areas of ability and responsibility.

> *Man presents a picture of Christ.*
> *Woman presents a picture of the church.*
> *God makes them joint-heirs.*

God designed the woman as a weaker vessel to enable her to satisfy the man's deepest needs. Then when He presented Eve to Adam, Adam immediately recognized her as the answer to his problem--someone he needed. Thus, God commands modern husbands to follow in the steps of their father Adam and to appreciate how much they need their wives' weaknesses.

A woman's feelings and emotional involvement with others make her the perfect guardian of love. At times, however, such feelings and single-mindedness distress a woman as she agonizes over the welfare of others.

Fortunately, when a guardian of authority rules over the home with love, a woman feels secure to go to him with her worries and problems. She knows that he will put matters back into their proper perspective and help her balance her feelings with the facts. Because of this, when a husband shows understanding for his wife's feminine nature and realizes that it is the source of her strength, he binds her ever more closely to himself.

But let a husband walk all over his wife's feelings, and she will resent him. His wife's weaknesses or femininity make her very vulnerable to his strength. If she fears his strength, she builds defenses around herself, and he loses his helper. If she feels securely protected by his strength, she lets down her guard, and he finds a wonderful helper meet just for him.

Every home needs a man--a real man--a man who dares to think, act, talk, and dress like a man--a man who knows his place--a man who stands firm as the guardian of authority--a man who leads, protects, and provides for his family. But such a man needs a loving wife more than anything else in this world.

The job of being an adequate helper for a man takes all the strength, intelligence, imagination, and love that a woman possesses. God didn't give the woman a simple job that she can do in spite of herself. Her job takes twenty-four hours a day, seven days a week for a lifetime of hard deliberate work and thought to meet the tremendous challenge of being a woman.

Every house on every block doesn't contain a helper meet for her husband as the feminists claim. In fact, one can look and search and hunt and still not find a woman who functions as God created women to be. Not a single secular job in the world offers the potential for fulfillment, the rewards for service, or requires the talent to accomplish the work that the job of being a loving wife, mother, worker at home, and servant of others offers a woman. Truly, God bestows upon the woman the greatest honor and challenge on earth--that of being the weaker vessel--the answer to man's problem.

STUDY EXERCISE

Answer all questions in your own words.

1. Give two examples of how the woman is biologically weaker than the man.

2. Give two examples of how the woman is physically weaker than the man.

3. Give two examples of how being the weaker vessel qualifies a wife to love her husband.

4. Give two examples of how being the weaker vessel qualifies a mother to love her children.

5. Give two examples of how being the weaker vessel qualifies the woman to be a worker at home.

6. How does subjection help the woman fulfill her responsibilities?

7. How many women fulfill their potentials as human beings? How can women enjoy their femininity more?

8. What seven things are involved in making a husband and wife one flesh with each other? Give an example for each one of how you are suitable to do your half of one flesh.

9. Do you disagree with anything in this lesson? If so, explain in detail giving scriptures for your reasons.

PERSONAL EXERCISE

Since God created the woman to fulfill a specific job, write a job resume to find out if you are qualified to work for God or not. Remember, God authorized your husband to do the hiring so you may want to get his help on this project. However, do not ask your husband for help unless you sincerely want to please him. Some suggestions follow:

Experience: 5 years marriage, 2 children, sewing and cooking classes, etc.

Outlook on life: Striving to be a faithful Christian, support husband and children, etc.

Ambitions for success: Prefer to work for success rather than someone handing it to you. Willingly work overtime when necessary instead of striving to do the least amount of work possible.

Pay desired: Happy husband, well-balanced children, inner peace and contentment, good reputation, heaven, etc.

Specialties: Sewing, joyful nature, children's birthday parties, gourmet cooking, etc.

Qualifications: List each part of one flesh and write your assets and training needs under each. You may want to ask your husband what he considers your assets and weak points for each section.

Plans for advancement: Study Bible, take special courses, read books, etc.

OPTIONAL CREATIVE EXERCISE

Some women enjoy making plaques using the sayings for the seven parts of one flesh. You can cross stitch them on a sampler, type them, or do them in calligraphy. Either list the sayings in a single column with the border decorated or draw pictures for each part and put the verses under them. Then you can decoupage them or frame them under a glass painting.

SOLUTION III:

TRUE LOVE

vs.

SENSUOUS LOVE

**(How to Lay the Foundation
for a Happy Marriage)**

"I adjure you, O daughters of Jerusalem, by the gazelles or by the hinds of the field, that you will not arouse or awaken my love, until she [it] pleases." (Song of Solomon 2:7)

CHAPTER 9

THE WOMAN'S SEARCH FOR TRUE LOVE

What about sex education in the schools? How can a girl know if she is marrying the right man or if she will make a good wife? How can a boy know if he is marrying the right girl or if he will make a good husband? Can a bride and groom really expect to live happily ever after? God answers all of these questions in the beautiful Song of Solomon.

I. THE PURPOSE

Studying the Song of Solomon benefits men and women and boys and girls in six major ways. In fact, God inspired the Song of Solomon to bless the lives of every man and every woman regardless of their age.

A. FASCINATING LOVE TRIANGLE

The story tells about a beautiful young vineyard keeper who loves a young shepherd who pastures his sheep close by. However, rich and powerful King Solomon comes to the country to check on his vineyards. When he sees the Shulammite maiden, he begins to woo her aggressively and brings her to his camp.

The young girl is caught in the middle. Solomon's prestige, wealth, and power tempt her to say, "Yes." But her love for the Shepherd continually nags at her. In a dilemma, she agonizes over who to marry--the Shepherd or King Solomon. Thus, the Song of Solomon presents an exciting triangle of personalities to expose the differences between true love and sensuous love.

In addition, the Song of Solomon not only teaches about an emotionally-charged subject--who to marry--but it edifies through emotionally-captivating writing techniques. For example, the story follows the formula for a perfect romance. Writing instructors say that good romances always contain three elements: (1) an innocent girl, (2) a good man who wants to marry her but whom she resists, and (3) an evil man whose charms tempt her. Then the story unfolds as the girl struggles to choose between the two men.

While the Song of Solomon follows this formula for a thrilling romance, it differs in one significant point--*the Shulammite was a real girl who really wrestled with who to marry*--rich, powerful King Solomon or the poor shepherd who offered her only his love.

The story also uses three action-type writing techniques to captivate its readers and to influence their emotions. First, the story is written as a play to be acted out and watched. Second, the story contains only dialogue with no narration at all. Third, the story is written in the form of poetry. Any one of these three techniques by itself adds action and power to a story. Yet all three combine in the Song of Solomon to make it a very moving and enthralling love story that beckons its readers to read it over and over again. In the process, the story arouses its readers' emotions so that they declare, "I want to be like the Shulammite" or "I want to be like the Shepherd."   By God inspiring the Song of Solomon to be written in such a stimulating manner, it enables the book to accomplish the very purpose for which it was written:

B. GUIDE FOR TEENAGERS

This book addresses one of the most difficult times of a teenager's life--the transition from parental love to romantic love. Parents normally give their children lots of physical and verbal love as babies, toddlers, and grade-schoolers. However, as the children mature, they become more independent of that love. Yet everyone needs to be patted, hugged, admired, and kissed. But children reach an age when father and mother's love isn't enough. They begin reaching out toward romantic love in search of a spouse.

During this time, the teenagers are too old for father and mother's love, but still too young to get married. It often becomes a very trying time, simply because everyone needs love--even teenagers who feel
embarrassed to kiss their parents. Likewise, it becomes an easy time for teenagers to get into trouble
by choosing the wrong friends. Thus, the Song of
Solomon guides teenagers through perhaps one of the
most difficult times of their whole lives.

When teenagers study the Song of Solomon before
they become romantically involved with someone, it
helps them analyze their dates. A girl asks herself, "Is
he like Solomon or like the Shepherd? Do I really love
him or is this just infatuation?"

A boy wants to know, "Does she have the qualities
of a good wife? Do I really love her, or do I just want
her body?" In this way, the book helps teenagers successfully cross the bridge from parental love to romantic love to married love.

C. SENSUOUS LOVE VS. TRUE LOVE

Solomon presents the best opportunity ever to test
the value of sensuous love. For instance, Solomon ac-
cumulated a vast wealth to spend on his women. Plus
his political prestige gave him access to the most desirable women of his time. If ever a man could succeed at sensuous love, Solomon should be able to. So
God's people don't have to grope through life trying to
find out if sensuous love holds the promise of blissful
happiness or if true love does. The story exposes
many of the pitfalls that trap lovers even today and
which deny them marital joy.

Through contrasting sensuous love with true love,
the Song of Solomon teaches how to choose a lifelong
sexual partner that one will not grow tired of. Solomon
actively pursued the Shulammite in belief that she
possessed the perfect body to satisfy his deepest
needs. Yet Solomon never understood the secret of true
love even though the Shulammite told him.

D. THE ANSWER TO SEX EDUCATION

The beautiful poetic language of the book permits
parents to use it to teach their children about sexual

love at each stage of their development. For example, parents can teach the drama of the story to very young children. They can tell them a true story about a young farmer's daughter who loved a poor shepherd. Then one day a rich and powerful king came and took her to his palace. He wanted to marry her but she still loved the Shepherd. And on the story goes catching the interest of young children and teaching them the basics of true love.

As the children mature, the poetic form allows the parents to insert more and more details. When the children ask intimate questions about lovemaking, the parents can use the Song of Solomon to supply the answers. This helps the parents protect their children from bad choices when they begin reaching out to romantic love. In addition, the Song of Solomon protects students against sex education classes that leave love out of the sexual embrace by placing the emphasis on the body.

Thus, God wondrously designed the Song of Solomon for parents to use with their children regardless of their age. Sex education classes in the schools can't begin to compare with such a truly marvelous book!

E. UNIVERSAL APPLICATION

Ideally, the Song of Solomon should be everyone's own love story as everyone must choose between sensuous love or true love. As Ecclesiastes says, people are the same from generation to generation (Eccl. 1:4, 10). The tools they use to subdue the earth change, but the people remain the same.

When parents teach the Song of Solomon to their children, they should be able to say, "When mommy and daddy fell in love, we did...just like the Shulammite and the Shepherd. And someday you'll fall in love, too. You'll know if he's the right person or not just like the Shulammite did." In this way, the Song of Solomon becomes everyone's own love story which they pass down from generation to generation.

F. DEMONSTRATION OF GOD'S LOVE

The Song of Solomon shows that God cares about the daily lives of His people. He wants His people to be happy and to enjoy wonderful marriages. Ideally, if a couple learns the Song of Solomon in their youth, then they can lay the proper foundation in courtship for a joyful marriage. The story gives some of the best advice available for courting couples. It teaches a girl how to choose a husband and a boy how to choose a wife so that they might live happily forevermore.

Young women who study about their role as a wife before marriage and who lay the proper foundation in courtship start off marriage on a high plain. Young brides of six months or a year, in whose eyes love still shines, likewise, enjoy beautiful marriages when they study God's plan for them. But their happiness doesn't begin to compare with that of the young women who learn their role *before marriage* and who lay the proper foundation *in courtship*. The ones who learn what God expects of them before marriage start off with fewer problems. And when problems appear, they know how to handle them instead of just reacting to them.

However, it's not too late for the ones already married. The Song of Solomon teaches the formula for laying the foundation for a happy marriage at every stage--courting, newlywed, silver and golden anniversaries. At whatever stage a couple happens to be, they can examine their relationship and marriage. Did they build their marriage upon a foundation of true love or sensuous love? If not, they can still lay that foundation in their marriage. It's not too late to enjoy the happiness of the Shulammite and the Shepherd and to thrill to the marital love that God designed. Thus, the Song of Solomon beautifully demonstrates God's love and care for all those who wish to serve Him.

G. ORIGEN'S DECEIT

In spite of God's great love in providing the Song of Solomon, the book is probably one of the most neglected books in the Bible. The depreciation of the book began with an ancient second-century theologian named Origen who held a low view of marriage and the sexual relationship. Pat E. Harrell explains Origin's attitude toward sexual love in his book *Divorce and Remarriage in the Early Church:*

> Christianity, as Origen reminded Celsus, actually transformed a man's conduct. He describes this as meaning:...from the time they adopt it, (they) have become in some way meeker, and more religious and more consistent, so that certain among them, from desire of exceeding chastity, and from a wish to worship God with greater purity, abstain even from the permitted indulgences of (lawful) love.[1]

Origen harbored such a strong distaste for physical love that he actively discouraged sexual intercourse between husbands and wives. This abhorrence of anything sexual led him to campaign against keeping the Song of Solomon in the collection of inspired writings that was being assembled into one volume at that time. He refused to believe that God inspired a book which recommended married lovemaking.

However, the authenticity of the book proved so strong that competent scholars rejected Origen's proposal to leave the book out. As the only alternative left for him, Origen resorted to covering up all references to the sexual relationship. Thus, Origen mutilated God's word by devising an allegory of Christ and the church. Since most of the religious leaders of Catholicism at that time shared Origen's views of extreme prudery, they embraced his allegory.[2] *Vol. II: Learning to Love* devotes a whole chapter to tracing the evil effects of their condemnation of married lovemaking.

Then in 533 AD the Catholic church denounced all literal interpretations of the book. As a result, the allegorical theory "reigned supreme" for the next thou-

---

[1]Pat E. Harrell, *Divorce and Remarriage in the Early Church* (Austin, TX: R. B. Sweet Company, Inc., 1967), pp. 205-206 quoting *Against Celsus, i*, p. 26.
[2]Albert Reville, *The Song of Songs*, p. 6 as quoted by Homer Hailey, "Syllabus on the Song of Solomon," Florida College class notes, p. 2.

sand years among Christian interpreters.[3] During this time, the Roman church subtly substituted the Virgin Mary for the church.[4] In the ninth century, the Jews invented a similar theory. They claimed that the story taught about Jehovah God and the Israelites.[5] In 1544 Sebastian Castellio dared to revive the literal interpretation of the book. However, the allegorical view remained dominant until the 19th century.[6] Sadly, many godly people today are still woefully ignorant of the book's beautiful story of courting love and its practical uses.

Just reading the story through for the first time, makes a literal interpretation seem impossible. However, the problem doesn't rest with the Song of Solomon, but with a lack of knowledge of Hebrew expressions and Jewish customs. By defining words and looking up unfamiliar customs, the story quickly unfolds into a logical sequence of events, and the mystery is lost.

One quality of the drama which makes the book particularly hard to understand is the division of speakers since the original Hebrew manuscript did not assign parts. To the Jew, this didn't cause a problem because the context made the divisions obvious to him.

Modern translators tried to solve the problem by writing who they thought the speakers were in the margins of their translations. However, this only created more confusion because the different versions seldom agreed on who was speaking: Some believed the book taught about Christ and the church while others thought it portrayed Solomon and one of his queens. Others recognized that the drama had to speak of two men--the Shepherd and King Solomon. Thus, the breakdown of speeches in the individual translations between the "bride" and the "groom" is *only the opinion*

---

[3]*The International Standard Bible Encyclopedia* (Grand Rapids, MI: Wm. B. Eerdmans Publishing Co., 1939), *v.*, p. 2832.
[4]Reville, *The Song of Songs*, pp. 8-9.
[5]Reville, *The Song of Songs*, p. 6.
[6]*The International Standard Bible Encyclopedia*, *v.*, p. 2832.

of the translators and is not an inspired division of speakers.

However, through a careful study of the context, an English-speaking Bible student can determine for himself where the divisions take place. For example, the use of singular and plural pronouns shows when the chorus speaks as opposed to one of the principle characters. For instance, the first two lines of chapter one, verse four use the singular pronoun "me" when the Shulammite speaks. The last two lines change to the plural pronoun "we" when the chorus of maidens answer her. Both the context and the grammar affirm that a division of speakers takes place even though the words are combined in one verse.

The changing of speakers in the middle of a verse creates another confusing element for some students. Yet the separation of the Bible into chapters and verses is not inspired. Instead, some of the first scholars who translated the Bible into other languages assigned chapters and verses to make the text easier to read and to help find quotations. For this reason, modern students should allow *the context* to determine when the speakers change rather than strictly adhering to a man-made guide.

In addition, the story seems to demand that two men are involved, rather than one. If one only man is represented, God shows approval of polygamy which allows a man to simply add another wife to his family when he tires of the previous wife's sexual charms. Polygamy violates the creation account where God designed one woman to satisfy all of Adam's needs. In addition, the Song of Solomon clearly demonstrates that many wives cannot satisfy a man who builds his relationships on the wrong foundation. On the other hand, only one wife can easily captivate her husband all of her life when the marriage follows God's laws and regulations.

God chose Solomon as a perfect representative of the sensuous, rich, influential man, while the Shepherd represents the poor, hard-working, honest man who gives true love to a woman. The problem? Both men love the same woman, but for different reasons. And she doesn't know who to marry.

The story begins:

II. THE SHULAMMITE'S DILEMMA

The story takes place in the vineyards of the countryside around Jerusalem. Solomon camped there while he inspected his vineyards which he had leased to farmers. Always on the lookout for a pretty face and figure, Solomon immediately noticed the young Shulammite vineyard keeper. The maiden so captivated him that he had her brought to his chambers.

But the Shulammite loved a shepherd. And no matter how Solomon wooed her, she could not quit thinking of her shepherd boyfriend. She continually compared the Shepherd to Solomon to see which she should marry. This is the story of her heart-felt search for an answer to her dilemma:

A. MEMORIES OF THE SHEPHERD

Song of Sol. 1:1-4: "The Song of Songs, which is Solomon's. 'May he kiss me with the kisses of his mouth! For your love is better than wine. Your oils have a pleasing fragrance, your name is like purified oil; therefore the maidens love you. Draw me after you and let us run together! The king has brought me into his chambers.'..."

The Shulammite maiden has just been brought to the king's chambers. And like anyone in a strange situation, she wishes for a friend to hold her hand and to confide in. Her mind immediately goes to the Shepherd. He is her best friend. She longs for his soothing kisses to still her nervousness. As she thinks of him, she feels torn between her desire for his comfort and the flattery of being brought to the King. The Shepherd was not an ordinary boy--many girls would be glad to belong to him. But after all, the King didn't invite just any girl to his chambers for his personal inspection. This might be the chance of a lifetime.

Even so, the Shulammite can't get the Shepherd out of her mind. She explains to the maidens that she is emotionally involved with the Shepherd--his love is better than wine. Society uses wine as a tranquilizer to get rid of the problems of life. A drink numbs a person's senses and life doesn't seem so bad anymore.

Yet true love does the same thing. It pacifies a person and offers more relief than a cocktail.

Everything about the Shepherd appeals to her, from his after-shave lotion to his name. The Shulammite fits the picture of a young girl dreamily writing the Shepherd's name over and over with a "Mrs." in front of it. She will be proud to wear his name--no "Ms." title for her!

When my mother was in high school in California, one of her teachers married a man by the name of Snodgrass. My mother and her schoolmates talked about what a horrible name Snodgrass was! They didn't see how anyone could ever love a man with that name! The next summer my mother went to Oklahoma to help her grandmother cook during harvest. Her grandfather employed a young man that summer by the name of Snodgrass. My mother fell in love with him and became Mrs. Snodgrass. And through the years, my mother has proudly worn the name of Mrs. Snodgrass. True love makes a man's name seem like "purified oil" to the woman who loves him, even if his name happens to be Snodgrass.

As the Shulammite thinks of the Shepherd she pleads to him in her mind, "Draw me after you and let us run together! The king has brought me into his chambers." She would really rather be with him than in Solomon's tent awaiting his inspection.

B. THE MAIDENS' EXCITEMENT

Song of Sol 1:4: "...We will rejoice in you and be glad; we will extol your love more than wine. Rightly do they love you."

The maidens who wait upon the King exclaim excitedly over the Shulammite. She is perfect! The king has such good taste in women! She is just what he needs!

C. BLACK BUT LOVELY

Song of Sol. 1:5-6: "I am black but lovely, O daughters of Jerusalem, like the tents of Kedar, like the curtains of Solomon. Do not stare at me because I am swarthy, for the

**sun has burned me. My mother's sons were
angry with me; they made me caretaker of
the vineyards, but I have not taken care of
my own vineyard."**

Because the Shulammite had been taking care of
one of Solomon's vineyards, her skin is sunburned and
black. She isn't lily-white like girls who sit at home
and primp all the time. Yet her swarthiness only adds
to her beauty and charm. Since her brothers make her
work in the vineyard, she has no time to groom herself
as other girls do.

However, she enjoys a healthy self-image. She
recognizes and accepts her own unique brand of
beauty. At the same time, she does not place all her
hopes in her attractiveness.

The Shulammite provides a good example for girls
today who place their confidence in their external
beauty. While physical loveliness attracts a boy's attention, appearance will not keep his attention if
beauty of character does not go with it.

D. THE LOVE OF HER SOUL

**Song of Sol. 1:7: "Tell me, O you whom my
soul loves, where do you pasture your flock,
where do you make it lie down at noon? For
why should I be like one who veils herself
beside the flocks of your companions?"**

While the Shulammite feels flattered that the King
finds her attractive, she loves the Shepherd. She
yearns for him and wishes that she could go with him
instead of with the King. What a dilemma! Can her
love for the Shepherd begin to compare with a life
with the King?

The Shulammite asks herself, "Should I be like one
who veils herself beside the flocks of your companions?" In other words, "Should I do what all the girls
do?" Girls this age try to accidentally on purpose happen to wander over to where the boys are. Then maybe
one of the boys will accidentally happen to notice
them. Girls are the same from generation to generation.
So the Shulammite asks if she should act coy and play
hard to get? Should she just happen to walk by the

place where he pastures his flocks with her veil innocently in place? Or should she just openly declare that
she is ready to marry him, putting an end to their
courtship and the intentions of the King? Before King
Solomon came along, she was sure about what she
wanted--now she isn't so sure.

The expression "make it [his flock] lie down at
noon" shows how successfully the Shepherd takes care
of his sheep. For example, sheep refuse to lie down at
noon to rest if they feel the least bit hungry, if some
kind of disease or bugs bother them, if any kind of
danger presents itself, or if friction exists between
their own social orders.[7] A shepherd who makes his
flock lie down at noon must meet all four of these
conditions. Thus, the Shulammite knows that the Shepherd is a hard, dependable worker.

E. FREEDOM TO CHOOSE

> **Song of Sol. 1:8: "If you yourself do not
> know, most beautiful among women, go forth
> on the trail of the flock, and pasture your
> young goats by the tents of the shepherds."**

Many people think that Jewish parents forced their
daughters to marry whoever they choose. That's not
true. For example, Rebekah's mother and brother gave
her a choice about marrying Isaac after Abraham's servant discussed it with them (Gen. 24:57–58). Each girl
made her own choice to either accept or reject the
arrangements her parents made.

For this reason, the maidens who wait upon the
King assure the Shulammite that she is free to go to
the Shepherd. If that is what she really wants, the
King won't force himself upon her. The choice is hers
to make. But since the King already showers his attentions upon her, wouldn't it be better to find out
what he wants before she makes her decision? The
Shulammite lingers.

[7]Philip Keller, *A Shepherd Looks at Psalm 23*, (Grand
Rapids, MI: Zondervan, 1970), p. 35.

III. SOLOMON'S FIRST PROPOSAL

King Solomon apparently enters the tent and begins to the court the young maiden. He boldly tells her exactly what he thinks of her--she is no ordinary beauty:

A. LIKE HIS MARE

> Song of Sol. 1:9-10: "To me, my darling, you are like my mare among the chariots of Pharoah. Your cheeks are lovely with ornaments, your neck with strings of beads."

Solomon knows that all women like to be told that they are beautiful, so he begins by praising her beauty. Why, she is to all the other maidens as his mare is to all the other horses. A girl today probably wouldn't appreciate her boyfriend telling her she reminded him of a nag. But Solomon pays the young vineyard keeper quite a compliment. He says that Pharoah can line up all of his horses and chariots, and his mare will stand out instantly. The same is true with her. She's the best! She'll stand out in a crowd of beautiful women.

As such a captivating creature, she deserves special treatment. He owns lots of ornaments and beads to enhance her natural beauty and desirability. Solomon assures her that he fully appreciates her charms.

B. PROMISES OF LUXURIES

> Song of Sol. 1:11: "We will make for you ornaments of gold with beads of silver."

The maidens sweeten the King's offer with promises of gold and silver ornaments. A life of luxury, ease, and splendor awaits her. She'll find it hard to choose something to wear in the mornings--she has so much. How can she turn down the chance of a lifetime? In Solomon's palace she will never worry about dishpan hands or the ironing piling up. Servants will gladly pamper her. She can spend her time reading or engaging in outside activities. What a life with Solomon!

C. MEMORIES OF THE SHEPHERD

> Song of Sol. 1:12-14: "While the king was at his table, my perfume gave forth its fragrance. My beloved is to me a pouch of myrrh which lies all night between my breasts. My beloved is to me a cluster of henna blossoms in the vineyards of Engedi."

Next King Solomon wines and dines the young maiden. But this is no ordinary meal. I Ki. 10:21 says that all of Solomon's drinking vessels were gold because silver was too common. Bakers knew how to make pastries that make modern gourmet food look like a peasant's rations (Prov. 23:1-3). In addition, the Jews' tents contained as many rooms as the owner wanted. So even though Solomon is camping out in the countryside, luxury beyond description surrounds the Shulammite.

In the midst of such grand splendor, one whiff of her perfume makes the Shulammite's mind flash back to the Shepherd. He is to her as "a pouch of myrrh which lies all night between my breasts." At night, the Jews often tied a small sack of flower petals or herbs around their neck. This gave off a pleasant smell during the night to replace the unpleasant odors of their hot, sweaty land. As a result, they slept better on hot nights.

The Shepherd was also like a cluster of henna blossoms in the vineyards of Engedi. The Jews planted flower gardens outside their cities. Then in the evening they would stroll through them to meditate. They also liked to pick clusters of flowers to carry home with them. Then if they passed something with a bad odor, they could smell the flowers instead.

The Shepherd is like these comforting smells to her that replace the unpleasant things in life. The Shepherd cannot give her gold ornaments and silver beads. But he bestows something better upon her. He offers her great pleasure and comfort. Should she give up the emotional delight that she enjoys with the Shepherd for the physical comfort of the King's house? She can't keep them both. She can choose either true love on the one side or sensuous luxury on the other. Such a dilemma!

D. HER GREAT BEAUTY

Song of Sol. 1:15: "How beautiful you are, my darling, how beautiful you are! Your eyes are like doves."

"Darling" means "a female associate:--fellow, love" (Strong, p. 109).

Solomon interrupts her thoughts to tell her again how beautiful she is. Solomon consistently refers to her as "my darling" or "my love," showing his shallow involvement with her. The term resembles the word "honey" which sales clerks sometimes use lightly with their customers.

Every girl likes to be told that she is attractive, and when a man notices her, his compliments make her more desirous of pleasing him. The Shulammite is not immune to the charms and flattery of King Solomon, for he appeals to her vanity and pride.

E. MEMORIES OF THE SHEPHERD

Song of Sol. 1:16-17: "How handsome you are, my beloved, and so pleasant! Indeed, our couch is luxuriant! The beams of our house are cedars, our rafters, cypresses."

"Beloved" means "properly to boil, i.e. (figuratively) to love; by implication, a love-token, lover, friend" (Strong, p. 30).

The young girl faces a big decision. She must choose between two completely different kinds of love, lives, and husbands. Before Solomon came to inspect the vineyards, the Shulammite knew that she loved the Shepherd and planned to marry him some day. Now the King offers her a life in his palace surrounded by servants.

But the Shulammite can't get the Shepherd out of her mind. Even in the presence of Solomon's grand offer, she still consistently refers to the Shepherd as "my beloved," showing her deep emotional attachment to him. She remembers how handsome and pleasant he is.

Every bride enjoys dreaming about her future home and how she will decorate it. In like manner, the Shulammite compares the house that the Shepherd will give her to Solomon's fancy tents and ornate palace. She knows that the Shepherd will never be able to provide her with anything more than a humble home constructed from rough planks of wood. But their love will transform the outdoors into a magnificent show-place in which to play, live, and work. True love converts even the most humble dwelling into a palace, while sensuous love gives a castle all the warmth of a drafty shack.

F. THE ROSE OF SHARON

Song of Sol. 2:1: "I am the rose of Sharon, the lily of the valleys."

Then the Shulammite makes a remarkable statement about herself as she voices self-respect, without which no girl is safe. She is a peasant girl burned by the sun, but she doesn't have to take just anyone who comes along for the sake of getting married. She can afford to exercise great care in selecting a husband. After all, she is the rose of Sharon, the lily of the valleys.

One encyclopedia describes the "rose of Sharon" as a very special flower:

> The meaning of the original excludes from our consideration the true rose and several other plants suggested. It is the opinion of some of the best authorities that the polyan- thus narcissus (*Narcissus tazetta*) is intended in Cant. ii.I, and Is. xxxv.I, where alone the rose is mentioned. The beautiful and fragrant narcissus grown in the plain of Sharon, as is required by these references, and during its season of bloom is sold in the bazaars of the East and carried by everybody as a specially favorite flower.

Tournefort mentions fifty-three kinds of roses, of which the damask rose and the rose of Sharon are among the finest. The essence of damask roses is an excellent perfume.[8]

The Jews also esteemed the "lily of the valleys." However, modern scholars don't know much about it. Some authorities suggest that the Jews used the lily of the valleys as a favorite wedding flower.

Of a certainty, the Shulammite maiden considers herself far superior to a weed. While only a humble vineyard keeper, she displays dignity and strength of character. The opposite of cheap, she radiates wholesome beauty in her conduct, attitude, and appearance. She considers herself as one of the most beautiful flowers in the land. Her self-respect protects the Shulammite from hastily accepting the proposal of any boy who desires her--even King Solomon! She can afford to wait for the right husband.

Several young women who nearly fell away from Christ as teenagers only to come back with strength and dedication in their twenties, manifested several similarities. For example, they all came from homes where their mothers and fathers obviously loved each other. They had several brothers and sisters whom they loved. Their parents actively participated in the work of their local congregations as class teachers and serious Bible students. Yet these young women all went through a very rebellious stage where they nearly rejected serving God.

Each of these young women was asked, "Did you like yourself during your rebellious years?"

Each replied, "No, I didn't like myself. I had a very low self-image."

One girl who came from an exceptionally loving home said, "My parents drummed it into our heads, 'Don't get to thinking too highly of yourself, lest you fall.' So my parents constantly emphasized that something was wrong with us if we liked ourselves."

The Bible contains balances--it teaches people how to balance their lives without going to one ex-

---

[8]*The Popular and Critical Bible Encyclopedia and Scriptural Dictionary* (Chicago, IL: The Howard-Severance Company, 1902), p. 1492.

treme or another. Many people go to extremes in the
area of self-respect. Many parents refuse to pay their
children deserved compliments for fear their children
will develop "big heads."

God wants His people to look at themselves realistically as people with both strengths and weaknesses. *God's people must accept their talents before
they can properly use them in service to God.* When a
person thinks more lowly of himself than he really is,
he inhibits his ability to serve God with all his heart,
soul, and might. After all, God created men and women
in His own image. As a person becomes more God-like,
he first admires the qualities in God and then appreciates the value of them in his own life when he masters them. So God wants His servants to have a balanced view of themselves--not better than they really
are, but not lower either--healthy self-images.

One father told about his teenage daughter's struggles with her self-image. She was going through a rebellious stage where things had gotten so bad at home
that her parents sent her to live with another family.
While there, his daughter confided in the lady about
wanting to marry a young man who everyone thought
was beneath her. So the lady asked her, "Why do you
want to marry him?" This was a legitimate question
which the Shulammite answers later when the maidens
ask her the same thing.

The young girl replied, "Because he proposed to
me, and I'm afraid it will be the only proposal I'll
ever get. I don't want to end up an old maid." Yet this
young woman was the kind of girl that everyone
thought would make a good wife someday. She should
have her pick of young men and be able to say, "I'm
the rose of Sharon, the lily of the valleys." Unfortunately, her low self-image made her vulnerable to the
marriage proposal of any boy who came along. She
didn't have a realistic view of herself and didn't recognize her qualities that gave her the right to be particular about who she married.

Just the opposite, another young woman maintained
a proper self-image. While everyone thought she'd
make someone an excellent wife, she kept turning
down marriage proposal after proposal. No one understood why until she finally told them, "Serving God is

very important to me. And I'm not going to marry anyone who doesn't want to become a gospel preacher."

Many girls who share this same ideal of wanting
to marry a preacher don't know what they're wishing
for. They see only the love and fruitfulness in a
preacher's life. They don't know about the great
heartaches that come from working with people who
don't share that same zeal for serving God. Many
preachers and their wives yearn for a normal life
where everyone else's problems aren't theirs as well.

However, this young woman felt strongly about her
goal and kept turning down proposal after proposal. At
the same time, she kept getting older and older making
people really worry about her. Finally, when she was
twenty-six, the right man proposed to her and she became a preacher's wife. Throughout this time she
thought, "I'm the rose of Sharon, the lily of the valleys. I'm going to be particular about who I marry."

Truly, any girl who respects herself and the job
God gave her to do is a lovely person. A certain tranquility, peace, and serenity surrounds a woman who
enjoys her womanhood. Although her features may be
imperfect, her character and inner happiness give her a
radiant beauty that prettier girls with rebellious hearts
cannot duplicate with makeup. And such a girl can
choose who she wants to marry; she doesn't need to
accept the first proposal that comes her way.

G. A LILY AMONG THORNS

**Song of Sol. 2:2: "Like a lily among the
thorns, so is my darling among the maidens."**

The Bible frequently uses thorns to describe
worthless things. For example, Prov. 15:19 pictures the
sluggard as a hedge of thorns and Heb. 6:7-8 portrays
unfruitful Christians as thorns and thistles. Thus,
Solomon quickly agrees that the Shulammite will be a
prize of a wife for any man. In comparison, all the
other girls seem like worthless thorns. "That's right,"
he says, "you can be particular who you marry." So
Solomon gives her time to consider his proposal because she is special.

Men esteem a woman with a sense of self-worth. If a girl doesn't respect herself, others seldom admire her. Men who open doors for some women don't even think of being considerate of others. Boys who would never pet with some girls expect others to go all the way. Men generally treat women as the women expect to be treated.

When a woman expects men to treat her as a lady, then generally even the harshest of men treat her with respect. On the other hand, when she fails to conduct herself with self-respect and dignity, even gentlemen sometimes refuse to show consideration for her. When men use crude language around a woman, she should carefully consider her conduct to see if she provokes such response.

IV. MEMORIES OF THE SHEPHERD

Again the Shulammite's thoughts go back to the Shepherd as she compares him to Solomon. The Shulammite carefully weighs both men, for the choice she makes affects the rest of her life. In like manner, girls today should carefully examine the boys they date and not rely completely on their feelings. In fact, every girl should compare her dates with Solomon and the Shepherd, for they represent the two types of men--the sensuous and the loving.

A. LIKE AN APPLE TREE

> Song of Sol. 2:3-4: "Like an apple tree among the trees of the forest, so is my beloved among the young men. In his shade I took great delight and sat down, and his fruit was sweet to my taste. He has brought me to his banquet hall, and his banner over me is love."

The other boys act like the "trees of the forest" which fight each other for the sunlight. When they date girls, they worry about what's in it for them. In contrast, the Shulammite views the Shepherd as her "apple tree." An apple tree spreads out it's branches to provide shade for others. In like manner, the Shepherd shows genuine concern for her welfare rather than

looking out only for himself. He protects her and encourages her to lean upon him. He gives her fruit in
the form of strength, pleasure, and love. All of his
ways exhibit kindness and consideration of her needs.

When the Shulammite dined at the King's table she
enjoyed a feast served in the most elegant style. Such
banquets usually included music, dancing, and merri-
ment unlike any a vineyard keeper ever experienced.
No doubt, Solomon also followed the pattern of the rich
and the royalty by decorating his banquet hall with
banners. These flags and streamers proclaimed political
offices and the ensigns of their fathers' houses much
like the speaker's stand of the president displays the
seal of the United States of America. Whenever
Solomon traveled or went to battle, servants carried
his banner so that everyone would recognize his importance.[9]

Yet, after that impressive feast, the Shulammite
stops in her thoughts to consider the Shepherd's banquet hall. Too poor for banners, let alone singers and
dancers and gold or silver cups, the Shepherd serves
his humble meal with only a banner of love over her.
But what a banner! Love turns the Shepherd's simple
food into a source of pleasure. As a result, the maiden
delights in the Shepherd's plain meal more than in
King Solomon's elegant one.

After marriage, a woman needs to feel secure in
her husband's love so that she can let her guard down
and allow her love to flow freely. She needs the security of knowing that her husband really cares about
her and acts in her best interest. A wife cheerfully
serves a husband who makes his love obvious. However, if these qualities are lacking in courtship,
they'll probably be missing after marriage as well.

B. LOVESICK

Song of Sol. 2:5-6: "Sustain me with raisin
cakes, refresh me with apples, because I am
lovesick. Let his left hand be under my head
and his right hand embrace me."

[9]The International Standard Bible Encyclopedia, i, pp.
384, 385.

People have always associated sweets with romance. And as the Shulammite remembers the Shepherd, she feels lovesick. Since the vineyard keeper is emotionally involved with the Shepherd, she can hardly bear the thought of leaving him. Only something sweet will help her get through this time with Solomon.

Even then, the maiden continues to look forward to the Shepherd's embrace and touch in marriage. Due to her emotional attachment to the Shepherd, she eagerly anticipates sexual love with him. This reveals a healthy attitude on her part. While other passages show that she protects her purity, her sexuality is maturing properly.

If a young woman does not look forward to uniting physically with her fiance in marriage, something is wrong. Either she fails to make a proper emotional bond with him or she clings to some bad attitudes toward sexual love. God created girls with sexual feelings that, ideally, should be *awaken in courtship.* However, God plans for young women to satisfy these desires in marriage.

When young women understand the role of purity in sexual satisfaction, they can enjoy the awakening of their desires in courtship. They know that their budding sexuality makes them yearn for marriage as the Shulammite does. For the Shulammite says, "Let his left hand be under my head and his right hand embrace me." The sexual purity of young women also makes their suitors covet marriage as the Shepherd shows later on. Because of these physical needs, young women must guard against getting into situations where they might lose self-control and damage their chances for complete marital happiness and sin against themselves, their boyfriends, and God.

C. THE THEME: DO NOT AROUSE OR AWAKEN LOVE

> **Song of Sol. 2:7: "I adjure you, O daughters of Jerusalem, by the gazelles or by the hinds of the field, that you will not arouse or awaken my love, until she [it--NAS footnote] pleases."**

"Arouse" and "awaken" come from the same root word which means "(through the idea of opening the eyes), to wake" (Strong, p. 86).

The expression "by the gazelles or by the hinds of the field" refers to the male and female deer or antelope and exemplifies intelligent mating. Even the animals understand enough about love not to force themselves upon each other. All animals go through a courting period of getting acquainted before they mate. Male animals perform fancy rituals of showing off their beautiful colors, dancing, fighting to impress their chosen females, etc. Mating takes place only after the females' emotions become sufficiently aroused.

As a country girl, the Shulammite understands the way of animals and the importance of courtship. So she turns to the maidens and begs them to give her and Solomon time to fall in love with each other before they force her to marry him. She repeats this plea two more times in the book. Thus, it comprises the theme of the Song of Solomon: By the example of nature, don't force a couple to marry before their love has a chance to develop naturally.

People force love in many ways. For example, one woman who divorced her husband said, "When I married my husband, I didn't really love him. But he just loved me so much, I thought I'd learn to love him after marriage. But I never did." She found out the hard way that it's much easier to learn to love a man before marriage than afterwards.

Another woman with a horrible attitude toward her husband referred to him as "a big fat slob." She dealt with her marriage frustrations by physically abusing her child. When asked if she loved her husband when she married him, she replied, "No, I married him only because I was pregnant with his child." She never learned to love him.

Marrying a certain man just because a woman is going to bear his child is one of the poorest reasons imaginable for marrying someone. The greatest gift parents can bestow upon their children is to give them parents who truly love each other. But trying to correct the sin of fornication by marriage often backfires and causes more heartaches than ever.

Thus, the Shulammite cautions the maidens not to awaken or arouse love until "it," referring back to "love," pleases. She begs the maidens to let her love grow naturally. Love must be allowed to develop of its own accord. It would be better to never marry than to marry a man whom a woman did not love and risk not being able to learn to love him later. To the Shulammite, men and women ought to exhibit as much common sense as the gazelles and hinds by building an emotional bond before marriage if they want to succeed at loving and being loved.

D. LIKE A GAZELLE OR A YOUNG STAG

> Song of Sol. 2:8-9: "Listen, my beloved! Behold, he is coming, climbing on the mountains, leaping on the hills! My beloved is like a gazelle or a young stag. Behold, he is standing behind our wall, he is looking through the windows, he is peering through the lattice."

"Gazelle" means "in the sense of prominence; splendor (as conspicuous), also a gazelle (as beautiful)" (Strong, p. 98).

"Stag" comes from a word which means "strength, hence anything strong, specifically a chief (politically), also a ram (from his strength), a pilaster (as a strong support), an oak or other strong tree:-- mighty (man), lintel, oak, post, ram, tree" (Strong, p. 11).

No doubt, the news of Solomon taking the young Shulammite maiden to his camp has spread over the countryside. The peasants curiously wonder what she will do. Such excitement has not come their way in a long time. Then as if she catches a glimpse of her shepherd boyfriend checking on her, the Shulammite declares, "Behold, he is standing behind our wall, he is looking through the windows, he is peering through the lattice." She confidently knows that he stays close by and waits for her decision.

The Shulammite regards the Shepherd as like the "gazelle," the male antelope, and the "young stag," the male mountain goat. Both of these animals lead and protect their females. Nothing sissy or questionable characterizes her beloved, for he is a man's man--a man on whom a woman can safely trust and rely.

Solomon told her that she has time to consider his proposal. With both the King and the Shepherd close by, she knows that she can choose either one. So her thoughts turn to the Shepherd as she considers their feelings toward each other. And she remembers when he discussed marriage with her:

V. THE SHEPHERD'S FIRST PROPOSAL

As the Shulammite considers the Shepherd, she thinks about how he brings out and enhances her femininity and how much she enjoys his masculinity--important attitudes for a successful marriage:

A. A HELPER MEET FOR HIM

> **Song of Sol. 2:10-13: "My beloved responded and said to me, 'Arise, my darling, my beautiful one, and come along. For behold, the winter is past, the rain is over and gone. The flowers have already appeared in the land; the time has arrived for pruning the vines, and the voice of the turtledove has been heard in our land. The fig tree has ripened its figs, and the vines in blossom have given forth their fragrance. Arise, my darling, my beautiful one, and come along!'"**

Everywhere flowers bud and the fragrant smell of spring fills the air, and as the saying goes, "a young man's fancy turns to love." In her thoughts, the Shulammite hears the Shepherd beg her to marry him now and to end their wait. Rather than a romance where the girl carried a crush on a boy who didn't know she existed, the Shepherd wants to marry the maiden tomorrow. He patiently awaits her answer.

The Shepherd wants the Shulammite to go with him to help him subdue the earth. Together they will prune the vines and enjoy the great outdoors. For to be successful, shepherds both cared for their sheep and plant and harvest crops. They use the grain to feed their sheep during the winter and for their own food.[10]

[10]Robert Henderson and Ian Gould, *Life in Bible Times*, (Chicago: Rand McNally & Company, 1967), pp. 6-7.

Through working together, the Shepherd and the maiden will reap the fruitful blessings of hard work.

B. HIS SOURCE OF COMFORT

> **Song of Sol. 2:14: "O my dove, in the clefts of the rock, in the secret place of the steep pathway, let me see your form, let me hear your voice; for your voice is sweet, and your form is lovely."**

The Shepherd calls to his dove in "the clefts of the rock" and "the secret place of the steep pathway," for the Shulammite stays beyond his reach. Although they share a deep love for each other, they aren't yet married. The Shepherd pleads with her to end their separation and come down from her inaccessible place into his home to be his wife.

The young maiden puts a sparkle in the Shepherd's life and he wants to see her and be near her every day. Her sweet comforting voice soothes him after a hard day of work. Her lovely form delights him. Her soft, tender, loving nature that makes her a weaker vessel makes him want to rush home from work to her--his dove--his haven of peace--his refuge from the world--his sanctuary for renewing his strength.

C. HER PROTECTOR

> **Song of Sol. 2:15: "Catch the foxes for us, the little foxes that are ruining the vineyards, while our vineyards are in blossom."**

The Shulammite responds by asking the Shepherd to take care of her. Just as he needs her, she depends upon him. The new little foxes are coming out of their dens to play among the vines. They are running up and down the rows in the vineyard, and knocking off the tender blossoms. The Shulammite needs the Shepherd's help and asks him to catch the foxes, for that is a man's job. Just as the Shepherd longs for the comforts of a woman, she yearns for the strength and courage of a man.

D. HER PROVIDER

> Song of Sol. 2:16: "My beloved is mine, and I
> am his; he pastures his flock among the
> lilies. Until the cool of the day when the
> shadows flee away,..."

Not a lazy individual, the Shepherd works hard all day long until "the cool of the day" or the evening. He pastures his flock among the lilies and takes good care of them. While the Shepherd's job seems common, he is a giant of a man when it came to plain, hard work. *His attitude toward work, not his college degrees, position in some company, or family name, make him dependable.*

In fact, Gilder says in his book *Men and Marriage* that marriage and a man's attitude toward work help him succeed far more than a college degree does. He states that statistics show that men with large families and only a high school education or less outearn female college graduates. Rather than resulting from sex discrimination, "the greater motivation and persistence of men with families--working overtime and often taking more than one job in their struggle to overcome the adverse economics of child support--generates income and productivity far beyond the 'worth' of their credentials." On the other hand, single men earn about the same as single women with the same education. Gilder concludes that parents might be ahead to encourage their sons to marry rather than sending them to college.[11]

A husband who refuses to work steadily burdens his wife by making it impossible for her to place total confidence in him. Without trust, a wife cannot completely let go of the reins to fully love her husband. Sometimes a woman makes the mistake of placing her confidence in her husband's job rather than in his ability and willingness to work. Jobs are only as secure as the economy and the goodwill of the employer. Therefore, a wise wife places her trust in her husband's determination to work rather than in the size of his paycheck.

[11]Gilder, *Men and Marriage*, p. 94.

E. HER LEADER

> **Song of Sol. 2:17: "...Turn, my beloved, and be like a gazelle or a young stag on the mountains of Bether."**

Some women want their husbands to give in weakly to their demands and guidance. These women fear the aggressive strength that God gives men to aid them as they lead, provide for, and protect their families. But not the Shulammite! She pleads with the Shepherd to "be like a gazelle or a young stag on the mountains of Bether." Rather than enslaving her, she knows that his strength allows her to depend upon him. She shows her appreciation by complimenting the Shepherd's vigor and aggressiveness. She gladly encourages the Shepherd to be masculine so that she can bask in his care.

The Shulammite compared herself to the rose of Sharon and the lily of the valleys; now she compares the Shepherd to the powerful gazelles and stags. She contrasts their natures and roles in life. As a delicate flower, she adds meaning, comfort, and beauty to his manliness. As a strong, supporting protector, he shields her womanliness. Since beautiful flowers cannot survive trampling, he rejects all forms of mental or physical abuse. Instead, he cherishes and nourishes his weaker vessel. Manly protection enables femininity to bloom all the more beautifully in a woman.

As the Shulammite contemplates marriage to King Solomon, she realizes that true love is more important than his money or prestige. After tasting of true love with the Shepherd, she is unwilling to settle for just Solomon's flattery. And so her search for true love continues.

STUDY EXERCISE

Answer all questions in your own words.

1. What value does the Song of Solomon have for teenagers?

2. What value does the Song of Solomon have for married couples?

3. Why is there so much misunderstanding about the Song of Solomon?

4. What was the Shulammite's opinion of herself? Is it a good opinion for women to have today? Why?

5. What were the important parts of Solomon's first proposal?

6. What were the important parts of the Shepherd's first proposal?

7. What is the significance of the gazelles and hinds of the field? And why did the Shulammite caution the maidens not to awaken love?

8. In what ways did the Shulammite want the Shepherd to function as a man?

9. Do you disagree with anything in this lesson? If so, explain in detail giving scriptures for your reasons.

RESEARCH EXERCISE

Each week as you study the Song of Solomon, begin with chapter one, verse one and read the story through to where you finished at the last class. Rather than busy work, this exercise helps make the Song of Solomon belong to you. Doing this on a regular basis instead of just one time for class makes the words and the story more familiar to you. It also helps you better understand the overall story line.

Then as you go about your daily life, your mind will automatically recall passages from the Song of Solomon. The events of life will remind you of the Shulammite, the Shepherd, or King Solomon. When that happens, the Song of Solomon belongs to you. This will enable you to use it effectively to teach your children and your neighbors about how to lay the proper foundation for a happy marriage.

OPTIONAL EXERCISE

Make a scrapbook with your children using pictures from magazines and hand-drawn ones to illustrate the Song of Solomon. Even very young children love projects like this. Women who have done this project report that both they and their children especially enjoyed it.

CHAPTER 10

THE MAN'S SEARCH FOR TRUE LOVE

When King Solomon went to the country to inspect the land that he leased to the farmers, he saw a beautiful vineyard keeper. He thought, "She has the most beautiful body I've ever seen! Surely, she is the answer to all my problems!" So he invited her to join his harem and brought her to his camp.

Once there, the Shulammite realized that she would have to make a decision about whether or not to marry Solomon. She also recognized that the choice she made would be a lifelong commitment. Yearning for true love as all young girls do, she begged the maidens to not force Solomon upon her before she learned to love him.

Then she told Solomon that she was the rose of Sharon, the lily of the valleys--that she could be particular about who she married. Solomon agreed and said that she was a lily among thorns. Then Solomon gave the Shulammite time to think. But rather than falling in love with Solomon, a certain dream kept recurring:

I. THE SHULAMMITE'S DREAM

Surrounded by Solomon's flattery and glamour, the Shulammite's love for the Shepherd refuses to be stilled. In spite of the life of luxury and ease that Solomon offers her, the maiden can't get the Shepherd out of her mind. Even when she tries to sleep, her dreams dwell upon the Shepherd. And so night after night, dreams about the Shepherd haunt her.

A. SEARCHES FOR THE SHEPHERD

> Song of Sol. 3:1-3: "On my bed night after night I sought him whom my soul loves; I sought him but did not find him. 'I must arise now and go about the city; in the streets and in the squares I must seek him whom my soul loves.' I sought him but did not find him. The watchmen who make the rounds in the city found me, and I said, 'Have you seen him whom my soul loves?'"

Dreams of marriage comprise a natural part of a young girl's transition into womanhood. After she starts dating, her dreams center around her boyfriend as she visualizes life with him. These dreams help her sort out her feelings and prepare her for marriage.

Thus, the Shulammite imagines married life in the city. But rather than revolving around Solomon as they would if she truly loved him, her dreams focus on the Shepherd. Instead of giving her peace, her dreams tell her of the emptiness she will feel without the Shepherd. Her whole being loves the Shepherd and refuses to let her forget him even for the riches of King Solomon.

In her dreams she sees herself overcome with sadness at night. Tormented so much that she can't sleep, she gets up and searches for her beloved. In her desperation to find him, she asks everyone she meets, even the guards of the city, if they've seen him.

B. FINDS THE SHEPHERD

> Song of Sol. 3:4: "Scarcely had I left them when I found him whom my soul loves; I held on to him and would not let him go, until I had brought him to my mother's house, and into the room of her who conceived me."

Finally, when the Shulammite finds the Shepherd in her dreams, she refuses to let him go until she brings him home for her mother to meet. The Shulammite wants her parents' approval because she wants them to love the Shepherd as she loves him.

Young couples today should seek their parents' approval of the one they plan to marry. Most parents have lived at least twice as long as their children and have met a variety of different people and have experienced marriage firsthand. Parents can point out qualities in a prospective marriage partner that emotional love sometimes fails to see.

The Shulammite wants to marry the Shepherd with all of her heart, but what about Solomon? She can't take lightly the honor he bestows upon her by asking her to marry him. Fortunately, she is not yet committed to either Solomon or the Shepherd, so she can choose the one she wants. She can choose the splendor of the city and the prestige of being Solomon's wife, or she can choose true love with a humble dwelling in the country. Such a big decision for a young girl.

After her dreams, the Shulammite realizes that she isn't ready to give up the Shepherd. So once again, she begs the maidens not to force her to marry Solomon before she loves him:

C. THE THEME: DO NOT AWAKEN OR AROUSE LOVE

Song of Sol. 3:5: "I adjure you, O daughter of Jerusalem, by the gazelles or by the hinds of the field, that you will not arouse or awaken my love, until she [it--NASV footnote] pleases."

The Shulammite pleads with the maidens not to force marriage upon her. If Solomon and the Shulammite learn to love each other the same way the Shulammite and the Shepherd love each other, it will take time to build an emotional attraction to each other. On the other hand, if she marries Solomon before true love develops between them, she'll continue to dream about the Shepherd and be miserable. She might never find true love again. So she tells the maidens, "Please, don't force Solomon and me together until we truly love each other with all our hearts!"

While the right choice for the Shulammite might seem obvious to the readers, even a shallow man often possesses a disarming charm that captivates innocent girls. Since flattery often influences a girl to make an unwise choice for a marriage partner, a girl should spend as much time as possible getting to know the man she wants to marry.

One woman said, "My grandmother gave me some good advice: 'Never date a boy you wouldn't want to be the father of your children.' She understood that once I started dating a fellow and spending time with him, I could easily fall in love and end up marrying him. So she warned me not to take a chance on falling in love with someone who wouldn't make a good husband and father."

Many wives started dating their husbands when they didn't even like them at first. They simply regarded their dates as a way to keep from staying home. One such wife admonished girls to never let a boy kiss them if they didn't want to fall in love with him. She said, "When I dated my husband, I let him kiss me good night to be polite. I had no intention of getting emotionally involved with him or anyone else. But soon afterwards, we were making marriage plans."

It is almost impossible for males and females to kiss without arousing passion for one another which can easily be mistaken for love. It would be better to love before kissing than to kiss and be fooled into thinking it is love. Love is too precious to gamble with losing it through careless dating habits.

II. SOLOMON'S SECOND PROPOSAL

After finishing the inspection of his vineyards, Solomon gathers his party together and starts back to his palace in Jerusalem. As he nears the city, the people line the road in front of their houses to see this magnificent parade march by. They excitedly ask, "Who is this coming up from the wilderness?" Once they recognize King Solomon, they call to their daughters, "Hurry! Come see the young vineyard keeper who has stolen the King's heart!"

A. RETURNS TO JERUSALEM

Song of Sol. 3:6-11: "What is this coming up from the wilderness like columns of smoke, perfumed with myrrh and frankincense, with all scented powders of the merchant? Behold, it is the traveling couch of Solomon; sixty

mighty men around it, of the mighty men of
Israel. All of them are wielders of the sword,
expert in war; each man has his sword at
his side, guarding against the terrors of the
night. King Solomon has made for himself a
sedan chair from the timber of Lebanon. He
made its posts of silver, its back of gold and
its seat of purple fabric, with its interior
lovingly fitted out by the daughters of
Jerusalem. Go forth, O daughters of Zion, and
gaze on King Solomon with the crown with
which his mother crowned him on the day
of his wedding, and on the day of his gladness of heart."

The description of King Solomon's traveling party
presents a very realistic picture of the traveling style
of royalty. For example, the Jews went to great
lengths to counteract the offensive odors of their hot
climate. When nobility travelled in their litters, atten-
dants tossed up "columns of smoke" or handfuls of
spices to perfume the path as a forerunner of modern
room-fresheners.

Surrounded by mighty men to protect him from
harm, Solomon rides in the grandest comfort of his
day. His maidens and servants carefully and lovingly
decorated his sedan chair just for him with gold and
silver and expensive purple cloth. Solomon, wearing
the wreath of a bridegroom (Isa. 61:10), presents an
impressive sight as he triumphantly takes the Shulammite through the city to his palace.

The daughters of Jerusalem swoon over the King
and his splendor. What wealth! What elegance! What
luxury awaits the lucky bride! Any one of them would
jump at the chance to marry Solomon and to share his
riches and prestige. Why, then, does the Shulammite
hesitate and not wear her wedding crown?

B. ADMIRES HER GREAT BEAUTY

Song of Sol. 4:1-5: "How beautiful you are,
my darling, how beautiful you are! Your eyes
are like doves behind your veils; your hair is
like a flock of goats that have descended
from Mount Gilead. Your teeth are like a flock

of newly shorn ewes which have come up from their washing, all of which bear twins, and not one among them has lost her young. Your lips are like a scarlet thread, and your mouth is lovely. Your temples are like a slice of pomegranate behind your veil. Your neck is like the tower of David built with rows of stones, on which are hung a thousand shields, all the round shields of the mighty men. Your two breasts are like two fawns, twins of a gazelle, which feed among the lilies."

Once Solomon brings the Shulammite back to his home, he begins wooing her in earnest. He tries every trick he knows to awaken her love for him. His speech flows smoothly from practice, charming the inexperienced young vineyard keeper. He tells her, "How beautiful you are, my darling, how beautiful you are!" Solomon told the young maiden this before, but now he adds more. His proposal takes the form of a description of her beauty which reveals only a sensuous infatuation with her. Her beauty is so great to behold, and he is so luck to have it all for himself to enjoy.

Solomon's description brings the Shulammite's beauty to life: Her eyes, like "doves," radiate peace and happiness. Her long black curly hair, like "a flock of goats [usually black] that have descended Mount Gilead," flows beautifully down her back. Her white, even teeth, like a flock of sheep "which have come up from their washing, all of which bear twins," enhance her smile. Her red lips, like a "scarlet thread," innocently invite his kisses. Her temples and flawless complexion, like "a slice of pomegranate," presents a picture of health and youth. Her long slender neck, like "the tower of David," adds beauty and grace to her necklace, like "the round shields of the mighty men." Her breasts, like "two fawns, twins of a gazelle, which feed among the lilies," reveal a girl who has become a woman. In other words, Solomon tells the Shulammite that she possesses everything necessary to make a good wife--the perfect body.

Then the Shulammite tells Solomon what every girl should say after such a proposal:

C. WANTS TIME TO THINK

> **Song of Sol. 4:6: "Until the cool of the day when the shadows flee away, I will go my way to the mountain of myrrh and to the hill of frankincense."**

The Shulammite needed time to think about Solomon's proposal, so she asked him to wait until evening, "until the cool of the day when the shadows flee away." "The mountain of myrrh and the hill of frankincense" refer to the numerous gardens outside the city. Thus, the vineyard keeper wants to take a walk among the sweet-smelling herbs and plants to try to figure out what she should do. In fact, the Jews enjoyed their gardens as special places to meditate:

> Gardens were dedicated to various uses among the Hebrews, such as we still find prevailing in the East. One most essential difference between them and our own is that they are not attached to or in any way connected with the residence, but are situated in the suburbs. We have gardens from half a mile to a mile distant from the houses of the persons to whom they belonged. It is manifest that all the gardens mentioned in scripture were outside the several towns. This is, however, to be understood of regular gardens, for shrubs and flowers were often planted in the open courts of the dwelling-houses.

> People repair to their suburban gardens to take the air, to walk, and to refresh and solace themselves in various ways. For their use there is mostly in each garden a kind of summer-house or pavilion, fitted up with much neatness, gaily painted, and furnished with seats, where the visitants may sit and enjoy themselves...

It is very evident that the gardens of the
Hebrews were in a very considerable degree
devoted to the culture of medicinal herbs,..."[1]

Since the Shulammite doesn't want to rush into
marriage, she wisely refuses to allow Solomon to pressure her into making a quick decision that will affect
the rest of her life. Likewise, a thoughtful boy gives a
girl time to think his proposal through, since her decision affects the rest of his life, too. A whirlwind romance often precedes an unhappy marriage.

D. PRAISES HER FLAWLESS BEAUTY

**Song of Sol. 4:7: "You are altogether beautiful,
my darling, and there is no blemish in you."**

Solomon tells the Shulammite, "You can think about
it all you want, but I won't change my mind." Why?
"Because you are physically perfect! There's not even
one blemish in you!" Thus, Solomon searches for love
by trying to find the perfect feminine body. Then with
Solomon's flattery ringing in her ears, the young
maiden goes to the garden to think:

III. THE SHEPHERD'S SECOND PROPOSAL

Later, strolling through the garden of spices reminds the Shulammite of her country home. Her
thoughts naturally turn to the Shepherd, and she compares his proposal to Solomon's. Every girl should
think seriously about the implications of a man's proposal of marriage before she accepts.

Indeed, every young man who searches for true
love should also examine his own proposal: If he
seeks a lifelong companion and lover as the Shepherd,
he should look for the same characteristics that attract
the Shepherd to the Shulammite. But, if his desires for
marriage center around sensuous lusts like Solomon
who searches for the perfect body, let him beware. For
when physical attractions begin to diminish (and they
will if an emotional foundation doesn't support them),
nothing will sustain the marriage.

---

[1]*Popular and Critical Bible Encyclopedia, ii,* p. 689.

It this way, the Shepherd's proposal provides universal application: Every man who searches for true love should make the same proposal to his beloved. Thus, the Shepherd wants to marry a woman whom he will enjoy all of his married life:

A. ENJOYS HER COMPANY

Song of Sol. 4:8: "Come with me from Lebanon, my bride, may you come with me from Lebanon. Journey down from the summit of Amana, from the summit of Senir and Hermon, from the dens of lions, from the mountains of leopards."

"Bride" means "a bride (as if perfect), hence a son's wife:--bride, daughter-in-law, spouse" (Strong, p. 55). "Bride" comes from a word which means "to complete:--make perfect."

While Solomon proposes to the Shulammite as "my darling," which refers to "a female associate" and shows his shallow view of her, the Shepherd proposes to her as "my bride." The Shepherd's name for her shows that he doesn't view her as a passing delight. Instead, he considers her someone to spend the rest of his life with. As a helper meet for him, she will complete him and make him perfect--she is the answer to his problem of loneliness. Wherever life leads him, the Shepherd wants the Shulammite to go with him.

He begs her to come down from the summit of Amana, Senir, and Hermon and the dens of lions and leopards. These inaccessible places symbolize the obstacles that separate the two lovers. She is not an easy mark for him; he respects her purity. Now he wants to remove all hindrances and unite with her in marriage. Rather than an immoral relationship, he desires a pure and holy covenant that lasts a lifetime.

B. TREASURES THE GLANCE OF HER EYES

Song of Sol. 4:9: "You have made my heart beat faster, my sister, my bride; you have made my heart beat faster with a single glance of your eyes,..."

"Sister" means "a sister (used very widely, literally and figuratively):--another, sister, together" (Strong, p. 10).

While the word "bride" shows the Shepherd's desire for a permanent relationship with the Shulammite, the term "sister" refers to their common backgrounds. The Shepherd and the Shulammite enjoy many compatible qualities that a brother and sister share: their nationality, family upbringing, religion, economic status, enjoyment of nature, personal integrity, worldly ambitions, and respect for marriage and the home. Men and women contemplating marriage should examine one another--do they partake of a common background as the Shepherd and the Shulammite did? When different values exist, problems quickly arise.

Each time the Shepherd sees the love and approval shining in the Shulammite's eyes, his heart beats faster than ever. She excites him! She captivates him! He hopelessly loves her! The butterflies that stir within the Shepherd testify to his emotional involvement with the maiden or his *philo* (affectionate love). While he feels great responsibility toward her which causes him to act in her best interest, the Shepherd enjoys the pleasure of coupling *philo* (tender affection) with *agape* (responsible love). (Review chapters 7 and 8 for the distinctions between *philo* and *agape*.)

The Shulammite's eyes play an important role all the way through the Song of Solomon. The way she looks at both the Shepherd and Solomon affects both men. Earlier, Solomon described her eyes as peaceful doves. Now the Shepherd says her eyes make his heart beat faster. Both want to see love shining from the Shulammite's eyes.

More important than the color of a woman eyes is the way she looks at a man. A woman says many things with her eyes that may never cross her lips. For example, a woman's eyes convey love, admiration, contentment, and acceptance or boredom, contempt, disgust, and hatred. Thus, the way a woman looks at a man tells him about her feelings toward him.

In addition to boyfriends, many a husband likes to see a demonstration of affection glowing in his wife's eyes. Proverbs says, "Bright eyes gladden the heart; good news puts fat on the bones" (15:30). For these reasons, a wife should learn how to control the expression of her eyes by controlling her thoughts. If she stands in front of a mirror and deliberately thinks loving thoughts of her husband, she sees firsthand how loving pleasant emotions make her eyes sparkle. Then during their times together, she can let her eyes radiate her love for her husband and caress him without saying a word.

C. NOTICES HER APPEARANCE

Song of Sol. 4:9: "...You have made my heart beat faster with a single glance of your eyes, with a single strand of your necklace."

In addition to the glance of her eyes, a single strand of the Shulammite's necklace also captivates the Shepherd. Although the Shulammite isn't one of the ten best-dressed women in the land, she takes time to add feminine touches to her appearance. These the Shepherd notices and appreciates. They make his heart beat faster.

When dating, most women pay attention to their dress, hair, cleanliness, and the little extra touches that tell their dates, "You're special." For some reason, many of these same women feel free to neglect their appearance after marriage and expect their husbands to remain hopelessly attracted to them. However, even when couples build their marriages upon an emotional commitment of concern, husbands still want their wives to attract them physically.

Many times little things make a lot of difference. For example, one wife said, "Someone gave me some dark nail polish. I tried it only because my regular polish was drying up. To my surprise, my husband immediately noticed it and said something about it. I told him I thought it was too dark. Then he said, 'That's why I like it, because it's dark.' Now I enjoy wearing dark polish all the time because I know my husband notices it and likes it."

Since women place more emphasis upon emotional rather than physical attraction, many fail to appreciate the value of keeping themselves attractive and feminine for their husbands. Yet even if wives fail to fully understand the importance of physical appeal to their husbands, the noble Shepherd testifies in the pages of inspired scripture that a loving man notices and reacts to his wife's appearance.

True love revolves around a commitment to always act in the best interest of the one loved plus satisfaction of the five senses. Rarely will a man take time to become emotionally involved with a woman who does not satisfy his five senses--taste, smell, sight, hearing, and touch. Fortunately, different men prefer different clothing, hair styles, makeup, and physical characteristics. So a woman must seek to please *her own husband*--not herself, her mother or father, the fashion designers, or other women--*but her own husband.*

One husband liked shirtwaist dresses on his wife, but she thought they made her look fat so she wore more slenderizing garments. Each time that she put on a shirtwaist dress her husband grumbled, "Well, you finally wore something for me!" Her husband interpreted her feelings for him by what she wore. He didn't think his preferences mattered to her and, unfortunately, he was right.

Many husbands enjoy their wives adding feminine frills to their appearance such as lace, soft or bright colors, hair ribbons and barrettes, jewelry, etc. In short, feminine clothing contrasts with garments and accessories that men wear. A wife makes herself attractive to her husband by wearing colors and styles that please him. A single strand of the Shulammite's necklace captivates the Shepherd.

In a similar manner, a wife makes herself unattractive and even repulsive to her husband by what she wears or refuses to wear. For example, a sloppily dressed woman who adorns herself with curlers or uncombed hair or worn out or dirty clothing or who uses no makeup or wears too much turns many men off. A wife who makes no attempt to satisfy her husband's five senses places a strain upon her marriage.

D. VALUES HER LOVE

> Song of Sol. 4:10-11: "How beautiful is your love, my sister, my bride! How much better is your love than wine, and the fragrance of your oils than all kinds of spices! Your lips, my bride, drip honey; honey and milk are

under your tongue, and the fragrance of your garments is like the fragrance of Lebanon."

Solomon said, "How beautiful is your body, my darling!" but the Shepherd said, "How beautiful is your love, my sister, my bride!" Winning the Shulammite's love is the ultimate accomplishment for the Shepherd, for her love intoxicates him more then the best wine. As long as she gives her love freely to him, he will never lack for any comfort in life. The tender expressions that come from her mouth, the words that only a loving woman knows how to say--he thrives on them. From her lips come "honey"--sweet comforting support and admiration, and "milk"--life-sustaining encouragement and confidence in his ability to care for her.

The Shulammite's garments give forth the soft, sweet aroma of an appealing woman. Again the Shepherd notices her appearance and her delight in her femininity. He tells her that the fragrance of her oils smell better than all kinds of spices. The scent of her garments reminds him of Lebanon--refreshing and soothing. The Shulammite may not spend countless hours grooming each day, but she keeps herself and her clothing clean and generously uses perfume. One hundred percent a woman, she proudly emphasizes her femininity.

The Jews used different kinds of oils as grooming aids in much the same manner that people use them today as hair and skin conditioners. Esther's beautification program provides an example of this practice: "Now when the turn of each young lady came to go in to King Ahasuerus, after the end of her twelve months under the regulation for the women--for the days of their beautification were completed as follows: six months with oil of myrrh and six months with spices and the cosmetics for women..." (Es. 2:12). Grooming aids didn't originate with modern women.

Keeping clean and sweet-smelling require little time or expense, but they offer great rewards as Solomon wrote in Prov. 27:9: "Oil and perfume make the heart glad, so a man's counsel is sweet to his friend." Thus, cleanliness and perfume perk up a person as much as visiting with a kind and helpful friend. The Shepherd praises the Shulammite for exhibiting both of these traits. Her fragrant cleanliness increases his enjoyment of associating with her and makes it easy for him to love her.

The perfume also holds special benefits for the Shulammite. When her "perfume gave forth its fragrance" while she dined at the King's table, it reminded her of the Shepherd--the one who she wore it to please (1:12). Perfume means romance to many men and women and helps put them in a mood for love. Certainly, wearing pleasing aromas benefits both the husband and wife by making their hearts glad. In fact, this ability of perfume to affect the emotions has been proven by scientists. Dr. Robert L. Pettus Jr. explains in his book, *As I See Sex Through the Bible,* how this happens:

> Recent research in neuropsychology and in neurochemistry has pointed out that the rhinencephalon, which is a part of the brain that has to do with smelling, has an important part in the regulating of emotions. This means a person can be stimulated positively or negatively by what they smell. Positive stimulation in sex is what we want without a doubt--a clean body, clean clothes and perfumes. Negative stimuli are body odors, halitosis and smelly clothes. You can readily see the difference between the two types of stimulations.[2]

People with a sensitive sense of smell know this. A person often doesn't even want to look to see if someone is pretty or handsome who radiates an offensive odor. In fact, he usually keeps his head turned the other way to avoid as much of the smell as possible. But the same person enjoys riding in the country where the wild flowers and pines fill the air with fragrance. Such a drive often stirs affectionate emotions toward the mate.

One husband divulged one reason why a perfumed wife attracts her husband. He said, "I usually don't notice how things smell unless they smell bad. When

[2]Robert L. Pettus Jr., M.D., *As I See Sex Through the Bible* (Madison, TN: Pettus, 1973), p. 66, quoting David N. Rotnavale, M.D., *Medical Aspects of Human Sexuality*, p. 63, April 1970, Vol. IV, No. 4.

my wife smells good, it's a delightful change from the ordinary. I like it." In fact, he complimented his wife more on smelling nice than anything else.

Any woman can smell sweet regardless of her physical characteristics. Since everyone gets used to smells after awhile and ceases to detect them, wearing a variety of perfumes helps insure that a husband continues to notice them. Even the Song of Solomon mentions more than one kind of perfume.

Another husband always noticed when his wife hung the sheets on the line to dry because they smelled clean and fresh. His wife said that when she put them in the dryer, he always commented when he got into bed, "What happened to the clean-smelling sheets?" He liked the smell of clean sheets so much that when they moved to a new house, he put up a clothes line first thing.

A wise woman learns the lesson about appealing femininity that the Shepherd teaches as he comments about the Shulammite's perfume. The woman who wants to awaken her husband's love or keep it passionate makes a special effort to put honey and milk on her tongue and to keep an air of fragrance about her.

F. GUARDS HER PURITY

Song of Sol. 4:12: "A garden locked is my sister, my bride, a rock-garden locked, a spring sealed up."

The Jews referred to both the husband and wife's sexual charms as "springs" as found in Prov. 5:15-18: "Drink waters from your own cistern, and fresh water from your own well [the wife's sexual favors--PRD]. Should your springs [the husband's sexual favors--PRD] be dispersed abroad, streams of water in the streets [shared with other women--PRD]? Let them be yours alone, and not for strangers with you [protect your purity--PRD]. Let your fountain be blessed, and rejoice in the wife of your youth [happiness comes when the husband preserves himself just for his wife--PRD]." *Vol. II: Learning to Love* devotes two chapters to studying this whole chapter of Proverbs. One chapter discusses "The False Promise of an Affair" and the other teaches about "The Older Wife, an Exciting Lover."

The self-respecting rose of Sharon locks her sexual garden to save her refreshing waters for only her husband. Earlier the Shulammite said that she looks forward to sexual love so there is nothing wrong with her desires. However, she controls her desires and her life. Because of his esteem for the sexual relationship and his deep admiration for the Shulammite as a person, the Shepherd doesn't try to force her into allowing him to drink from her spring before marriage. Thus, the Shepherd tells the Shulammite that he respects and values her purity.

This shows a healthy attitude toward the sexual relationship on the part of both the Shepherd and Shulammite. God didn't create the sexual relationship for a few stolen moments during courtship. Instead, God designed sexual love to bless a couple *all of their married life*. Doctors now recognize that the best lover may well be the older husband--not the young bridegroom. Thus, in the ideal situation, if a couple patterns their marriage after God's wisdom, the older they become, the better lovers they both become.

Problems resulting from premarital sex comprise the hardest marriage problems of all to overcome. Premarital sex affects the mind in a negative way that often causes problems from guilt and a lack of trust. On the other hand, a husband and wife who keep themselves pure during their courting years free their minds and bodies to start sexual love off on a high plane in marriage. Then they can build upon that purity and love through the years so that the joy they experience in each other continually increases.

Doctors report that one of the most common causes of premature ejaculation comes from premarital sex. Frequently, the boy feels guilty about what he does in the back seat of a car. So instead of relaxing and enjoying himself as a husband does with his wife, he tries to hurry up the act. As a result, his body learns to respond in that unnatural manner which causes him problems for the rest of his life. Thus, for just a few years of stolen pleasure during the courting years, many couples rob themselves of many, many years of delight in married lovemaking.

Vol. II: Learning to Love shows over and over that God places the emphasis upon the mind. *When a husband and wife take care of their minds through purity and healthy attitudes toward sexual love, then their bodies automatically take care of themselves.* This is what the Shulammite and the Shepherd are doing--taking care of their attitudes and preserving their purity in courtship so that they'll enjoy this relationship in marriage.

Many husbands enjoy their wives' gullibility and playfully tease them and play pranks on them. Unfortunately, simple-minded men play on this natural innocence and try to seduce girls without taking on the duties and obligations of a husband. A boy who insists on self-gratification without responsibility gives the girl no reason to assume that he will become reliable after he tastes irresponsible pleasure. When problems arise or he gets bored, he will be inclined to run away from them. Dr. Pettus cautions girls against this danger:

> When we are advising our children in reference to sex, we should remember that in general the attitudes of boys and girls differ greatly. Girls usually equate the desire to have intercourse with love. Boys do not think like this, despite what they tell the girl. I have been told many times by the non-virgin girl, "Dr. Pettus, he told me he loved me." Since girls equate desire to have intercourse with love, they conclude that the boy truly loves them if he wants to have intercourse. They are indeed naive. The girls are not aware that the male wants sexual relations because of a strong physical sexual drive, a need for release. This drive is usually not as strong in the female as it is in the male. Our girls do not know these things. Because of the extreme persistence and insistence, girls are persuaded to go too far mistaking passion for love. We should tell our girls that the boys are only seeking a release or a new person to conquer.
>
> I think we ought to emphasize to our girls that no matter how much a boy says he loves

her that he will often betray her. Certainly at the time of seduction it is not his plans, but once he accomplishes his goal he can hardly wait to brag about it.

To the male it is a game. One he hopes to win. He hopes to score or at least get to first base. The boy has less to lose than the girl. If he succeeds he has a sense of accomplishment. On the other hand, he cannot get pregnant. His reputation is not as likely to be damaged. In certain adolescent, teenage and adult groups a boy's or man's reputation is enhanced when it is known that he has made out or gone all the way with some girl. This raises his prestige in his peer group.[3]

A high-principled boyfriend doesn't try to steal what doesn't rightfully belong to him. He refuses to exploit his date with such lines as "If you love me, you'll prove it" which not only shows a lack of love on his part, but also asks the girl to participate with him in sin. Or "How do you know if you're passionate, unless you experiment?" which proves nothing because the embrace of passionate love differs from the embrace of sensuous lust. Or "Come on and have some fun" which leads to misery and guilty feelings because sexual activity doesn't equal sexual enjoyment. Or "Let's find out if we're compatible" because the lack of commitment to a lasting marriage makes the test results unreliable. Or "Everybody is doing it" because true Christians aren't doing it.

Many a young girl fails to realize the value of her purity to a responsible man. When a girl permits a boy to taste her sexual favors before marriage, she loses her self-respect, respect from the boy, and respect from her future husband. A wise girl who cares about herself puts the same stipulations on her body that the Shulammite put on hers. If a young man willingly assumes the responsibilities of a husband by providing, leading, and protecting her as his wife, then after their marriage, lovemaking blesses their union. Then if sexual problems arise after marriage, acceptance of

[3]Pettus, *As I See Sex Through the Bible*, p. 33.

their responsibilities helps them achieve compatibility through study and application of God's word.

The Shepherd demonstrates his love for the Shulammite by expecting her to save herself for him until marriage. Sexual love provides one of the most happy and enjoyable experiences on earth when entered into under the proper conditions--those established by God when He designed the sexual union. When sexual contact deteriorates into a sensuous affair, it often becomes one of the most miserable and frustrating relationships that a man and woman ever experience.

Thus, the Shepherd reveals the secret for finding sexual satisfaction with a woman--honest respect for her. Minds and bodies cannot blend into harmony and sexual bliss unless respect reigns. The Shepherd places a high value on womanhood and the duties of a woman. The Shulammite's womanly qualities make her dear to him. The Shepherd finds in her a helper who is meet for him and who chases away all his loneliness.

F. MAKE A GOOD MOTHER

> **Song of Sol. 4:13-14: "Your shoots are an orchard [park or paradise--NASV footnote] of pomegranates with choice fruits, henna with nard plants, nard and saffron, calainus and cinnamon, with all the trees of frankincense, myrrh and aloes, along with all the finest spices."**

The Jews often referred to their children as "plants" or "shoots." For example, Ps. 128:3 says, "Your wife shall be like a fruited vine, within your house, your children like olive plants around your table."

The Shepherd thinks the Shulammite possesses excellent qualifications for becoming a loving mother. He tells her that he wants her to be the mother of his children as he refers to their children as pomegranates, henna, nard plants, affron, calainus, cinnamon, and trees of frankincense, myrrh, and aloes.

One student remarked, "It sounds like the Shepherd wants to have a lot of children!"

By referring to their children as different plants, the Shepherd recognizes the uniqueness of each child and the individual care required. Each plant that he names denotes a valuable service--some provide food, others supply dyes, others serve as spices, and others furnish perfumed ointments. The Shepherd confidently believes that each child will receive the proper care and loving guidance necessary to grow up into a useful, productive adult at the hands of the Shulammite.

Not only will their children become valuable citizens, but the Shepherd also knows assuredly that the Shulammite will transform their home into an "orchard" or, "a park or paradise." What a woman! Not only will the Shulammite raise their children to be a credit to her, but she will make their home a paradise at the same time. The Shepherd expects to live in a well-run, organized orchard--not some run-down garden patch with weeds taking over. What a challenge to a woman!

G. HIS SOURCE OF LIFE

> Song of Sol. 4:15: "You are a garden spring, a well of fresh water, and streams flowing from Lebanon."

In addition to using springs and wells to refer to sexual favors, the Jews also used water to symbolize a life-sustaining quality. For example, God referred to Himself as a "fountain of living waters" which the Jews had forsaken (Jer. 2:13). Jesus called Himself living waters (Jn. 7:37-38).

The Shepherd sums up his proposal by declaring that the Shulammite is a garden spring, a well of fresh water, and streams flowing from Lebanon. Just as men go to springs for nourishment and to quench their thirst, he seeks her. Likewise, as men enjoy the beautiful streams of water that cascade into waterfalls down the slopes of Lebanon, so he finds refreshment for his spirit with her. Her purity, her feminine ways, her mothering qualities, and her industry all combine to make her his own private cistern of clear bubbling waters. The Shepherd knows that after marriage he will come to her time and time again to drink from her refreshing waters and be satisfied.

Gilder explains in his book, *Men and Marriage*, that statistics show that marriage increases a man's life span. He goes on to show just how wives give length of days to their husbands lives:

Single men have almost double the mortality rate of married men and three times the mortality rate of single women from all causes: from automobile accidents and other mishaps, as well as from the whole range of conventional diseases. Most of the illnesses do not become evident until after age forty-five.

In analyzing the high death rate of single men, sociologists normally focus on the bachelors' lack of the kind of "personal maintenance" married men enjoy from their wives. Sexual liberals talk of the failure of sexist society to teach male children how to cook and take care of themselves. But the maintenance theories are inadequate to explain the all-encompassing reach of single male afflictions. Altogether the pattern of mortality among single men is so various and inexorable that it suggests an organic source: *a failure of the will to live,* [emphasis added--PRD] a disconnection from the life force itself as it arises in society.[4]

Then Gilder sums up his discussion of how badly men need wives just to give purpose to their lives and to spur them on to greater accomplishments in the workforce:

In short, when a man, accepting an honor at the company banquet--or prefacing a book--gives much of the credit to his wife, he is not merely following a ritual. He is stating a practical fact. In all likelihood he would not have succeeded--and possibly not even have survived--if he had been single or divorced.[5]

Thus, through the words of inspired scripture, the poor Shepherd recognizes the Shulammite as his source of life. For she gives him enthusiasm, purpose, and encouragement to do his best as he subdues the earth.

[4]Gilder, *Men and Marriage,* pp. 65-66.
[5]Gilder, *Men and Marriage,* p. 66.

When he lacks courage, she points out his strengths. When he suffers defeat, she dwells on his successes. When he worries, she soothes him with her confidence in his leadership. Whatever he needs, she willingly supplies. In this way, she adds meaning and purpose to his daily life and becomes his source of life.

The Shepherd's beautiful proposal of marriage speaks to the deepest longings of every feminine woman--her desire to be needed and appreciated for her womanly qualities. With such words of love and need stirring within her bosom, the Shulammite makes an important promise to herself:

IV. THE SHULAMMITE'S PROMISE

Two men love the Shulammite, but for different reasons. One loves her body; the other loves her person. The Shulammite must make the choice that every bride must make. She must choose between sensuous love with Solomon or pure love with the Shepherd. While the choice seems easy to modern readers, the Shulammite is emotionally involved in her dilemma. She's living it, and the choice is not so easy for her. Nor is the choice easy *for any girl* in the midst of dating and strange new feelings of love and passion rising within her breast.

So the Shulammite chooses first to remain true to herself. Even though Solomon's flattery and offers of splendor please her, deep in her heart she wants a marriage built upon true love and blessed with children. Thus, the Shulammite makes an important promise to herself, a promise which every young girl should, likewise, make to herself:

A. TO EMBRACE FEMININITY

> **Song of Sol. 4:16: "Awake, O north wind, and come, wind of the south; make my garden breathe out fragrance, let its spices be wafted abroad. May my beloved come into his garden and eat its choice fruits!"**

Every young girl has a reputation in regard to her future as a wife. People look at some girls and say, "She'll make some fellow a good wife when she mar-

ries! I hope she marries someone just as special."
They look at other young women and say, "I feel sorry
for whoever marries her. He won't know what happened
to him!" When they see other maidens, they say, "I
hope she doesn't get married for awhile. She still has
some growing up to do."

The Shulammite calls to the north and south winds
to spread her reputation as a woman who is ready for
marriage and who will make a good wife. More than
anything, she wants true love and a happy marriage.
She considers herself as valuable as the rose of
Sharon and the lily of the valleys. So she pledges to
herself that she will be a good wife. She will do her
part to create a successful marriage.

Then she visualizes herself succeeding in her
pledge. She says, "Let me get married, and let the man
I marry be glad he married me! Let him eat the choice
fruits that I grow and that I create through loving him,
caring for the children, and overseeing the home. Let
him be so happy, he's beside himself!" The Shulammite
makes this promise to herself even though she doesn't
yet know who she will choose--whether Solomon or the
Shepherd.

Thus, she pledges to be a garden to which her
chosen beloved comes and finds peace and refreshment. She delights in the prospects of becoming a
comforting helper for her husband. Understanding her
feminine role, she begs the north and south winds to
tell everyone what kind of woman she is. Just as they
dreamily carry her perfume in the air to entice her
suitors, let them also broadcast that she will make a
good and faithful wife. If she can just be a wife who
satisfies all of her husband's mental, sexual, and
spiritual needs for companionship--then her life will
be a worthwhile one. She recognizes her potential in
being a wife, mother, and homemaker. She prays that
she might meet that challenge.

Some women feel that their lives are menial when
spent taking care of a husband, children, and a home.
But not the lily of the valleys! She reaches toward the
glory and honor of being a woman and doing a
woman's work. She cheerfully works at developing the
insights and courage necessary to fulfill her role. She
wants to lean and depend upon a husband someday;

and more than anything, she wants him to come to her for comfort and refreshment.

All young girls should adequately prepare for marriage. Yet many spend their school years learning the skills for a man's occupation instead of developing their natural talents for a woman's specialties. To make matters worse, many mothers fail to teach their daughters how to cook, budget grocery money, or clean a house efficiently. Young girls who would rather play than work feel fortunate when their mothers don't make them clean house. But as married women, they seldom appreciate their mothers' negligence. Their husbands show even less gratitude for their wives' inept home-making abilities.

The Shulammite places her hopes in her aptitude for performing her jobs well rather than in her looks or popularity. Physical attractiveness doesn't always endure, and popularity is only as secure as the emotions of the trend setters. Unfortunately, feminine competency is becoming more and more rare, too.

A girl with feminine abilities need not hide her head in shame. Instead, she should boldly call to the north and south winds to advertise her purity of body and mind and her delight and desire to function as a complete woman. Likewise, a girl should promise herself that she will gladly satisfy all of her future husband's emotional, sexual, and spiritual needs for companionship as the Shulammite does when she prays, "May my beloved come into his garden and eat its choice fruits!"

B. TO SUCCEED IN MARRIAGE

> **Song of Sol. 5:1: "I have come into my garden, my sister, my bride; I have gathered my myrrh along with my balsam. I have eaten my honeycomb and my honey; I have drunk my wine and my milk..."**

The Jews used comparisons with perfumes to describe actions which especially pleased others. For example, Paul said, "Walk in love, just as Christ also loved you, and gave Himself up for us, an offering and a sacrifice to God *as a fragrant aroma*" (Eph. 5:2). Paul also wrote, "I have received everything in full, and have an abundance; I am amply supplied, having received from Epaphroditus what you have sent, *a fragrant aroma*, an acceptable sacrifice, well pleasing to God" (Phil. 4:18).

The Shulammite realizes that she holds the power to satisfy all of the Shepherd's desires for a wife. In her mind, she visualizes marriage with him. She hears him tell her how satisfied he is. Indeed, more than satisfied! Happy beyond measure! Not only will she be like a refreshing garden to him, but she will stimulate and please him as the two most precious perfumes in the land, myrrh and balsam, give pleasure.

The Shepherd also tells the Shulammite that he finds honey and a honeycomb with her. The honeycomb and honey refer to the quality of the Shulammite's words since the Shepherd said earlier, "Your lips, my bride, drip honey" (4:11). People who raise bees know that the presence of a honeycomb helps prevent the honey from turning to sugar and keeps the honey usable longer.

The adulteress' lips drip honey (Prov. 5:3) only for the purpose of trapping and exploiting a man. But a wife preserves her sweet words of loving sympathy and understanding *with a honeycomb* to benefit her husband. A man eats his honey and honeycomb when his wife gives him sweet, innocent, honest love twenty-four hours a day, seven days a week. Everyday company manners makes a wife peaceful and pleasant to live with.

The Shulammite also envisions the Shepherd telling her that she is better than wine, for she gives him the highest form of happiness. He finds in her milk, as she becomes his source of life and sustains him throughout the years. He looks forward to growing old with her.

C. TO PLEASE GOD

Song of Sol. 5:1: "...Eat, friends, Drink and imbibe deeply, O lovers."

"Imbibe deeply" means "to become tipsy, in a qualified sense, to satiate with a stimulating drink or (figuratively, influence:--be filled with) drink (abundantly), (be, make) drunk (-en), be merry" (Strong, p. 116).

God, who inspired the recording of this true story, puts His stamp of approval on the proposal of the Shepherd rather than the sensuous proposal of King Solomon. Since the Shulammite and the Shepherd have built their relationship on a firm foundation of true love, God tells them to drink and become drunk on married love. In a marriage built on mutual respect for each other's role in life and inherent abilities, blessings abound from God.

God created marriage and the marriage bed. He created the sexual desires between a husband and wife. God cares about who a person marries, just as He cared about who the Shulammite married. Because of His great love and care for the happiness of men and women, God inspired the Song of Solomon to teach His people how to pick the right marriage partner and how to build a foundation of true love in a marriage. God wants His people to be happy in their marriages. So God tells the Shulammite and the Shepherd, "Get married and get drunk on married love!"

But in spite of God giving His blessing, the Shulammite has not yet accepted the Shepherd as her husband-to-be. She still lives in King Solomon's palace, and she still wrestles with her confusion about who to marry. So after her stroll in the garden to mediate, the Shulammite makes her way back to the palace and to bed. But sleep comes fitfully as her subconscious agonizes over who to marry:

V. A NEW DREAM

This time her dream takes a different form from her previous dreams and torments her in a new way. Before she was still in the country close to the Shepherd. When she dreamed about him, she felt that she could go to him whenever she wanted. Now she is in the city in Solomon's palace while the Shepherd still lives in the country. As a result, she can't go to him as easily as before. Her new dream reflects her uneasiness.

A. HEARS THE SHEPHERD'S VOICE

> Song of Sol. 5:2: "I was asleep, but my heart was awake. A voice! My beloved was knocking: 'Open to me, my sister, my darling, my dove, my perfect one! For my head is drenched with dew, my locks with the damp of the night.'"

In her previous dreams the Shulammite searched for the Shepherd and found him. In this dream, the Shepherd begs the vineyard keeper to marry him and not King Solomon. He addresses her with expressions which befit her dignity: He calls her "my sister"--they share a common background and purpose of life, "My darling"--he wants her to accompany him through life as his lover, "My dove"--he views her as his sanctuary and refuge from the world, and "my perfect one"-- he respects and values her purity.

The Shepherd tells her that his head is drenched with dew and damp from the night which refers to his work as a shepherd. During dry spells, shepherds rose early in the mornings before the sun came up and took their sheep out to graze on the dew-drenched grass. In this way, when the sheep ate the grass, they also got the dew. This satisfied their needs for water. Then after the sun came up, the sheep spent the rest of the day sitting in the shade ruminating.[6]

Obviously, while the Shulammite slept in, the Shepherd went to work early. Now as he comes in from working the night shift, he needs her. He wants her to be the answer to his problems--the one he comes home to. Rather than some passing fancy with him, she is his whole purpose in life. Begging her, he pleads, "Open to me!" He wants the Shulammite to say that she will become his bride and put a sparkle into his life.

B. THE SHULAMMITE RESISTS

> Song of Sol. 5:3: "I have taken off my dress, how can I put it on again? I have washed my feet, how can I dirty them again?"

[6]Keller, *A Shepherd Looks at Psalm 23,* pp. 51-53.

The Shulammite hears the Shepherd's plea, but she is in the palace now, sleeping in a beautiful bedroom all her own. Far away from the familiar sights, sounds, and smells of the country, she easily dismisses her feelings of intense longing for the Shepherd. Solomon has proposed to her, so why should she get excited because the Shepherd can't live without her? Does the Shepherd really want her to give up the glamour and the security of the palace and say, "Yes," to him?

The overwhelming flattery and attention of the King makes her unsure of her feelings. So she resists the Shepherd's plea for her to come back to him. In her dream, the Shulammite tells the Shepherd to go away. She is already in bed and doesn't want to bother getting dressed again. She has already washed her feet so that she won't get her bed dirty (Lk. 11:5-8).

Thus, the Shulammite shows how a girl can get so emotionally involved in a romance that she no longer thinks clearly. Although God and the readers all know that Solomon is the wrong choice, and although she should know it too, she is ready to accept Solomon's proposal. But then something happens to bring her back to her senses:

C. SEES THE SHEPHERD'S HAND

Song of Sol. 5:4: **"My beloved extended his hand through the opening, and my feelings were aroused for him."**

After rejecting the Shepherd, the Shulammite dreams that only his hand reaches in to her, and suddenly all the intense feelings of affection flood back to her. She doesn't need to see his face to know how she feels about him--just the sight of his hand awakens her love for him. She thought that she could forget the Shepherd in the palace, but she realizes that she cannot.

D. OPENS TO THE SHEPHERD

Song of Sol. 5:5: **"I arose to open to my beloved; and my hands dripped with myrrh, and my fingers with liquid myrrh, on the handles of the bolt."**

Now that she knows for sure what her feelings are, the Shulammite jumps up and eagerly runs to let the Shepherd in. On the way to the door, she dips her hands into the liquid myrrh and splashes herself with it. Wearing perfume is such a natural habit with her that even on this spur-of-the-moment event, she quickly makes herself fragrant for her beloved. Happiness and excitement tingle through her! Thus, the Shulammite reaches the turning point of her affections, but she still has problems.

E. THE SHEPHERD LEAVES

> **Song of Sol. 5:6: "I opened to my beloved, but my beloved had turned away and had gone! My heart went out to him as he spoke. I searched for him, but I did not find him; I called him, but he did not answer me."**

By the time the Shulammite decides to open the door, the Shepherd is no longer waiting. She lives in the city now while he lives in the country. Her heart aching with the separation, she searches and calls. But her true love is nowhere to be found.

F. THE WATCHMEN STOP HER

> **Song of Sol. 5:7: "The watchmen who make the rounds in the city found me, they struck me and wounded me; the guardsmen of the walls took away my shawl from me."**

Marriage is a lifetime commitment, not a frivolous adventure to be shared with one partner after another. The full implication of that fact hits the Shulammite when the watchmen stop her. In her previous dream, the watchmen helped her find the Shepherd. Now the situation is different. Once the Shulammite marries Solomon, she can never go back to the Shepherd and his way of life. If she wants the Shepherd, she must decide now before entering a lifelong covenant with the King.

While both the Shepherd and King Solomon earnestly seek a wife to end their loneliness, only the Shepherd searches on the basis of true love. While the Shepherd finds satisfaction of his five senses with the Shulammite, he also makes a commitment to act in her best interest. Likewise, he appreciates the Shulammite's commitment of responsibility toward him.

On the other hand, Solomon cares only about satisfying his five senses. He does not make any commitment to the Shulammite or require any from her except for sexual satisfaction. All he cares about is her body. He thinks that the perfect feminine body will replace the emptiness in his life.

Thus, the Shulammite finally realizes that Solomon is not the one for her in spite of his great wealth and prestige. So she turns to the Shepherd who values her as someone to work alongside him to subdue the earth, to fill it with people, and to glorify God. Even in view of his poverty, he offers her more than Solomon ever could. To Solomon she is a toy, but to the Shepherd she is a valuable person. But the Shulammite is still in Solomon's palace in Jerusalem and the Shepherd is still in the country. What can she do now that she has made up her mind?

———

STUDY EXERCISE

Answer all questions in your own words.
1. What is Solomon's view of marriage?
2. What is the Shepherd's view of marriage?
3. Why should a girl guard her purity?
4. Is purity important for a boy? Why?
5. In what ways did the Shepherd want the Shulammite to function as a woman?
6. Explain how the Shepherd's description of the Shulammite is of universal application in your marriage. You may want to get your husband to help you with this project. However, do not ask for his help unless you sincerely want to know what he thinks.

(1) Enjoys her company.
(2) Treasures the glance of her eyes.

(3) Notices her appearance.
(4) Values her love,
(5) Respects her purity.
(6) Thinks she would make a good mother.
(7) Considers her his source of life.

7. Did God approve of Solomon or the Shepherd? Why?

8. Why did the Shulammite have such a hard time deciding who to marry? Do girls have this same problem today?

9. Do you disagree with anything in this lesson? If so, explain in detail giving scriptures for your reasons.

GOAL–ACHIEVING EXERCISE

Change the following points to fit your individual needs. Review this exercise as you study the next two chapters and make additions as necessary.

Purpose: To increase romance in your marriage by helping love grow naturally and fully and by developing the universal characteristics of the Shulammite.

Goals: To see the look of love and admiration shining in your husband's eyes by achieving the following personal goals:

1. The Shepherd enjoyed her company—develop a pleasant disposition and learn to enjoy your husband's company.

2. The Shepherd treasured the glance of her eyes—make a special effort to let love shine from your eyes every time you look at your husband.

3. The Shepherd noticed her appearance—satisfy your husband's five senses by keeping yourself clean and sweet-smelling and by dressing to please your husband.

4. The Shepherd valued her love—be genuinely concerned about your husband's problems and always act in his best interest. Show affection openly.

5. The Shepherd respected her purity—do not act in a sensuous and provocative manner around other men.

6. The Shepherd thought she would make a good mother--strive to make the home a paradise, no matter how many children you have.

7. The Shepherd considered her his source of life--keep milk and honey along with a honeycomb on your tongue.

Priorities:

1. Always keep your appearance neat, clean, and sweet-smelling when in the presence of your husband.

2. Always be refreshing when your husband comes home by rearranging your schedule where necessary.

3. Keep your evening time free to revive your husband from his day's work.

Plans:

1. Take care of appearance by fixing face, combing hair, and putting on perfume before fixing breakfast and before your husband comes home in the evening. Take a bath if necessary. Even if you have more housework, canning, sewing, etc. to do after your husband comes home, you can still take care of these basic grooming needs and be a pleasant sight at the door and through supper.

2. Take extra steps to please your husband's five senses by overhauling your wardrobe where necessary to please him. For example, some men like for their wives to own several robes for morning wear. You might do some extra sewing. Or you may need to restyle your hair, etc.

3. Lie down for fifteen minutes before your husband comes home to soothe your nerves and to mentally get excited about his homecoming. Greet him at the door in a pleasing and happy manner with the look of love in your eyes. After all, he worked all day for you and needs you to be his dove.

4. Have the house picked up and the children quiet and calm when your husband comes home. Fix supper on time and allow the whole family to relax together for an hour or more.

5. Continue to set aside a time everyday for Bible study and prayer.

CHAPTER 11

THE EMPTINESS OF SENSUOUS LOVE

After a night of tossing and turning and dreaming, the Shulammite realizes that she can't sell the chance for true love with the Shepherd for all of King Solomon's money and prestige. However, her problems aren't over. She must let the Shepherd know that she wants to marry him. And she must also tell King Solomon that she cannot marry him. It won't be an easy day for the young vineyard keeper.

First, she finds the maidens who wait upon Solomon and tells them of her choice:

I. THE SHULAMMITE'S CHOICE

Song of Sol. 5:8: "I adjure you, O daughters of Jerusalem, if you find my beloved, as to what you will tell him: for I am lovesick."

The Shulammite lets the maidens know in no uncertain terms that she no longer enjoys the attentions of the King. She is lovesick for the Shepherd, the one she wants to marry with all her heart.

Then as the Jews customarily sent friends of the bride to communicate with the groom, she begs the maidens to promise to send word to the Shepherd for her. She implores them to tell him that she chooses him over Solomon. Tell him, she pleads, that she is in anguish with love for him and for him to please come get her.

A. HER BELOVED

Song of Sol. 5:9: "What kind of beloved is your beloved, O most beautiful among women? What kind of beloved is your beloved, thus you adjure us?"

The maidens cannot believe what they hear. So they ask the Shulammite what kind of man is her beloved to cause her to give up Solomon. Surely, no man deserves such a sacrifice! What kind of a woman yearns for a shepherd over a king? A silly one, no doubt! They view the Shulammite with the same disdain that popular girls regard a girl who turns down a date with the captain of the football team or the president of the student council to date an obscure, poor boy.

In the same way, girls of loose morals and low ideals often ridicule other girls who save themselves for their husbands. Yet girls with high standards place more value on the happiness of their whole lives than on the few passing pleasures of the courting years.

Ignoring their taunting, the Shulammite answers the maidens with an impressive description of the Shepherd which provides universal application for every husband. For she describes a woman's attitude when true love fills her heart. Therefore, if a woman cannot feel this same way about the man she wants to marry, she should carefully ponder whether or not she really loves him.

Likewise, if a married woman doesn't view her husband in this same way, she needs to work on her attitudes. A marriage cannot be all that God desires if a woman doesn't manifest these attitudes toward her husband. Fortunately, a wife can learn these attitudes after marriage.

B. OUTSTANDING AMONG TEN THOUSAND

Song of Sol. 5:10: "My beloved is dazzling and ruddy, outstanding among ten thousand."

The Shulammite esteems the Shepherd as the greatest man that ever lived! "Why," she says, "you can line up ten thousand of the best men, and none of them can compete with him! You can pick him out in an instant! He's the most perfect man that ever lived!"

Older women often respond, "That's what all young girls think when they're dating. It's easy to think that when you're in love. But after they get married, they find it's not so easy to think that anymore!"

Yet God commands wives to reverence or respect their husbands in Eph. 5:33. Reverence basically means to go beyond the limit in esteeming the person. *While optional before marriage, reverence becomes mandatory after marriage.* Even if the husband is not a Christian, God still expects the wife to show reverence for her husband ("respect"--I Pet. 3:1-2). A woman who doesn't adore her husband beyond measure before marriage may find this command hard to obey after marriage.

However, to the degree that a woman truly reverences her husband, to that same degree she experiences a wonderful marriage. All husbands absolutely must have their wives' honest appreciation before they can fulfill their potential as providers and loving, caring husbands. For these reasons, a woman should choose her husband so that she will enjoy obeying all of God's laws after marriage.

Reverence is such an important ingredient of a successful love relationship that *Vol. II: Learning to Love* devotes a whole chapter, "Satisfying the Man with Reverence" to discussing the mechanics of obeying it. True reverence increases both the husband and wife's delight in each other sexually.

After stating how much she admires the Shepherd, the Shulammite begins to describe him and to give details which prove that he is outstanding. First she turns to his appearance which satisfies her five senses. Then she talks about his character and his commitment of accepting responsibility for her.

C. IMPRESSIVE APPEARANCE

Song of Sol. 5:11-15: "His hand [head--KJV] is like gold, pure gold; his locks are like clusters of dates, and black as a raven. His eyes are like doves, beside streams of water, bathed in milk, and reposed in their setting. His cheeks are like a bed of balsam, banks of sweet-scented herbs; his lips are lilies,

dripping with liquid myrrh. His hands are rods of gold set with beryl; his abdomen is carved ivory inlaid with sapphires. His legs are pillars of alabaster set on pedestals of pure gold; his appearance is like Lebanon, choice as the cedars."

While this poetic description easily fits Charles Atlas, it also portrays a ninety-six pound weakling who possesses an important quality of true masculinity--respect for hard work. When a man uses his body to provide for his wife and to protect her from harm, he makes her rich. Her wealth doesn't depend upon the size of his paycheck, but on his ability and desire to work. The Shepherd savors honest labor. Thus, any man who takes his place among men should fit this manly description in the eyes of his wife. The Shulammite glories in the Shepherd's appearance of masculinity.

Most translators render verse 11 "his head is like gold, pure gold," but a few translate it "his hand." Since the rest of the sentence definitely talks about the Shepherd's head and his hands aren't mentioned until verse 14, "head" fit the context and pattern of the description better than "hand."

So the Shulammite describes her beloved from the top of his head all the way down to the bottom of his feet. Then beginning with his head she says that it is "like pure gold" and his locks are "like clusters of dates and black as a raven." In other words, she admires his lustrous, curly, black hair. In this day of changing hair styles, many claim that the way a man wears his hair is unimportant. Yet the Shulammite notices the Shepherd's hair and is impressed. The apostle Paul says in I Cor. 11:4-15 that a man's hair reveals his masculinity, for long hair is a glory to a woman, but letting the hair grow dishonors a man.

The Shepherd's eyes remind the Shulammite of "doves" because peace and tranquility radiate from them. She feels enveloped in softness and tenderness when he looks at her. A woman should not feel uncomfortable or out of place when the man she loves gazes at her. One way a man shows his love for a woman is by the way he looks at her.

His eyes appear to be "beside streams of water, bathed in milk," for the whites of his eyes make the blue appear brighter. While the Shulammite's basic description provides universal application for all husbands, she points out some individual characteristics that especially appeal to her--his ruddy complexion, curly black hair, and blue eyes. She likes the unique way he looks. Yet other women find different physical characteristics attractive. For example, a woman might find red hair and brown eyes along with a fair complexion becoming.

Even though related, balsam and myrrh contain one main difference. The Jews usually extracted balsam in an oil form while they made myrrh into a liquid to add to other ingredients. Thus, the expression "his cheeks are like a bed of balsam, banks of sweet-scented herbs" seems to refer to the oil he puts on his face in the manner of the Jews who oiled their heads and faces to protect them from the sun. One commentator suggested that the words "bed" and "banks" of herbs refer to his beard. Whether he sports a beard or not, she likes his grooming habits and the way he smells.

The expression "his lips are lilies, dripping with liquid myrrh" probably refers to the shape of his lips and to the use of a sweet-smelling mouthwash. Since myrrh had a very bitter taste, the Jews usually mixed it with something else. Mark mentions myrrh mixed with wine in Mk. 15:23 as being the drink offered to Jesus when He hung upon the cross. The parallel passage in Mt. 27:34 describes the same drink in the King James translation as "vinegar mingled with gall." This combination sounds very much like modern mouthwashes that are made of alcohol and perfumes and still taste terrible.

The Jews lavishly used perfumes for everything from anointing their heads, faces, feet, clothes, and beds to carrying sprigs of flowers for added fragrance. The men used scents as much as the women. In effect, the Shulammite tells the maidens that her beloved smells sweet and clean instead of dirty and sweaty.

The Shepherd's fingers are as "rods of gold" with "beryl" fingernails in the Shulammite's love-colored picture. Rods symbolize strength and protection whether used by a shepherd to protect his sheep or by a peasant to hold the front door of his home closed. A mechanic's hands often appear rough and stained with grease, but since he earns a living with them, they look beautiful to an appreciative wife. A doctor's hands frequently seem soft and smooth, but they emulate precious gold if they provide for a wife and protect her from harm.

Describing the hippopotamus in Job 40:16, God said, "Behold now, his strength in his loins, and his power in the muscles of his belly." When the Shulammite says that the Shepherd's "abdomen was like carved ivory inlaid with sapphires," she no doubt refers to his muscular chest and self-confident posture. Certainly, muscles developed through hard work represent strength and power.

The Jews considered alabaster as the best possible material for making vases for precious perfumes. Oils stored in alabaster jars often retained their fragrances for an indefinite period of time. In fact, archaeologists verified this trait of alabaster when they opened some of the ancient tombs of Egypt. Four-thousand-year-old jars often contained sweet-smelling substances as fragrant as the day they were poured. Thus, the Shulammite describes the Shepherd's legs as "pillars of alabaster"--dependable and capable of doing their work.

Pure gold, refined with fire to remove all impurities, symbolizes guiltlessness along with preciousness throughout the whole Bible as in Job 23:10 and I Pet. 1:7. To the Shulammite, the Shepherd's whole person and character rest solidly on his righteous conduct, for she describes his feet as "pedestals of pure gold." In fact, she began her description with the same observation: "his head is like gold, like pure gold." From head to toe, the Shepherd presents a picture of godly masculinity.

Then the Shulammite summarizes his physical description by stating "his appearance is like Lebanon, choice as the cedars." Dr. William Smith explains the significance of cedars of Lebanon:

> ...firmly rooted and strong tree,...the cedar of Lebanon, as being the firmest and grandest of the conifers. As far as is at present known, the cedar of Lebanon is confined in Syria to one valley of the Lebanon range, viz., that of the Kedisha river, which flows from near the highest point of the range westward to the

Mediterranean, and enters the sea at the port of Tripoli. The grove is at the very upper part of the valley, about 15 miles from the sea, 6500 feet above that level, and its position is moreover about that of all other arboreous vegetation.[1]

A very impressive, scenic, snow-capped mountain range, Lebanon combines with the rare cedars that grow there to make the Shulammite's description even more emphatic--no one compares to the Shepherd! She began by telling the maidens that the Shepherd was "outstanding among ten thousand." Now as if being distinguished among men were not enough, the Shulammite ends her physical description by saying that the Shepherd equals the most majestic and awesome sight in nature--the strong, beautiful rare cedars standing tall and proud on Lebanon. The Shepherd embraces all of manhood: His appearance and manner suggest strength, determination, purity, dependability, resourcefulness, endurance, and wealth in character.

Together, the Shulammite and the Shepherd represent femininity and masculinity as described in Prov. 11:6: "A gracious woman attains honor, and violent [strong--KJV] men attain riches." (Review chapters 7 and 8 for a discussion of this verse.) The Shulammite graciously offers comfort in all realms, for the Shepherd views her as a refreshing garden stream. The Shepherd presents a picture of strength as a wise leader, protector, and provider for the Shulammite. Together, they possess all the qualities necessary for a successful marriage and to subdue the earth and fill it with people.

D. WHOLLY DESIRABLE

Song of Sol. 5:16: "His mouth is full of sweetness. And he is wholly desirable..."

"Desirable" means "delightful, hence a delight, i.e. object of affection or desire:--beloved, desire, goodly, lovely, pleasant (thing)" (Strong, p. 64).

[1]Smith, *Dictionary of the Bible*, pp. 101-102.

The Shulammite tells the maidens that the Shepherd's mouth is full of sweetness. Just as bad body odors turn most men off, they also turn off most women. Women often complain in the lovelorn columns about their husbands coming to bed smelling bad, but expecting their wives to be warm, receptive, and eager for closeness.

Many people today falsely assume that since body odors are a natural part of humanity, people should just ignore them. Some claim that the men and women in ancient days lived with such smells, so to be natural and to go back to the "good old days," people should not worry about foul odors.

With the naturalists' scorn for defying nature with baths and perfume to make the body appealing to the spouse, many people feel confused about how much attention to pay to grooming. However, an important occupation of the Jews three thousand years ago was that of the perfumer as mentioned in Neh. 3:8. Other historical evidence verifies that ancient, civilized men lavishly used perfume and perfected elaborate methods of making it.

Taking baths is not a modern invention, either. Unfortunately, according to Stuart Babbage in his book, *Sex and Sanity,* man's ignorance during the Dark Ages of the purpose of sexual intercourse in a Christian's life led men to fear taking a bath:

> There were some monks who regarded it as a snare, if not a sin, to bathe, because of the danger of seeing themselves undressed. Athanasius boasted that Anthony "never changed his vest nor washed his feet," and his example was held up for pious emulation. Cleanliness of the body, it was held, was the pollution of the soul. Antonius proudly related that such was the holy asceticism of Simeon Stylites that when he walked, vermin dropped from his body. "The church killed the bath," Havelock Ellis accuses.[2]

[2]Stuart Barton Babbage, *Sex and Sanity, A Christian View of Sexual Morality* (Philadelphia: The Westminster Press, 1965), p. 15, quoting Herbert Workman, *The Evolution of the Monastic Ideal*, pp. 63-64.

In their fierce determination to subdue the body and to escape the enticements of the flesh, these ascetics systematically neglected hygiene and health. What W. E. H. Lecky bluntly calls this "hideous maceration of the body" found its horrifying culmination in Origen's barbaric act of self-emasculation.[3]

Ironically, the same group of religious leaders who regarded the Song of Solomon as an immoral book, also considered taking a bath a sin. Their abhorrence of a relationship that originated within the mind of God to bless husbands and wives led them to many strange and extreme practices, even the mutilation of their own bodies.

However, studying the Song of Solomon clears up questions concerning the proper attitude toward fragrant hygiene. Both the Shulammite and the Shepherd keep themselves sweet-smelling to enhance their desirability to the other. Both of them, in the pages of inspired scripture, notice the efforts of the other and express appreciation.

In fact, the Song of Solomon begins with the Shulammite saying, "May he kiss me with the kisses of his mouth!" and adds, "Your oils have a pleasing fragrance" (1:2-3). Any man who fails to learn the lesson that the Shepherd teaches about satisfying a woman's five senses should not be surprised if his wife acts less than enthusiastic when he makes advances.

The wife of such a man should tell her husband in a kind and dignified way that this causes a problem. Likewise, a man should let his wife know when it presents a problem for him. Wise husbands and wives understand that some people possess a more sensitive sense of smell than others. Thus, one spouse may be offended by odors that the other partner doesn't even notice. Surely, removing all unpleasantness for the spouse reaps many benefits in the bedroom.

To reinforce these good habits, the Shepherd and the Shulammite frequently tell each other how much

[3]Babbage, *Sex and Sanity*, p. 15, quoting William H. Lecky, *History of European Morals from Augustus to Charlemagne*, ii, p. 107.

they enjoy the other's fragrant oils. Without any hesitation, they both look forward to all that the embrace of love promises them in marriage.

To the Shulammite, the Shepherd is completely desirable with nothing repulsive or detestable about him. She looks forward to satisfying his physical needs because he is the object of her own sexual desires. Love builds within her a desire to give her whole self to him.

If a woman does not share this feeling of the Shulammite before marriage, she should search for the source of the problem and correct it, whether by changing her attitudes toward sexual love or by realizing that she simply doesn't love the man. A man needs more than a female body to find satisfaction. He needs sexual warmth and playful seduction from his wife.

A woman who fails to understand God's place for the sexual union in marriage or who feels emotionally cold toward the man she plans to marry weakens the foundation of her marriage and may cause the whole structure to crumble. She also shows a lack of sympathy and understanding for her future husband because her indifference will deprive him of the sheer ecstasy of mutually sharing love in each other's arms.

Likewise, if *a married woman* fails to enjoy making love, she needs to examine her attitudes toward sexual love and her husband, and then correct them. If she has fallen out of love, she must reactivate love before sexual intercourse will give her full pleasure. While a woman can kill love or allow it to die through neglect, she can also rekindle it.

E. HER BELOVED AND HER FRIEND

Song of Sol. 5:16: "...This is my beloved and this my friend, O daughters of Jerusalem."

"Friend" means "an associate more or less close)." It comes from a root word which means "to tend a flock, i.e. pasture it, to graze, generally to rule, to associate with (as a friend)" (Strong, p. 109).

Too many times lovers are only lovers--not friends. For a marriage to survive the bad times as well as the good, the lovers must also be true friends.

They must delight in each other and enjoy each other's company during the day as well as during the night. They must trust each other enough to confide their deepest secrets to one another.

The Shulammite shares such a relationship with the Shepherd. He genuinely cares about her welfare and doesn't exploit her for his own selfish purposes. She pleads with him to be a man, to take the lead, to protect her, and to provide for her. She feels no fear of his leadership over her because he is not drunk with power. He will not dominate her as a tyrant, nor talk to her as to a child, nor treat her as a feeble-minded slave. She can confidently place herself in his care because he is full of sweetness, kindness, and consideration, and because he is her friend.

One of the greatest causes of marriage problems is an inability to talk with the spouse. If the couple talks to each other, they can solve some problems in one hour. But without communication, simple problems grow worse. Courtship presents the best time to learn how to talk and to build a friendship before problems become serious. God created husbands and wives to treat each other like bosom buddies.

On the other hand, the advice columns contain letter after letter from young women who want to know the wisdom of marrying someone whom they argue with all the time. If a woman fears a man or feels uncomfortable in his presence before marriage, she had better not marry him. Many people put forth their best behavior during courtship only to revert to old habits after marriage. Before marriage, a woman should say with the Shulammite, "His mouth is full of sweetness. And he is wholly desirable. This is my beloved and this is my friend."

During the espousal of a Jewish maiden and young man, the couple avoided seeing each other. They did all of their communication through friends of the bride and the bridegroom who made all the wedding preparations.[4] Thus, the Shulammite implores the maidens to find the Shepherd for her and to tell him that she is ready to marry him. Now after listening to such a beautiful description of her beloved, the maidens are

[4]Smith, *Dictionary of the Bible,* pp. 382-383.

eager to befriend the Shulammite and to find the Shepherd for her.

II. THE MARRIAGE PREPARATIONS BEGIN

Song of Sol. 6:1: "Where has your beloved gone, O most beautiful among women? Where has your beloved turned, that we may seek him with you?"

As the friends of the bride, it becomes the maidens' job to find the Shepherd and to bring him back. Then following the custom of the Jews, the Shulammite will accompany the Shepherd back to his home in the country and to the actual marriage ceremony.[5] So the maidens ask where the Shulammite's beloved has gone so that they may bring him to her.

A. THE SHEPHERD'S WORK

Song of Sol. 6:2: "My beloved has gone down to his garden, to the beds of balsam, to pasture his flock in the gardens and gather lilies."

The Shulammite knows exactly where to find her beloved. As a responsible person, he is surely taking care of his flocks.

A wise girl looks for this same characteristic in her future husband. If he works steadily as a dependable worker, he probably won't require her to forsake her feminine role to help him earn a living. On the other hand, if he does as little as possible, she may end up supporting him.

One young woman felt uneasy about the work habits of a college-age boy who proposed to her. She said that he habitually worked for a few months, then quit his job and lived on his earnings for the next several month. When his money ran out, he looked for another job and worked for a few more months. This pattern repeated itself over and over again. When he asked the girl to marry him, she told him that she didn't want to live that way. The boy promised her

[5]Smith, *Dictionary of the Bible*, pp. 382-383.

that after marriage he would change his lifestyle. But the girl wisely decided not to take a chance on him. Deeply ingrained during childhood, work habits often require much effort to change them. Promises made before marriage are often forgotten afterwards if they are not a natural part of the person.

Many parents become upset when their daughters marry lazy, shiftless men. With forethought, however, parents can often avoid such a tragedy. Parents can instill both respect for work in their children, and also delight in associating with hard-working people.

My father did this without ever lecturing any of his children. Not only did he set an example of hard work himself, but at mealtimes he praised his employees who delighted in good, honest labor. I remember him bragging about a high school boy who always saw jobs that needed to be done and did them without being asked. My father's verbal appreciation of the boy's industry made me desire to do the same quality of work.

When I began dating my future husband, Sam, I asked my father to give him a job during wheat harvest. My father agreed on one condition: If my boyfriend was not a hard worker, then that would be the end of him. I agreed to the bargain, but I didn't tell Sam so that it would be a fair test. Only after we were married did I tell him about the test he passed. Thus, my father prevented me from entering into a marriage that could have made me unhappy.

One father said, "Before my daughter begins to date and becomes emotionally involved with boys, I plan to take her out to dinner from time to time to discuss what kind of man would make the best husband. It should be easy to help her think through her plans and to get her to agree that her future husband must possess certain qualities." Before emotions become aroused and create a chance for feelings to be hurt, a father and daughter can make a pact to find the best possible husband for her. Mothers can help their sons choose a good wife in much the same way.

However, if parents wait until their children begin dating to try to teach them how to choose a marriage partner, they may find that their children will reject any suggestions they make. Parents should begin preparing their children for marriage before they even begin school. The Song of Solomon presents the perfect beginning place.

B. BELONG TO EACH OTHER

Song of Sol. 6:3: "I am my beloved's and my beloved is mine, he who pastures his flock among the lilies."

The Shulammite and the Shepherd share kindred hearts, minds, and purposes--they belong together. A bond of mutual love and respect surrounds them so that no one else can intrude. True love offers a man and woman the highest form of happiness throughout their life together.

III. SOLOMON'S THIRD PROPOSAL

The night before Solomon had given the Shulammite time to think while she strolled in the garden. While there she remembered the Shepherd's proposal and how it differed from Solomon's. That night she fretted over a dream about life without the Shepherd. Then early the next morning she sent the maidens to find the Shepherd and to tell him that she wanted to marry him.

Later that same morning Solomon requests that the Shulammite come to him. More than likely, she finds him in a large ornate room. Whether or not he knows that she has already sent for the Shepherd, Solomon tries a third time to convince her to marry him. He also wants her to meet all of his other wives and concubines seated around him. More than anything, he wants to persuade the Shulammite maiden to enter his harem. He boldly describes her with flattering and erotic terms of passion--the best proposal sensuous love can ever make. With all his might, he attempts to seduce her.

In spite of all of his wealth, prestige, and glory, Solomon illustrates perfectly how to fail in love and marriage. Sensuous love thrives on the external and superficial, but lacks depth to sustain it over a long period of time. Thus, the shallowness of Solomon's proposal:

A. AS BEAUTIFUL AS TIRZAH

> **Song of Sol. 6:4: "You are as beautiful as Tirzah, my darling, as lovely as Jerusalem, as awesome as an army with banners."**

Tirzah and Jerusalem, two of the royal cities, attracted crowds of people just as beautiful cities today appeal to tourists. Solomon knows that the people will make special trips to view his latest wife who is as awesome as an army with banners. And just as people stop to watch an army parade by with flying flags, the people will stop to gaze upon the Shulammite when Solomon leads her around the city. Solomon wants to marry the Shulammite so he can display her as a trophy that will make everyone jealous of him.

B. HER EYES CONFUSE SOLOMON

> **Song of Sol. 6:5: "Turn your eyes away from me, for they have confused me;..."**

The Shulammite's eyes dishearten Solomon as he begins his flattering plea to her, for he no longer sees the look of eager trust shining in her eyes. Before the Shulammite completely committed herself to the Shepherd, the King's flattery charmed her. Now at last, she is immune to Solomon's smooth, polished words. However, since Solomon usually sees women swooning before his graceful speech, the Shulammite's lack of interest confuses him. So he asks the country lass to turn her eyes from him. He doesn't want to forget his lines before he can finish his prepared proposal.

In contrast, the Shepherd told the Shulammite, "You have made my heart beat faster with a single glance of your eyes" (Song of Sol. 4:9). The look of love and admiration radiating from the Shulammite's eyes turned him on. It made him want to be with her and to partake of her comforting nature.

A woman often reveals her feelings to a man by the way she looks at him. When a young girl really loves her suitor, other men don't interest her at all. As long as other men can turn her head, she is not ready for marriage. Girls often write the advice columnists about what do when they're engaged to one man and still want to date others. While such a girl's fiance might be deeply hurt if she breaks the engagement, her desire to date others exposes her lack of readiness for marriage.

C. EXCEEDINGLY BEAUTIFUL

> Song of Sol. 6:5-7: "...Your hair is like a flock of goats that have descended from Gilead. Your teeth are like a flock of ewes which have come up from their washing, all of which bear twins, and not one among them has lost her young. Your temples are like a slice of a pomegranate behind your veil."

Solomon continues his description after the Shulammite turns her eyes away. No ordinary beauty, her features appear perfect in every way. Oh, she is the most beautiful woman Solomon has ever seen!

But something seems wrong. Didn't Solomon describe her in this same sensuous way when he first brought her to his palace (Song of Sol. 4:1-5)? He speaks as if he knows the words by heart. Can this be just a line that he perfected on other women? Solomon's next words take away the mystery:

D. ONLY SIXTY WIVES

> Song of Sol. 6:8-9: "There are sixty queens and eighty concubines, and maidens without number; but my dove, my perfect one, is unique: she is her mother's only daughter; she is the pure child of the one who bore her."

At this time Solomon has *only* sixty queens, eighty concubines, and maidens without number waiting to go into his chambers. The queens differ from the concubines in that concubines are always slaves while the queens or wives are free women like the Shulammite. Sometimes the concubines belong to the wives who rule over them. Any children born to a concubine also belong to her mistress. The stories of Leah, Rachel, and Sarah provide examples of these differences.

However, Solomon assures the Shulammite that now he can quit looking for satisfaction in variety and new thrills. The vineyard keeper is, indeed, the best wife he could ever find. He insists that she differs from all his other wives--she is perfect, unique, the best of her mother's daughters.

What a line Solomon feeds the Shulammite! All his other wives failed to satisfy him for long, but he promises the Shulammite, "It will be different with you!" How many times has he used this same line? Probably as many times as he used the one to describe her beauty--sixty queens plus eighty concubines equals one hundred and forty wives plus maidens without number! Can the Shulammite believe him? Dare any woman believe any man who tells her, "It'll be different with you"?

Solomon makes the dilemma of sensuous love obvious. At this time, he has one hundred and forty wives to satisfy his needs, but none of them can hold his interest for long. He probably *honestly believes* that the Shulammite maiden will end his search for fulfillment and happiness. He hopes that she will be the one to end his loneliness and frustrations.

Solomon spent his whole life thoroughly testing sensuous love. He enjoyed access to the most beautiful women in the known world from the daughters of kings to peasants to slaves. Neither did he lack in money to spend on them. If any man could ever succeed at sensuous love, Solomon should have been that man.

In his search for the perfect feminine body, Solomon eventually married "seven hundred wives, princesses, and three hundred concubines"--one thousand women in all! (I Ki. 11:3) Instead of making Solomon happy, his multitude of wives turned his heart away from God. If one thousand of the most beautiful and desirable women could not satisfy the needs of a man who founded his marriages upon sensuous desires, it is folly for two people to build their own marriage on a sensuous foundation. Thus, modern couples don't have to go through life looking for the most perfect body because Solomon has already demonstrated the emptiness of sensuous love.

Solomon's search for true love and his resulting harem seen unreal to the average man and woman. Yet many modern men of wealth and prestige try to find happiness with the same formula that Solomon used. Perhaps the most famous in recent year was the multi-billionaire Howard Hughes. Soon after his death, the newspapers and magazines published articles about his habits and lifestyle. He resembles Solomon in a remarkable, but tragic way.

For example, Howard Hughes used women in much the same way that Solomon did, but he employed modern technology to locate the most perfect bodies know to man. When Hughes found a picture in the newspapers or magazines of a woman with all the right dimensions, he launched a thorough investigation complete with a background study and blown up pictures of her. If the woman still met his specifications, Hughes sent for her. He kept the woman on call twenty-four hours a day to satisfy his sexual desires. Even with this intense and painstaking search to find the perfect body to turn him on, Hughes quickly became bored with the women.

Neither Solomon nor Howard Hughes are fictitious characters, but real, warm-blooded men who spent their whole lifetimes searching for the perfect body with which to find fulfillment and supreme happiness. But all their money, intelligence, and fame were useless in the pursuit of love.

Men of more limited means still try this same formula to a lesser degree by constantly changing girlfriends. Many of them claim that it's impossible for a man to find satisfaction by restricting himself to one sexual partner for the rest of his life. However, countless poor, common, and obscure men succeed where the playboys flounder. *The secret is not in finding the perfect body to make love to, but in truly loving the woman.*

IV. THE QUEENS' PRAISE

Song of Sol. 6:9-10: "...The maidens saw her and called her blessed, the queens and the concubines also, and they praised her, saying, 'Who is this that grows like the dawn, as beautiful as the full moon, as pure as the sun, as awesome as an army with banners?'"

Strangely, the queens and concubines praise the Shulammite who will share their husband and lover if Solomon gets his way. Yet some modern wives, who don't enjoy sexual intercourse, encourage their husbands to read sensuous magazines or to engage in affairs. In fact, Carol Botwin, the author of *Is There Sex After Marriage,* wrote in a recent *Redbook* article that many husbands and wives have an implied understanding that the husband can engage in all the affairs he wants as long as he doesn't embarrass the wife.[6] Some husbands and wives even engage in partner swapping and group sex or sexual orgies. The women Howard Hughes selected agreed to live apart from him and occasionally got together with him. So perhaps these queens and concubines aren't much different from some of the women living today.

If the Shulammite marries Solomon, she must willingly share him with the one hundred and forty women he already has and the maidens without number who await their turns. Solomon definitely is not a one-woman man. He doesn't know how to become emotionally involved with a woman and give her emotional support. Likewise, the women Solomon marries probably aren't able to love on an emotional basis either, thus their approval of the Shulammite.

A girl should determine if her fiance is a one-woman man before marriage rather than risk finding out later that he cannot be true to his vows. When a young man makes a sensuous proposal to a girl, he should realize that she will find it next to impossible to satisfy him completely.

When a relationship rests upon a sensuous foundation, love needs variety and perfected techniques to keep its base from crumbling. A man needs more than a glamorous body for sexual satisfaction. Thus, a sensuous husband places a great burden on his wife to keep him interested in only him. As Solomon observes in Prov. 27:20, the eyes of a man are never satisfied.

However, in praising her, Solomon's wives ask, "Who is this? Why, the more we look at her, the more

[6]Carol Botwin and Edward L. Parsons, M.D., "Good Women, Bad Marriages," *Redbook* (2/87), p. 95.

beautiful she becomes! Tell us who she is! Where did you meet her?"

A. MET IN THE VINEYARDS

> **Song of Sol. 6:11-12:** "I went down to the orchard of nut trees to see the blossoms of the valley, to see whether the vine had budded or the pomegranate had bloomed. Before I was aware, my soul set me over the chariots of my noble people."

Solomon tells the queens and concubines that he met the Shulammite when he went to inspect his orchards. Before he knew what happened, his soul set him over the chariots of his noble people when he saw the young Shulammite maiden. It was love at first sight! Although he felt no emotional attraction for the girl, her beautiful body made Solomon's heart beat faster than the chariots at the races. Her appearance completely captivated him!

Since the Shulammite had already given her heart to the Shepherd, Solomon's sensuous proposal repulses her. When a woman is emotionally involved with a man, the playboy antics and sensuous flattery of other men alienate her. For the first time, the Shulammite understands Solomon's intentions, and she doesn't want to hear any more. Disgusted, she turns to leave the room.

B. BEG HER TO STAY

> **Song of Sol. 6:13:** "Come back, come back, O Shulammite; come back, come back, that we may gaze at you!..."

Solomon, his queens, and concubines can't understand why their flattery fails to impress the Shulammite. Doesn't every woman want to feel needed and appreciated? Who desires her more than they? They beg her, "Come back, come back, that we may gaze at you!"

The plea of Solomon's wives only repulses the Shulammite even more. And she tauntingly throws their sensuousness back at them:

C. WANT ONLY TO LOOK AT HER

Song of Sol. 6:13: "...Why should you gaze at the Shulammite, as at the dance of the two companies?"

The rose of Sharon mocks the queens and concubines by asking if they want to gaze at her in the same way they watch someone dance seductively. Do they only want her to amuse them with her bodily movements? Is she just some toy for them to play with? Is her physical beauty the only thing they care about?

Solomon's wives answer with a resounding "YES! What's wrong with that?" To prove their point, the queens and concubines describe her, showing how perfect she is to dance for them:

D. THE QUEENS' PRAISE

Song of Sol. 7:1-5: "How beautiful are your feet in sandals, O prince's daughter! The curves of your hips are like jewels, the work of the hands of an artist. Your navel is like a round goblet which never lacks mixed wine; your belly is like a heap of wheat fenced about with lilies. Your two breasts are like two fawns, twins of gazelle. Your neck is like a tower of ivory, your eyes like the pools in Heshbon by the gate of Bath-rab-bim; your nose is like the tower of Lebanon, which faces toward Damascus. Your head crowns you like Carmel, and the flowing locks of your head are like purple threads; the king is captivated by your tresses."

Hastening to point out her feminine features, Solomon's wives admire her hips, navel, belly, hands, breasts, neck, eyes, and nose. They can hardly wait to watch her perform in an Oriental seductive dance!

While most people may not find a nose that looks like the tower of Lebanon attractive, various facial features appeal to different peoples. Her flowing long dark hair especially captivates the King. Only a rare man doesn't enjoy a woman's well-kept long hair. "Yes!" they want to gaze at the Shulammite and let her amuse them.

V. SOLOMON'S FOURTH PROPOSAL

After such a tantalizing description of the Shulammite and visualizing her dancing provocatively before him, Solomon tells the young maiden exactly what he wants:

A. HER DELIGHTFUL CHARMS

> Song of Sol. 7:6-7: "How beautiful and how delightful you are, my love, with all your charms! Your stature is like a palm tree, and your breasts are like its clusters."

Solomon excitedly tells the Shulammite, "You're so beautiful! You've got such a sexy body! You've got everything it takes to make a man happy!" Sadly, King Solomon completely overlooks the Shulammite's great wealth of character and focuses only on her looks. What a great pity! In contrast, the Shepherd briefly mentions her looks, but highly praises her ability to perform her feminine role well.

Solomon's feelings revolve entirely around his sensuous lust for the maiden's beautiful body. Comparing her stature to a palm tree, he undoubtedly refers to her stateliness. A woman's posture portrays her inner condition. A slumping, shuffling, indifferent posture indicates boredom and lack of self-respect. A woman who loves life and who enjoys her femininity emits an aura of inner beauty and dignity that charms a man.

B. ONLY WANTS SEX

> Song of Sol. 7:8-9: "I said, 'I will climb the palm tree, I will take hold of its fruit stalks.' Oh, may your breasts be like clusters of the vine, and the fragrance of your breath like apples, and your mouth like the best wine!..."

Solomon's expression "I will climb the palm tree, I will take hold of its fruit stalks" refers to the Oriental method of fertilizing palm trees. Since the male and female flowers were born on separate trees, someone had to climb the female trees and tie some of the pollen-bearing male flowers among their blossoms.[7] Thus, Solomon very graphically says, "I told myself, 'I've just got to go to bed with you!'"

Solomon cares only about sexual intimacies with the Shulammite. Just as playboys today care only about getting well-developed bosoms and bodies into bed, so does Solomon. He thinks that the perfect female body will solve all of his problems. Surely, her beautiful body, breasts, and sweet breath will make the sexual embrace that much more ravishing. In effect, Solomon tells the Shulammite, "Baby, you've got a beautiful body, and we're going to have a wonderful time in bed!"

But the Shulammite thinks differently:

C. THE SHULAMMITE SAYS, NO

Song of Sol. 7:9: "...It goes down smoothly [sweetly--KJV] for my beloved, flowing gently through the lips of those who fall asleep."

"Smoothly" means "evenness, i.e. (figuratively) prosperity or concord, also straightness, i.e. (figuratively) rectitude:--agreement, aright, that are equal, equity, (things that are) right (-eously, things), sweetly, upright (-ly, -ness)" (Strong, p. 66).

"Flowing gently" means "to move slowly, i.e. glide:--cause to speak." It comes from a word which means "to be sluggish, i.e. restful, quiet:--strength" (Strong, p. 29).

"Desire" means "stretching out after, a longing:--desire" (Strong, p. 126).

The King James translation combines the end of Solomon's previous speech with the beginning of the Shulammite's response in one sentence. However, the original Hebrew and Greek manuscripts don't contain

---

[7]Joseph P. Dillow, *Solomon on Sex* (Nashville: Thomas Nelson Publishers, 1977), p. 136.

any punctuation. Thus, the translators must supply punctuation as the context indicates. The scholars who translated the New American Standard version broke verse nine into two speeches and put a period between them.

Even if these scholars did not separate the verse, a careful study of the context reveals that Solomon ceases to speak and the Shulammite responds. For example, throughout the book, only the Shulammite uses the expression "my beloved." But she never addresses Solomon with this tender name. That is one reason why she begged the maidens not to force Solomon upon her--she didn't yet feel any emotional attraction for him. She calls only the Shepherd "my beloved." Since neither the Shepherd nor Solomon use the term "my beloved," the context demands that the last half of verse nine belongs to the Shulammite's speech.

Thus, completely revolted by Solomon's intentions toward her, the Shulammite interrupts his erotic attempts to possess her body. She rebuffs him with, "It goes down smoothly for my beloved." Realizing that Solomon just considers her as a body, a toy, and a technique, she can't stand the thought of his hands on her body.

On the other hand, she appreciates the Shepherd's intentions toward her. He pledges to forsake all others and to live with just her for the rest of his life. He loves her and values her love for him. While looking forward to uniting physically with her, the Shepherd respects her purity and regards her as a clear bubbling spring at which he can refresh himself. He wants her to be the mother of his children, and he has confidence in her ability to make their home a paradise. The Shepherd considers her the source and purpose of his life, while Solomon only views her as a sex object.

Solomon offers the Shulammite everything that sensuous love can offer a woman. But the thought of sexual contact with a man whom she doesn't love or who doesn't love her repulses her. She knows that true love makes sexual intercourse smooth and blissful. What a blow to Solomon's ego! Out of one hundred and forty-one women, only this common vineyard keeper dares to tell him that she can't stand the thought of sexual intimacy with him.

Since "smoothly" refers to "things that are right" and "righteous," the Shulammite describes sexual love as a righteous act for a loving husband and wife to participate in. Lovemaking also presents the perfect means of telling the other, "I love you! I need you! And I appreciate you!"

"Smoothly" also means "evenness, equal, equity." Sexual contact between true lovers produces equal enjoyment and release of tension for both of them. Throughout the Bible, God makes no distinction between the sexual desires of men and women or their abilities to experience supreme pleasure. Thus, the Shulammite recognizes that she will delight in the sexual embrace with her beloved as much as he does because of their emotional attraction to each other. It won't be the one-way attraction that Solomon feels for her.

Then she tells Solomon that sexual love will flow gently through the lips of those who fall asleep. Gently means sluggish, restful, quiet, strength, etc. The Shulammite and Shepherd will have to work hard for their living, but sharing love at the end of the day in each other's arms will reward their labors. In this way, God gives a husband and wife the perfect way to relax that doesn't require any money--just love for each other.

However, two teenagers in the back seat of a car seldom experience the gentleness of sexual love. Fear of being caught and pregnancy destroy their tranquility. On the other hand, a husband and wife can spend as much time giving and receiving pleasure as they desire. Afterwards, their bodies release hormones which help both the husband and wife sleep peacefully.

This beautiful sexual harmony of the male and female bodies originated within the mind of God and shows His love and concern for the welfare of mankind. For God rewards men and women with blissful lovemaking when they accomplish the work He created them to perform.

D. BELONGS TO THE SHEPHERD

Song of Sol. 7:10: "I am my beloved's, and his desire is for me."

Then the Shulammite rejects King Solomon even more completely when she tells him that she belongs to the Shepherd and he belongs to her. She states flatly that no other man can have her. Her garden is locked until the Shepherd opens it in marriage, for she knows that the Shepherd longs for her as a person-- not just as a body.

Joseph C. Dillow, the author of *Solomon on Sex,* suggests that her statement corresponds with I Cor. 7:2-4, God's law of compatibility:[8] "But because of immoralities, let each man have his own wife, and let each woman have her own husband. Let the husband fulfill his duty to his wife, and likewise also the wife to her husband. The wife does not have authority [power--KJV] over her own body, but the husband does; and likewise also the husband does not have authority [power--KJV] over his own body, but the wife does."

Paul states that a wife does not possess what it takes to satisfy her own sexual desires--it takes a husband loving her with both his body and mind to satisfy a wife's deepest needs. Likewise, a husband does not possess what it takes to satisfy his own sexual desires--it takes a wife who gives both her body and mind in love to truly satisfy him.

Thus, the Shulammite and the Shepherd gladly recognize their obligations to satisfy each other's sexual desires and needs. In marriage, the Shulammite's body will no longer belong to her, but to the Shepherd. In the same way, his body will belong to her. She pledges to fulfill this duty cheerfully and with warmth. Likewise, she accepts his promise to gladly satisfy all of her needs.

Three times, the Shulammite repeats this commitment that she and the Shepherd made to each other (Song of Sol. 2:16; 6:3; 7:10). This shows the importance of a couple determining *before marriage* to always satisfy the other's sexual needs. The Shulammite and the Shepherd do not plan to leave up to chance the happiness of their sexual life together.

A good sexual relationship deepens existing love while expressing love. Platonic love or even a partially platonic relationship prevents the marriage from

[8]Dillow, *Solomon on Sex,* p. 144.

growing into perfect, total emotional and physical rapture.

While the Shulammite begs the maidens to learn a lesson from nature concerning letting love grow, animals cannot reach the height for emotional love that humans can. Only men and women can make love for love's sake alone. Animals can only snuggle and groom each other; they must reserve their sexual contacts for procreation. Thus, the Shulammite turns her back on Solomon and the emptiness of sensuous love.

———

STUDY EXERCISE

Answer all questions in your own words.

1. How do a woman's eyes either comfort or confuse a man?

2. Why did the Shulammite tell the maidens to go get the Shepherd?

3. What was the Shepherd's attitude toward work?

4. Is a boy's work habits an important consideration before a girl marries him? Why?

5. Explain how the Shulammite's description of the Shepherd is of universal application in your marriage:

     (1) Her beloved
     (2) Outstanding among ten thousand
     (3) Impressive appearance
     (4) Wholly desirable
     (5) Her beloved and her friend

6. Why did the queens and concubines praise her? Do women have this same attitude today? Why?

7. What are the dangers of building a marriage on sensuous love?

8. Why is the sexual relationship beautiful when both of the participants love each other?

9. Do you disagree with anything in this lesson? If so, explain in detail giving scriptures for your reasons.

RESEARCH EXERCISE

To help you analyze the difference between sensuous and true love make four charts. For each chart, turn an 8 1/2 x 11 inch sheet of paper sideways and make six columns. Label the columns as follows: (1) Hear, (2) See, (3) Smell, (4) Taste, (5) Touch, and (6) Commitment. Then analyze each of the following relationships on a separate chart:

1. Solomon Rates the Shulammite
2. The Shulammite Rates Solomon
3. The Shepherd Rates the Shulammite
4. The Shulammite Rates the Shepherd

On the charts, list each example in the Song of Solomon of satisfying the five senses and the commitments to act in the other's best interest. Include the verses for reference. Then write a one to two page summary of the advantages and disadvantages of true love vs. sensuous love. *Remember that physical stimulants plus a commitment of responsibility equal true love. However, physical stimulants only equal sensuous love.* Continue this project through the end of the next chapter. An example follows:

The Shulammite Rates Solomon

Hear: flattery--1:9-10; 4:1-5; 6:5-7; 6:11-12; 7:6-9
See: saw his chambers--1:4, sitting at his table--1:12, saw his traveling couch--3:7, powerful--3:8, everyone gazed on him with his crown--3:11, spent the night in the palace--5:2-7
Smell: perfumed with myrrh and frankincense--3:6
Taste: dined with him--1:12
Touch: couldn't stand the thought of him touching her--7:9
Commitment of Responsibility: tried to force love--1:4; 6:11-12, promised her gold and silver--1:10-11, sensuous--4:1-5; 6:4-9, only wanted sex--7:6-8

PERSONAL EXERCISES

1. Make two additional charts to analyze the foundation of your marriage and to find out how you rate

with your husband and how he rates with you. On one chart write down how your husband pleases your five senses and makes commitments to provide for you and to satisfy your needs. If you have a sincere desire to please your husband, ask him to fill out the second chart on you listing your assets and weaknesses in each area. If you are not comfortable asking your husband to do this, fill out a chart for yourself. If you are single, fill out a chart about the qualities you will bring to marriage.

2. When you answer question 5 about how your husband fits the universal description of the Shepherd, give it to your husband to read. You may prefer to answer the question more intimately for him than for class.

CHAPTER 12

THE TRIUMPH OF TRUE LOVE

The day has barely begun, but already the Shulammite is impatient for the Shepherd to arrive. Very early that morning she sent the maidens away to tell him that she wants to marry him. But before he could come, King Solomon called her to his court to introduce her to all his wives and to propose to her again. This time she saw through his sensuous flattery--he didn't care about her at all. He just wanted to make love to her body! She'd never been so repulsed by anything in her life!

And imagine his wives! They didn't care about her either even though they welcomed her into the harem with them. She doesn't want to end up like them and have to share her husband with other women.

But where can the Shepherd be? It's been hours since the maidens left. She needs him to come rescue her from Solomon and his sensuous plot. She meant what she said when she told Solomon, "I am my beloved's, and his desire is for me." If only she could just see the Shepherd, she would tell him how much she loves him.

I. THE WEDDING PROCESSION

Then right in the midst of this ordeal with Solomon, the Shepherd walks in. Perhaps he pastured his flocks nearby so he could keep an eye on her in case she needed him. At any rate, the maidens found him quickly, and he has come. She is so thrilled to see him standing there that she calls out to him without shame, "Come, my beloved, take me away from all this mockery! You're the one I want to marry."

A. THE BLESSINGS OF FEMININE LOVE

> **Song of Sol. 7:11-12: "Come, my beloved, let us go out into the country, let us spend the night in the villages. Let us rise early and go to the vineyards; let us see whether the vine has budded and its blossoms have opened, and whether the pomegranates have bloomed. There I will give you my love."**

As the Shulammite calls to the Shepherd, she says, "Come, my beloved, let us start the wedding procession right now. I don't want to wait another minute before becoming your bride." She wants to spend the rest of her life helping him subdue the earth and filling it with people. She prefers to live simply and work hard for everything she owns and to enjoy true love, than to live in luxury and worry about what new techniques she must employ to keep Solomon interested in her.

Then placing her arm in his (Song of Sol. 8:5) the Shulammite and the Shepherd leave Solomon's palace to begin the walk back to his home. Dr. Smith explains how this begins the wedding procession and follows the typical Jewish wedding customs:

> When the fixed hour arrived, which was generally late in the evening, the bridegroom set forth from his house, attended by his groomsmen (A.V. "companions," Judg. xiv.11; "children of the bride-chamber," Matt. ix.15), preceded by a band of musicians or singers (Gen. xxxi.27; Jer. vii.34, xvi.9; 1 Macc. ix.39), and accompanied by persons bearing flambeaux (2 Essdr. x.2; Matt. xxv.7; compare Jer. xxv.10; Rev. xviii.23, "the light of a candle"). Having reached the house of the bride, who with her maidens anxiously expected his arrival (Matt. xxv.6), he conducted the whole party back to his own or his father's house, with every demonstration of gladness (Ps. xlv.15). On their way back they were joined by a party of maidens, friends of the bride and

bridegroom, who were in waiting to catch the procession as it passed (Matt. xxv.6).[1]

Until now, the Shepherd and the Shulammite spoke to each other only in the thoughts of the maiden. From now on, as the story follows the pattern for an actual Jewish wedding, they speak directly to each other in much the same way as any young couple pledges their love and devotion during their wedding.

So the Shulammite tells the Shepherd that she wants to spend her honeymoon in the countryside. She's had enough of city life. Instead she wants to see if the vines are budding or if the spring flowers are blooming.

Then the Shulammite begins telling the Shepherd about some of the blessings they will share in marriage. For one, she promises to give her love freely to the Shepherd both emotionally and physically when the wedding ceremony is over. This is very different from the attitude of many brides today. Many approach the wedding night with apprehension and do not enjoy it. However, the Shulammite's healthy attitude enables her to eagerly look forward to giving her whole self in love to the Shepherd.

Feminine love is not a timid emotion that lies still and lets the man show all the affection. God created the woman as an active participant in love making. *Promising to follow God's plan, the Shulammite assures the Shepherd that she will lovingly and affectionately initiate the act of love upon occasion.* With such an attitude, her wedding night and honeymoon will generate many delightful memories of shared love for them both.

B. THE BLESSINGS OF MARRIAGE

> **Song of Sol. 7:13: "The mandrakes have given forth fragrance; and over our doors are all choice fruits, both new and old, which I have saved up for you, my beloved."**

The Shulammite's mention of "mandrakes" held special significance to the Jews who regarded it as a

[1]Smith, *Dr. Smith's Dictionary of the Bible*, pp. 382-383.

plant with the powers to insure conception. Dr. Pettus describes this plant:

> Mandrakes are called "May apples" and "devil's apples." It is a plant which grows about a foot high, has purple blooms in May, has a tubular root, and is akin to the potato family. The plant blooms with a purple flower in May which turns into a two-inch large apple. The roots of the plant and the fruit of the plant both have been used to promote fertility in the female.[2]

Dr. Pettus recounts the story of Jacob and his two wives, Rachel and Leah found in Gen. 30:14. Reuben brought his mother Leah some mandrakes in the days of the wheat harvest, the same time that the mandrake's apples grew ripe. Then Rachel bargained with Leah for the mandrakes by allowing Jacob to spend the night with her. Soon afterwards Rachel conceived. Dr. Pettus explains how the mandrakes may have helped Rachel become pregnant:

> Rachel's desire to have a child bordered on the psychotic. She "said unto Jacob, 'Give me children or else I die'" (Gen. 30:1). If not psychotic she was certainly irrational. We know anxiety, tension and worry will affect fertility. Perhaps the mandrakes Rachel obtained from Reuben and Leah served no purpose, however, it is interesting to me as a physician to think about it in the light of the following. Mandrake roots and "May apples" have been used throughout the ages as sedatives, soporifics and fertility potions. A nervous, tense, worried woman sometimes does not conceive. When the tension over being childless is relieved by the adoption of a child, these women frequently conceive. Perhaps the sedative effect which the mandrakes had, helped Rachel conceive.[3]

---

[2]Pettus, *As I See Sex Through the Bible*, p. 122.
[3]Pettus, *As I See Sex Through the Bible*, p. 123.

The Shulammite confidently tells the Shepherd that they will enjoy a happy home. Children will abound for her to care for and to bless their union. The Shulammite stored up both new and old delights for the Shepherd which she saved just for him. He has already tasted her emotional involvement with him and eaten her honey and milk. Now he will taste the new fruit of uniting physically with her as he drinks from her pure garden spring.

C. THE BLESSINGS OF AN UPBRINGING OF LOVE

Song of Sol. 8:1: "Oh that you were like a brother to me who nursed at my mother's breasts..."

Solomon offers the Shulammite only sensuous love, but she expects to experience real love for a lifetime with the Shepherd. Why? Because they both grew up in affectionate homes, so similar that the Shepherd could easily pass for one of her brothers. The Shulammite gives their mothers credit for teaching them how to express tenderness and love by nursing them. Ps. 22:9 and Is. 66:11-13 show the effects of nursing upon infants in addition to feeding.

Nursing and breastfeeding aren't always the same. Breastfeeding, the simple act of offering a baby the breast instead of a bottle, differs from nursing which includes the tender loving care that accompanies breastfeeding. Some breastfed babies are not surrounded by tenderness, while some bottle-fed babies receive emotional nourishment as well. The Shulammite simply states that both of their mothers provided loving homes for them to grow up in and to bless their future marriage.

Hence, when parents lay the proper foundation for affection through example and parental love, their children grow up to reap the natural blessings of sexual love in marriage. This foundation begins to form in infancy as the mother nurses, cuddles, plays with, and talks to her children. As the children mature, the foundation continues to build through the free reign of love in the home as the parents kiss and openly express love for each other and their children.

Sadly, Solomon did not grow up in such a loving home. His father and mother, David and Bathsheba, began their marriage on the basis of sensuous lust. For after watching Bathsheba bathing, David committed adultery with her. Later when she discovered that she was pregnant, he killed her husband to cover up his sin. After they married, God took their first child as punishment for their wickedness. Then Bathsheba, *only one* of David's many wives, gave birth to Solomon (II Sam. 11:2-12:24).

The scriptures also record jealousy, fighting, rape, and murder among David's children by his different wives. While Solomon was probably breastfed by either his mother or a wet nurse, nursing alone cannot replace an emotional void in the home. As a result of not seeing his parents set an example of love and devotion to each other and growing up in a home filled with sibling rivalry, Solomon never learned how to build an enduring relationship with any woman.

In a recent newspaper article modern psychologists claimed that divorce statistics prove that adults who failed to get along with their brothers and sisters as children, usually also failed to develop the proper skills for getting along *with anyone*. Their lack of regard for others especially wrecked havoc in their marriages. The psychologists said that parents can protect their children from growing up and joining the marriage, divorce, and remarriage merry-go-round by teaching them how to love and appreciate each other.

Many couples expect to marry and to enjoy one glorious, unruffled, happy union forever. More often than not, this is not the case because few couples come from ideal homes in this age of leftover Victorian morals, divorced parents, working mothers, and feminists who do not want babies in the first place. Then when inevitable problems arise, many couples are too embarrassed to seek help. They falsely assume that they are the only ones in the whole world with sexual problems.

However, modern researchers say that more than fifty percent of all marriages suffer from sexual problems. They claim that the problems increase steadily rather than declining.[4] Fortunately, couples can solve many of these problems very easily if they acknowledge them and obtain proper help. But the longer they put off facing their difficulties, the harder it becomes to solve their problems.

Ideally, a couple should begin discussing these potential problem-areas in courtship before sensitivities develop in marriage. If either of their parents failed to lay a foundation of love in the home, the adult child should not expect to know how to love properly. Likewise, if either of them came from a broken home, then the couple should expect to encounter some adjustment problems. Therefore, if a couple wants to partake of all that true love offers, they should examine the home life of each of them *before marriage*. In addition, they should make sure that they share similar attitudes toward marriage so that one's solution to problems is not prayer while the other's is divorce. If they both grew up in stable homes, they will agree more readily on what to do or not to do in marriage.

During courtship, a man or a woman can easily say, "I've never seen my parents kiss. And I can't remember them ever telling me that they loved me. I don't want to be like them. I want to show affection to you and our children. I probably won't overcome twenty years of upbringing overnight, but I'm willing to work at it. I hope we can always talk to each other without accusing the other of not loving or caring."

When couples discuss their home upbringing and feelings toward giving and accepting love before marriage, they find it easier after marriage to discuss problems as they arise. However, failure to lay a foundation of open communication about sexual love in courtship often leads to hurt feelings after marriage. Then instead of a loving rapport developing between the couple as together they learn to love, they begin accusing each other, "You're just like your parents—cold and unloving!" As a result, resentments and stubbornness replace the desire for closeness and block the road to complete happiness.

[4]Don Luftig, "The Sex Test," Condensed from a WNBC-TV Feature, *Reader's Digest* (Sept, 1977), pp. 78-70.

On the other hand, when a couple approaches problems of this nature openly and honestly, they usually can solve them quickly. With God's love and help, expressing affection can become spontaneous in adulthood regardless of the kind of homes the couple grew up in. Some counselors recommend memorizing scriptures dealing with love from the Song of Solomon, etc. to help free the mind of childhood-caused inhibitions. *Vol. II: Learning to Love* deals with the subject of sexual love in detail.

The Song of Solomon implies that the Shulammite and the Shepherd thoroughly talked about sexual matters before marriage. For example, they made a commitment to each other to keep themselves sexually pure for their wedding night. The Shepherd not only valued the Shulammite's virginity, but he also helped preserve both his and her purity. Likewise, they made a commitment to each other to satisfy the other's sexual desires as indicated by her three statements, "I am my beloved's and my beloved is mine." In addition, the Shulammite knew what kind of loving home the Shepherd grew up in. *Thus, their verbal sexual communication, rather than sexual experimentation, assures them of a wonderfully ecstatic relationship of rapture in each other's arms until death do they part.*

D. THE BLESSINGS OF DISPLAYING AFFECTION

Song of Sol. 8:1: "...If I found you outdoors, I would kiss you; no one would despise me, either."

Because they base their actions toward each other on true love, the maiden can impulsively kiss the Shepherd and no one will despise her even if they are outdoors. Many times a display of affection between courting couples appears offensive because they are not married. After marriage, however, the situation changes. Then a tasteful display of affection for one's spouse often pleases the observers.

Many a husband embarrasses his wife by becoming cranky when company visits stretch out over several days. This usually happens, not because the company overstays their visit, but because the couple refrains from their usual hugs and kisses in front of the visitors. Whether company visits or not, a husband needs a certain amount of patting, hugging, squeezing, and kissing. But when a wife waits endlessly upon the company by fixing fancy meals and seeing to their every need while leaving her husband to shift for himself emotionally, the husband quickly becomes irritable.

On the other hand, when a wife puts her husband's emotional needs first by openly kissing him and patting him on the knee, he enjoys the company more. Likewise, the company sees a good example of an affectionate wife and enjoys their visit more. Everyone knows that when the man of the house gets grouchy, no one relaxes and enjoys a good time.

The Shulammite recognizes the need for a woman's touch of love and willingly promises to make the first move. Too many wives expect their husbands to make all the affectionate advances. If the husband didn't grow up in an affectionate home and isn't inclined to put his arms around his wife, many a wife wrongfully withholds her affection from him.

Such a wife often considers it unwomanly to make the first move toward tenderness. However, the Bible plainly teaches that the woman sets the loving atmosphere in the home, and the man responds to it (Tit. 2:4-5). A wise wife doesn't wait for her husband to create the mood for love, she freely bestows her love upon him as the Shulammite promises to do. If she finds him outdoors or in front of company, she will kiss him. And no one will despise her either--especially not her husband! The woman's tender emotions make her the perfect one to literally fill the air with love.

E. THE BLESSINGS OF A LOVING MOTHER

> **Song of Sol. 8:2: "I would lead you and bring you into the house of my mother, who used to instruct me; I would give you spiced wine to drink from the juice of my pomegranates."**

"Instruct" means "properly, to goad, i.e. (by implication) to teach (the rod being an Oriental incentive)" (Strong, p. 60).

The Shulammite's mother set a good example for her daughter and taught her how to make a man happy.

But some mothers, who set good examples, fail to teach their daughters the principles behind their actions. A mother should verbally instruct her daughter and not assume that her daughter instinctively understands how to do everything right just from watching her.

Redbook magazine featured a questionnaire for their readers concerning how they felt about sex, motherhood, housework, men, and the women's liberation movement. Over 120,000 women responded. One of the results of that survey revealed the importance of a mother teaching her daughter the joys of being a wife and homemaker:

> Women who put considerable emotional investment in children are, logically, more likely to believe that being a wife and mother is a full-time occupation. They are happy with the routine work in housekeeping and child care as well. But we found a significant factor of their contentment with marriage and children was a prior knowledge of and planning for this role. Women who had no clear expectations about marriage (or whose expectations were not met) and who were not able to plan their children are much less happy than women who knew what they were getting into. They are dissatisfied with the role of wife and less positive about their experiences with pregnancy and childbirth.[5]

Thus, mothers who teach their daughters how to be good wives, mothers, and homemakers bless their daughters and future sons-in-law in a tremendous way. They lay the foundation for their daughters' contentment with the work and role of a woman. Women who fail to accept their responsibility for teaching their daughters how to enjoy their femininity handicap their daughters' marriages and future happiness.

The *Redbook* survey offers encouragement for women whose mothers failed to instill love for the

[5]Carol Tavris and Toby Jayaratne, *How Do You Feel About Being a Woman? The Results of a Redbook Questionnaire,* *Redbook* booklet (Jan, 1973), p. 5.

family and the home within them. For education, obviously, plays an important role in a woman's contentment. Thus, if a woman missed out on receiving proper training as a child about her feminine role, correcting that ignorance as an adult enables her to better relish the special jobs God gives her.

The feminists insist that sex role stereotyping harms women, but it is exactly that type of training that helps women reach their full potential. Doctors, lawyers, dentists, and teachers must receive specialized education before they can practice their professions efficiently and reap the greatest personal benefits. In exactly the same way, women must receive expert instruction in the art of homemaking.

Some mothers argue that their daughters show little interest in learning how to work around the house. However, the word "instruct" means "to goad" and implies the use of a "rod" to discipline when necessary. If children always knew what was best for them, God would not have commanded them to obey their parents in Eph. 6:1-3. For this reason, a loving mother *not only tells her daughter* about her feminine role, but she *also makes her daughter* carry out her jobs.

For example, when a mother makes her daughter keep her room clean, she teaches her how to prevent clutter from accumulating, helps her develop self-discipline, and gives her self-confidence through doing a good job and becoming organized. Likewise, a mother encourages her sons to imitate their father by bragging on jobs the sons do well. She also help her sons become good husbands by letting them hear her praise her husband.

One woman, whose parents share a beautiful and enviable relationship with each other, married a fine man. But she expected him to do everything her father's way. She didn't understand the principles which her mother practiced to bring out the best in her father. Her mother never explained to her how to get long with a man. As a result, this young wife didn't know how to bring out her husband's better side. Instead, through unrealistic expectations and ignorance, she brought out an ugliness in him that no one knew existed.

Fortunately, the Shulammite's mother instructed her how to create love and tranquility within the home.

She promises to do little acts of love for the Shepherd such as bringing him pomegranate juice to drink. She knows that these small acts of kindness are just another way of saying, "I love you." She won't feel mistreated or that she does menial work when she pampers her husband.

Horrified at the thought of bringing a man something to drink, the feminists charge, "He has two legs of his own!" It is precisely because a man has two legs of his own that waiting upon a husband serves as such a valuable act of love. Anytime a woman, of her own free will, does something for a man that the man can do for himself, she shows her love. If the man has no legs and depends upon the woman to bring him a cold drink, it becomes more an act of necessity rather than an act of love.

One wife, who had begun to do little extra loving deeds for her husband, overheard him talking to a neighbor. Her husband told his friend, "You won't believe the change in my wife. Watch!" Then he called to his wife, who was in another room, "Honey, would you bring me something cold to drink?" The wife quickly brought him a drink from the refrigerator. After she left, she heard him exclaim to the neighbor, "See!"

However, this same wife couldn't believe the change that came over her husband when she started showing more affection for him through little things. He began talking to her instead of to the dog when he came home from work. He started keeping their car in better running condition. He got a promotion at work after being passed over several times. And her father asked her, "Are you pregnant?" when her husband pulled out the chair for her at a restaurant.

No, she wasn't pregnant. She was just a wife who was reaping the benefits of creating an atmosphere of love in the home. The feminists may try to tell her that bringing her husband a cold drink is menial and undignified. But she will answer like the Shulammite, "I am my beloved's, and his desire is for me."

F. THE BLESSINGS OF SEXUAL LOVE

Song of Sol. 8:3: "Let his left hand be under my head, and his right hand embrace me."

Because of her mother's teaching, the Shulammite longs for the Shepherd's touch and embrace and to unite physically with him. Oriental or Jewish people are well known for their natural affection for one another. This partly stems from the older women teaching the younger women about the physical side of love. Not influenced by Victorian morals, Oriental women aren't afraid of loving their husband physically as Western women often are. Robert Chartham explains in his book, *Mainly for Wives: The Art of Sex for Women,* how the Orientals give careful attention to preparing their children for sexual love:

> ...in the Orient...the girl is prepared for marriage much more carefully than the man. A large part of her preparation is devoted to learning from older and experienced women the technique of making love. She is taught that it is part of her wifely duty to satisfy her husband sexually; and not merely to satisfy his urge but to help him to experience the most refined and pleasurable erotic sensations. In addition, the Oriental woman is made deeply aware of the pleasure to be gained for herself.

> In Oriental marriages the woman is the more experienced, or at least the more sexually knowledgeable partner, at the outset, though the man has not been entirely forgotten...He is taught a few very simple caresses and it is he who, like his Western counterpart, makes the first approaches. But it is a polite fiction in which the couple are indulging, necessary to the husband's self-respect; for just like the Western husband, the Eastern husband believes himself to be the master of his household, the dominant partner of his marriage and his marriage-bed.

> But once the husband has made the initial approach, and met the other conditions required of him, it is not long before the wife takes over the conduct of the intercourse. She does it unobtrusively, and if challenged would depreciate any praise of her art. From the very

CHAPTER 12: THE TRIUMPH OF TRUE LOVE

first act of love she demonstrates to her husband the sweet pleasure that can come from skillful lovemaking. Within a short time, the husband realizes that there are other skills which he can contribute. There is a period of experimentation during which the heights of erotic sensation are sought, and because, during this period, a complete frankness inevitably develops between husband and wife, the sexual relationship of the couple becomes an equal partnership in which the technique of both is deemed to be an essential contribution.[6]

The Oriental people or the Jews about whom the Song of Solomon was written learned from their parents the art of lovemaking. Thus, they entered the marriage union with a great capacity to enjoy complete marital bliss. The Shulammite knows that God created the sexual embrace for women as well as for men. She isn't afraid to kiss the Shepherd or to give her love to him. In fact, she longs for his left hand to be under her head and his right hand to embrace her.

Proper sex education in the home leads to wholesome attitudes in men and women which allows them to enjoy the sexual embrace when they marry. God created sexual love for His people to delight in *with clear consciences* and to use in service to Him. Loving parents, especially mothers, teach their children how to build their marriages on the solid foundation of true love so that they can reap all the blessings of married love.

At this time, the Shulammite and the Shepherd have left the palace and are making their way to his home in the country. Excited to see him, she shared with the Shepherd her joy at their approaching marriage and her eager anticipation of the consummation of their love. Finishing her intimate conversation with him, the Shulammite turns to the maidens who accompany them to their wedding. She cannot resist warning them one more time:

[6]Robert Chartham, *Mainly for Wives: The Art of Sex for Women* (New York: Signet Books, 1969), pp. 24-25.

G. THE THEME: THE BLESSINGS OF TRUE LOVE

> Song of Sol. 8:4: "I want you to swear, O daughters of Jerusalem, do not [Why should you--NASV] arouse or awaken my love, until she [it--NASV footnote] pleases."

"Swear" is the same word translated "adjure" in 2:7 and 3:5 and means "to be complete, to seven oneself, i.e. (as if by repeating a declaration seven times)" (Strong, p. 112).

The Shulammite's expression of the theme of the book changes somewhat as she makes her final plea for the case of true love to the maidens. The New American Standard footnote says, "Why should you arouse or awaken love until it pleases?" Most of the commentators seem to agree with this translation.

Thus, after seeing what nearly happened to her and how she almost fell for Solomon's line, the Shulammite asks the maidens, "What good reason can you possibly have for forcing love in your own lives? Can't you learn from my experience with Solomon? Swear to me that you will wait for true love in your own lives." Under no circumstances should they force love--they must allow love to take its natural course.

The italics on the word "my" in the various translations shows that the scholars added it to make the meaning clearer. Unfortunately, the addition of the word "my" limits the theme of the book to the arousal of just the woman's heart and body. However, as the story demonstrates, the main difference between Solomon and the Shepherd was that the Shepherd's love for the Shulammite had been awakened while Solomon's had not been.

For example, the Shepherd had developed an emotional bond with the Shulammite that made him want to take care of her--to provide for her, protect her, and to lead her in addition to joining with her sexually. In contrast, Solomon hadn't known her long enough to develop an emotional bond. Furthermore, he was so intent upon making sexual contact with her that he really wasn't concerned about taking care of her--except to adorn her body with jewels.

Both males and females need time to get to know each other before their love can become truly aroused for each other. If sexual activity begins before this happens, as in premarital sex, the relationship may well be destroyed before it even really begins.

Many a girl bemoans this fact when she writes to an advice columnist, "I gave in to keep him, but he left. How can I win him back?" Sadly, such a girl lost her virginity and her boyfriend, and she *probably won't be able to win him back* because she violated the theme of the Song of Solomon. She gave in to his pressure for intercourse before he developed an emotional bond with her that demanded that he take care of her in marriage. So he left her to search for new conquests in hopes of finding the perfect feminine body to satisfy his desires.

A renowned psychologist in the field of male sexual problems, Dr. Bernie Zilbergeld, states over and over in his book *Male Sexuality* that a man absolutely must feel an emotional attraction toward a woman before sexual contact is meaningful or even highly pleasurable. *However, after sexual intimacy without true love, most men quickly became bored and lose interest in developing an emotional bond with the woman.*[7]

In addition, George Gilder claims in his book *Men and Marriage* that sexual purity in women is the greatest gift that women can give their boyfriends and future husbands. Rather than saying "because all men want to marry virgins" he states:

> In a world where women do not say no, the man is never forced to settle down and make serious choices. His sex drive--the most powerful compulsion in his life--is never used to make him part of civilization as the supporter of a family. If a woman does not force him to make a long-term commitment--to marry--in general, he doesn't. It is maternity that requires commitment. His sex drive only demands conquest, driving him from body to body in an unsettling hunt for variety and excitement in which much of the thrill is in the chase itself.[8]

[7]Bernie Zilbergeld, Ph.D., *Male Sexuality* (New York: Bantam, 1978), chapters 1-4.
[8]Gilder, *Men and Marriage,* p. 47.

Thus, Gilder explains that sexual purity on the part of women becomes a great gift to their boyfriends because it motivates them to settle down, to become responsible, and to make something of their lives. As stated earlier, nearly all men who rise to the top of their professions are married men. *Men need wives.* However, without sexual purity on the part of women, men, in general, aren't motivated to seek marriage and its responsibilities. So without purity, which leads to marriage, women cannot fulfill the desperate need in men for wives.

The abuse of true love begins in junior highs and even grade schools as the youngsters begin early courting. The students force love on each other by regarding anyone without a steady boy or girlfriend as a social outcast. While going steady provides security, it also forces love by denying emotions the freedom to grow naturally and purely.

In addition, going steady adds a dangerous element to dating by leading to familiarity. Each date overcomes more and more of the initial bashfulness and awkwardness of the first meeting. The couple talks about matters and engages in activities on the twentieth date that they avoided on the first one. Going steady makes it hard for teenagers to maintain pure minds and bodies.

As an added disadvantage, a teenager who dates only one person narrows down his field of choice for a marriage partner. He forfeits the privilege of learning about people with different moods, various temperaments, and assorted intellects. A personality that fascinates him in courtship may quickly become boring or even get on his nerves in marriage.

Obviously, both boys and girls force love through going steady. After going with each other for so long, they sometimes feel obligated to marry. Or they fear hurting the other's feelings or disappointing their parents if they break up. Likewise, both men and women marry for career purposes. And on and on go the ways to force love.

Hence, the Shulammite implores the daughters of Jerusalem, "Can't you learn from my experience not to force love?" True love and marriage are too wonderful to throw away the chance for happiness by forcing love.

II. THE WEDDING FESTIVAL

Song of Sol. 8:5: "Who is this coming up from the wilderness, leaning on her beloved?..."

Since wilderness refers to an uninhabited area, the wedding party finally enters the Shepherd's village. The country people come out of their homes to see who is getting married. They ask themselves who the radiantly happy bride is, for the way she leans on the Shepherd makes her love for him obvious. Not afraid for others to see her deep affection for her beloved, the Shulammite is consistently pictured as the giver of love.

Now the stage is set for the actual wedding festivals to begin. Dr. Smith explains the customs of the Jews which the Shulammite and the Shepherd follow:

> The inhabitants of the place pressed out into the streets to watch the procession (Cant. iii.11). At the house a feast was prepared, to which all the friends and neighbors were invited (Gen. xxix.22; Matt. xxii.1-10; Luke xiv.8; John ii.2), and the festivities were protracted for seven, or even fourteen days (Judg. xxii.11), and the feast was enlivened with riddles (Judg. xiv.12) and other amusements.[9]

Several days earlier, these same country folks probably witnessed Solomon and his traveling party take the Shulammite to Jerusalem to marry the King. Now she is marrying the Shepherd. What could have happened to cause the vineyard keeper to give up the King? What would make any woman give up wealth and prestige to marry a poor shepherd? Whether or not they actually ask the Shepherd what happened, they can hardly wait to find out. Before the Shepherd spoke only through the thoughts of the Shulammite; now he

[9]Smith, *Dr. Smith's Dictionary of the Bible*, pp. 382-383.

personally reveals the secret of how he won the Shulammite's love when King Solomon couldn't:

A. AWOKE HER LOVE

> Song of Sol. 8:5: "...Beneath the apple tree I awakened you; there your mother was in labor with you, there she was in labor and gave you birth."

"Awakened" is the same word used in the theme of the book in 2:7, 3:5, and 8:4 and means "(through the idea of opening the eyes); to wake" (Strong, p. 86).

The Shepherd didn't force himself upon the rose of Sharon by asking her to prove her love to him with premarital sex. Instead, he awoke her affections under the apple tree in her yard, when he visited her home. There he spent time talking with her, getting acquainted with her, understanding her, and being considerate and kind to her. In this way, he took the time to develop the emotional bond that cements a lasting relationship and that awakens a woman's sexual desires for a man.

On the other hand, Solomon didn't spend time at all getting to know the maiden. He just praised her physical beauty and tried to get her in bed as soon as possible. Marriage only legalized his lecherous lust.

Wise men today follow the Shepherd's secret for winning a woman's love. *Fact of feminine nature: a woman's love must be awakened.* Therefore, if a courting man or a married man wants his sweetheart to love him more, he must spend time with her, go places with her, talk to her, get to know her, and let her get to know him better. Above all, he must show consideration for her needs. A woman needs to feel deep in her heart that her beloved's banner over her is love.

B. THE POWER OF LOVE

> Song of Sol. 8.6: "Put me like a seal over your heart, like a seal on your arm. For love is as strong as death, jealousy is as severe as Sheol; its flashes are flashes of fire, the very flame of the Lord."

The Shepherd understands the seriousness and per-
manence of the marriage bond. He knows how much he
needs the Shulammite's emotional involvement with him
and how much he depends upon her love. So the Shepherd tells the Shulammite, "Make a pledge to me that
you *will never* hide your love from me--that you will
make your love for me so obvious that you might as
well wear an arm band that reads, 'I love the Shepherd.'" Earlier the Shulammite promised to freely bestow her love upon the Shepherd--now he tells her
that he cannot live without her keeping her promise.

Wives today need to listen to the Shepherd's plea
because their husbands might not feel free to make the
same plea to them. But the Shepherd tells all wives
through the pages of inspired scripture that *all husbands need an obvious display of affection from their
wives.*

Then the Shepherd reminds the Shulammite that
"love is as strong as death." How strong is death?
Death is so strong that everyone must die someday.
True love is as dependable as death because it rests
upon satisfaction of the five senses plus an emotional
bond of commitment to always acting in the best interest of the other.

However, sensuous love, which depends upon the
sexual act for happiness, is not as strong as death.
When the sexual embrace is over, the love is gone
until the next union. The strange women in Prov. 7:18
told the young man, "Come let us drink our fill of love
until the morning; let us delight ourselves with caresses." Thus, their love depended solely upon the
sexual delights that they could give each other. Sensuous love desires anyone who satisfies the sexual
tensions, perhaps only tensions of frustration or boredom.

While true love enhances the sexual embrace, it
doesn't depend upon it for its existence. The act of
love only deepens and expresses the love that already
exists. As a result, true love continues to bind the
husband and wife together emotionally after lovemaking. Prov. 5:19-20 tells the husband to "be exhilarated
always" with his wife's love in contrast to desiring
the strange woman's bosom.

As the Shepherd continues to explain his feelings
about love, he cautions the Shulammite that "jealousy

is as severe as Sheol." Sheol refers to destruction in either this life or the life to come. Jealousy--wondering where he fits in, wondering if she really loves him, wondering if she wishes she'd married someone else, wondering if she regrets leaving Solomon--that's destructive. To function as God desires in a marriage, a husband and wife must openly trust each other.

"Its [jealousy] flashes are flashes of fire, the very flame of the Lord," emphasizes how jealousy destroys everything in its path. The Shulammite tested Solomon and decided not to marry him, now she must set her mind on making a success of her marriage with the Shepherd. She can never go back--even in her mind. If the Shulammite cannot keep herself just for the Shepherd, then jealousy will surely overtake and destroy him. His love for her is strong, but he does not want a possible lack of devotion on her part to devastate him.

1. CAN'T DESTROY LOVE

Song of Sol. 8:7: "Many waters cannot quench love, nor will rivers overflow it;..."

Since "many waters cannot quench love, nor will rivers overflow it," true love lasts through the bad times as well as the good times, through riches and poverty, through sickness and health, until death do they part. When a couple builds their marriage on the foundation of true love along with mutual respect and admiration for each other, nothing can destroy the bond between the husband and wife.

The POW's who came back after up to nine years of imprisonment in Vietnam demonstrate the strength of true love. Some men came home to the loving arms and tender sympathy of wives who truly loved them and who remained faithful during their ordeal. Sadly, other men came back only to find that their wives had divorced them and started new families. Powerful enough to withstand pounding rains and raging floods, true love weathers the tortuous tests of life and marriage.

2. CAN'T BUY LOVE

Song of Sol. 8:7: "...If a man were to give all the riches of his house for love, it would be utterly despised."

Many a man buys a beautiful companion or a glamorous wife, but none of them can buy true love. For after a man buys a woman's love, her love becomes utterly despised. She cannot hide what she loves the most--his money. Solomon, with all his wealth and prestige and the many wives it bought, could not buy what the Shulammite gave freely to the lowly Shepherd.

True love is not for sale. True love is a free gift that flows spontaneously to the one who awakens it. Since true love cannot be bought or demanded, few husbands ask their wives for love. Unfortunately, even fewer wives realize just how much their husbands need their open display of verbal and physical affection or how much their husbands hate to ask for love. Thus, the wise wife listens to the Shepherd's plea to the Shulammite to make her love for him obvious. Willingly, the wise wife makes her love unmistakably plain to her own husband. But when a wife forces her husband to ask for love or attention, her love seldom satisfies him. To be of value to the receiver, love must be given freely.

After the Shepherd told the wedding guests how he won the Shulammite's love over King Solomon, the guests turn their attention to the radiant bride. They have an important question for her that cannot wait:

III. THE WEDDING RIDDLE

Song of Sol. 8:8: "We have a little sister, and she has no breasts; what shall we do for our sister on the day when she is spoken for?"

Following the custom of posing questions and riddles at weddings, the guests ask the Shulammite about their little sister who is still too young to care about boys. What can they do for her when she begins to think about boys and marriage? How can they prevent her from making a disastrous mistake like the Shulammite nearly made? Then the guests answer their own question to see if the Shulammite agrees. After all, the rose of Sharon made the choice between sensuous lust and true love that every wife must make. They value her opinion.

A. IF SHE CAN SAY, "NO"

Song of Sol. 8:9: "If she is a wall, we shall build on her a battlement of silver;..."

To the Jews, a "wall" symbolized security because the walls around their cities kept their enemies out. A "battlement," a parapet built on top of the walls, protected the soldiers who guarded the wall. The battlements usually contained small openings for the soldiers to see through or fight. Sometimes the battlement served mainly as decoration for the walls. In addition, lattice-type battlements adorned the tops of the flat-roofed houses as protection against falling.

If a girl is a "wall" with the self-control to say, "no," to the sensuous offers of her dates, then her parents should build a "battlement of silver" on her. They do this by teaching her, restricting her activities, and by giving her only the amount of freedom that she is mature enough to handle. A battlement of silver conveys just how precious a girl's self-control becomes when coupled with her parents' guidance.

One woman said, "My parents built a battlement of silver on me by limiting the number of times I could date each week and by setting a definite time for being home. They also regulated where I went and what I did. When my husband and I dated, some of his friends told him, 'I sure wouldn't date a girl with so many restrictions!' So, boys who were interested in a different kind of a good time than I was didn't even bother to ask me for a date."

Thus, this woman's parents automatically narrowed down her choices for a future husband by eliminating the sensuous and undesirable dates. In effect, they built a battlement of silver on their daughter which helped give her a reputation of high principles.

God gives parents the responsibility to prepare their children for dating and to instill within them a determination to preserve their purity. Parents can do this by explaining the ways of sensuous men and women. Likewise, young people need to hear from their parents the special blessings of sexual love in marriage. This gives them the confidence and support to say, "no," when needed.

Ideally, parents should begin their children's sex education before the teenage years. Unfortunately, some parents fear that discussing sexual matters with their children leads to experimentation. However, many teenagers get into trouble because of ignorance and from learning about sexual intercourse from their friends at school. When parents teach their children honestly and clearly about sex from the Bible, it instills in them a determination to wait for marriage.

Thus, wise parents answer their children's questions honestly and clearly. Perhaps more than anything else, the parents' embarrassment about discussing sexual matters discourages their children from going to them for information. However, if parents truly want to protect their children from harmful influences, they will work to make their children feel comfortable asking questions. Biblical sex education builds a battlement of silver on young people for protection--ignorance destroys many of them before they are old enough for marriage.

B. IF SHE CAN'T SAY, "NO"

Song of Sol. 8:9: "...But if she is a door, we shall barricade her with planks of cedar."

By providing entrance into something, a "door" represents a gullible, naive girl who remains open to all the boys' suggestions. The Jews considered the doors the weakest part of their defense. As a result, they used strong bars of wood or bronze to secure the whole gate by passing them transversely into sockets in the gateposts. Thus, parents whose daughter easily follows the lead of boys must barricade her with planks of cedar. They must fix the door so it can't swing open without supervision.

It doesn't matter what big sister got to do on dates. It doesn't matter how old big sister was when she went out on her first date. It doesn't matter how many dates each week big sister got to go on. It doesn't matter how late big sister got to stay out. It doesn't matter about anything big sister did with boys. What matters is how much responsibility little sister is ready to accept--is she a wall or a door?

The parents' responsibility is to look at each of their daughters individually and to limit their activities according to their emotional growth. Where they see weaknesses in their daughter, they must build rein- forcements--either battlements of silver or planks of cedar--whatever it takes to protect their daughters from sexual harm. Thus, wise parents either grant or deny privileges for each girl on the basis of her personal maturity.

Both daughters and sons need their parents' pro- tection because, when sexually excited, people commit many foolish acts. One man described the problem of irrational sexual desires as like the man who jumped off of a ten-story building. As he went by each floor he said, "All is going fine so far."

Many teenagers falsely assume that if they stop short of the sexual act, they are not sinning. However, God provides a word for that type of sin in II Cor. 12:21--"lasciviousness" (KJV) or "sensuality" (NASV). "Lasciviousness" or "sensuality" means "unbridled lust, excess, licentiousness, lasciviousness, wantonness, outrageousness, shamelessness, insolence, wanton (acts or) manners, as filthy words, indecent bodily movements, unchaste handling of males and females, etc." (Thayer, pp. 79-80).

"Lasciviousness" doesn't refer to the sexual act, but stops short of it. Yet the word includes some of the actions that husbands and wives engage in as foreplay which leads to intercourse. For example, Prov. 5:19-20 encourages the husband to enjoy fondling his wife's breasts in love play, but forbids him to embrace the bosom of the strange woman. Likewise, the Shu- lammite looks forward to the Shepherd's hands on her body after marriage, but was horrified of Solomon's sensuous hands touching her (Song of Sol. 7:9; 8:3).

In addition, girls can get pregnant from mutual masturbation of the genitals. Sperm is not concerned with how it finds its way into the vagina. Its only goal is to unite with the egg, and it will do so if given half a chance.

Petting is a privilege of marriage, not an entertainment for courtship. Not only sinful in courtship, petting also makes it extremely hard for the couple not to go all the way and commit fornication. Affection that results from casual kissing has a weak foundation. But kisses that respond to true love have an intelligent foundation to build a successful marriage on. A girl should use her brain, not her free kisses and breasts to get a date. And to make matters worse, when carried over into marriage, loose morals create one of the most difficult marriage problems to solve. In fact, sexual immorality is the only reason God allows for divorce and remarriage (Mt. 19:9).

Thus, the wedding guests ask the Shulammite if this is the right thing to do for their little sister who has no breasts--to treat her one way if she is a wall and another if she is a door. The Shulammite answers them from her personal experience:

C. SHE COULD SAY, "NO"

Song of Sol. 8:10: "I was a wall, and my breasts were like towers; then I became in his eyes as one who finds peace."

The Shulammite agrees with the guests, for she proved that she was a wall who was able to say, "no," even to King Solomon's sensuous plea. Although her breasts were well-developed and she was definitely ready for love, she wasn't gullible. When Solomon overwhelmed her with provocative flattery, she told him that she wanted time to think about it. She didn't react impulsively to what he told her.

Apparently, part of what her mother taught the Shulammite was, "By the gazelles or by the hinds of the field, do not arouse or awaken love until it pleases." So before she got emotionally involved in the dilemma of who to marry, she already knew that love must grow naturally for true love to result. Thus, her mother's battlement of silver protected her from making a serious mistake.

Then through her self-respect and self-control she found inner peace and happiness. She found true love with the Shepherd to bless the rest of her adult life. If, instead, she had married King Solomon, she would have found a house full of riches and prestige, but she would have forfeited tranquility of spirit in the process.

Saying, "no," doesn't mean that a girl misses all the fun in life. A lifetime lasts much longer than the few years spent in school battling the temptations to join the crowd and partake of loose morals. Each time a girl says, "no," she makes a wise investment in her future happiness and fulfillment in the marriage union. If a girl wants to enjoy a happy ending to her marriage, she must build it upon the foundation of pure, intelligent love.

D. SOLOMON'S VINEYARDS

Song of Sol. 8:11: "Solomon had a vineyard at Ball-hamon; he entrusted the vineyard to caretakers; each one was to bring a thousand shekels of silver for its fruit."

The Shulammite goes on to explain her relationship to Solomon. Solomon leased his vineyard at Ball-hamon, about halfway between Jerusalem and Shunem, her home, to caretakers who paid him a thousand shekels of silver as rent for farming his land. While the caretakers farmed the land and harvested its fruit, the land belonged to Solomon and was under his jurisdiction.

E. CONTROLLED HERSELF

Song of Sol. 8:11: "My very own vineyard is at my disposal; the thousand shekels are for you, Solomon, and two hundred are for those who take care of its fruit."

Just as Solomon supervises his property, the Shulammite oversees what belongs to her--her body. She gladly pays Solomon a thousand shekels for rent on the vineyard because it belongs to him. She cheerfully gives the harvesters two hundred shekels because they worked to earn it. But she is under no obligation to give Solomon her personal vineyard--her body.

Every girl has the right to protect her virginity as her own private property and as her responsibility. She can neglect her purity and allow it to become overgrown with weeds so that no worthy man wants her for a wife, or she can protect her virginity with a lock to keep it pure and clean for her husband. The girl alone makes the choice.

IV. THE WEDDING CEREMONY

Modern marriages conclude with saying, "I do," by both the man and woman as they pledge lasting love for each other. Then the preacher pronounces them husband and wife. The Jews enjoyed a similar custom along with witnesses of the vows:

> The bridegroom now entered into direct communication with the bride, and the joy of the friend was "fulfilled" at hearing the voice of the bridegroom (Jn. iii.29) conversing with her, which he regarded as a satisfactory testimony of the success of his share in the work. The last act in the ceremonial was the conducting of the bride to the bridal chamber (Judg. xv.1; Joel ii.16), where a canopy was prepared (Ps. xix.5; Joel ii.16).[10]

The time has finally arrived for the Shulammite and the Shepherd to consummate their wedding vows. So as the custom of the Jews dictates, the Shepherd speaks to the Shulammite:

A. THE SHEPHERD'S CALL

Song of Sol. 8:13: "O you who sit in the gardens, my companions are listening for your voice--let me hear it!"

The Shulammite made her choice and the Shepherd doesn't want the conclusion of the ceremony delayed any longer. As they sit in the garden, one of the most common places for the Jews to conduct their weddings, he calls to her to let his companions hear her agree to complete their union.

---

[10]Smith, *Dr. Smith's Dictionary of the Bible*, p. 383.

B. THE SHULAMMITE'S ANSWER

> **Song of Sol. 8:14: "Hurry, my beloved, and be like gazelle or a young stag on the mountains of spices."**

The Shulammite responds to the Shepherd's plea to complete the marriage with "Hurry!" She is eager for love and the responsibilities of marriage. Then she tells him to be like a gazelle or a young stag on the mountains of spices which is similar to a modern bride's promise to honor and obey her husband. The Shulammite is ready to reverence her husband by following his leadership. She wants him to be like the magnificent male animals who lead the females in the herd.

All the way through the Song of Solomon, the Shepherd pleads with the Shulammite to give her love to him freely, for he values it above everything else. All the way through the story, the Shulammite begs the Shepherd to be a man and take care of her.

In order for the Shulammite to let her guard down so that her love flows freely to the Shepherd, she must feel protected. She recognizes that the aggressiveness and desire to lead which God placed in the Shepherd is for her protection, not her enslavement. The Shulammite will not be a domineering and complaining wife, but rather a submissive one who happily fulfills the role God places before her.

Just as the Shulammite selected her husband according to the principles of God, she governs her actions toward the Shepherd according to God's wisdom. The Shepherd and the Shulammite will enjoy the blessings God created in marriage because they respect the differences between masculinity and femininity.

What happened to the Shulammite was a very well known event since the town people saw Solomon take her to Jerusalem and the Shepherd bring her back. Obviously, they were curious about what happened as their questions at her wedding indicate. No doubt, she quickly became somewhat of a folk hero to the peasants and repeated her story many times.

For this reason and because the story is written as the Shulammite would have told it, the Shulammite may well be the one God used to write it down. In addition, the story does not record the thoughts of anyone other than the Shulammite. Since I Cor. 2:11 says, "For who among men knows the thoughts of a man except the spirit of the man, which is in him?" these thoughts had to come directly from the Shulammite. Likewise, all recorded dialogue took place in the Shulammite's presence--words she heard.

If Solomon wrote the book, he wrote about something he didn't know anything about at that stage of his life--true love. The story certainly does not cast Solomon in a favorable light with all of his wives and his attitude toward marriage. However, God used Solomon to write wonderful passages about love in the book of Proverbs. But Solomon probably wrote those in his early years when he still looked to God for wisdom. If Solomon or some other man wrote the Song of Solomon, *he wrote it as if he were the Shulammite, as if he were a woman.* So whether or not a woman actually wrote the book, the book is written as if a woman wrote it.

If the Shulammite wrote the Song of Solomon, she did so through inspiration, through God giving her perfect remembrance of the events as He did the apostles of Christ (Jn. 14:26). This would not violate any of God's teachings concerning the woman's subjection to men in the spiritual realm. In both the Old and the New Testaments, women prophesied (Acts 2:17; Jg. 4:4). Yet in each case, the women exercised their spiritual gifts in ways that supported their femininity and their roles within the spiritual realm. As a giver of love (Prov. 5:19) and as a teacher of their daughters (Song of Sol. 8:2) and young women (Tit. 2:3-5), what more fitting book for God to use a woman to write than the Song of Solomon? But regardless of who wrote the Song of Solomon, God inspired a wonderful story of love for His people to learn from and to use to teach others. Thank you, God!

———

STUDY EXERCISE

Answer all questions in your own words.

1. Who promised to initiate love in the Song of Solomon after marriage? Do you think this is a good idea? Why?

2. How did the mothers of the Shulammite and the Shepherd teach them how to love? How can modern mothers teach their children to love?

3. Why should engaged couples examine their attitudes toward marriage and their home backgrounds before marriage?

4. How can a couple determine if they are sexually compatible in courtship?

5. Name some ways a couple can solve sexual problems when they arise?

6. What advice would you give courting couples?

7. What does the Shepherd teach a woman about giving love to her husband?

8. How can parents protect their daughters from making mistakes in love?

9. Do you disagree with anything in this lesson? If so, explain in detail giving scriptures for your reasons.

PROBLEM-SOLVING EXERCISE

The Problem: The following excerpts come from the article "Couple Now 'Partners,'" *The Spokesman-Review* (12/7/72).

On the day after Thanksgiving, Mr. S and Ms. C signed a partnership agreement--that is, a contract to become partners in marriage. It calls for separate bank accounts, independent management and control of all financial assets and a division of space in a large old frame house they're buying.

Birth control is listed as a mutual obligation and an unwanted pregnancy as unacceptable. To resolve serious conflicts a third-party mediator is specified. And the entire 10-article document is subject to amendment and mandatory reevaluation each year.

Mr. S, 26, a schoolteacher, and Ms. C, a 27 year-old law student at the University, say it took six months of living together and another six months of negotiations to work out the contract.

"It's not a guarantee of anything. We recognize that," she said. "The pledges made in the contract call for emotional support and mutual consent to share household tasks, make independent friendships, pursue our separate careers and even live apart if necessary."

"But we wanted to go through a process whereby our expectations were articulated. We didn't want marriage to be a big crisis experience."

The Exercise: Discuss the above newspaper article in detail telling whether or not you believe the reasonings and safeguards of the couple are sound. Give scriptures for your reasons.

SOLUTION IV:

SUBJECTION

vs.

SERVITUDE

(How to Become Truly Beautiful to Your Husband)

"An excellent wife is the crown of her husband, but she who shames him is as rottenness in his bones." (Prov. 12:4)

CHAPTER 13

SUBJECTION FOR BOTH MEN AND WOMEN

Just the mention of the hated word "subjection" fills the minds of many women with imagined horrors while others express rage, double over in laughter, or break into tears. Thus, subjection is *the most unpopular* aspect of marriage in the Bible among both feminists with their marriage contracts and Christians with their rationalizations against it.

Women with marriage problems often think that subjection only leads to grief. Others fear that they will become puppets who must always say, "Yes, Dear" even when they really want to say, "No, Dear." To many women, subjection means pure misery and torture at the hands of their husbands.

Some women assume that they know what subjection is all about--that while a husband has the power of veto, his wife can argue with him up to the point of his final decision. Other women surmise that a submissive wife simply fades into the woodwork never to raise an objection to anything her husband says or wants to do.

However, many of these women fear subjection because they really don't understand it. While the enemies of subjection profess to know its evils, it still remains one of the least understood subjects in the Bible. Prejudices and myths surrounding subjection close the minds of many women to an honest investigation of it.

In addition, many women fear subjection because most men, likewise, do not understand it. Some men think subjection means that a man should tell his wife "no" all the time while making sure that she doesn't do anything without his permission. Others speculate that subjection means that a man does whatever he wants while his wife pretends to like it. Still others suppose that subjection means that a man gets to boss his wife around all the time. Other men believe that subjection means that their wives can never disagree with them about anything.

With all the confusion between men and women about what subjection involves, no wonder women tremble at the mention of subjection. Yet chapter 6 shows that God gave the law of subjection to protect women and to make their lives more comfortable. Subjection actually liberates a woman and frees her to do the important jobs that God created her for.

However, contrary to what both men and women often believe, God designed subjection *for men, too.* Subjection is not just a feature of marriage. Rather it is a way of life for both men and women in every realm of life--the government, the marketplace, the family, and the church. *In all of these realms, with the exception of the family and some aspects of the church, men have as much responsibility to be submissive as women have.* In addition, the quality of subjection does not differ between what God requires of men or from women. Subjection is not a feminine issue! Subjection applies to *both men* and women. The difference comes from *where* they practice subjection. Subjection begins with the universal law of authority:

I. UNIVERSAL LAW OF AUTHORITY

I Cor. 11:3: **"But I want you to understand that Christ is the head of every man, and the man is the head of a woman, and God is the head of Christ."**

Rather than the main topic being the woman's covering, I Cor. 11:3-16 teaches about subjection--how a woman shows subjection in both the family and the spiritual realms. For this reason, the section begins with a universal law of authority. This line of authority begins with God who delegated authority to Christ to serve as the head of man. Then Christ delegated authority to the man to serve as the head of woman.

A. GOD OVER CHRIST

This line of authority represents a tremendous amount of wisdom, for God is a God of order. For example, the divine relationship of God the Father to God the Son and to God the Holy Spirit rests upon authority and subjection. God exercises supreme authority, Christ submits to Him (Mt. 26:39; Jn. 5:30; Heb. 5:8), and the Holy Spirit submits to Christ (Jn. 14:26, 16:13-14) and to God. This efficient organization results in a very powerful working unit that has blessed and continues to bless the world.

For example, working together through subjection and leadership, the divine team of God, Christ, and the Holy Spirit designed and created the earth with its plant and animal life. In addition, they designed and created humans with intricate bodies and mental abilities. Continuing to work together, the Godhead gave these complex organisms the Bible to guide their lives into complete happiness. By working together, by practicing subjection and leadership, they accomplished this tremendous work that continues to astonish the minds of mere humans.

A God of order in His own life, God ordained that every single human relationship likewise follow a pattern of order. In other words, God placed someone in authority over the others in every realm of human endeavor--civil government, the marketplace, the family, and the church. Over all of these realms, God placed Christ over man in the line of authority:

B. CHRIST OVER MAN

Mt. 28:18: "And Jesus came up and spoke to them, saying, 'All authority has been given to Me in heaven and on earth."

Jesus said, "All authority *has been given* to Me." Thus, God delegated all of the authority to Jesus that He possesses in heaven and on earth. All mankind must submit to Christ. Then Jesus delegates certain authority to men to aid them in living orderly lives on earth.

However, all of the authority that God through Christ gives man, in every single realm, *is confined to specific areas of human opinion.* The definition of the word "subjection," the same word used for subjection to the government, the employer, the husband, parents, and the elders shows this. "Be subject" means "to subject one's self, to obey, to submit to one's control, *to yield to one's admonition or advice"* (Thayer, p. 645). Thus, God gives man certain areas of dominion over other people *only in the realm of human opinion.*

In addition, the line of authority confirms this same principle. For instance, the line of authority places the divine judgments of God and Christ over men. Obviously then, God's authority overrides man's and all conflicts are settled in favor of God. *Consequently, the only authority left for man to exercise is in selected areas of human opinion.* All other authority belongs to God. Thus, man's authority in the civil government, the marketplace, the family, and the church is limited to designated areas of human opinion.

Anything that can be proven from the Bible constitutes the authority of God and Jesus and is not within man's authority to change. If a man tries to make changes in God's authority, those under him must obey God rather than man. Thus, they obey the higher authority when disagreements occur. These principles control the man's authority over the woman:

C. MAN OVER WOMAN

> I Cor. 11:11-12: "However, in the Lord, neither is woman independent of man, nor is man independent of woman. For as the woman originates from the man, so also the man has his birth through the woman; and all things originate from God."

Chapter 5, "The 'Very Good,' Lost and Found" discusses the two reasons why the woman owes subjection to the man, because (1) she was made from man's side and (2) she was made for man as a helper meet for him (I Cor. 11:7-10). Now Paul sums up these principles by affirming that "in the Lord" subjection does not make the woman a second-class citizen. To prove this, he explains how the man depends upon the woman. They both need each other as they work together to serve God. From the beginning of creation,

God determined that the man and woman would share a relationship of order, just as God, Christ, and the Holy Spirit share an orderly working arrangement. God created men and women to work and to reach goals in their personal lives. Subjection and leadership simply allows them to become their most productive selves.

However, the expression "in the Lord" qualifies the woman's subjection. A similar phrase occurs in each of the realms where God delegates authority to man--civil government, the marketplace, the family, and the church. In each instance, "in the Lord" tells the one in subjection to obey God's divine judgments over man's opinions. Just as the woman being taken out of man shows her need to submit to him, the fact that both the man and woman originated from God shows their need to submit to Him. God's authority overrides man's opinions in every instance of conflict.

II. SUBJECTION IN THE EARTHLY REALM

Understanding the basic universal law of authority clears up many misunderstandings in the earthly realm. As a God of order, God designates that certain people exercise leadership in the many areas of life upon the earth. The following domains of man's authority are listed in descending rank, for the highest order of authority on earth is the civil government:

A. CIVIL GOVERNMENT

> Rom. 13:1-2: Let every person be in subjection to the governing authorities. For there is no authority except from God, and those which exist are established by God. Therefore he who resists authority has opposed the ordinance of God; and they who have opposed will receive condemnation upon themselves."

God through Christ gives the civil government the job of rendering vengeance against evildoers (Rom. 12:19; 13:4). For example, since the flood God ordains that men respect life by taking the life of any man or animal who sheds man's blood (Gen. 9:5-6). Since this is not in the realm of human opinion, but a divine

judgment which can be read in the Bible, man has no
say in the matter. Thus, when men fail to cover up the
blood of the slain by refusing to exercise capital
punishment, God brings down His wrath upon the nation
involved (Num. 35:29-34, Isa. 26.21).

On the other hand, God gives civil governments a
certain amount of authority in the realm of human
opinion. As with the wife, the regulating factor for
obeying the civil government is God's laws--do the
government's opinions contradict God's ordinances as
recorded in the Bible. If not, Peter says, "Submit yourselves *for the Lord's sake* to every human institution:
whether to a king as the one in authority; or to governors as sent by him for the punishment of evildoers
and the praise of those who do right" (I Pet. 2:13-14).
Thus, "for the Lord's sake" shows that the authority of
God and Christ overrides the civil government's opinions.

Paul mentions the most common area where civil
governments exercise their opinions--collecting taxes
(Rom. 13:7). God gives governments the right to determine the amount of taxes that they collect and to establish the procedure. In addition, modern governments
set speed limits. While opinions vary on what is the
safest speed, the government's opinion overrides the
motorist's opinion. That's why policemen issue tickets.
The government also enjoys the right to require mo-
torists to wear seat belts or citizens to license their
firearms. All of these areas are in the realm of opinion
and do not conflict with divine laws.

Unfortunately, some governments prohibit people
from worshiping God. Other governments prohibit parents
from disciplining their children. In these instances,
plain Bible commands (Heb. 19:23-25; 12:8-11; etc.)
indicate that God's authority overrides the government's. As a result, God's people must obey God rather
than man.

Underneath the civil government's authority rests
the husband's authority over his wife:

B. HUSBANDS

Col. 3:18: "Wives, be subject to your husbands, as is fitting in the Lord."

God gives the husband-wife team the important work of subduing the earth, bearing children, and glorifying God. So to help them realize their goals, God places the man in authority over the woman in the realm of opinion. However, again the overriding factor is "as is fitting in the Lord." While part of a wife's duty to the Lord is obeying her husband, if her husband tells her to do something that contradicts what the government or God says, she must obey the overriding authority.

For example, if a woman's husband tells her to drive seventy miles per hour when the speed limit is fifty-five, then she must obey what the government says. Likewise, if her husbands wants her to sign a fraudulent income-tax form, she must refuse out of obedience to the government's opinion.

This same principle holds true in the woman's service to God. If a woman's husband forbids her to attend worship, she must obey God rather than her husband (Heb. 10:23-25). If her husband tells her to lie to cover up something he did wrong, she must obey God and tell the truth no matter how unhappy it makes her husband (Rev. 21:8). However, when a wife feels that she must disobey her husband, she should make sure that she is not substituting her opinion for a divine ordinance. She should be able to read in the Bible where her husband's wishes contradict God's desires.

Sometimes a wife thinks, "I can argue and argue with my husband all I want. And if I can finally persuade him to my way of thinking, then really, I'm submissive. After all, he changed his opinion, didn't he?" Such wifely logic ignores the meaning of subjection--yielding to the admonition and advice of others. An argumentative wife doesn't yield; she just outlasts her husband. Husbands who give in just to keep the peace think their wives are anything but submissive.

This does not mean, however, that a wife can never express an opinion. To the contrary, wise husbands value their wives' opinions and different perspectives. Even so, the husband may decide to do something different. In that case, God gives the husband the right to make judgments in the realm of human opinion. The second time a wife repeats herself, and especially the third time, she treads on dangerous ground. Although perhaps unintentionally, she fails to recognize her husband's right to rule in the realm of human opinion.

One Saturday morning a young bride of a college student politely asked, "Honey, would you please empty the trash for me?" Even though her husband was studying, she expected him to stop and immediately empty the trash for her. He didn't do it, but kept studying. After waiting an hour or more, she again said, "Please, Honey, would you empty the trash for me?" She felt proud of the way she was handling the matter because her tone of voice was so nice and she didn't feel any animosity toward him. She thought, "This is what subjection is all about." She waited another hour or so for her husband to stop studying and empty the trash. When he didn't, she asked him a third time making sure that she asked him as sweetly as the two previous times.

This time her husband replied, "You have asked me three times, and I heard you each time." In recounting the incident, the wife said, "It really made an impression on me because I didn't realize I was nagging. I thought I was being sweet and patient. But it came across as nagging him. I also realize in looking back on it that I wasn't being considerate of his study needs. I expected him to drop whatever he was doing and do what I wanted."

By ordaining the law of subjection, God has done away with the power struggle in marriage so that couples can get busy doing His work. Likewise, God has eliminated the power struggle in regard to raising children:

C. FATHERS

> **Eph. 6:4: "And, fathers, do not provoke your children to anger; but bring them up in the discipline and instruction of the Lord."**

God gives a father authority over the discipline and upbringing of his children. Yet a father exercises this authority only in the realm of opinion. For example, speaking of fathers, Heb. 12:18 says, "For they disciplined us for a short time as *seemed best to them.*"

God gives the father lots of room for opinion in the realm of discipline. For example, Prov. 29:15 says, "The rod and reproof give wisdom, but a child who gets his own way brings shame to his mother." This obligates the father to look at his child and to ask the question, "Do I need to use the rod, or should I just set him down and talk to him, or should I take away some privileges?" Whatever the father decides will be an opinion--an opinion God gives him the right to make.

However, God tells fathers not to exasperate their children or to provoke them to anger (Col. 3:21). The father needs to base his opinions on the elements of wisdom discussed in chapter 4 -- righteousness, justice, and equity. Treating a child with the same courtesies afforded other people such as "please" and "thank you" go a long way in promoting harmony in the home.

A mother exercises authority over her children being in subjection to her husband's opinions unless God's divine judgment or the government's laws override her husband. However, being submissive in the realm of raising children causes women perhaps more problems than any other area of subjection. Most of this stems from the mother's tender emotional nature. She finds it much easier to side with her children than her husband does. Thus, the proverb reads, "a child who gets his own way *shames his mother.*"

One wife asked, "But suppose you *just know* your husband is wrong?" When asked how she knew he was wrong, she stated more emphatically, "But suppose you *just know* he's wrong?" When asked a third time how she knew he was wrong, she answered, "I guess I don't know *for sure* that he's wrong. It's just my opinion against his opinion."

Mother-father conflicts have always existed and they always will as long as men and women are different in their mental makeups. Usually the mother thinks the father is too overbearing and the father thinks the mother is too lenient. Fortunately, when the mother and father work together as God designed, they balance each other by bringing overlooked facts to the other's attention. A wise father appreciates his wife pointing out details he missed. Having all the facts helps him make a wise decision.

Furthermore, in giving men authority in matters of opinion, God nowhere says that men can't make mistakes. The civil government makes plenty of mistakes in judgment, thus the continual changing of laws. Likewise, husbands make lots of mistakes in establishing budgets, choosing cars, etc. Even fathers make mistakes in setting discipline standards for their children. Yet God gives wise men the right to make mistakes (Prov. 9:8-9).

For this reason, a wife's obedience to her husband doesn't depend upon his perfect judgment. Anytime that a wife feels that she must disobey in any of these areas, she should do so on the basis of scripture rather than her opinion.

In like manner, God directs children to obey their parents in the Lord:

Eph. 6:1: "Children obey your parents in the Lord, for this is right."

God commands children to obey their parents. How long? As long as what their parents tell them to do doesn't conflict with what Christ tells them to do. As long as it's in the realm of human opinion, and not in the realm of divine judgment.

Sometimes parents tell their children to do things that conflict with divine judgment. For example, when somebody calls and the child answers the phone, sometimes a parent says, "Tell them I'm not at home." Such a parent wants his child to tell a lie to make life a little easier. However, when a child tells a lie for his parents, it is still telling a lie. When the child obeys God first, he tells his parents, "I'm sorry Mother," or "I'm sorry, Daddy, that I can't lie for you. I can tell them that you don't want to talk to him or something like that. Or you could come talk to them and take care of the situation. But I must obey God rather than man."

D. EMPLOYERS

I Pet. 2:18: "Servants, be submissive to your masters with all respect, not only to those

**who are good and gentle, but also to those
who are unreasonable [perverse--NASV foot-
note]."**

Subjection plays an important part in the way a
man earns a living. The word "submissive" is the same
word studied all the way through this chapter which
refers to yielding to the opinions of others. The word
"respect," showing the man's attitude toward his employer, is the same word as "respectful" in I Pet. 3:1
and "reverence" in Eph. 5:33 which describes the
proper attitude of a wife toward her husband. In addition, God wants a man to even respect an unreasonable
or perverse employer (I Pet. 2:18) just as He wants a
wife to respect an unbelieving and possibly wicked
husband (I Pet. 3:1). The main difference, God gives
husbands the right to change employers, but He
doesn't give wives the right to change their husbands
just because they don't like their opinions.

In other words, God expects a man to show exactly
the same attitude toward his employer that He requires
a wife to show toward her husband. *Thus, God wants
both men and women to be submissive in their individual
realms of work.* Just as God expects the wife to be
submissive within her realm of work within the home--
caring for her husband and children, God also expects
the husband to be submissive within his realm of work
outside the home--subduing the earth.

When the wife works outside the home, she just
takes on an additional area of subjection. So a woman
who flees marriage to get away from subjection just
exchanges one realm of subjection for another. However, one leader loves her; the other one doesn't.
Many a homemaker who previously worked at an exciting secular job claims that she enjoys more freedom
to be creative and fulfilled in the home than she ever
found submitting to a boss who cared only about making money.

Both men and working women share *equal responsibilities* to submit to their employers with one exception: A wife must recognize her husband as the higher
authority when submitting to her employer. For example, a woman's husband might want her to avoid
working nights or certain hours or days. Or he may tell
his wife that he doesn't want her to do a certain kind

of job. In those cases, the husband's opinion overrides the employer's.

In all other areas, men and women submit in exactly the same manner to their employers in the realm of human opinion. As before, "as to Christ" in Eph. 6:5-8 provides the controlling factor. When the employer's opinion contradicts the opinions of God or the civil government, an employee must obey the overriding opinion.

Sometimes the employer's opinion conflicts with the government's, such as when he wants his employee to file false tax statements or to lie to the customers about a problem. In all of these cases, the employee must chose to obey the higher authority. Other times, an employer's opinion may conflict with his employee's opinion. For example, some employers ask their employees to dress a certain way or wear their hair a certain length. This is in the realm of human opinion and God gives employers the right to make this judgment. Yet some employees resist their employers' right to set dress policies. Some employees even sue their employers when they fire them for not getting a hair cut.

Thus, God requires exactly the same type of subjection from men in the earthly realm as He does from women except for two areas--marriage and children. In only these two instances, God requires submission from women that He doesn't require from men. Obviously, subjection has nothing to do with shame, inferiority, or respecter of persons--it is a matter of orderliness and productivity in the Godhead and the earthly realm *for both men* and women.

III. RELATIONSHIP TO GOD

Wives frequently complain, "Why do I have to make *all* the sacrifices, and my husband doesn't have to do anything? He just sits back and soaks it all up!" However, God requires as many sacrifices from the man under his half of leadership as He expects from the woman who practices subjection. Besides that, the man's part demands more personal sacrifices than the woman's half.

Instead of fearing their role as many women do, most men fear failing in their role. Thus, the focus of many men and women is reversed: Women are afraid of what will happen *to them* if they succeed at subjection while man are afraid of what will happen *to their families* if they fail at leadership.

God wonderfully designed subjection and leadership to balance and support each other to make a very productive working unit within marriage. However, ignorance of subjection on the part of both husbands and wives renders many couples ineffective in serving God with their marriages. Perhaps the best way to counteract this ignorance and to show the harmony of subjection and leadership is to study them together by combining their similar qualities. In fact, subjection and leadership utilize *the same attributes of character*. The only difference is the focus. But even here, they are similar, too, because both focus on the other.

In addition, subjection and leadership share similar characteristics with Christians in general. The same attributes which make a person a mature Christian also make that same person a better husband or wife. Even if God never told wives to be submissive or husbands to be loving leaders, Christians would still practice these principles because these are basic principles of Christianity. The same qualities that help a person get along with people in the world also make living with a spouse a pleasant experience.

Fortunately, God has not left it up to Christians to decide to apply the principles of Christianity to their marriages. Instead, God applies the basic principles of Christianity to the marriage relationship for husbands and wives. This shows God's love for men and women. God wants His people to be happy and to enjoy wonderful marriages.

Thus, this section on the mechanics of subjection and leadership starts with the general principle of Christianity followed by the man's part in leadership and the woman's part in subjection. This pattern continues throughout the next two chapters. However, if a wife feels tempted to say, "When my husband does all the number one's, I'll do the number two's," she should pay careful attention to where subjection and leadership begin:

A. BEGINS WITH DEVOTION TO GOD

> **Rom. 6:17-18: "But thanks be to God that though you were slaves of sin, you became obedient from the heart to that form of teaching to which you were committed, and having been freed from sin, you became slaves of righteousness."**

Paul thanks God for Christians who are completely dedicated to serving God in all areas of their lives to the point of becoming God's slaves. When a situation comes up where what they want to do conflicts with the word of God, they gladly forfeit their desires in preference to God's will.

One of the paradoxes of marriage is that although it affords great opportunities for happiness and personal fulfillment, it also provides a perfect breeding ground for unhappiness and personal sins. The closeness in the home quickly brings to light character defects which often lie hidden from public sight.

For instance, many people who exercise self-control in public let their guards down with their families, allowing their tempers to rage out-of-control. Afterwards, some even apologize profusely to their families. But the apologies mean little to the families who know that a another outburst will soon follow. So marriage, which God designed to bless both men and women, often becomes a battleground where anything goes and; consequently, sin runs rampant behind the closed doors of the homes.

A home cannot function as the wonderful emotional paradise that God intends unless husbands and wives dedicate themselves to serving God twenty-four hours a day, seven days a week, fifty-two weeks a year, for a lifetime. Delighting in a successful marriage begins with the right attitude toward God and His word.

1. THE HUSBAND'S DEVOTION TO GOD

> **I Pet. 3:7: "You husbands likewise, live with your wives in an understanding way, as with a weaker vessel, since she is a woman; and grant her honor as a fellow-**

heir of the grace of life, so that your prayers may not be hindered."

"Hinder" means "properly, a cutting (made in the road to impede one's course by cutting off his way, hence universally to hinder)" (Thayer, p. 166).

Peter tells husbands that if they fail to treat their wives properly and living with them according to understanding, God will not hear their prayers. Thus, it doesn't matter how long or how beautifully a man prays or how many times he is called upon to lead public prayers. If he fails to treat his wife right, his prayers don't go any higher than the ceiling.

"Likewise" indicates that God expects husbands to work at making their marriages happy just as He expects women to. When husbands neglect treating their wives properly, they adversely affect their relationship with God. The apostle John explains: "We know that God does not hear sinners; but if any one is God-fearing, and does His will, He hears him" (Jn. 9:31). God classifies a man who wrongs his wife as a sinner, and He promises that no sinners will enter heaven. How can a woman then say that God does not love women? God demands that men treat women properly if they expect to live with Him throughout eternity.

Since the way a man treats his wife affects his relationship with God, a man's leadership does not hinge upon whether or not he married a good or a bad wife, a warm or a cold lover, a good or a poor cook, an efficient or a careless housekeeper, an affectionate or an indifferent mother of his children, or a pleasing or a repulsive companion. A man's relationship with his wife reflects his attitude toward serving God regardless of what his wife does.

Unfortunately, many men get it backwards. They govern their actions by the way their wives treat them instead of treating their wives right because they love and trust God. But regardless of what a husband does or doesn't do, God holds the wife responsible for her own actions:

2. THE WIFE'S DEVOTION TO GOD

Col. 3:18: "Wives, be subject to your husbands, as is fitting in the Lord."

"Fitting" means "to have come up to, arrived at, to reach to, pertain to, what is due, duty" (Thayer, p. 45).

A wife doesn't practice subjection because she's not smart or because she's a coward or because she's inferior to her husband. Instead, a wife practices subjection to her husband because she loves God, and it is her "duty" to the Lord. God created a wife to be a helper who is meet for her husband. Without subjection, or adapting herself to her husband's mood and spirit, she cannot become meet for her husband. In this way, submitting herself to her husband's opinions enables a wife to work with him and to accomplish what God created her to do.

As a result, subjection becomes part of a woman's service to God and glorifies God as a good work. Realizing that subjection is a good work and in reality is subjection to God makes subjection easier for the woman who fears it. This means that God is the woman's overriding authority. If her husband asks her to commit a sin, she obeys the supreme authority-- God. Obviously, sometimes a wife may have to disobey her husband to obey God. In that instance, she still submits "as is fitting in the Lord."

This doesn't give a woman the right to thumb her nose at her husband and self-righteously declare, "I don't have to obey you in this matter!" or "I'm better than you are so I don't have to do what you say!" Instead, a submissive wife who cannot obey her husband in order to obey God, feels grieved. She tells her husband, "I'm sorry that I cannot obey you in this matter. I want to please you with all my heart. But I must please God and do what He says. Thus, I cannot obey you in *this instance* although it deeply pains me." She still maintains a submissive attitude toward her husband even when she cannot carry out his will.

However, if a wife's mind *is not* in subjection, telling her husband that she cannot obey him will probably offend him. He will view it as just another example of how she refuses to submit. On the other hand, if she always submits to him and then must disobey him, her husband knows that she really wants to please him, but can't out of conviction.

Sometimes a wife assumes that her husband's sins cancel her personal responsibilities. For example, many a wife reasons, "He's selfish and doesn't consider my needs, so why should I do what he wants?" Such a woman seems to think that two sins add up to a happy marriage. Instead, they usual result in a fight.

Just as a man's obedience of God doesn't depend on how his wife treats him, neither does a woman's obedience. God doesn't command a wife to submit because she married a wonderful husband, a good provider, a warm lover, a diligent father for her children, or an exciting companion. God commands a wife to submit because she loves Him. If a woman truly loves God, it affects the way she submits to her husband:

Eph. 5:22: "Wives be subject to your own husbands, as to the Lord."

The fact that subjection is a good work in service to God makes it more important to please the Lord than to please a husband. While a husband doesn't know what his wife does when he is gone, God knows. Therefore, a wife who loves the Lord submits herself to her husband *at all times* to please God.

Paul uses a parallel expression to "as to the Lord" to discuss the relationship of a servant to his master. He explains that "as to Christ" means "not by way of eye-service, as men-pleasers, but as slaves of Christ, doing the will of God from the heart" (Eph. 6:5-7). Accordingly, a wife who submits "as to the Lord" obeys from her heart--she keeps her mind in subjection. A truly submissive wife obeys even when her husband is not watching instead of saying, "What he doesn't know won't hurt him or me."

While many women desire to obey God, permanently changing thinking and conduct takes deliberate effort over a prolonged period of time. Thus, it may take a wife many hours of study and practice before she can truly render heart-felt service to God in the area of subjection. For example, many women become encouraged about their marriages when they begin learning their role and start noticing some improvements. However, those with deep problems usually reach a plateau somewhere in the middle of their journey to happiness.

They become discouraged because their husbands have not completely changed the way they think they should. Sometimes these women fume, "It's not fair! Why do I have to make all the sacrifices and my husband doesn't have to give up anything?"

As they blame their husbands for many problems, the plateau suddenly turns into a crisis. Often very angry, they blame God, too, and want to reject His plan for their lives as unfair and unworkable. *Yet this crisis point signals the opportunity for the women to step across the threshold of misery into God's glorious light.* Typical of many women who begin studying their role, they want a better marriage, but they don't want to give up too many of their rights in the process. However, their emotional crisis makes it impossible for them to keep straddling the fence that sits between having it their way or God's way.

Emotional pain radiating from the very core of their being drives these women to make *a permanent decision.* Whether they like it or not, these wives must make a choice *to find peace within themselves.* They must choose to either obey God wholeheartedly even though their husbands have quit responding, or they must choose to revert back to doing things their own way. If the wives face this crisis of commitment and deliberately choose to obey God regardless of how their husbands treat them, they win the battle of the will. Only after they deliberately choose to serve God no matter what the cost can dramatic changes take place in their minds and marriages.

This phenomenon has been observed time after time in students taking these classes. While many women make this transition alone, others need the reassurance of a teacher or an older woman who knows her subject and who has confidence in the word of God. These wives need help to sort through many false attitudes toward both God and men that they have harbored for perhaps years. Continuing to study God's plan for women while engaging in frequent interview-type prayers along with doing the study exercises encourages these women to keep working instead of giving up.

Sadly, the failure to make this commitment to God is one of the greatest stumbling blocks confronting the happiness of modern marriages. Today many a couple marries with the idea of trying marriage for awhile. Then if it doesn't work out, meaning if the spouse doesn't treat them as nice as they want, they feel free to divorce and start the cycle all over again. Such an attitude prevents the true solving of problems. Yet once women truly surrender their will to God and submit to their husbands because God said to, they stop trying to manipulate their husbands with subjection. And husbands respond to heart-felt subjection.

In summary, both subjection and leadership begin with devotion to God. For the woman, subjection begins when she subjects *herself* to the word of God regardless of what her husband does. For the man, loving leadership begins when he subjects *himself* to the will of God regardless of what his wife does. Neither subjection nor leadership reflect a person's love for his spouse or the spouse's love for him. *Subjection and leadership demonstrate the individual's love for God.*

B. PROMOTES MARITAL SUCCESS

> **I Tim. 4:8: "...for bodily discipline is only little profit, but godliness if profitable for all things, since it holds the promise for the present life and also for the life to come."**

In this passage God states a general principle of Christianity: Just as following a regular exercise program builds good physical health and stamina, godliness is profitable for all things in the present life and the one to come. In other words, godliness—an attitude of always trying to please God—improves the quality of a person's life in every realm. In effect, God guarantees the person who seeks to obey Him wholeheartedly success on earth and in heaven, too.

As chapter 2 shows, the context of this passage deals specifically with foods and marriage, things God created to be gratefully shared in, but rejected by many people. If a person wants a sanctified or happy marriage, he must practice from his heart the rules for marriage that God ordained. In addition, God cautions the husband and wife each individually that they must obey His laws if they want a successful marital union:

1. THE HUSBAND PROMOTES MARITAL SUCCESS

Eph. 5:28-30: "So husbands ought also to love their own wives as their own bodies. He who loves his own wife loves himself; for no one ever hated his own flesh, but nourishes and cherishes it, just as Christ also does the church, because we are members of His body."

"Nourish" means "1. nourish up to maturity; 2. nurture, bring up" (Thayer, p. 200).

"Cherish" means "1. properly to warm, keep warm; 2. cherish with tender love, foster with tender care" (Thayer, p. 282).

That little word "ought" refers to a debt owed to someone else. What debt? The debt a husband owes his wife to love her as his own body! The word "love" comes from the Greek word *agapeo* discussed in chapters 7 and 8 and refers to the husband's attitude of always acting in the best interest of his wife. "As his own body" means that a husband places his wife's needs on an equal plane with his own desires. A leadership position leaves no room for selfishness.

Paul said "for no one ever hated his own flesh, but nourishes and cherishes it." A man's attitude toward his physical body shows what his attitude should be toward his marital body, his wife: When hungry, he feeds his body. When cold, he clothes his body. When tired, he rests his body. When bored, he amuses his body. When sad, he comforts his body. When sick, he takes his body to the doctor. When sexually aroused, he seeks satisfaction for his body.

By paying his marriage debt, a husband defuses his wife's greatest fear in regard to subjection--selfishness on his part. While a husband possesses a very strong authority antenna that homes in on any breech of submission in his wife or children, a wife possesses a very sensitive selfishness antenna. She immediately perceives any selfishness on her husband's part, even if unintentional, as a threat to her well-being. Just as the physical body depends on the head for satisfaction of its needs, so a wife depends on her head, her husband, for satisfaction of her needs.

Thus, when a husband considers his wife's needs and readily supplies them, he takes away her fear of yielding totally to him. Many a wife gladly forgoes necessities when she believes her husband honestly considers her needs in his decisions. Such a loving husband causes his wife to delight in her feminine role. He makes her want to love him, to take care of his children, and to clean his house--to cheerfully do whatever he bids. Indeed, a husband who loves his wife as his own body loves himself because of the benefits he reaps from his wife.

On the other hand, many a woman demands the moon simply because her husband looks out for his own interests while ignoring hers. When a wife becomes busy defending herself from the selfishness of her husband, she loses her ability to give spontaneous love and to express tender sympathy for him. Every woman knows that Paul spoke the truth when he said, "a man who loves his wife loves himself" because of the response it creates in a wife's heart.

One wife deliberately overspent the food budget because her husband spent badly needed money on a luxury item for himself. She reasoned, "If he isn't going to take care of the children and me, then I'm not going to worry about staying within the budget!"

Another woman resented her husband because he refused to let her buy a luxury item she really wanted on the grounds, "We can't afford it." Yet he bought luxury item after luxury item for himself. Some wives periodically go on shopping sprees to even the score.

A selfish husband hurts himself most of all. He may surround himself with luxuries and get to do whatever he wants, but he also enfolds himself in his wife's coldness. A husband's selfishness makes his wife fear subjection.

The word "cherish" is the same word as "tenderly cares" in I Thess. 2:7 where a nursing mother "tenderly cares for her children." A woman's emotional nature makes her a perfect giver of affectionate love to her family. But her emotional nature also makes her crave that same obvious love from her husband. One wife confided, "I would do anything for my husband to come up to me when I'm washing the dishes and kiss me on the neck."

When a man surrounds his wife with warmth and tenderness, he enhances her loving nature. He makes his wife feel secure in giving her love freely. A woman's emotional love needs security because her love involves giving her total self to her husband.

A wife doesn't want her husband to keep her warm with an electric blanket. She wants obvious evidence of his tender feelings for her such as pats, hugs, squeezes, kisses, caresses, and lovemaking to make her "feel" loved. When a husband forces his wife to analyze whether or not he loves her, he hampers her ability to love him. A wise husband remembers every day of his marriage that *women crave obvious affection from the heart.*

Certainly, God hands the husband a grave responsibility to be a capable, loving leader. Rather than a position of selfishness, competent leadership requires doing what is best for the followers. When a man properly assumes his position of authority, his wife feels protected. In return, such a man reaps love from his wife for his labors.

If a wife lives with a selfish or a cold husband, obviously combating the problem with selfishness and aloofness of her own only makes the problem worse. Instead of criticizing her husband, a wise wife looks to her own areas for promoting success in her marriage:

2. THE WIFE PROMOTES MARITAL SUCCESS

I Pet. 3:3-5: "And let not your adornment be external only--braiding the hair, and wearing gold jewelry, and putting on dresses; but let it be the hidden person of the heart, with the imperishable quality of a gentle and quiet spirit, which is precious in the sight of God. For in this way in former times the holy women also, who hoped in God, used to adorn themselves, being submissive to their own husbands."

"Adornment" means "1. an apt and harmonious arrangement or constitution, order; 2. ornament, decoration, adornment" (Thayer, p. 356).

432   MARRIAGE: A TASTE OF HEAVEN: VOL. I

Peter cautions women not to place their hopes for attracting and keeping a husband in their external appearance such as "braiding the hair, and wearing gold jewelry, and putting on dresses." However, some people misuse Peter's instructions to teach that women should not braid their hair or wear gold jewelry at all. If that is what Peter means, then the verse *also condemns wearing dresses,* for Peter puts dresses in the same category with braided hair and gold jewelry. And if Peter condemns wearing dresses, he also contradicts the previous verse which tells women to conduct themselves in a chaste manner.

Understanding the purpose of an ellipsis, a "not-but" construction with a common verb, takes away the mystery of Peter's condemnation of braiding the hair and wearing jewelry. The Orientals (including the apostles of Christ) used ellipsis to show a relationship between two things that were both true. However, they placed the emphasis on the second item preceded by the "but." As a result, the Jews understood Peter to say, "While a woman pays *some attention* to her outward adorning, to fixing her hair and wearing jewelry and pretty dresses, *let it take second place* to her putting on the inner beauty of a gentle and quiet spirit."

The Shulammite maiden demonstrated the principle Peter teaches. For example, she said that she did not spend countless hours primping in front of the mirror as other girls did (Song of Sol. 1:6). Yet she took time to dress attractively, for a single strand of her necklace made the Shepherd's heart beat faster (Song of Sol. 4:9).

In the same way, the woman of great price made clothing for herself out of fine linen and purple (Prov. 31:22). A busy woman, she was a loving wife, an excellent housekeeper, a devoted mother, a helper of the needy, and even a part time business woman. While she did not have time to waste maintaining an extravagant appearance, she took time to keep her appearance appropriate and attractive.

While Peter condemns the vanity of extravagance, he does not promote drab dress for a woman. Rather, he teaches women to keep their grooming habits in proper perspective with their goals in life and to place their priorities on dressing the inner person as the Shulammite and the woman of great price did.

Indeed, a woman's true beauty comes from within-- from her heart. Beautiful outer garments look cheap on a woman who lacks inner beauty, for inner beauty balances and supports physical beauty. Inner beauty is imperishable and causes even older women to radiate attractiveness. One preacher said that an older woman who does not possess inner beauty cannot compete in attractiveness with eighteen-year-old girls. But an eighteen-year-old girl, no matter how pretty, cannot compete with the loveliness of older women who are filled with spiritual beauty and maturity. Lottie Beth Hobbs adequately sums up how women attain true beauty in her book *You Can Be Beautiful*:

> A lovely life must be deliberate; it never happens accidentally. Making the most of ourselves requires a lifetime of constant vigilance and diligence. Pleasing physical traits may be inherited, but true beauty must be acquired. A wise teacher told her class of high school girls: "You may not be pretty at twenty, but at forty there is no excuse." Every admirable trait can be developed. We have within us the power to be all God intended. When we walk in righteousness, we appropriate an eternal power and fulfill an eternal purpose. God gives us life and a "do it yourself" kit. The rest is up to us.[1]

In addition, the context makes Peter's instructions concerning clothing easy to understand. The two verses immediately preceding the passage on dress definitely teach about subjection. Likewise, the two verses following Peter's comments also refer to subjection. Obviously, assuming that the instructions about dress have nothing to do with subjection, lifts them completely out of context and, thereby, misses a very important principle of subjection.

---

[1]Lottie Beth Hobbs, *You Can Be Beautiful (with the Beauty of Holiness)*, (Ft. Worth, TX: Harvest Publications, 1959), p. 15. Used by permission.

Many women object, "But I'm not a clothes horse! I don't primp in front of the mirror every day. I'm too busy! How can these passages possibly affect my relationship with my husband? What does wearing too much jewelry, expensive garments, or fancy hair-dos have to do with subjection?"

The problem with subjection and clothing is that many modern wives, while not slaves of the fashion industry, still place their hopes for a happy marriage in the wrong place--in their looks. Many a wife thinks that if she can only lose thirty pounds, wear contacts, change the color of her hair, get a new outfit, buy a revealing negligee, or go the beauty shop once a week; all her marriage problems will disappear. The fact is, many women blame their marriage problems on their appearance no matter how minor or overwhelming their physical defects might be.

Therefore, Peter cautions women not to fall into the trap of blaming their troubles on the outer man. While appearance is important, personality and attitude defects cause a lot more marriage problems than what a woman wears. Peter emphasizes this point with his statements about the gentle and quiet spirit. Then Peter proves his point by holding up the holy women of old as perfect examples of beautiful and successful wives.

Peter says, "For in this way"--in the ways just described of adorning the heart with a gentle and quiet spirit, "in former times the holy women also, who hoped in God"--the women who desired and expected to go to heaven, "used to adorn themselves"--they made themselves beautiful both to God and their husbands by "being submissive to their own husbands"--these women made themselves beautiful with subjection that reflected a gentle and quiet spirit.

When a woman wants to make herself attractive, she doesn't wear the ugliest dress in her closet, nor act like an ill-bred barbarian. Instead, she wears the prettiest dress she owns and puts on company manners. An intelligent woman finds attractive garments to use to make herself even more appealing to others. In fact, Webster says that the word "adorn" implies taking something attractive and putting it on something else to make it even more beautiful.

So it is with subjection. Subjection, a beautiful quality when practiced properly, turns an attractive woman into an even more lovely wife. While women fear subjection, men readily recognize the power it holds over them. Just as a husband loving his wife as his own body makes sense to women, being submissive makes sense to men. They know that a wife's subjection makes her husband want to do more things than ever for her. It makes him love and value her more. It makes her precious in his sight. Men recognize that a wife's subjection brings out the best in them and makes them become better husbands.

At the same time, the strong authority antennae of men refuse to let them acknowledge lip-service on the part of their wives. Thus, Peter teaches women how to abolish the number-one reason many husbands act selfishly toward their wives: Many men ignore their wives' legitimate needs simply because they think their wives aren't submissive. Their bodies may do everything right, but they have not adorned themselves with a gentle and quiet spirit by putting their minds in subjection. As a result, many husbands try to prove their right to lead their wives by lording it over them and by restricting their lives.

Unfortunately, the wives frequently respond, "I'd better stand up for my rights or he'll treat me worse than ever." Then when they stand up for their rights, their husbands often mistreat them worse than ever. Thus they start a vicious circle of each bringing out the other's worst features instead of their better sides.

In summary, when a man does what God commands him to do as a husband, he makes his wife love him more and want to please him. When a woman does what God commands her to do as a wife, she makes herself more beautiful and desirable to her husband who in turn wants to please her. Even if only one spouse obeys God's laws of subjection and leadership, he creates an environment that brings out the best in the other. The marriage becomes better than if neither one obeyed God. *When both subjection and leadership are practiced, personal happiness and a successful marriage results.*

B. PORTRAYS THE HEAVENLY MARRIAGE

> **Gen. 1:26–27: "Then God said, 'Let us make man in our image, according to our likeness; and let them rule over the fish of the sea and over the birds of the sky and over the cattle and over all the earth, and over every creeping thing that creeps on the earth.' And God created man in His own image, in the image of God He created him; male and female He created them."**

In the very beginning, God created the man and woman in His image, but sin separated them from the image of God. However, when a man and woman strive to imitate God in love, patience, abhorrence of sin, good works, etc., they reflect the image of God for those outside of Christ to see (II Cor. 3:18; Eph. 4:13).

In addition, the marriage relationship presents a special opportunity for husbands and wives to portray the heavenly marriage. While the opportunities for men and women differ, they balance and support each other and utilize the unique characteristics and talents of each:

1. THE HUSBAND, A PICTURE OF CHRIST

> **Eph. 5:23: "For the husband is the head of the wife, as Christ also is the head of the church, He Himself being the Savior of the body."**

Part of the wonderment of marriage stems from the way it parallels heavenly figures. For God designed the marriage relationship to present a picture to the world of Christ's relationship to the church. Just exactly as Christ leads the church, God wants a husband to lead his wife. This means that when others look at a husband's relationship with his wife, they see *a living picture* of Christ's relationship with His bride, the church. God designed for the life of a husband to match the life of Christ in love, sacrifice, devotion, provision, tenderness, thoughtfulness, and hard work.

What an example to imitate! Christ loves the church deliberately. He loved the church before the foundation of the world. He loves Christians before they become Christians. No one forces Christ to love Christians, He does it voluntarily. When the world looks at a husband, it should see the great richness of character that originated in Christ and a picture of Christ's love for the church. Likewise, God gives the woman a special image to portray to the world:

2. THE WIFE, A PICTURE OF THE CHURCH

Eph. 5:24: "But as the church is subject to Christ, so also the wives ought to be to their husbands in everything."

Just exactly as the church submits to her husband Christ, so God wants a wife to submit to her own husband. For example, the church submits "herself" to her "own" husband, Christ, calling Him "Lord." The church "obeys" in "everything" with "meekness" and "quietness" with "reverence." Thus, when a person looks at a wife, he should see *a living picture* of the church's obedience to Christ.

Both the husband and wife preach a strong sermon to the world by the way they treat each other. When they follow God's plan for their lives, they proclaim God's love and wisdom to everyone they come in contact with. What better way can men and women teach a lost world about a loving Savior?

God choose the institution of marriage to describe life in heaven with Him and Christ (Rev. 19:7-8). Obviously then, when husbands and wives delight in wonderfully happy marriages, they take a small taste of the joys of heaven, thus the title of this series of lessons: *Marriage: A Taste of Heaven*. In a similar manner, the mutual ecstasy that husbands and wives feel for each other presents a visual-aid of heaven to non-Christians. It gives them a taste of heaven too.

When husbands and wives fully realize that their relationship to Christ in heaven parallels their marriages, it makes them appreciate their earthly marriages that much more. Likewise, that realization creates eager anticipation of entering the heavenly marriage. It also arouses their desire to work at improving their earthly marriages even more. And the more they strengthen their earthly marriages, the more they desire to enter the heavenly one.

In summary, *both subjection and leadership have a tremendous power for evangelism by portraying examples of spiritual truths about the church--Christ's love for His people and the church's absolute obedience to Him.* Together, the husband and wife become a highly effective team for converting others to Christ. God wants His people to be happily married in this life and in the life to come.

STUDY EXERCISE

Answer all questions in your own words.

1. What is God's universal law of authority? What is the order of authority in the earthly realm?

2. In what realm does God give men the right to exercise authority?

3. In what areas must men practice subjection? In what ways is subjection similar for both men and women?

4. What does "as to the Lord" mean?

5. Give three everyday examples of how a wife might not subject herself "as to the Lord."

6. How does the way a person practices subjection or leadership affect his relationship with God?

7. If a woman's opinion conflicts with her husband's opinion, whose opinion does she know *for certain* is right? What should she do?

8. How does a wife placing herself in subjection to her husband make her fulfill God's purpose for creating her in Gen. 2:18?

9. Do you disagree with anything in this lesson? If so, explain in detail giving scriptures for your reasons.

GOAL-ACHIEVING EXERCISE

Change the following points to fit your individual needs. Review this exercise as you study the next three chapters and make additions as necessary.

Purpose: To portray the heavenly marriage through proper use of subjection and leadership.

Goals:

1. To conduct yourself in a submissive manner at all times even when your husband is not aware of your actions.

2. To *enjoy* being submissive even when your husband's will conflicts with yours. If you are not enjoying subjection, you are doing something wrong. Do not blame your husband, but look for the fault within yourself.

Priorities:

1. Give your husband's opinions priority over yours.

2. Give God's divine ordinances priority over your husband's opinions.

3. Give the governments laws priority over your husband's opinions.

Plans:

1. Each morning when you put on your makeup, make a definite commitment to God to be submissive that day. Then if a conflict arises, your mind will already be in subjection and you will be better able to handle it properly.

2. Each night go to God in prayer. Thank Him for giving you strength when you needed it and ask His forgiveness when you failed to be submissive. Ask Him to help you be stronger the next day.

3. Talk to your children about your relationship with your husband. Explain how you must obey him just as they obey both you and him. Tell them that this is God's plan so that mothers and fathers will not fight about who gets to do what. Explain how their father works hard to provide for them as God wants him to.

4. If you are aware of some areas of conflict in the past, you will want to correct them. You may need to apologize to your husband and ask his forgiveness for some incidents. Likewise, you may need to change some of your habits in order to conform to his wishes. Make plans accordingly.

CHAPTER 14

FINDING THE BLESSING IN SUBJECTION

Women often complain, "In theory subjection sounds good, but in practice it is an entirely different story." The reason subjection does not always seem good in practice is because few men and women fully understand the mechanics of subjection and leadership, how they support, balance, and protect each other.

Not only do subjection and leadership benefit each other, but when properly practiced, they produce an highly efficient organization for accomplishing the work God gave men and women to do--subduing the earth, filling it with people, and glorifying God. Likewise, they create an environment which frees men and women to become their most intelligent, creative, and productive selves.

I. RELATIONSHIP TO SELF

However, subjection and leadership demand that both the husband and wife manifest certain attitudes toward themselves. Without proper attitudes toward himself, it becomes impossible for a husband to truly love his wife as his own body. In the same manner, without proper attitudes toward herself, a wife cannot submit in spirit as well as body to her husband. Developing proper attitudes toward themselves enables a husband and wife to find a blessing in subjection instead of enduring a self-made curse.

This chapter follows the pattern of the last chapter by giving a general principle of Christianity and then applying it to the man's leadership and the wife's subjection. Thus, it becomes ever more clear that God makes as many demands upon the husband as He makes upon the wife.

A. ACCEPT PERSONAL RESPONSIBILITY

II Cor. 13:5: "Test yourselves to see if you are in the faith; examine yourselves! Or do you not recognize this about yourselves, that Jesus Christ is in you--unless indeed you fail the test?"

This passage, a basic principle of Christianity, applies to men and women alike, married or unmarried: God expects everyone to examine His word for themselves, and then to put themselves on trial to find out whether or not they obey Him. Thus, Christians who please God accept personal responsibility for their conduct. They don't blame society's evil influence, their parents' lack of teaching, the elders' failure to foresee their problems, the minister's neglect to preach what they needed, the older women for not providing proper role-models, or their spouses for withholding love. Regardless of what anyone else does, God holds His people personally accountable for their own actions.

The same holds true with subjection and leadership. While designed to function as a team, husbands and wives have individual responsibilities toward God that they cannot share. A man cannot delegate his obligations for serving God in his marriage to his wife nor can he serve God for her. Both must examine themselves individually.

Consequently, a godly wife doesn't study the man's half of marriage to help her improve her husband. Rather, she learns about her husband's role so that she can properly support him. In a similar way, better understanding of his wife's responsibilities enables a husband to cherish her more. By taking care of their own duties instead of the other's, a husband and wife become a marvelous working team.

1. THE HUSBAND PROVES HIMSELF LOVING

Col. 3:19: "Husbands, love your wives, and do not be embittered against them."

This verse doesn't say, "Wives, see to it that your husbands love you and aren't embittered against you." Instead, it says, "Husbands, love your wives." Likewise, God directs every other verse that deals with a husband loving his wife toward the husband, not the wife, as for example, Eph. 5:25-33. God places the responsibility for a husband loving his wife upon the husband's shoulders.

As explained in chapter 7, the word "love" comes from the Greek word agapao which refers to an attitude of always acting in the best interest of the object loved. Thus, the word love portrays the opposite of selfishness.

When a wife maintains an active list of complaints about her husband, she frequently tries to remake him. Or if she keeps her unhappiness to herself, she at least wishes he were different. In truth, when a wife tries to remake her husband, she places herself in a position of leadership and ceases to show subjection.

This is probably one of the hardest part of subjection--completely letting go of the man's responsibilities. Many a woman wants subjection on her terms--not her husband's or God's. She tries to make her husband worthy of subjection by nagging him into assuming his rightful role. However, even when a man fails to consider his wife's needs, God still holds him responsible for his behavior, not his wife. At the same time, God tells the wife to pay attention to her own conduct, even if her husband has rejected serving Him:

2. THE WIFE PROVES HERSELF SUBMISSIVE

I Pet. 3:1-2: "In the same way, you wives, be submissive to your own husbands so that even if any of them are disobedient to the word they may be won without a word by the behavior of their wives, as they behold your chaste and respectful behavior."

Many husbands falsely assume that they are to force their wives to be submissive. Yet the verse does not say, "Husbands, place your wives in subjection," but "Wives, be subject to your own husbands." In all the commands concerning subjection, God tells the wife to submit herself (Eph. 5:22; Tit. 2:4-5; Col. 3:18; I Pet. 3:6; and Gen. 3:16). *The fact that subjection is a free will act on the wife's part is probably the most misunderstood aspect of subjection.*

The only time anyone ever commanded a husband to put his wife in subjection occurs in Es. 1:18-22. Here King Ahasuerus commanded the men to put their wives in subjection after his wife refused to obey him. However, this command came from man, not God. God nowhere gives men the authority to force subjection upon their wives, but consistently commands women to place themselves in a sphere of obedience.

God gives every wife the choice of being submissive or contentious. As hard as it may be to let a wife make her own choice, every husband should give his wife the same choice God gives her. He may force her body to obey him, but he cannot force her mind to submit willingly to him. In fact, the more a husband pushes his wife toward subjection, the harder he makes it for her to submit to him. The best way a husband can help his wife become submissive is by following the commands that apply to him and by letting her be responsible for the commands that apply to her.

For example, one wife said that soon after she and her husband married, the men at work gave her husband all kinds of advice to help him avoid marriage problems. They told him, "Don't ever let your wife get the upper hand! Get your thumb down on her right from the beginning and make sure she's in subjection to you. If you ever let her get out of subjection, you'll be sorry."

So when her husband came home from work, he started talking tough to her instead of tenderly. He began bossing her around, and soon they had marriage problems. She believed in subjection and tried to practice it before he started trying to force it on her. Now all of a sudden, it was very hard for her and she found herself resisting subjection.

When a husband tries to force subjection on his wife, she needs to realize that he does it out of ignorance of his role. Even so, the fact that he tries to force subjection on her shows that he doesn't view her as submissive. If a husband *doesn't think* his wife is submissive, she needs to carefully consider the situation. Perhaps she really wants to please her husband, but she doesn't always know what he wants. In that case, she needs to tell him that she's not a mind reader and he needs to communicate his will to her. Or she may have to disobey her husband in order to obey God. However, generally speaking, a woman's *attitude of resisting subjection* while her body obeys frequently makes a husband think she is not submissive.

When a wife finds herself in such a position, she needs to ignore her husband's misunderstanding of subjection and rise to the challenge of obeying God in spite of the stumbling-block her husband places before her. If she can talk to her husband, she should tell him how his actions make it hard for her to submit cheerfully to him. Regardless of what her husband does, she should go ahead and place herself in subjection.

When she stands before God, she cannot point her finger at her husband and say, "But he was unreasonable in his demands on me." Or at her mother and say, "But she taught me to be domineering." Or at the soap operas and say, "But they made contention look like such fun and the smart thing to do." Or even at the feminists and say, "But they ridiculed subjection until I felt stupid." God gives the command to be submissive to the wife and He holds her, not the man, responsible for obeying it.

Not only do some men think they are to force subjection upon their wives, but some women also believe that their husbands should force subjection upon them. These wives excuse their contentiousness with, "But my husband isn't man enough to make me be submissive."

This attitude reflects the same ignorance of subjection. God doesn't give the husband the job of placing his wife in subjection. God expects the wife to place herself in subjection. A wife who wants her husband to force her to do her role greatly handicaps her husband and the success of their marriage. She draws her husband's attention away from fulfilling his own obligations and occupies him with worrying about her role. A man simply cannot be strong in his own role while forcing his wife to maintain hers. Neither can a woman be strong in her own role while overseeing the man's obligations. It is just not humanly possible.

Ironically, the characteristic men and women complain the most about in each other is one God assigns to each individually. And this same area is one where husbands and wives are often reluctant to trust each other. For example, men chide that if they give a woman an inch, she will become a ruler. Women counter that if they give a man an inch, he will take a mile.

In summary, subjection and leadership accept responsibility for one's own actions regardless of what the spouse does. When this step is taken, the husband and wife can complete the next part of subjection and leadership:

B. DEVELOP SELF-CONTROL

Mt. 5:5: "Blessed [happy--PRD] are the gentle [meek--KJV], for they shall inherit the earth."

While a popular passage, many people fail to comprehend the great truth it teaches due to a false conception of the word "meek." The Greeks originally used "meek" to describe a wild horse who had been gentled or broken for a riding. When the rider pulled the reins one way, the horse went that way. When the rider pulled the reins the other way, the horse went the other direction. While the horse's spirit was not broken, it was placed in harmony with the man's spirit so that he could be ridden. Thus, the horse retained his power to provide transportation or to give the advantage in war or to plow the fields.

A person becomes "meek" in the same way. Rather than someone else breaking his rebellious nature, he exercises self-control and takes charge of his influence and his life. In this way, meek refers to man's control in horses and to self-control in humans.

Thus, Jesus said in the sermon on the mount, "Happy are the people who take control of their lives." While men put horses in subjection, God commands Christians to put themselves in subjection to the will of God. Part of the fruit of the Spirit mentioned in Gal. 5:22 is self-control. Being a Christian is controlling one's own life rather than allowing the circumstances of life to control him.

The Christian who possesses self-control inherits the earth and becomes blessed. His life on earth grows ever more productive. He finds happiness and enjoys life more, simply because he solves his problems rather than reacting to them like most people do.

Some people exercise no self-control at all over their lives. They study and learn what they should do, but when it comes to doing it, they never get it done. They may call others up to give them a pep-talk so that they can go ahead and do what they need to. Yet in a few days, they desperately need another pep-talk to help them over the same hurdle they faced the day before. Such a person wants someone else to control his life for him instead of controlling it himself.

However, trying to control another person's life for him never works. As long as someone else bails him out of trouble either emotionally or physically, a dependent person never develops self-strength. This soon becomes emotionally draining on the one he consults who has his own life to control in addition to his. The dependent person eventually become an emotional leech who simply goes from person to person exhausting their personal resilience before moving on to the next victim. Yet little progress is ever made despite years and years of effort to help him.

Rather than allowing themselves to be devastated by unrealistic emotional demands, godly people must insist that emotional leeches exercise self-control as God says. Spiritually minded people can never help emotionally dependent people until they take charge of their own lives.

One preacher said that every New Year's Eve for several years someone would call him in the middle of the night. Although different people called each year, they always followed the same pattern: In tears, they were upset at how messed-up their lives were. They wanted the preacher to counsel them on how to make their lives right with God. So each time someone called, the preacher spent several hours that night calming the person down. Then he set up another session in a day or two. After spending countless hours helping these people and showing them how to straighten up their lives, the people always gave up in the end and didn't want to correct their lives.

The preacher finally concluded that people who don't exercise enough self-control to decide to get help and then to wait until the morning to call someone, probably don't possess enough self-control to apply God's principles to their lives. Just hearing how to solve problems, doesn't change anything. A person must exercise enough self-control to implement the truth into his life.

Even though exercising self-control is a very important principle of Christianity which encompasses a person's entire life and relationship to others, God specifically tells husbands and wives to take control of the way they live with each other. When husbands and wives practice self-control, they inherit the earth as it diminishes their problems:

1. THE HUSBAND LIVES BY KNOWLEDGE

I Pet. 3:7: "You husbands likewise, live with your wives in an understanding way,..."

"Live with" means "to dwell together (Latin--*cohabito*):--of the domestic association and intercourse of husband and wife" (Thayer, p. 605).

"Understanding way" means "knowledge and signifies in general intelligence, understanding" (Thayer, p. 119).

God tells husbands not to joke with one another and say, "Who can understand a woman?" or not to throw up their hands in despair and become workaholics or engage in affairs when they encounter problems. Rather, God tells husbands to learn the rules for living with a wife.

Women seem confusing only when a man doesn't understand Biblical teachings about the husband-wife relationship. Happily, God makes the man's job of understanding the feminine nature easy by revealing countless mysteries about women in Proverbs, the Song of Solomon, Eph. 5:22-33 and Tit. 2:3-5. A man who says he cannot understand the female personality, in effect, says that he doesn't want *to take the time* to understand women, for the Bible is the greatest teacher of all about the peculiarities of women. In fact, Solomon wrote many of the passages in Proverbs about love primarily to men--not women. Even Prov. 31:10-

31, which describes the woman of great price, and which women have loved for ages, is written to help men understand the needs of their wives and to teach them how to appreciate the feminine role.

However, God requires much more than for a man to just understand a woman--that's the easy part. After a man understands his relationship with his wife, then God expects him to "dwell with" her according to that knowledge. "Dwell with" requires action. A man not only knows, but he also follows through. He lives according to God's truth about women. That's self-control.

Obviously, leadership is not for weak, spineless men who fear women, but for men who possess a tremendous amount of self-control. This is especially true in a society that puts ugly labels on men who dare to be leaders in their homes such as "male chauvinist," "enemy," "oppressor," "task master," and "eighteenth century tyrant." At the same time, if a man does kind deeds for women, the feminists accuse him of harboring ulterior motives and of using the "iron hand of chivalry" to manipulate and use women. Yet, if a man goes about his business and ignores women, the feminists still brand him as a user of women for his own selfish purposes. How can a man win with today's logic?

Most of society refuses to honor a man who dares to be a real man--a man who both loves and leads his wife. Thus, it would be easy for a man to yield to the propaganda of the feminist movement, the ridicule of his peers, and the nagging of his wife by deserting his responsibilities in the home.

But no matter how hard it seems to hold his ground and be what God designed, God commands the husband not to theorize about what makes a good marriage, but to *live* a good marriage by *living* with his wife according to knowledge. For example, if his wife mistreats him, God expects him to exercise enough self-control to continue to act in her best interest rather than retaliating to please himself. *Living* God's word requires self-control for both the man and the woman who would achieve success in the home.

2. THE WIFE HAS A GENTLE SPIRIT

I Pet. 3:3-4: "And let not your adornment be external only...but let it be the hidden person of the heart, with the imperishable quality of a gentle [meek--KJV] and quiet spirit, which is precious in the sight of God."

"Meek" means "gentle, mild, meek" (Thayer, p. 534).

"Spirit" means "universally, the disposition or influence which fills and governs the soul of any one, the efficient source of any power, affection, emotion, desire, etc." (Thayer, p. 523).

Rather than placing her hopes for a happy marriage in her external beauty, God tells wives to exercise self-control. Unfortunately, many women think that possessing a gentle or meek spirit means that a woman becomes a spineless coward who jumps at her husband's every command. Nothing could be further from the truth!

A woman needs to control her spirit so that she can help the man subdue the earth, fill it with people, and glorify God. While men must break horses, God nowhere commands husbands to break their wives, but to love them. God tells the wife to control herself, to exercise great strength of character by placing herself in subjection to her husband. When a woman develops a gentle spirit, she gains control of her will and forces herself to obey God's laws of marriage.

Developing a gentle spirit resembles setting the alarm clock at night. When the alarm goes off, few women think, "Oh boy! I get to get up and work hard today! What fun!" Instead, they think, "Oh, no! Is it six o'clock already? If only I could sleep another fifteen minutes, I would feel so much better." But the woman *forces* herself to get up because she knows she must. She drags herself into the bathroom to brush her teeth; then she stumbles into the kitchen to make breakfast.

Before long, however, she is enjoying the clean smell of the early morning air, the quietness, maybe the birds singing, and even seeing the sun rise. She begins to think, "It's great to get up early and get started on my work!" And just a few minutes earlier she was complaining about having to get out of bed. This cycle repeats itself many times over a period of weeks or perhaps months. Then one morning, the woman's eyes pop open five minutes before the alarm goes off, and she feels refreshed, ready to get up and tackle the day.

Subjection works the same way. Often in the beginning a woman must *force* herself to be submissive just as she forces herself to get out of bed in the morning. Subjection may go against her deepest feelings. She may say, "But I don't want to be submissive! I don't feel like it! When my husband tells me to do something, I want to do anything but what he says!" Thus, in the beginning, many a woman wants to reject subjection because her feelings aren't in tune with it. But she is getting things backwards. When a woman tries to control her feelings first and then her actions, she'll experience a very hard time. Yet when a woman exercises self-control and places the emphasis on making her actions conform to God's word, her feelings respond.

Then after she practices subjection for a while, it becomes second nature. She begins to enjoy subjection in the same way that she enjoys the early morning hours. A woman must be strong, take control of her will, and force herself to do what is right whether or not it makes sense to her and whether or not she wants to do it. This is what having a gentle spirit is all about--controlling the will.

The feminists accuse submissive women of being weak. But there is nothing weak about subjection. It takes a tremendous amount of character for a woman to submit to the opinions of another human being who makes mistakes occasionally, who often doesn't understand her point of view, or perhaps doesn't even care what she thinks. Thus, it takes a heroic amount of strength to rise to the challenge of subjection.

In summary, *both subjection and leadership require self-control to force themselves to obey the will of God even in the face of mistreatment or selfishness on the part of the other.* When self-control of the actions takes place, the next step is control of the emotions:

C. RADIATE INNER PEACE

> **Phil. 4:7: "And the peace of God, which surpasses all comprehension, shall guard your hearts and your minds in Christ Jesus."**

As a general principle of Christianity, a flood of peace beyond description flows over Christians when they serve God. Obviously then, if a Christian lacks inner peace which surpasses all comprehension, something is wrong. Perhaps he doesn't fully understand God's will in certain areas of his life. Or maybe he knows what God wants him to do, but he refuses to apply God's teaching to his life. Fortunately, when he begins living as God desires, it brings inner happiness, serenity, and contentment to his daily life. Then the peace that comes from following God's wisdom guards a Christian's heart and mind while preserving his emotional well being and protecting him from all harm.

Unfortunately, the marriage union which God designed to bring great happiness and peace to men and women often leads to bitterness and emotional turmoil. However, instead of leaving husbands and wives to wallow in self-torment, God commands them to face the inner conflicts that ruin their marriages:

1. THE HUSBAND NOT TO BE EMBITTERED

> **Col. 3:19: "Husbands, love your wives, and do not be embittered against them."**

"Embittered" means "embitter, exasperate, i.e. rendered angry, indignant, irritated" (Thayer, p. 208-209).

Often a wife fails to understand why her husband grows bitter toward her over the years. After all, she does all kinds of things for him in the home to make his life happy. So why are some husbands not happy?

When asked that question, one husband replied, "Men continually make sacrifices for their wives to provide for them and to give them the things they need and want. But if a man has the idea that his wife doesn't appreciate those sacrifices, then he starts building resentments and bitterness toward her."

While conscious of the sacrifices she makes for her husband, many a wife often has no idea of the sacrifices her husband makes for her. Yet just going to work day after day is a sacrifice. Worrying about paying the bills and making sure the children grow up right also weigh heavily on a husband. Even a husband who isn't a Christian feels these pressing responsibilities. He also wants to be a good leader for his family. A wife seldom realizes how much her husband fears failing in his role. Thus, a wife's appreciation lightens her husband's burdens.

Sometimes, however, a husband comes home from work to find that his wife doesn't know what to fix for supper. Busy doing her thing all day, she just hasn't taken time to worry about a good hot meal. A wife doesn't think of this as not appreciating her husband, but many a man does. The husband thinks, "I've been working hard all day and looking forward to a good home-cooked meal. Is that too much to ask?"

One husband harbors bitter feelings toward his wife because she sleeps while he gets up and fixes himself a cold bowl of cereal every morning before work. He says, "I'm going off to work to provide for the family, and *the least* she can do is get up and fix my breakfast." The husband voices a legitimate complaint. Eccl. 3:13 says that just earning the money to put food on the table rewards a man for all his labors. In fact, Ecclesiastes says that enjoying the food he earns "is the gift of God." Food is important to a husband, more so than many a wife realizes.

Likewise, many a wife doesn't even bother to greet her husband at the door when he comes home. Such a wife becomes so wrapped up doing her own things that she wants her husband to find her and give her a kiss. Yet God gives the woman her tender sympathetic feelings to help her see the little things that mean a lot to her husband--things that say, "I appreciate you and the sacrifices you make for me and the children."

Besides feeling hurt when his wife fails to show appreciation, a husband easily becomes bitter when his wife acts contentious. Sometimes a husband feels as if, "Everything I do or want to do, she opposes it." Instead of working with her husband to satisfy his great need for companionship and help, many a wife makes her husband feel neglected and looked down upon.

Whatever the cause, once a man lets ill-feelings find a place in his heart, love soon leaves to make room for the bitterness. Love and bitterness cannot exist in the same heart--even in a strong masculine heart. Thus, God tells the husband to replace the bitterness with love--love *(agape)* that causes him to act in his wife's best interest regardless of how she treats him.

So even if his wife takes him for granted, God still expects the husband to continue sacrificing himself for her and acting in her best interest. Even if his wife makes no pretense of loving him, God still commands the husband to love her as his own body and to lead her wisely. In addition, God wants a husband to deny himself for his wife's benefit even if she makes his life miserable. Certainly, subjection does not demand any more of a wife than leadership demands of a husband.

Since love and bitterness cannot exist in the same heart, a wise wife makes her husband feel free to voice his complaints. If she compels him to harbor his resentments for fear of unleashing her scorn, she encourages him to build bitterness instead of love for her. No one likes criticism, but it is far better for a husband to get his complaints out into the open where both he and his wife can deal with them, than to build resentments toward his wife.

If a woman's husband feels bitter toward her, she can help him best by making sure that she controls her own attitudes. Many a husband becomes bitter in response to a wife who constantly wages inner battles of her own. A man detects resentments and ill-feelings easily in his wife. For that reason, a quiet spirit makes a woman beautiful to both her husband and God:

2. THE WIFE HAS A QUIET SPIRIT

I Pet. 3:4: "...but let it be the **hidden person of the heart, with the imperishable quality of a gentle and quiet spirit, which is precious in the sight of God.**"

"Quiet" means "1. quietness (descriptive of the life of one who stays at home doing his own work and

does not officiously meddle with the affairs of others-
-II Thes. 3:12); 2. silence" (Thayer, p. 281).

Being "quiet" requires the same strength of character that meekness demands. Any weak-kneed woman
can be afraid to speak up to her husband, but that is
not what being quiet is all about. Being quiet means
that a woman controls her feelings and attitudes so
that she does not silently bad mouth her husband or
openly criticize his leadership.

This verse strikes home to all women because of
their emotional nature that makes it easy for them to
turn their feelings inward to feel sorry for themselves
instead of turning them outward to appreciate and love
their husbands. A woman who truly practices subjection
controls her spirit, her emotional nature, so that she
finds inner peace and happiness.

A submissive woman's inner peace keeps her from
being argumentative while making her content to do her
own work and to let her husband do his. Many a
woman who claims to be submissive is actually rebellious. She may do what her husband wants, but her
mind stays far away from obedience. If a woman appears submissive, but seethes on the inside toward her
husband, she fails to practice true subjection.

For example, if a wife does any of the following
things to get her way, she does not possess a quiet
spirit: mentally rehearses her husband's failures, domi-
nates her husband, takes matters into her own hands
and does not consult her husband, gives in to hysteri-
cal fears about what might happen, refuses to let her
husband fail without saying, "I told you so," argues
with her husband and tries to force him to see things
her way, questions her husband's decisions, harbors
resentments toward her husband, feels irritated or impatient with her husband, belittles her husband's actions, manners, personality, looks, etc., ungrateful for
the things her husband does for her, raises her voice
to her husband, manipulates her husband with compliments, quotes scriptures to force her husband to give
in, compares her husband to herself or others in a
derogatory way, throws temper tantrums, cries to intimidate her husband, gets sick when opposed, threat-
ens to leave her husband, pouts and gives her husband
the silent treatment, or cuts her hair to punish her
husband.

The emotional aspect of subjection represents one of the hardest parts of all to master. Many a wife fails at this point simply because she allows her emotions to determine her actions which is backwards. Peter tells a wife to first put on a gentle or meek spirit (to exercise self-control) and then to develop a quiet spirit (to completely conquer her feelings). A wife usually must force herself to take the first step toward subjection, but after a while, her emotions respond which enables her to embrace God's complete doctrine of subjection.

Then a wife finds wonderful peace that surpasses understanding from knowing that she serves God with all her heart, mind, and soul. In addition, she becomes beautiful to her husband--someone for him to cherish instead of harboring resentments against. Thus, peace floods her marriage, too.

In summary, Solomon said in Prov. 16:32 that "He who is slow to anger is better than the mighty, and he who rules his spirit, than he who captures a city." It takes a strong man and woman to practice true Bible subjection. and leadership. It requires real character to respond properly to a spouse who occasionally makes mistakes, who seems unreasonable at times, and who is a human being. *Subjection and leadership are for men and women who dare to rise to all their human potentials as children of God.*

D. REQUIRES SACRIFICES

I Pet. 3:13-15: "And who is there to harm you if you prove zealous for what is good? But even if you should suffer for the sake of righteousness, you are blessed [happy--PRD]. And do not fear their intimidation, and do not be troubled, but sanctify Christ as Lord in your hearts, always being ready to make a defense to every one who asks you to give an account for the hope that is in you, yet with gentleness and reverence;..."

Under normal circumstances, following God's word brings out the best in other people, thereby improving the quality of a Christian's life. However, since God gives everyone a freewill choice, some people may

choose to mistreat those who serve God wholeheartedly. Rather than cowering before undeserved ill-treat-
ment, God promises that a Christian can find happiness. How? When a Christian determines to serve
Christ no matter what the cost, it gives him inner
peace in the face of persecution. In addition, if a
Christian thoroughly knows why he believes as he
does, it gives him the ability to explain his actions to
everyone with kindness and respect. This imparts great
confidence and happiness to a Christian even if the
oppression continues.

However, Peter adds, "For it is better, if God
should will it so, that you suffer for doing what is
right rather than for doing what is wrong" (I Pet. 3:17).
Thus, sometimes God requires Christians to make sacrifices to serve Him. God nowhere promises that becoming a Christian relieves a person of the stresses
and trials of life. Yet God assures the Christian that
he can face affliction without sin and with peace of
mind.

Many of the temptations to sin come from within
the marriage relationship, especially if one of the
partners is not committed to serving God. While God
expects Christians to remain faithful in every area of
their lives, He gives special instructions to help them
not let their marriage deteriorate into a source of sin:

1. THE HUSBAND GIVES HIMSELF UP

**Eph. 5:25: "Husbands, love your wives, just
as Christ also loved the church and gave
Himself up for her;..."**

Christ set the supreme example of a loving husband by dying in His wife's place. In this same manner, God expects a husband to deny himself to the
point of giving up his life to preserve the life of his
wife. While many wives accuse their husbands of
selfishness, few wives fully appreciate the sacrifices
their husbands gladly make for them.

For example, many a wife wails, "My husband gets
to go to work everyday and I'm stuck here at home!"
No, a husband doesn't *get to go* to work, a husband
has to go to work to provide for his family. Even if a
man works at a job he really likes, he still fights

pressures. Some days he may rather stay home and read his latest mechanic magazine, go mountain climbing, go for a drive, or just sleep late. Yet a responsible man keeps working even after his job loses its glamour. A dependable man keeps working even when he doesn't like his boss. A trustworthy man goes to work even when spring fever hits and makes him feel lazy.

A self-denying husband spends the majority of his life providing for his family. One preacher said that a man spends the first twenty-five years of his life getting an education in order to support his family, the next twenty-five years ruining his health to support his family, and the last twenty-five years trying to regain his health to keep supporting his family, and all the while he pays on life insurance to support his family after he is gone.

Listening to a high school boy's dreams for the future shows how many sacrifices the normal husband makes for his wife. Years ago one such teenager excitedly told about his plans: He had already chosen a college where he could earn advanced degrees and enjoy a fulfilling career. He loved the thought of traveling all over the country in a fancy sports car. He even described the luxury apartment he wanted to outfit with nice furniture and stereo and sports equipment. Of course, he would buy whatever he wanted in the way of clothes.

Then one day he fell in love with a girl and his dream began to fade as he planned how to support a wife. He forgot his advanced educational goals as the babies came long. He settled for a station wagon instead of a sports model. He wore the same suit year after year to buy clothes for his children. Tricycles and baseball gloves replaced the stereo and sports equipment. He traded the luxury apartment for a modest house near the schools. And he resigned himself to taking the children home to see their grandparents instead of going on extensive trips.

In a similar way, the normal husband makes sacrifices for his wife. Perhaps he's never shared his boyhood dreams with her and she doesn't know what he gave up to love her. Not only does many a husband willingly make these sacrifices for his wife, but God expects him to continue making sacrifices all of his married life for her benefit.

For example, a husband who genuinely looks out for the needs of his wife *may never get to do what he wants to do,* for God obligates him to place the needs of his wife above his own needs and desires. What is best for his wife may not be what he wants to do, yet God expects him to sacrifice his own interests in favor of doing what is best for her. Even if a man delights in a submissive and loving wife who totally supports him, *he still may never get to do what he wants to do.* He still must place his wife's needs above his own just as Christ did the church's.

Likewise, what a wife *wants* may not be what she *needs.* Even so, God expects the husband to face her displeasure and to go ahead and do what is best for her. Thus, a husband might never get to do what either he or his wife wants, because God obligates him to act in his wife's best interest.

And some wives have the nerve to say, "It's not fair! Why do I have to make all the sacrifices?" So what does a husband get when he sacrifices all his ambitions to love his wife? Certainly bills and often a nagging and complaining wife who doesn't appreciate him. In view of the sacrifice God commands husbands to make, wives cannot rightfully claim that God expects too much of them by commanding them to submit without fear:

2. THE WIFE SUBMITS WITHOUT FEAR

> I Pet. 3:6: **"Thus Sarah obeyed Abraham, calling him Lord, and you have become her children [daughters--KJV] if you do what is right without being frightened by any fear."**

"Do what is right" means "1. do good, do something which profits others, show one's self beneficent, do some one a favor, benefit; 2. do well, do right (used in I Pet. 2:15, 20; 3:6, 17; III Jn. 11)" (Thayer, p. 2).

"Frightened" means "terrified, frightened, put to flight by terrifying (scared away); 1. put to flight, to flee; a. fear, be afraid, struck with fear, seized with alarm (of those who fear harm or injury), fear one,

afraid of one lest he do harm, displeased, etc."
(Thayer, p. 655).

"Fear" means "afraid with terror, put in fear by any
terror" (Thayer, p. 556).

Women argue profusely against subjection. Many
fear that subjection will degrade them or cause their
husbands to mistreat them. Others fear men in general
and tremble at their own femininity--afraid of being a
complete woman. Many fear that feminist friends will
accuse them of being doormats. Others fear sexual
closeness and giving themselves completely to their
husbands. But William Barclay explains how the wives
to whom Peter wrote this letter had many *real reasons*
for feeling terrified at the thought of subjection:

> If a wife became a Christian, while her
> husband did not, she had taken a step which
> in the ancient world was unprecedented, and
> which produced the most acute problems. In
> every sphere of ancient civilization, women
> had no rights at all. Under Jewish law a
> woman was a thing; she was owned by her
> husband in exactly the same way as he owned
> his sheep and his goats; on no account could
> she leave him, although he could dismiss her
> at any moment. For a wife to change her reli-
> gion while her husband did not, was unthink-
> able. In Greek civilization the duty of the
> woman was "to remain indoors and to be obe-
> dient to her husband." It was the sign of a
> good woman that she must see as little, hear
> as little, and ask as little as possible. She
> had no kind of independent existence and no
> kind of mind of her own, and her husband
> could divorce her almost at caprice, so long
> as he returned her dowry. Under Roman law a
> woman had no rights. In law she remained for-
> ever a child. When she was under her father
> she was under the *patria potestas,* the father's
> power, which gave the father even the right of
> life and death over her; and when she married
> she passed equally into the power of her hus-
> band. She was entirely subject to her husband,
> and completely at his mercy. Cato the Censor,
> the typical ancient Roman, wrote: "If you were

to catch your wife in an act of infidelity, you can kill her with impunity without a trial." Roman matrons were prohibited from drinking wine, and Egnatius beat his wife to death when he found her doing so. Sulpicius Gallus dismissed his wife because she had once appeared in the streets without a veil. Antistius Vetus divorced his wife because he saw her secretly speaking to a freed woman in public. Publius Sempronius Sophus divorced his wife because once she went to the public games. The whole attitude of ancient civilization was that no woman could dare to make any decision for herself. What, then, must have been the problems of the wife who became a Christian while her husband remained faithful to the ancestral gods? It is almost impossible for us to realize what life must have been for the wife who was brave enough to become a Christian.[1]

With all of these seemingly logical excuses for fearing subjection, Peter told these women to trust God and "do what is right." In reality, a wife's fears say, "God, you didn't know what you were doing when you ordained the law of subjection. Surely, you didn't know what my husband would be like." Thus, she claims to be smarter than God. But dare any woman make such a claim, even if she lives with an unbelieving husband?

God expects a wife to practice exactly the same type of subjection whether her husband is a Christian or an atheist. The principles for enjoying a successful marriage are the same for both Christians and non-Christians. God's ways work because He deals with the basic inherent natures of men and women--natures so complex that scientists still work at unraveling all the mysteries.

Peter says that a woman becomes the daughter of Sarah *if she does what is right*. Paul reveals the significance of becoming a daughter of Sarah in Gal. 3:29: "And if you belong to Christ, then you are Abraham's

---

[1] William Barclay, *The Letters of James and Peter* (Philadelphia, PA: The Westminster Press, 1958), pp. 258-259.

offspring, heirs to the promise." Thus, when a woman does what is right in service to God, she becomes the spiritual daughter of Abraham and Sarah and confidently expects to go to heaven. Having this hope set before her, a daughter of Sarah refuses to allow any man or woman to intimidate her so that she cowers in a corner and ceases to serve God with her marriage.

Unfortunately, some Bible teachers misuse Sarah's lies about her marriage to Abraham (Gen. 12:11-20; 20:1-18) to promote an untruth about subjection: That God condones a wife's sins when her husband tells her to commit them. These people falsely conclude that because God uses Sarah as an example for women to follow, He approves of her as a sinless person.

However, assuming that God approves of *every* action of people He praises is not good logic. For example, even though God describes David as a man after His own heart (Acts 13:22), God was not pleased with all of David's actions such as when David committed adultery with Bathsheba and later killed her husband Uriah (II Sam. 11:2-27).

Like David, Sarah was a human being who stumbled upon occasion. God was not always pleased with her, and He rebuked her when necessary. For instance, God promised to bless Abraham and Sarah with an heir to the promise that someday Abraham's descendants would inherit the land of Canaan. Many years later, when both Sarah and Abraham were very old, Sarah overheard God say that she would give birth to the promised child. Sarah laughed in unbelief. Then when God rebuked her about laughing, Sarah denied that she laughed and sinned again (Gen. 18:9-15).

Even though some people view Sarah's lies as an excuse for wives to sin to please their husbands, God says in Rev. 21:8 that all liars, along with the cowardly will be in the lake that burns with fire and brimstone. The verse does not say, "liars, except for wives who lie to please their husbands" or "the cowardly, except for wives who fear their husbands' displeasure more than God's." Peter says, "You have become her [Sarah's] children *if you do what is right,"* not if you do *everything exactly as she did.* God doesn't hold up the example of Sarah's lying for women to imitate; He commends her calling her husband "Lord."

Instead of being an excuse for sinning, Sarah's example gives a wife encouragement. For if Sarah, who made mistakes and corrected them, was pleasing enough in the sight of God to be used as an example for women to follow, then women should take heart. When they make mistakes, they can correct their mistakes and go on to become beautiful examples of true subjection as Sarah did.

The example of Ananias and Sapphira clearly shows God's attitude toward a wife sinning to please her husband (Acts 5:1-10): Ananias sold some property and gave part of the money to the church. However, Ananias lied by telling the apostles that he gave "all" the money to the church when in fact he kept part of it for himself. As a result, he was struck dead, not for keeping part of the money which he had a right to do, but for lying about how much he sold the property for. Sapphira went along with Ananias' plan and lied to the apostles, too. As a result, she likewise was struck dead for agreeing with her husband to lie.

Jesus tells Christians to fear God, who can both kill the body and cast the soul into hell, rather than fearing the one who can only kill the body (Lk. 12:4-5). A woman is to be in subjection to her husband because she fears God, not because she fears her husband. But anytime a husband's wish or command conflicts with the word of God, God's word overrides the husband's opinion. Thus, a wife must obey God first.

In summary, *both subjection and leadership require sacrifices in service to God.* Even if the spouse mistreats the other and the sacrifices seem unpleasant, a true Christian always strives to do what is right in the sight of God. God does not ask any more of a wife than He asks of a husband. In this respect they are equal, for God requires them both to make a commitment to do what is best for the other without thought of reciprocation.

II. THE RESULT

I Pet. 2:12: **"Keep your behavior excellent among the Gentiles, so that in the thing in which they slander you as evildoers, they may on account of your good deeds, as they**

**observe them, glorify God in the day of vis-
itation."**

As God's people work and live among the Gentiles,
people who care absolutely nothing about serving God,
God wants them to always make sure that they follow
His laws. Why? Because as the Gentiles observe the
Christians' good conduct, they see the difference between Christians and themselves. In this way, Christians have an opportunity to become good influences.

For example, people in the world often endure terrible marriages without ever a thought of turning to
God as a possible solution to their anguish. But when
they look at Christians, whom they ridicule for worshiping God, and see the beautiful relationships of joy
that they share with their spouses, it attracts their
attention. They want to know, "Why are we so miserable and you are so happy?" Then when the Christians
answer the question with scriptures and examples from
their own lives, even the Gentiles glorify God.

Greater than their influence upon the Gentiles, a
husband and wife exert more influence on each other
than anyone else in their lives, even their own parents. A couple celebrating their silver anniversary can
look back on their high school days and see how their
attitudes changed over the years: Their views toward
finances differ from their parents who lived through the
depression. In addition, they may reject their parents'
discipline standards as too harsh or too lenient. Many
couples even dare to support different political parties
than their parents do.

As a couple faces the problems of life together
and discusses them in each other's arms in the middle
of the night, their attitudes change--they change drastically over the years. The forty-three-year-old wife is
nothing like the eighteen-year-old bride who couldn't
wait to have babies. The forty-five-old husband is
nothing like the twenty-year-old groom who set out to
conquer the world. Along the way, their attitudes toward honesty and personal integrity either became more
entrenched or were given up as impractical. Their
commitment toward serving God either became stronger
or weaker. In many ways, the older couple doesn't
even resemble the honeymooners because the marriage
relationship exerts tremendous influence on the part-

ners. And when they celebrate their golden anniversary, they will find that the next twenty-five years will have also changed their attitudes even more.

When a husband and wife are both dedicated to serving God, they exert a tremendous amount of spiritual influence on the other. When one is a Christian and the other is not, they still exert tremendous influence on each other. Either the stronger influences the weaker to become stronger, or the weaker influences the stronger to become weaker. The marriage does not remain unaltered. Unless the spiritual partner accepts his personal responsibilities and determines to influence the other for good, more than likely, he absorbs the other's worldly influence.

But through true subjection and true leadership, a husband and wife help their influence produce good in the other's life. Nowhere are good examples more needed than in the marriage realm. Unfortunately, many husbands and wives do not even try to set good examples for the other, but simply resort to treating their spouses as their spouses treat them. Yet God gives husbands and wives the opportunity to set good examples for the other:

A. THE HUSBAND INFLUENCES HIS WIFE

> **Eph. 5:25-27: "Husbands, love your wives, just as Christ also loved the church and gave Himself up for her; that He might sanctify her, having cleansed her by the washing of water with the word, that He might present to Himself the church in all her glory, having no spot or wrinkle or any such thing; but that she should be holy and blameless."**

"Present" means "place beside or near, set at hand, present, provide, (place a person or thing at one's disposal), present or show (with an acc. of the quality which the person or thing exhibits)" (Thayer, p. 489).

As a result of Christ loving the church and acting in her best interest to the point of giving Himself up to die, He "presents" her to Himself "in all her glory, having no spot or wrinkle or any such thing, but holy and blameless." Christ's good deeds powerfully affect the church. The church finds glory because Christ honors her. She becomes holy and blameless because Christ protects her with complete leadership. She enjoys being set apart from sin because Christ is set apart from sin.

The same principle holds true in the husband-wife relationship. The way a husband treats his wife affects what she becomes over the years. If he leads with selfish and inconsiderate decrees, he stifles his wife's femininity. Even worse, he may bring out an ugliness in her that he didn't know existed. So if a husband wants a selfish wife, he should do everything he wants to do and ignore her needs. If a husband wants a bitter wife, he should communicate resentment to her. If a husband wants a nagging, contentious wife, he should refuse to be a loving leader.

Even if his wife possesses tremendous strength of character and refuses to let him pull her down into hateful nagging or bitterness, she loses her ability to give *her complete self* to him in love. To survive emotionally, she must withhold part of herself to withstand his evil influence. Keeping her loving and tender qualities intact in such circumstances requires a tremendous amount of emotional energy. While a wife can remain loving in spite of her husband's evil influence, many quit trying along the way.

On the other hand, when a husband treats his wife properly, he creates an environment that makes it easy for her to yield to her true feminine nature. This frees her to channel her emotional energy into loving him and their children. As a result, she becomes a more satisfying wife over the years because she does not have to fight to control her feelings or to keep from sinning. For this reason, if a husband wants a loving wife, he should give her a loving leader. If a husband wants a wife who places his needs above her own, he should regard her needs before his. And for his efforts, he presents to himself a wife in all her glory. Therefore, if a husband wants a wife who is meet for all of his needs, he should present one to himself as Christ did the church by being a loving leader.

The Bible continually portrays leaders, not as lording it over their subjects, but as examples and good influences upon those under their command. For instance, the Bible portrays Jesus as an example for

Christians to imitate. Peter says in I Pet. 2:21-23, "For you have been called for this purpose, since Christ suffered for you, leaving you an example for you to follow in His steps,..." Unlike many leaders who say, "Do as I say, not as I do," Christ's behavior demonstrated the doctrines He taught.

Following in the steps of Jesus, the apostles also set examples for Christians (I Cor. 4:16; 11:1; Phil. 3:17). In addition, Paul used Silvanus and Timothy along with himself as proper examples of what he taught through inspiration (I Thes. 1:6; II Thes. 3:7-9). In a similar manner, Peter admonished elders, "Shepherd the flock of God among you, not...as lording it over those allotted to your charge, but proving to *be examples* to the flock" (I Pet. 5:2-3). Likewise, Paul told Timothy, a young preacher, to make sure that he set a proper example for those he labored over (I Tim. 4:12).

Thus, a leader provokes good behavior in his charges not by bossing them around, but by leading them where they should go. Authority does not give leaders the right to dominate others, but the privilege of providing examples for them. As a leader, the husband also sets examples of subjection for his wife.

For instance, many a husband likes for the preacher to read passages about subjection to his wife. But as chapter 13, "Subjection for Both Men and Women," shows, the man practices exactly the same type of subjection in his realm of work outside the home as his wife practices in her realm of work within the home. Subjection is a way of life for both men and women and for both bread winners and bread warmers. God requires everyone, whether male or female, to submit to others in several realms.

Thus, through his example, a husband helps his wife become submissive by cheerfully submitting to his country and to his employer. Every time a husband drives his car, he demonstrates to his wife what he thinks about subjection. If he breaks traffic laws, his actions imply that the law of subjection should bend for personal desires and whims. When a husband bad mouths his employer or slacks off behind his boss' back, he shows that he believes a person can do whatever he wants as long as he can get away with it. If a man wants his wife and family to respect his

authority, he must respect those God placed in authority over him.

Perhaps by realizing that the attitudes are exactly
the same in the employee-employer and the husband-
wife relationships, a husband can understand a little
bit why many women find subjection hard to practice.
Such understanding helps him set a good example *by
treating his wife the same way he wants those in authority over him to treat him.* In this way he becomes
a more loving and considerate leader who influences
his wife for good instead of evil.

B. THE WIFE INFLUENCES HER HUSBAND

> **I Pet. 3:1-2: "In the same way, you wives,
> be submissive to your own husbands so that
> even if any of them are disobedient to the
> word they may be won without a word by
> the behavior of their wives, as they behold
> your chaste and respectful behavior."**

"Disobedient" means "not to allow one's self to be
persuaded, not to comply with; 2. to refuse or without
belief; b. to refuse belief and obedience" (Thayer, p.
55).

"Word" is the same Greek word both times and
means "2. what some one has said, a saying; a. the
sayings of man; b. the sayings of God; 3. discourse,
the art of speaking, speech" (Thayer, p. 380).

Paul says, "For I am not ashamed of the gospel,
for it is the power of God for salvation" (Rom. 1:16).
The word "power" comes from a Greek word which is
related to the English word "dynamite." Thus, the
gospel contains phenomenal power for transforming the
lives of sinners. However, sometimes even that mighty
power cannot budge the stubborn wills of some husbands.

On the other hand, by living her life according to
God's plan, a wife can frequently catch her husband's
attention and turn his thoughts toward obedience of the
gospel. This happens because God's laws improve a
marriage when practiced properly. What man wouldn't
pay attention to a gospel which gives him a wife who
truly appreciates his manhood, who enjoys her own
femininity, who becomes an exciting lover, who joy-

fully nurtures their children, and who turns his home into a wonderful haven of rest and peace? Thus, as a husband witnesses the changes in his wife when she obeys the gospel, he sees firsthand the tremendous power of God's word. Any right thinking man wants to be a part of that truth.

Subjection simply puts a woman's phenomenal power and influence under control so that she brings out her husband's better nature instead of his worst side. An older wife said, "I'm sure that if I weren't a submissive and loving wife, my husband would just be an old crank like his father. His sisters can't believe how good he is to me and how different he is from his brothers."

Peter doesn't prohibit a woman from discussing religion with her husband--only from nagging him about obeying the Bible. When a husband's lack of interest closes the door to further discussion, a wife still possesses an effective tool for influencing her husband for good--her life. Such is the power of a woman's influence over her husband as her life translates the Bible into language he can understand and appreciate.

The most effective way a wife helps her husband assume his responsibilities is not her tongue, but her life. Frequently, even an overbearing husband no longer feels that he must constantly monitor every move she makes when she willingly submits herself to him. His new trust in her devotion to him causes him to ease up on the reigns. This in turn makes subjection much more pleasant for the wife. In this way, the wife's subjection balances the husband's leadership, and they both enjoy their roles much more.

Unfortunately, many a woman ignores the trite saying, "I can't hear what you are saying because your actions are speaking too loudly."

Instead, she argues, "When he straightens up, then I will be a good wife!" That is backwards! God says for the wife to straighten up first and then perhaps her husband will be encouraged to straighten up, too.

A wife may protest, "But I've done everything right for a month now and he hasn't changed a bit!" When a wife submits to her husband only in order to manipulate him into reforming, she sets an example of selfishness instead of demonstrating her love for God. Sooner or later, she inevitably gets discouraged or they have a fight, and she reverts back to her old ways. When this happens, her husband loses confidence in her and the God she claims to follow.

This wifely attitude resembles that of a paroled convict who called a preacher for a handout. He threatened, "If somebody doesn't give me some money, I'll just go steal some!" He indicated that his good behavior depended totally on how others treated him rather than on how he ought to treat others.

Like the ex-convict, such a wife seems to think that her husband ought to buy her good behavior. However, since Jesus purchased the sins of everyone with His blood, a wife does not have the right to charge anyone for her good conduct. She owes good behavior to Christ whose name she wears. He bought her good deeds (I Pet. 1:17-19) before her husband ever came along. Therefore, God wants a wife to set a good example for her husband regardless of how he treats her or how he responds to her proper conduct because she is a Christian.

Many a wife sets an example like a yo-yo--good one day, terrible the next, mediocre the following day, excellent the next, but bad for two days in a row. Such a wife often cannot understand why her husband doesn't respond to her "good" days. Sometimes a wife even thinks that if she averages more good days than bad, her husband should declare a celebration and shout from the roof top what a wonderful wife he married.

But a wife who influences her husband for good doesn't bounce back and forth like a yo-yo from delight to anger to happiness to sadness and back to delight. Many a husband views such yo-yo emotions as a gimmick to manipulate him into changing. He not only resists his wife's influence, but he also resents her. Until a wife controls the example she sets, she does not know if she can enjoy a truly wonderful marriage with her husband, or if she can win him to Christ with her behavior.

In summary, neither a husband nor a wife can look to the other as an excuse to sin or for motivation to treat the other right. *Subjection and leadership set a good example for the other regardless of what the other does.* When a husband and wife accept their responsibilities to set good examples, they exercise a tremendous influence over the other.

By loving his wife as his own body, a husband can present to himself a wife who is "in all her glory, having no spot or wrinkle,...but holy and blameless" (Eph. 5:25-28). By a wife keeping her behavior chaste and respectful while submitting to her husband, her husband "may be won without a word" (I Pet. 3:1-2). Good examples come packed full of power for transforming evil into good and for bringing out the best in one's mate. Only in this way do marriages have a chance to become a literal taste of heaven.

STUDY EXERCISE

Answer all questions in your own words.

1. Does subjection indicate inferiority or superiority? Why?

2. Should a husband put his wife in subjection to him? Why?

3. What should a wife do if her husband fails his role of leadership?

4. How important is self-control in subjection and leadership? Why?

5. How does a wife develop a quiet spirit? How can a husband get rid of bitterness?

6. Which one gets to do everything he wants to do--the husband or the wife? Why?

7. How can a husband present a submissive wife to himself?

8. How can a wife bring out her husband's better side? Explain.

9. Do you disagree with anything in this lesson? If so, explain in detail giving scriptures for your reasons.

PROBLEM-SOLVING EXERCISE

The Problem: The following excerpts are from the article "Housewife Still on Strike," *The Spokesman-Review* (5/17/73), p. 26.

Mrs. H continued on Wednesday her strike against household chores. She began the work stoppage after listening to a Sunday sermon in which the minister quoted from the Bible that the man is the master of the house.

"I'm afraid that sermon stopped it," said Mrs. H, 30, mother of three children. After hearing the Mother's Day sermon, she refused to do housework, although she said she had made some concessions Wednesday.

"My demands are not met, but I did break down and pick up a few things," she said. "I've always fed the children, but I cooked breakfast this morning instead of making cereal. But I still haven't washed any clothes or made the beds."

"And I took my sign down." The sign she had put outside the house had read to passersby: "On strike!! For shorter hours...one day off per year and other humane consideration. Signed: Woman of the House."

She said her husband had "ignored my demands for a few days, so I put up the sign. The kids think the whole thing is a joke," Mrs. H said. "In a way it's a joke," she said, "but I'm also serious about it."

"I expect she'll give in soon," her husband said Tuesday, before the concessions.

"No, I'll never clean up the place. I have the nicest family and husband in the world," Mrs. H said. "But when I get mad, he just takes me lightly."

The Exercise: Discuss the above newspaper article telling what you would advise the above women to do if she were your friend. Use scriptures for your advice.

CHAPTER 15

AVOIDING THE CURSE OF SUBJECTION

Subjection and leadership blend and harmonize perfectly together and are filled with safety devices to protect both the husband and wife. The basic difference between them is the focus of attention. Subjection places the emphasis on protecting the husband's rights with the wife being sheltered from harm coming as a side benefit. On the other hand, responsible leadership places the emphasis on preserving the wife's rights, while the husband reaps personal protection as an added bonus.

Both subjection and leadership focus on the other instead of self. Indeed, when the husband and wife begin to think primarily of themselves instead of the other, they start failing in their individual roles. Selfishness is foreign to both subjection and leadership.

I. RELATIONSHIP TO SPOUSE

After looking at the husband and wife's relationship to God and to themselves, this chapter shows their relationship to each other. Ignorance brings misery to every realm of a person's life, whether repairing cars, driving a semi-truck, sewing, cooking, making love, or practicing subjection and leadership. Fear and ignorance turn subjection into a curse. Confidence in God and the truth transform subjection into a blessing. *Ignorance is the enemy, not subjection, and certainly, not the man.* But the question still remains, what is a husband and wife's relationship to each other?

A. ACCEPT EACH OTHER

Rom. 12:16: "Be of the same mind toward one another; do not be haughty in mind, but associate with the lowly. Do not be wise in your own estimation."

"Lowly" means "low in situation, humble, poor, mean, depressed, metaphorically of the mind, humble, lowly, modest" (Wigram, p. 347)

"Wise" means "a. intelligent, wise; b. prudent, i.e. mindful of one's interests" (Thayer, p. 658).

This verse reveals a general principle of Christianity that applies to every realm of life and dealings with others. Paul warns Christians about thinking that the world revolves around them or that they're the best there ever was. Rather than letting their own intelligence impress them, Christians should listen to the opinions of others. In short, God wants His people to accept the members of their spiritual family at face value with their mental and physical abilities, their idiosyncrasies, their talents, and their handicaps-- things upon which their soul's salvation does not depend.

Nowhere is such humility of conduct usually more lacking nor more desperately needed than in the home. Many a couple experiences problems simply because they fail to accept their spouse at face value. In addition, many a husband and wife expect greater feats from the other than they demand of themselves. In fact, a person often insists on perfection in a spouse while at the same time making excuses for his own failures. However, the commands to the husband to love his wife and the instructions to the wife to submit to her husband include the word "own," a word of great significance:

1. THE HUSBAND LOVES HIS "OWN" WIFE

Eph. 5:28: "So husbands ought to love their own wives as their own bodies..."

God tells a husband to love *the woman he married,* not the woman he wishes he married, not his ideal of the perfect wife, not women in general, not somebody else's wife, and certainly not his mother--but his "own" wife. A husband loves his "own" wife just as he loves his "own" body. While a man expects his wife to obey him, he cannot expect her to be exactly like other women. No two women are precisely alike, not even mothers and daughters.

A husband who expects his wife to do everything as his mother did places a tremendous burden on his wife that inhibits her own imagination and desire to do little acts of love for him. This doesn't prevent a husband from asking his wife to cook his favorite foods that his mother used to prepare. However, he avoids comparing and measuring his wife by his mother or other women. His wife probably has a different energy level, family responsibilities, homemaking talents, etc. than his mother. These differences require him to look at his *own* wife and to determine her individual needs. God said that a man shall *leave* his father *and mother* and cleave to *his wife* in Gen. 2:24.

A woman wants to know her husband's likes and dislikes, but she also wants her dignity preserved. For example, sometimes a husband talks down to his wife like, "You, idiot, don't you know anything?" Such a husband not only discourages his wife, but he also shows his own ignorance of the mental differences between men and women. Sadly, he expects his wife to think like a man and doesn't accept his *own* wife's femininity.

Loving his *own* wife doesn't require a husband to give up a single part of his leadership or to submit to his wife. Accepting his wife as the woman she really is simply regulates how a husband leads his wife. This acceptance enables him to lead her fairly and realistically as he recognizes both her virtues and limitations--qualities found in every human being-- even him. Accepting his *own* wife at face value prevents a man from falsely thinking that he is superior to his wife. It also keeps him from looking down on his wife and treating her like a child. A husband's failure to accept his wife as a person in her own right causes many a woman to resent her husband and his leadership. Yet a husband can turn that resentment into appreciation overnight by accepting his wife at face value.

If a husband fails to accept his wife at face value, the wife should examine her attitudes to make certain that she fully accepts him. For when one person refuses to accept the spouse at face value, it encourages the other to nit-pick. Thus, a husband may follow his wife's example when he compares her unfavorably to other women.

At the same time, a wife should remember that many of a man's preferences in the home stem from the way his mother kept house. He may detest some of his mother's habits and approves of others. Or a husband may see things on television, in magazines, or on other women that he likes and wishes his wife would do. These methods of formulating desires are natural and a wife should not take her husband's preferences as a sign that he doesn't accept her. In fact, *she must accept his preferences* if she sets a proper example of acceptance in the home:

2. THE WIFE SUBMITS TO HER "OWN" HUSBAND

I Pet. 3:1: "In the same way, you wives, be submissive to your own husbands..."

"Own" means "1. pertaining to one's self, one's own, universally of what is one's own as opposed to belonging to another" (Thayer, p. 296).

The Bible is more specific in the woman's acceptance of her "own" husband. For instance, the word "own" used for the wife in Eph. 5:22 and I Pet. 3:1 differs from the word Eph. 5:28 uses for the man. The Bible uses just a general possessive pronoun to describe the husband's acceptance while it uses a more definite term for the woman's relationship to her husband.

Even though a wife submitting to her *own* husband seems like an obvious part of subjection, the violation of it frequently causes marriage problems and leads to much bitterness and unhappiness for many women. Often a woman does not even realize that she fails to accept her *own* husband at face value.

God gives a husband the right to decide for himself matters on which his soul's salvation does not depend--these are the things within the realm of human opinion. But God does not give a wife the right to dictate these opinions and to make her husband over. Instead, He gives her the privilege of bringing out the best in her husband, encouraging him to achieve his ambitions, enjoying his social graces, and living with his idiosyncrasies.

Accepting a husband at face value involves understanding him, his fears, his parents, his education, his failures, his triumphs, and his moods. When a wife understands her husband and sympathizes with him, it enables her to accept him for who he is and to live contentedly with him.

No two men are exactly alike, not even fathers and sons, so a wife can't logically expect her husband to fit into another man's mold. Some men like to paint walls and houses--others splatter paint over everything. Some men like to put up curtain rods--others always smash their thumbs. Some men like to work on cars--others don't know what a timing light is. Some men like to cook spicy dishes--others don't know how to use baking powder. Some men don't mind changing diapers--others gag and feel clumsy. Some men like to take their wives to dinner and a movie--others prefer a quiet evening at home. Some men enjoy meeting the public as a salesman--others are nervous around strangers. Some men thrive on the challenge of being in business for themselves--others like the security of working for others with a regular paycheck.

Since God doesn't make a man's salvation depend on what he likes or dislikes in any of these realms, a wife doesn't have the right to make the happiness of his marriage depend on these things. When a wife tries to force her husband to conform to the standards of other men or to her own ideals, she fails to submit herself to her *own* husband.

In addition, submitting to her own husband means that a woman's husband comes before her parents. Anytime she must make a choice between the two, she chooses in favor of her husband. A submissive wife acts in such a way that her husband never wonders if she is on his side. When a woman grows up idolizing her father, it often causes marriage problems. For what young husband can adequately follow in the steps of an idolized father?

Some wives try to make their husbands act more like the preacher, elders, deacons, or other godly men.

Sometimes such wives go to the preacher, elders, etc. to ask questions of judgment about what their husbands should do in given situations. While God wants Christians to seek help with legitimate problems from mature Christians, these wives aren't interested in correcting their own behavior. Instead, they want to use the preacher's opinions to try to regulate their husbands' behavior. While these wives think this shows subjection because some other man disagrees with their husbands, in reality, it shows a failure to accept their husbands at face value and an attempt to manipulate all the men involved.

Some women fail to accept their husbands by looking enviously at the husbands of other women, not in a lustful way, but in a wishful manner. They long for their husbands to work the same hours, like the same foods, show the same affection, etc. Many of these wives neglect to consider that the successful men in other marriages are probably happy because the wives in those marriages apply themselves to fulfilling their feminine role.

These wives make the mistake of assuming that a happy marriage comes from being married to one man as opposed to another man. While the choice of a marriage partner is important, usually when a woman exchanges one husband for another, she only trades one set of problems for a different set. Every marriage experiences its own unique problems and areas of adjustment. Thus, to accept each other at face value seems like a better solution than replacing the husband. The divorce courts are full of people who failed in their second, third, and fourth attempts to find the perfect mate.

In summary, while men complain that their wives do not make biscuits like their mothers, women gripe that their husbands do not make dough like their fathers. However, memories of home usually begin after a person's parents have been married for several years. Over the years their mothers had learned a few cooking tricks and their fathers advanced financially. Both parents enjoyed the chance to mature and learn how to live with each other. To expect a new husband or wife to possess all the assets of an older married person is not realistic. *Both true subjection and leadership revolve around the acceptance of the other at face value which prevents the husband and wife from thinking too highly of themselves or looking down on the other.*

B. RESPECT THE HUSBAND'S ROLE

> I Cor. 12:18-20: "But now God has placed the members, each one of them, in the body, just as He desired. And if they were all one member, where would the body be? But now there are many members, but one body."

God gives everyone different talents and responsibilities. Thus, as a general principle of Christianity, God wants everyone to respect each other as He created them to be. The whole chapter of I Corinthians 12 deals with the proper attitudes for the various members of the body of Christ. Since God designed people with different inherent abilities, no one can say to the other, "We don't need you--you're different." Just as the physical body needs different parts--hands, eyes, ears, etc.--all Christians need each other. God takes the credit for assigning the various jobs from the apostles down to the lowliest members. So disregarding someone with different skills condemns God's wisdom.

The same holds true in marriage, for God designed men and women with different mental and physical characteristics along with different responsibilities. When either the husband or the wife shows disrespect for the other's role, he displays disrespect for God as well:

1. THE HUSBAND IS THE HEAD OF HIS WIFE

> Eph. 5:23: "For the husband is the head of the wife, as Christ also is the head of the church,..."

"Head" means "the head, (both of men and of animals), metaphorically (anything) supreme, chief, prominent, (of persons) master, lord" (Thayer, p. 345).

God created the husband to function as a "head," not as a "body." This makes it wrong for a husband to submit to his wife even if she wants to be the leader. Since God gave the husband his leadership, he doesn't have the right to give it to someone else. In the same way, when a wife refuses to let her husband exercise the leadership, she steals from both God and her husband. She takes something that belongs to someone else--not to her.

When a wife tries to take over the leadership, she puts her husband in a dilemma. If he gives in to her, she despises him as a weakling. If he resists her and fights for his rightful leadership, she hates him as she would a tyrant. No matter what the husband does, his wife refuses to be happy.

Most husbands dearly love peace. In fact, many a husband prefers to enjoy harmony in the home rather than to continually defend his right to lead. Consequently, such a husband often spurns confrontations with his wife when she usurps his authority. He simply suffers in silence and draws further away from his wife emotionally. Unfortunately, many a wife falsely assumes that her husband's silence means approval. As a result, the wife often becomes even more self-reliant and indifferent to her husband.

However, God expects a husband to respect the position of leadership which He gives him. Thus, a husband must refuse to let his wife take over his leadership. A husband does this by making his will known to his wife and then letting her decide whether to obey or disobey. If a wife acts contentiously, a husband may have to tell her, "no," even to requests he would like to honor simply because she asks or demands them in a belligerent manner. In such instances, the man's right to lead is more important than the woman's request, no matter how legitimate. In this case, the husband sacrifices what both of them want to act in his wife's best interest.

A wise wife thanks God for a husband who openly refuses to let her take his leadership away from him. Rather than fearing his determination to lead, she appreciates it like the Shulammite who told the Shepherd, "Hurry, my beloved, and be like a gazelle or a young stag on the mountains of spices" (Song of Sol. 8:14). Even if a husband doesn't understand all the mechanics of subjection and leadership, this trait demonstrates his recognition of his God-given role and his desire to fulfill his destiny as a man.

480 MARRIAGE: A TASTE OF HEAVEN: VOL. I

When a husband reaches toward full manhood, it frees his wife to become her most influential feminine self. As a wife embraces her own role, her subjection balances and supports her husband's leadership while bringing out his best qualities. In fact, when a husband possesses this strong determination to lead, his wife can often completely change the happiness of the marriage by just her learning God's will and applying it to her life.

On the other hand, a husband who weakly gives in to his wife makes it hard for her to return the leadership to him when she learns better. Many such a wife must plead with her husband to be a man and to lead. Far better to live with a husband who acts like a male chauvinist than one who lets his wife dominate him. So when a husband seems overbearing, a wise wife will put her arms around his neck, kisses him, and tell him, "I'm sure fortunate to be married to such a strong leader as you!"

Some husbands assume that their wives automatically know what they want them to do. But wives are not mind readers any more than husbands are. Even God does not expect Christians to automatically know His will. Paul says in I Cor. 2:10, "For who among men knows the thoughts of a man except the spirit of the man, which is in him? Even so the thoughts of God no one knows except the Spirit of God." If a husband wants his wife to know his thoughts and will, he must tell her.

In these ways, a man shows respect for his role by accepting his leadership and then by telling his wife what he wants. But God also expects the wife to respect her husband's role:

2. THE WIFE CALLS HER HUSBAND "LORD"

I Pet. 3:6: "Thus Sara obeyed Abraham, calling him Lord,.."

"Obey" means "listen, hearken; 1. properly of one who on a knock at the door comes to listen to who it is, (the duty of the porter); 2. hearken to a command, i.e. obey, be obedient unto, submit to" (Thayer, p. 638).

"Calling" means "to call; 2. to call aloud, utter in a loud voice, to call i.e. name, call by name, give a name to" (Thayer, p. 321).

"Lord" means "he to whom a person or thing belongs, about which he has the power of deciding, master, lord" (Thayer, p. 365).

Sarah provides an example of a holy woman who adorned herself with subjection and made herself beautiful to God and her husband. Sarah took the initiative for practicing subjection by calling her husband "lord." Sarah didn't force Abraham to announce, "Now, I'm going to be the head of the family and you must do what I say." Rather, Sarah willingly listened to Abraham's commands and hearkened to his voice. Calling him "lord," she placed her mind in subjection to his will. This is the key to subjection. When a wife places her *mind* in subjection, her actions and emotions take care of themselves.

The last meaning Webster's dictionary gives for "lord" is "7. Humorous. A husband; as, her lord and master." Unfortunately, many a wife views subjection as a laughing matter and treats her husband as lord according to Webster's meaning instead of God's. However, being God's steward of authority entitles a husband to his wife's esteem rather than her ridicule.

The word "sir" conveys similar honor in modern language. Instead of making a military procedure out of it, a wife shows respect for her husband's authority by using "Yes, sir" and "No, sir" upon occasion. Also by asking him, "Please, kind sir" or saying, "Thank you, sweet sir," she shows respect for his manhood.

Many times when a husband accuses his wife, "You're not in subjection to me," she can't understand why he thinks such a thing. After all, she does everything that he wants her to do. To make matters worse, often the husband cannot tell her exactly why he doesn't consider her submissive. Usually the problem stems from the fact that although the wife does everything her husband tells her to, her mind is not in subjection. Sarah obeyed Abraham "calling him lord." Sarah placed her mind in subjection to Abraham's mind.

The husband's strong authority antenna quickly senses when his wife's mind fails to submit to him. And when he senses a rebellious attitude, then she need do *only one little thing* wrong, and he immediately accuses her of not submitting to him *at all*. On the other hand, if a wife places her mind in subjection and she unintentionally does something that, in the truest sense of analysis, is not a submissive act, often her husband hardly seems to notice because her attitude is right.

The key to pleasing a husband with subjection is the wife's attitude. If a wife resents his opinions, it really doesn't matter to a husband what she does--he views it as contentious. But when a wife places her mind in subjection, her actions take care of themselves. Respect for the husband's God-ordained position in the family is one of the most important ingredients of subjection. When a wife masters it, the rest becomes easy.

A wife shows respect for her husband's leadership by *not telling him* what to do, but by *asking him*. This doesn't mean that a wife can never make suggestions to her husband; it only regulates *how* she does it. Most husbands want to hear what their wives think, and they value their different perspective of life. But expressing her views disrespectfully actually makes a husband want to do anything except what his wife proposes even when it is a good suggestion.

For example, when a wife *tells* her husband, "This is what you should do," or "Here is a great idea for you," or "If I were you," she fails to show respect for her husband's authority. But when a wife *asks,* "Would it work if you did...?" or "What will people think if you do...? Will they understand your reasons as I do?" or "Do you think...is a good idea?" she recognizes her husband's leadership. Most husbands genuinely consider respectful questions; few even listen to bold proposals.

Why does *asking* a husband win his endorsement when *telling* him the same suggestion earns his disapproval? Simply because when a wife *asks* her husband, she requires him to act as the head and make a decision. When a woman *tells* her husband, she acts as the head and requires him to follow as an obedient body. Telling him what to do places a wife in competition with her husband's leadership and offends his strong authority antenna.

Most husbands honestly consider suggestions made in a submissive manner. That doesn't mean that they *accept* every submissive suggestion, but only that they *consider* it. If a woman requires any more of her husband than *consideration of her ideas,* she needs to work on developing a meek and quiet spirit along with true respect for her husband's right to lead.

When a husband resents her suggestions, it may indicate that a wife is not offering them properly. In such cases, a wise wife refrains from making *any suggestions whatsoever* unless her husband asks for her opinion. Depending upon how much a wife has abused telling her husband what to do and how sensitive he is, she may need to wait several weeks or even months before making a single suggestion. This gives her husband's authority antenna time to pick up her new respect for his leadership.

In summary, *both subjection and leadership must respect the husband's role in order to function together.* The husband respects his role by leading, while the wife respects his authority by submitting. In this way, they both show respect for God who ordained the laws of subjection and leadership. However, God not only expects both the husband and wife to honor the husband's right to lead, but He also demands that they both recognize the wife's role as equally important:

C. RESPECT THE WIFE'S ROLE

Rom. 12:10: "Be devoted to one another in brotherly love; give preference to one another in honor;..."

"Honor " means "1. a valuing by which the price is fixed, hence the price itself; 2. honor which belongs or is shown to one, the honor which one has by reason of the rank and state of the office which he holds" (Thayer, p. 624).

As a general principle of Christianity, God wants Christians to maintain an attitude of devotion, brotherly love, preference, and honor for one another. Honor involves appreciating the value of a person and esteeming the role God gives him to fulfill. Although society sometimes looks down on the role of a wife, God commands the husband to honor his wife's special feminine abilities:

1. THE HUSBAND HONORS HIS WIFE

> **I Pet. 3:7: "You husbands likewise, live with your wives in an understanding way, as with a weaker vessel, since she is a woman; and grant her honor as a fellow-heir of the grace of life, so that your prayers may not be hindered."**

"Honor," the same word defined above, refers to the high value God wants a husband to place on his wife. Instead of making her inferior to her husband, a wife's weaknesses qualify her for her God-ordained jobs. Her differences turn her into a specialist, a guardian of love and a caretaker of the home. Thus, God tells the husband to view his wife intelligently and to recognize her as equally important as him in God's plans for life on earth and in heaven, too. So when a husband fails to fully honor his wife as a valuable asset in the home, he degrades himself and shows a lack of understanding about life.

As chapter 14 shows, both Gentile and Jewish men of Peter's time looked down on women. In modern times, many men still view women with disrespect—only for different reasons. Victorian morals, which caused women to withhold their love from their husbands, led many men to despise women in response. The leftover fruits of that extreme prudery still influences many husbands to consider their wives as second class citizens.

In addition, the feminist movement and the sexual revolution of this country kindled even more contempt in the hearts of men toward women. So while men no longer view women as property without any rights at all, bad attitudes toward women still remain. And sadly, while Jesus restored womanhood to its rightful place of honor through His own teaching and the apostles' writings, many men still fail to see the glory and honor of femininity.

But rather than demanding respect, God tells the wife to earn respect by the life she lives:

2. THE WIFE RESPECTS THE FEMININE ROLE

I Pet. 3:4: "...but let it be the hidden person of the heart, with the imperishable quality of a gentle and quiet spirit, which is precious in the sight of God."

"Precious" means "precious; a. requiring great outlay, very costly; b. excellent, of surpassing value" (Thayer, p. 530).

When a wife embraces the feminine role of subjection, she makes herself meet for her husband by placing her mood and spirit in harmony with his mood and spirit. At the same time, a wife makes herself indispensable by freely giving her love, support, comfort, and tenderness to her husband. Then she becomes a valuable assistant to help her husband subdue the earth, fill it with people, and glorify God.

The Bible consistently portrays the woman who yields to her destiny as a woman as precious in the sight of both God and her husband. For example, the Shepherd and the Shulammite pledged respect for both the masculine and feminine roles. The Shulammite prayed that she might rise to the height of feminine success (Song of Sol. 4:16). Likewise, the description of the virtuous wife said that her price was far above rubies and that the heart of her husband trusted in her. In fact, the woman of great price received honor and praise from God, her husband, children, and the members of her community (Prov. 31:10-31). Solomon said that the gracious woman attains honor (Prov. 11:16).

In the New Testament, Peter reminds Christian women that they become the daughters of Sarah when they do right and thus become joint-heirs with men of the grace of life (I Pet. 3:6-7). Paul compares submissive wives to the church, the beautiful bride of Christ (Eph. 5:24). Being a submissive wife is a privilege, an honor, and a wonderful opportunity to reap the most from the husband-wife relationship.

In summary, *both subjection and leadership require respect for the woman's role.* God, husbands, children, responsible members of the community, and other Christians highly prize the worth of women who dare to function as God designed. Can any woman intellectually look down on the Biblical role of a woman? Certainly, anyone who views the woman's place as an inferior position of no importance calls half of God's human creation worthless, thereby revealing his own ignorance.

D. ADAPT TO EACH OTHER

Eph. 5:21: "...and be subject to one another in the fear of Christ."

"Subject" comes from the same root as "subjection" and refers to yielding to the admonition or advice of someone else. Thus, as a general principle of Christianity, God expects His people to submit to the opinions of other Christians, yet "in the fear of Christ." Consistently, Christ's teachings override the opinions of man when conflicts arise.

God designed for His people to work together to teach the lost. But if they fuss and fight and engage in power struggles, no one will ever hear the gospel. So God tells Christians to submit to one another so that they can work together to bear fruit for His glory.

Marriage requires lots of adjustments on the parts of both the husband and wife before they blend into a marvelous working team. God even expects the husband to adapt himself to his wife in certain areas:

1. THE HUSBAND HONORS THE WEAKER VESSEL

I Pet. 3:7: "You husbands likewise, live with your wives in an understanding way, as with a weaker vessel, since she is a woman."

As chapter 8, "Honoring the Weaker Vessel," demonstrates, God created the woman as the weaker vessel to equip her for helping the man. While different and weaker both physically and psychologically, the woman possesses certain skills which the man does not. This enables the woman to become a wonderful guardian of love for her husband and children.

God tells a husband not to take advantage of his wife's weaknesses by looking down on her or by ridiculing her. Also, expecting her to think and do everything the way he does, fails to recognize her differences. God commands the husband to protect his wife's weaknesses. Thus, God holds each husband personally responsible for determining what his wife can and cannot do since she is a woman. He must make his decisions on *her capabilities*, not his. This requires a significant amount of knowledge and understanding to adapt himself to his wife.

Sometimes a husband forces his wife to do tasks she is not emotionally, physically, or spiritually suited to do. For example, one husband insisted that his wife work outside the home late into each evening. Then when she came home, he expected her to take the laundry to the laundromat and to do other major housekeeping chores. This wife's health rapidly reached the breaking point because her husband required her to work harder than she was physically able to.

Some books about marriage give lists of "do's" and "do not's" for women such as a woman should never mow the lawn, paint the house, etc. Such lists rest on human opinion--perhaps wise opinion, but opinion nonetheless. Yet God holds each husband responsible for making such a list for his own wife based on her unique abilities and weaknesses.

This doesn't give a husband the license to dissolve the distinctions between men and women or the right to treat his wife any way he chooses. Instead, God demands that a husband *understand the differences* between masculinity and femininity so that he can treat his wife as a feminine woman. God wants the husband to conduct his marriage according to intelligence, not prejudice or laziness.

Many people think that all the rights belong to the man, while all the duties belong to the woman. Contrary to that popular opinion, *as a weaker vessel, a woman possesses basic rights which the man does not have.* She enjoys the right to be provided for so that she can devote herself to caring for the children and the home; the right to be protected from mental, physical, and spiritual harm; and the right to look to her husband for leadership.

Being a weaker vessel doesn't prevent a wife from driving a truck, carrying out the trash, or earning a paycheck. However, it prevents her husband from forcing her to do any of those things which she is not physically, mentally, or spiritually suited to do. God commands each husband to make sure that he protects his wife's individual rights.

In like manner, God commands grown children to protect their widowed mothers, while the church protects a certain class of widows (I Tim. 5:3-5). Honoring the woman as a weaker vessel is not a denial of rights, but a guarantee of rights that a man cannot scripturally take away from his wife, mother, or a "widow indeed." While the husband protects the wife's rights, God expects the wife to protect her husband's rights:

2. THE WIFE SUBMITS IN EVERYTHING

Eph. 5:24: "But as the church is subject to Christ, so also the wives ought to be to their husbands in everything."

"Everything" means "everything, (anything) whatsoever, all things, wholly, altogether, in all respects" (Thayer, p. 492).

Even after such a definition of "everything," many a wife still asks, "What does *everything* mean?" "Everything" means that the husband makes *all decisions that he does not lawfully delegate to his wife*. In areas where a husband lawfully delegates authority to his wife, she is free to make decisions, yet with an attitude of desiring to please her husband. Fortunately, God provides a partial list of some of the items that come under a husband's jurisdiction of "everything":

Tit. 2:4-5: "...that they may encourage the young women to love their husbands, to love their children, to be sensible, pure, workers at home, kind, being subject to their own husbands, that the word of God may not be dishonored."

This list of a wife's duties and attitudes ends with "being subject to their own husbands" which modifies everything above it: "to love their husbands, to love their children, to be sensible, pure, workers at home, [and] kind." An examination of each of these qualities shows a wife how to submit to her own husband in "everything." In addition, subjection improves the quality of a wife's life in every area:

(a) SUBJECTION ENHANCES MARITAL LOVE

Chapter 8, "Honoring the Weaker Vessel," explains that the word "love" in Tit. 2:4 comes from the Greek word *philo* and includes both an emotional and physical involvement with the object loved. *The Septuagint* also uses *philo* to describe sexual love between a husband and wife (Prov. 5:19). While *philo* conveys a very expressive form of love, husbands differ greatly in their needs for affection. So without subjection, a wife cannot fully satisfy her husband's desires nor become the answer to his problem. Thus, subjection plays a major role in a wife's tender display of love for her husband.

For example, many a husband greatly enjoys his wife initiating love. Perhaps he wants her to entice him and turn him on more than he wants to initiate love himself. When a wife freely bestows physical love upon her husband, she pays him a high compliment--she makes him feel manly and desirable. So a submissive wife accepts this desire in her husband and gladly arouses him with her womanly charms.

On the other hand, while welcoming his wife's advances on occasion, many another husband wants to initiate most of the lovemaking. He prefers his wife to entice him subtly with good meals and staying clean and attractive along with coyness. In this case, a submissive wife cheerfully submits to her husband's lead in the embrace of love.

Subjection also plays a vital role in the wife's enjoyment of the sexual act. *Vol. II: Learning to Love* proves from the scriptures and medical documentation that the wife's attitude toward her husband affects the way her body responds. True subjection that comes from the heart liberates a wife's body to delight in an orgasm in her husband's arms. Thus, God rewards the submissive wife with wonderful sexual thrills. Once a wife experiences firsthand the effect of a submissive attitude on her body's response to her husband, she knows that subjection, indeed, enhances love.

(b) SUBJECTION PROMOTES MOTHERLY LOVE

Often after a newlywed couple works out subjection and leadership between them, children start coming along and the battle of the wills begins all over again, only more intense than ever. The wife's tender, sensitive nature readily identifies with her children and causes her to overlook offenses by sympathizing with them. On the other hand, the husband's strong authority antenna quickly picks up on disobedience and he punishes accordingly. Ideally, the two viewpoints of the father and mother balance and support each other. But when it's her little boy or girl that's being disciplined, many a wife resents her husband's leadership as being far too strict.

A certain husband, his wife, and four-year-old son ate dinner with another couple. During the meal the mother told about going shopping and how they hadn't eaten anything but junk food all day. "That's why," she explained, "our son isn't eating very much."

For dessert, a three-tiered plate filled with an assortment of candies was set on the table. When the little boy saw all the candy, he immediately wanted some. But his father said, "Unless you clean up your plate, you can't have any."

The wife turned to her husband and said, "But he's been eating junk food all day long. What would a little more hurt?"

The husband replied, "You may not make him mind when I'm not home, but I'm here, and he's going to mind."

Without another word, the wife took her fork and ate the rest of her little boy's food. When she finished cleaning his plate, she showed it to her husband. Then she gave the little boy some of the candy.

That little boy wouldn't have starved if his mother had denied him the candy. But he might grow up to be a rebellious teenager because his mother denied him respect for his father's authority. A wife's subjection protects her children by promoting motherly love that benefits them.

(c) SUBJECTION UTILIZES COMMON SENSE

Sober-mindedness or common sense also revolves around subjection. What is sensible for a wife depends to a great extent upon her own husband's finances, age, health, education, social preferences, etc.

For example, the wife of a company president might show sensibleness when she buys hundred-dollar dresses to look appropriate for her station in life. Yet another wife might sew clothes for the whole family on a hundred dollars to keep them looking presentable. One wife might sensibly serve tender cuts of steak several nights a week, while such actions would quickly bankrupt another husband. Hiring a maid might make sense for one wife, while another wife might need to take in ironing to help pay for unexpected expenses. True sensibleness cannot exist without subjection.

(d) SUBJECTION GUARDS PURITY

The difference in a man and a woman's sexual thinking often prevents many a woman from recognizing certain garments, habits, and language as impure. Yet purity not only results from the way a woman views herself, but also from the way others see her. For example, Peter said that an unbelieving pagan husband ought to be able to see purity shining in his wife's conduct (I Pet. 3:1-2). Consequently, the husband's opinions help establish his wife's purity.

Sadly, many a wife resents anyone telling her what to wear or not to wear. She doesn't want to give up anything that she can't see the harm in. On the other hand, sometimes conflicts arise when a husband fails to protect his wife from the lustful looks of other men. Instead, such a husband enjoys other men envying his wife.

For example, one woman's husband wanted her to wear extremely short skirts and tight pants. He told her, "When we walk down the street, I want every man to see what I have. I want them to be jealous of me and the wife that I've got." This wife was not a Christian and she went along with dressing the way her husband wanted. But a Christian recognizes that

God's laws about sensuous dress and conduct override her husband's opinion in such cases.

Another wife's wedding ring wore out, so for several years she did not wear a ring. During this time she often came home from work telling about the men who propositioned her that day. They thought she wasn't married, or if she was, she wasn't faithful to her husband because she didn't wear a wedding ring. Her husband said it didn't bother him because he trusted her fidelity. Yet this husband's trust violated God's laws of purity which consider the thoughts of others and avoid tempting them to sin. So even though this wife's husband didn't question her purity, her conduct caused others to.

However, in most cases a husband truly cares about both his wife's purity and her appearance of purity. Thus, a husband's manly way of looking at sexual things guards a wife's purity when she submits to him.

(e) SUBJECTION PROTECTS THE HOME

Many a wife refuses to surrender the leadership of her homemaking to her husband. She argues, "He has his say about everything else, but this is my domain! He doesn't have any say at all about what I do or how I do it!" In contrast to that dogmatic opinion of many wives, Tit. 2:4-5 plainly teaches that a woman is to be a worker at home, "being subject" to her own husband. Also, one of the qualifications for an elder or a deacon, "he must be one who manages his own household well," implies that a man exercises authority over the home (I Tim. 3:4, 12).

By requiring the wife to submit to her husband with her homemaking talents, God insures that the home becomes a haven of rest for the man and his children. For example, a husband wrote an advice columnist how disappointed he was in his wife's housecleaning abilities. He told about how when he looked under the bed and saw the dust balls, it nearly made him throw up. But most other husbands don't even know what a dust ball is, let alone look under the beds. Since men obviously vary in their needs for orderliness in their homes, the submissive wife seeks to satisfy her own husband. As a result, one wife may vacuum under the beds much more frequently than other wives.

However, the wise husband delegates a tremendous amount of authority to his wife in caring for the home. If he feels compelled to oversee every detail, he hampers his wife's ability to add feminine touches to her homemaking which in turn convey love and comfort to him. Yet God holds him responsible for making sure that he budgets his wife enough money to properly feed and care for the family.

(f) SUBJECTION REGULATES GOOD WORKS

"Kind" or "good" means "1. of a good constitution or nature (corresponds to the figurative expression 'good ground' in Lk. 8:15 and denotes a soul inclined to goodness, and accordingly eager to learn saving truth and ready to bear fruits); 2. useful, salutary; 3. pleasant, agreeable, joyful, happy; 4. excellent, distinguished; 5. upright, honorable" (Thayer, p. 2).

God places "kind," the wife's benevolent concern for other people, at the end of the list of "everything" in Tit. 2:4-5, for the passage ranks the wife's jobs in their order of proper priority. For instance, a woman is to be kind without neglecting her husband, her children, common sense, or her home while "being subject" to her own husband *even if he is not a Christian.*

The first chapter, "God's Plan for Men and Women," shows that God expects a wife's priorities to change with her family responsibilities. This enables the woman to care properly for her family, while at the same time rendering the best possible service to God.

Most husbands, even if they *are not Christians,* want their wives to show compassion for other people and to do good works. At the same time, most husbands, even if they *are Christians,* resent their wives neglecting their own families to supply the needs of other people. Thus, a wife's good works for people outside her family sometimes causes marriage problems. Many a wife gets her priorities mixed up and ceases to serve God in the home in order to serve God outside the home.

For example, one wife offered to take a widow shopping. But the widow only wanted to go on Saturday. The wife thought her husband didn't care about the widow when he objected to them going shopping on his day off. After all, he didn't plan to go anywhere that day. Yet God created the woman primarily to satisfy her husband's needs. And a husband who works hard all week has the right to look forward to spending a Saturday relaxing with his wife. Rather than going somewhere, he needed her company.

Besides, the wife could still take the widow shopping, but on her own time, not her husband's time. A submissive wife does not substitute her good deeds for others for her husband's needs. The widow didn't have a husband to schedule her activities around--she just had a preference. Subjection makes the husband's preference override the widow's.

Another wife observed a friend who didn't have enough to wear. So she asked her husband if she could give her some material to sew. Her husband said, "No, I don't think that's a good idea."

After stewing about it and continuing to feel sorry for her friend, the wife finally decided that God's law overrode her husband's opinion. So she gave her friend some material behind her husband's back. Later the wife learned that her friend's husband was neglecting to provide for his family. And by her giving the material to her friend, she was actually encouraging the husband in sin. In reality, she had done her friend more harm than good. The husband who said, "No," had recognized the other husband's obligation to provide for his family and that it was not a true case of need.

Submitting to her husband would have protecting the wife from participating in someone else's sin. However, if the wife had been right about God's laws on caring for the needy overriding her husband's opinion, she should have disobeyed her husband *openly, but regretfully* instead of going behind his back. This would have given the husband an opportunity to explain his reasons and to show that he actually understood the situation better than his wife did. When it comes to good works, a wife's tender, sympathizing nature needs the protection of her husband's more realistic way of looking at life.

(g) SUBJECTION GLORIFIES GOD

As a result of the wife submitting in everything, the husband-wife team turns into a very loving unit which supports, protects, and balances one another. Not only that, but the husband and wife become highly efficient in subduing the earth, filling it with people, and glorifying God because they work together instead of wasting their energies on power struggles.

Subjection and leadership are for Christians; contention and tyranny are for pagans. Subjection and leadership are for strong, mature, liberated people who exercise control over themselves; fighting and bickering are for weak people who are slaves of their emotional whims. True subjection and loving leadership glorify God by blessing every area of life which they touch.

However, when a husband and wife engage in power struggles, they bring dishonor upon themselves. For example, a fourth grade girl looked forward to spending the night with one of her school friends. But she came home the next day shocked at what she had seen: Her friend's mother spent the night sleeping in her daughter's bedroom. Then the next morning the parents got into a big fight, so the mother brought the girl home early. After she got home, the girl asked her mother about parents who didn't sleep together and who fought. "If that's the way it is," she said, "I don't want to get married." The mother explained that when husbands and wives serve God, it prevents a lot of fights.

In summary, *subjection and leadership require both the husband and wife to give up some of their preferences to adapt to the other.* As a result, the husband protects his wife's feminine nature by not asking any more of his wife than she can give. In return, the wife makes her mood and spirit harmonize with her husband's in everything. Thus, when a husband and wife practice subjection and leadership as God designed, they take the man-made curse out of subjection. Then they begin to enjoy their marriage as God intends and truly delight in each other.

II. THE RESULT

> **Phil. 2:3-4: "Do nothing from selfishness or empty conceit, but with humility of mind let each of you regard one another as more important than himself; do not merely look out for your own personal interests, but also for the interests of others."**

One mark of a true Christian is unselfishness-- genuinely caring for other people and making personal sacrifices for their benefit. Jesus did this when He died upon the cross for sinful people, some of whom helped kill Him. He gave himself up to do what was best for others without thought of Himself.

Unlike Christ, many people stubbornly fight for their rights, refusing to give up a single privilege regardless of what happens to others. In this way, the feminist movement tries to make sure that no one denies women a single right regardless of the consequences to men, children, or women. Likewise, both husbands and wives, battling for their rights to the bitter end, fill the divorce courts. But when a couple patterns their marriage after God's laws *both* the husband and the wife give up *all* their rights for the sake of their union and to protect the other:

A. THE HUSBAND FEARS HARMING HIS WIFE

> **Eph. 5:33: "Nevertheless let each individual among you also love his own wife even as himself;..."**

After drawing the beautiful parallels between the husband and Christ and the wife and the church, Paul sums up the key to a successful husband-wife relationship in Eph. 5:33. Through the guidance of the Holy Spirit, Paul commands the husband to love his own wife even as himself. Loving his wife as his own body demands that a husband have a wholesome dread of doing anything that might harm his wife--not "displease," but "harm" his wife.

Loving his wife as his own body does not mean that a husband never makes mistakes because he does no matter how hard he tries not to. Nor does it mean that a husband does everything his wife wants because God expects him to lead in the realm of human opinion. It means, however, that in all his decisions, he considers the effect upon his wife and does what *he thinks* (not she thinks) is best for her. In this way, a true leader in the home serves his followers, not himself, doing what he deems best for them.

One wife said, "Before my husband and I married, we both read several books about marriage. The books I read convinced me that the success of our marriage depended solely upon me and the way I treated my husband. After we were married, my husband remarked one day that he thought the success of a marriage depended primarily upon the man and the way he treated his wife. This really shocked me because I thought that he was more or less an innocent bystander and that I completely controlled the happiness of our marriage. But after thinking about his statement, I realized that for a marriage to be really successful, *both* the husband and wife must act as though the success of the marriage depended solely upon each of them and give one hundred percent to the happiness of the union."

When a husband has a wholesome dread of harming his wife, he helps his marriage prosper. But even if a husband fails to lead in the realm of happiness, God expects the wife to do her part. A marriage with only one spouse giving one hundred percent is happier than a marriage in which no one works for harmony.

B. WIFE FEARS DISPLEASING HER HUSBAND

> **Eph. 5:33: "...and let the wife see to it that she respect [reverence--KJV] her husband."**

"Respect" or "reverence" means "1. fear, dread, terror, (in subjective sense); 2. reverence, respect, (for authority, rank, dignity)" (Thayer, p. 656).

"Respect," is the same word translated "afraid" in Ac. 5:26 which says, "Then the captain went along with the officers and proceeded to bring them back without violence; (for they were *afraid* of the people, lest they should be stoned)." "Respect" and "afraid" mean to have a wholesome dread of displeasing someone. A wife shows respect for her husband's God-given leadership over her by being afraid to displease him, just as the soldiers were afraid to displease the people.

Not an option, God commands the wife to reverence her husband. Reverence includes every aspect of subjection by controlling the wife's attitude as she fears displeasing her husband in even one area of their life together. Reverence adds the finishing touch to subjection that turns it into a blessing.

The Amplified New Testament shows that reverence takes advantage of the wife's tender emotional nature by including feelings of esteem, veneration, love, and admiration to such a degree that they lead to verbal praise of her husband. Thus, the wife does not obey her husband out of resentment or duty, but out of admiration that goes beyond the limit in regarding the worth of him. Like the Shulammite, she both thinks and says, "My beloved is dazzling and ruddy, *outstanding among ten thousand"* (Song of Sol. 5:10).

Showing reverence for her husband allows a wife to unlock the door to supreme marital happiness. In fact, the majority of marriage problems cannot be completely solved without a wife manifesting this attitude of respect and admiration for her husband. A lack of reverence greatly magnifies even those problems that stem primarily from the husband, such as problems of supporting the family, child discipline, and certain sexual difficulties.

Since the wife's reverence and the husband's unselfishness are so important to the success of a marriage, *Vol. II: Learning to Love* devotes two whole chapters to the special mechanics of reverence and love (*agape*). First, however, the wife should concentrate on understanding the basic mechanics of subjection. When she masters them, reverence comes easier.

In summary, *subjection and leadership function together to protect both the husband and wife.* God asks the wife to submit to her husband so that she can work with him to subdue the earth, fill it with people, and glorify God. God asks the husband to completely forget himself and to always do what is best for his wife. God expects both a husband and wife to deny themselves for the good of the other and to protect the other. Consequently, leadership is not a matter of dominating the wife, but acting in her best interest. Neither is subjection cowardly servitude, but acting in the husband's best interest.

Thus, love and reverence go together and enable the husband and wife to remove all selfishness from their lives. And to the degree that a husband loves his wife as his own body and to the degree that a wife practices reverence, to that same degree they both enjoy a wonderful marriage that is a taste of heaven. Love and reverence remove the man-made curse in subjection and replace it with a blessing from God.

STUDY EXERCISE

Answer all questions in your own words.

1. What are some pitfalls that keep a wife from subjecting herself to her own husband?

2. What are some pitfalls that keep a man from subjecting himself to his own wife?

3. Which one has the most important role--the husband or the wife? Why?

4. What happens if a husband does not respect his own role?

5. How does a husband show respect for his wife's weaknesses?

6. What does it mean for a wife to submit to her husband in everything?

7. Why does true subjection and loving leadership go hand in hand?

8. Why is it necessary for a woman to place her mind in subjection? What will happen if she does not?

9. Do you disagree with anything in this lesson? If so, explain in detail giving scriptures for your reasons.

PERSONAL EXERCISE

Answer the following questions to determine if you accept your husband at face value. Give yourself the appropriate points for how often you do each thing (4 points--never, 3 points--once in a while, 2 points-- most of the time, 1 point--every chance you get):

1. Point out his faults in front of others.
2. Use other men as shining examples.
3. Use yourself as a good example.
4. Encourage him to improve himself and develop his character.
5. Let him know you deserve a better husband.
6. Let him know how he gets on your nerves.
7. Let him see your disappointment in him.
8. Get cool when he doesn't do things your way.
9. Drop hints about what you expect him to do.
10. Map out what you think he should do.
11. Analyze his problems and propose solutions.
12. Expect him to tell you everywhere he is going and what he'll be doing.
13. Remind him of how you struggle to live on his paycheck.
14. Tell him what to say at meetings of the church.
15. Tell him how to stand up to other people or his boss.
16. Tell him he is losing his masculine figure or getting fat.
17. Tease him about getting bald or the way he wears his hair.
18. Remind him of his past mistakes.
19. Make jokes about his home repair abilities.
20. Correct the stories he tells to others.
21. When he tells you about his ambitions, warn him of failure.
22. Let him know he could never succeed without you.
23. Use your higher education to defeat his ideas.
24. Work outside the home because his income does not cover your needs.
25. Pick apart his social graces or lack of them.
26. Be afraid to fully submit to him.
27. Feel hurt because he won't talk to you.
28. Complain about the way he takes care of the yard work or car repairs.
29. Refuse to follow his directions for disciplining the children.
30. Try to guide his thinking by sly questions.
31. Think what he doesn't know won't hurt him so don't tell him everything.
32. Make excuses for him to the children or your family.

33. Make him the brunt of jokes in public.
34. Make him the brunt of jokes in private.
35. Criticize the way he dresses.
36. Wish you had married someone else.
37. Refuse his help when he offers it.
38. Refuse to wear the clothes he likes on you.
39. Exchange his gifts.
40. Try to force him to go to church or quote scripture to him.
41. Think you would make a better man than your husband does.
42. Push him to get another job or raise.
43. Don't ask him about thinks you think he will say "no" on.
44. Spend more money than he budgets you.
45. Tell him "I told you so."
46. Refuse to be ready to leave the house when he is.
47. Compare him to your father or brothers.
48. Correct his grammar, spelling, or pronunciation.
49. Complain about his TV or reading habits.
50. Complain about his hobbies.
52. Look down on him taking naps or going to sleep in front of the TV.
53. Disapprove of the hours he works.
54. Accuse him of bragging too much in public.
55. Try to persuade him not to be bashful.
56. Belittle him for not showing you common courtesies such as opening doors, etc.
57. Be hurt when he forgets to buy you a gift.
58. Disapprove of his friends.
59. Insist that he like the same entertainment as you do.
60. Ask your husband to name other ways that you do not accept him at face value and subtract 2 points each.

Score: Add up your points to determine whether or not you accept your husband at face value.

      240–181 points = Face Value
      180–121 points = 3/4 Value
      120– 61 points = 1/2 Value
       60– 0 points = 1/4 Value

CHAPTER 16

FALSE CONCEPTS OF SUBJECTION

Poets write sonnets of love, popular vocalists sing about love, young women dream of love, young men compete for love, while all the world yearns for more love. Yet the divorce rate steadily rises as husbands and wives fight over custody and property rights. Something has happened to love; something has stolen the love out of marriages.

"Contention" is that sinister villain. In a country founded upon everyone's right to make their own choices, contention seems normal. Few people even suspect that contention might be the culprit who stole love from countless marriages. Instead, trusting wives gladly welcome contention into their homes to help them win their rights. But before they know it, contention escalates from simple fights to outright hostilities. Next contention fearlessly invades the bedrooms of unsuspecting couples to numb their joy of sexual love. Sadly, naive wives who can't understand what happened to the love they once felt find themselves speaking contemptuously to their husbands.

Contention easily finds a home with many wives. Since subjection has such a bad reputation in modern times, few people suspect that contention really makes people miserable. But from the beginning of time, contention has destroyed love in the home. Far too many times contention successfully has alienated a husband and wife and left them wallowing in pain and sorrow. Fortunately, contention flees when women learn the truth about subjection. Then once again, love flourishes.

I. CONTENTION HARMS EVERYONE

I Tim. 5:14-15: "Therefore, I want younger widows to get married, bear children, keep house, and give the enemy no occasion for reproach; for some have already turned aside to follow Satan."

"Get married" means "1. used of men to lead in marriage, take to wife; 2. used of women to give one's self in marriage; 3. of both sexes" (Thayer, pp. 108-109).

"Keep house" means "to be master (or head) of a house, to rule a household, manage family affairs" (Thayer, p. 439).

The word "get married" reflects the differences between a husband and a wife. When a man marries, he accepts the duty of "leading" a wife. On the other hand, when a woman marries, she "gives herself" over to the leadership of her husband. A submissive wife follows the opinions of her husband in order to work with him and to promote true love. Just the opposite, a contentious wife works against her husband by trying to force her opinions on him.

Thus, Paul told Titus to remind the young women of their duties, for God designed important work for women to do. God wants young women to seek husbands and to work alongside them. He desires for them to bear children and to become experts in managing their homes. When women neglect their responsibilities, the world suffers from a lack of their good influence while Satan profits.

When women turn aside from their God-given job, Satan quickly finds work for them to do. He outfits them with hard heads and gives them the best tool he ever designed--willfulness and selfishness, plain old contention. With Satan's help, contentious women foil the best efforts of men.

In addition, Satan also effectively uses women to destroy the influence of the church--to cause those outside of Christ to speak against God's word. When women seek sexual satisfaction outside of marriage, they bring reproach upon God (I Tim. 5:11-12). Likewise, when God's people endure miserable marriages just like people outside of Christ do, it brings re-

proach upon the God who designed marriage. By their
failure to use their single-mindedness and intuition to
work on their marriages as guardians of love, women
can completely undo all the efforts of others to teach
the lost.   History shows that Satan successfully
uses contentious women to defeat the best of men--
men with special unique qualities:

A. ADAM HEEDED THE ADVICE OF HIS WIFE

**Gen. 3:12: "And the man said, 'The woman
whom Thou gavest to be with me, she gave
me from the tree, and I ate.'"**

God created Adam in His own image as a perfect
man without mental, physical, or spiritual handicaps.
Then God made Eve to work alongside that first man
and to help him subdue the earth. But Satan went to
Eve and talked her into eating from the forbidden tree
of knowledge of good and evil. Then she gave to Adam
and he also ate. Thus, Adam readily heeded the advice
of his wife and sinned. When God exposed Adam's sin,
Adam acknowledged the influence of his wife over him,
for he said, "The woman whom Thou gavest to be with
me, she gave me from the tree, and I ate."
God also acknowledged the woman's influence over
Adam, for He said, "Because *you listened* to the voice
of your wife...cursed is the ground because of you..."
(Gen. 3:17). Even though Eve influenced Adam's decision to disobey God, God still held Adam responsible
for his own actions. Blaming his wife did not free
Adam from punishment. *Thus, a woman led God's perfectly created man into sin.*

B. AHAB SUBMITTED TO HIS WIFE'S COUNSEL

**I Ki. 21:25: "Surely there was no one like
Ahab, who sold himself to do evil in the
sight of the Lord, because Jezabel his wife
incited him."**

King Ahab desired Naboth's vineyard as recorded in
I Kings 21. When Ahab asked Naboth to sell his vine-
yard, Naboth refused. This depressed Ahab. His wife
Jezabel tried to cheer him up by asking him if he

were a king or a weakling with the words, "Do you now reign over Israel?" Surely, a ruler should be able to get what he wanted!

After shaming Ahab, Jezebel said, "I will give you the vineyard of Naboth." She apparently considered Ahab incapable of doing anything right, and took matters into her own hands to help him overcome his depression. Then Jezebel proceeded to frame Naboth and have him stoned to death. Later she told Ahab, "Arise, take possession of the vineyard of Naboth."

When Elijah cursed Ahab for the sin, Elijah said, "Have you murdered, and also taken possession?" (verse 19). Even though Jezabel conspired to commit murder, Ahab turned his rightful leadership over to her and became guilty of the sin in God's eyes. Ahab still bore the responsibility. *Thus, a woman overpowered a mighty king.*

C. SOLOMON SINNED BECAUSE OF HIS WIVES

> **Neh. 13:26: "Did not Solomon king of Israel sin regarding these things? Yet among the many nations there was no king like him, and he was loved by his God, and God made him king over all Israel; nevertheless the foreign women caused even him to sin."**

God blessed Solomon with so much wisdom that people from other lands traveled great distances to hear his proverbs. Even the queen of Sheba came to test Solomon with difficult questions (I Ki. 10:1-13). After Solomon answered all of the queen's question she replied, "It was a true report which I heard in my own land about your words and your wisdom. Nevertheless I did not believe the reports, until I came and my eyes had seen it. And behold, the half was not told me. You exceed in wisdom and prosperity the report which I heard."

However, Solomon, who knew God intimately, was led into idolatry by his many wives. In his old age he rejected the God he served in his youth. *Thus, the wisest man succumbed to the influence of his wives.*

D. SAMSON YIELDED TO A WOMAN'S NAGGING

> **Jg. 16:16-17: "And it came about when she pressed him daily with her words and urged him, that his soul was annoyed to death. So he told her all that was in his heart and said to her, 'A razor has never come on my head, for I have been a Nazirite to God from my mother's womb. If I am shaved, then my strength will leave me and I shall become weak and be like any other man.'"**

Samson, the strongest man, slew a thousand Philistines with the jawbone of a donkey. Yet the Philistines used a woman to defeat him. And what did she use for a weapon? Why, her tongue, of course. Delilah, a lowly harlot, pressed Samson daily with her words until he became annoyed to death and gave in and revealed the secret of his strength--his hair which had never been cut. Then while he slept, the Philistines cut off his hair and easily captured him. They put out his eyes and made him work grinding grain in the prison. Thus, *the tongue of a woman conquered the strongest man.*

E. JOB REFUSED HIS WIFE'S BAD ADVICE

> **Job 2:9-10: "Then his wife said to him, 'Do you still hold fast your integrity? Curse God and die!' But he said to her, 'You speak as one of the foolish women speaks. Shall we accept good from God and not accept adversity?' In all this Job did not sin with his lips."**

If ever a man could have felt justified at giving in to his wife, Job was that man. Job suffered with mental, physical, and spiritual anguish. A freak storm killed all his children, robbers killed his servants and stole his herds, boils from the top of his head to his feet made him writhe in pain, and he wondered if God still heard his prayers.

God allowed Satan to tempt Job with all these disasters to test Job's faith. But Satan did not kill Job's wife when he killed the rest of his family--she was more valuable to Satan alive than dead. She advised Job to do the very thing Satan wanted, "Do you still hold fast your integrity? Curse God and die!"

Many commentators suggest that Job's wife told him to commit suicide on top of renouncing God which would cinch Satan winning his contest with God. Job's wife served Satan well, but Job rebuked her and told her to be quiet. Of all these great men, only Job in all his anguish and loneliness refused the evil counsel of his wife.

As these examples show, a woman becomes a very powerful tool for Satan if she allows him to use her. All she need do is quit thinking rationally and yield to her emotions. Then she becomes selfish with her mind set on having everything her own way. When she does this, she becomes ripe for Satan to use to defeat her husband and children in particular and the church in general. A fact of human nature seems to be that failures in the home often fail in the church, too. Through a woman's influence, a perfectly created man, a mighty king, the wisest man, and the strongest man all suffered defeat. Both men and women need protection from the wrong kind of feminine influence:

II. SUBJECTION PROTECTS EVERYONE

Eph. 5:23: "For the husband is the head of the wife, as Christ also is the head of the church, He Himself being the Savior of the body."

The Jews used the word "savior" to talk about everyday men who protected others. For example, they referred to their kings as saviors because they protected them from political unrest and wars. But Christ represents the ultimate savior who saves people from their sins. In this same manner, God wants a husband to become his wife's savior--to love her as his own body and to protect her from all harm. And when a wife allows her husband to protect her through submission to him, she protects him, too.

God didn't design the influence of women to bring about evil. Fortunately, many Bible women used their influence for good. These women presented their suggestions and disagreements in a submissive way. Subjection protects a wife from misusing her influence by insisting that the husband make a decision regarding her suggestions. Through subjection, a wife promotes love in the home. In this way, God uses women to help men subdue the earth, fill it with people, and glorify God:

A. ABIGAIL STOPPED DAVID FROM SINNING

I Sam. 25:28: "Please forgive the transgression of your maidservant; for the Lord will certainly make for my lord an enduring house, because my lord is fighting the battles of the Lord, and evil shall not be found in you all your days."

The Bible describes Abigail's husband Nabal as "harsh and evil in his dealings." Yet Abigail was intelligent and beautiful in appearance. Even though Abigail lived with a wicked husband, she used subjection to protect herself, her husband, and her servants from a bloodbath and David from committing that massacre (I Samuel 25).

David and his men protected Nabal's sheep from robbers while the shepherds pastured them in the hills. When time for shearing the sheep came, David sent some of his men to ask for food from Nabal as was the custom of the people. For at shearing time the owners of the flocks prepared large banquets for the shearers and to repay those who helped the shepherds during the year. Thus, David and his men had earned the food.

Instead of honoring David's legitimate request, Nabal answered, "Who is David?" While everyone knew that David was the anointed king who would take Saul's place, Nabal refused to share his banquet with David and his men.

Angered, David determined to kill Nabal and all of his house. One of the servants quickly told Abigail about what Nabal had done and the certainty of David committing mass murder in revenge. Abigail could not warn Nabal of the impending disaster because he was drunk. Since Abigail could not support her husband's sin of refusing to honor the anointed king of Israel, she made sure that she did not sin too. She loaded donkeys with food from the banquet and personally took them to David.

Abigail approached David in a submissive way. She did not criticize him for planning a slaughter of innocent people along with Nabal. As the hostess of the banquet, she accepted responsibility for not knowing about his request and honoring it. She asked for his forgiveness for her oversight. Then she recognized David's authority as the anointed king who would some day rule Israel--she prayed that the deed he contemplated would not cause him shame later on. She let David see her shock that someone as good as him would do such a thing--he was too noble and righteous to stoop to Nabal's level by committing murder.

Through maintaining a submissive attitude by appealing to his God-given authority and by believing in the good in him, Abigail brought out the best in David. David praised her and said, "Blessed be the Lord God of Israel, who sent you this day to meet me, and blessed be your discernment, and blessed be you, who have keep me this day from bloodshed, and from avenging myself by my own hand" (verses 32-33).

When Abigail went home, she still could not tell Nabal what happened for "he was very drunk." The next morning after he sobered up, she told him what happened. Nabal reacted to the news that he had nearly been killed along with all his household by suffering some kind of attack and died. David reacted to Abigail's submissive correction of his imminent sin by asking her to become his wife.

Abigail maintained a proper attitude toward the relationship between men and women even when she was about to be killed. It would be easy to forget the principles of subjection in a case of impending disaster. Yet because Abigail was submissive, David listened to her and granted her request. Abigail's subjection replaced David's hate for her husband with love for her.

B. MANOAH'S WIFE GAVE HIM GOOD COUNSEL

Jg. 13:22-23: "So Manoah said to his wife, 'We shall surely die, for we have seen God.' But his wife said to him, 'If the Lord had desired to kill us, He would not have ac-

cepted **a burnt offering and a grain offering
from our hands, nor would He have showed
us all these things, nor would He have let
us hear things like this at this time.'"**

Before Samson was born, an angel appeared to his
mother and told her that she would conceive and give
birth to a son. The angel gave her special instructions
to follow during her pregnancy and after the birth of
Samson (Jg. 13:2–24).

Samson's mother told her husband all these things.
Manoah asked God to send the angel back to tell them
how to raise the boy properly. When the angel came
the second time, he came only to Manoah's wife. But
imagine! She told an angel of the Lord *to wait* until
she got her husband. That's subjection! Then when
Manoah came, he asked the angel how to raise the
child. Afterwards, Manoah made a burnt offering for the
angel. When the angel ascended in the flame of the
altar toward heaven, Manoah realized that he was the
angel of the Lord and told his wife, "We shall surely
die, for we have seen God."

Some women writers ridicule Manoah for being
afraid that he and his wife would die. They say, "This
is an example of a wife having to lead her husband
because she was smarter than he was. She had to give
her husband three reasons why God wouldn't kill them."
On the contrary, the story does not show a wife taking
over for a weak husband. Rather, the narrative shows
how a submissive wife points out certain facts to her
husband which he overlooked and which may change
his conclusion.

Every action of Samson's mother demonstrated her
subjection: She went to her husband after the angel
appeared and told him everything. The second time the
angel appeared she got her husband so that he could
talk to the angel, too. Then when Manoah drew a
wrong conclusion about the incident, she submissively
pointed out some facts he failed to considered.

Some people think that subjection means a wife
can never disagree with her husband. But a husband
doesn't want his wife to lie just for the sake of
agreeing with him. Neither does a husband want his
wife to flaunt her wisdom when he makes a honest

mistake. Subjection just *regulates the way* a wife disagrees with her husband.

A contentious wife would have corrected her husband differently than Samson's mother did. Contentious wives jump at the chance to make remarks such as, "You stupid man, don't you know anything? Why, God isn't going to kill us, or He wouldn't have shown us all these things!" or "I've never seen anyone so frightened of his own shadow! God is not going to kill us, or He wouldn't have done all these things!"

When a woman maintains a submissive attitude, her husband doesn't resent her pointing out facts that he fails to consider. Rather, a wise husband appreciates his wife when she honestly disagrees with him and tells him in a respectful manner. Men hate the contentious attitude, not the correction.

C. ESTHER SAVED A NATION

> **Es. 8:5: "Then she said, 'If it pleases the king and if I have found favor before him and the matter seems proper to the king and I am pleasing in his sight, let it be written to revoke the letters devised by Haman, the son of Hammedatha the Agagite, which he wrote to destroy the Jews who are in all the king's provinces.'"**

The story of Esther demonstrates the power of a submissive woman to defeat the best laid political plans. Briefly, Haman tricked King Ahasuerus into giving permission to kill all the Jews in the land on the thirteenth day of the first month (Es. 3:8-12).

Then queen Esther, a Jew, learned that she and all the other Jews would soon to be killed. She petitioned the king by first preparing a banquet for him and Haman. Then she prepared a second banquet the next day, at which time she approached the king with the submissive words, "If I have found favor in your sight, O king, and if it please the king..." The story continues on to tell how the king granted Esther's request and spared the Jews.

Who knows what would have happened if Esther had approached the king in a contentious manner to *demand* rather than to submissively *ask* him to spare their lives? Being submissive does not guarantee that the man will grant the woman's petition, only that he will listen and consider the request. Contention, on the other hand, nearly always guarantees that the man will do everything possible to avoid the demand. Subjection is the only safe course to follow in matters of life and death.

D. DEBORAH GAVE BARAK COURAGE

> Jg. 4:8-9: "Then Barak said to her, 'If you will go with me, then I will go; but if you will not go with me, I will not go.' And she said, 'I will surely go with you; nevertheless the honor shall not be yours on the journey that you are about to take, for the Lord will sell Sisera into the hands of a woman.' Then Deborah arose and went with Barak to Kadesh."

Deborah, a prophetess and judge over Israel, did not use God's favor with her as an excuse to become a domineering woman. Content to stay within the realm of authority God gave her, she delivered God's messages to His people. Thus, she told Barak that God wanted him to conquer Sisera and his army. But Barak lacked confidence and asked Deborah to come along, even though God assured him that He would give Sisera into his hand.

Barak did not want Deborah to command the army, but simply to give him confidence and self-assurance. This Deborah did. It would be easy for a woman to assume the leadership in a case like this when the man obviously lacked courage--especially since the woman was a prophetess, one through whom God spoke.

A contentious woman would have reasoned, "I know God gave the man this job, but he doesn't know how to do it and wants me to do it. He's afraid and I'm not, so why shouldn't I do it for him?" However, Deborah did *her job* and then encouraged Barak to do *his job*. God took care of Barak's lack of trust in Him by delivering Sisera into the hands of a woman.

A woman cannot build up a man's self-confidence by being domineering. A woman helps bring out the best in a man by sharing her wisdom with him in a submissive manner. A woman's sensitive nature helps her build up a man's self-confidence so that even when he is afraid, he still fulfills his obligations.

If ever human logic could rationalize a woman taking over a man's job, Deborah should have taken over Barak's job when he became afraid. But Deborah valued God's logic and recognized that God gave the job of conquering Sisera to Barak, not her. That is what subjection is all about: honoring God's wisdom in giving the man certain jobs even when the man is afraid.

E. RUTH FOUND REST WITH HER HUSBAND

Ru. 3:1: "Then Naomi her mother-in-law said to her, 'My daughter, shall I not seek security [rest--KJV and NASV footnote] for you, that it may be well with you?'"

"Rest" means "quiet, i.e. a settled spot, or (figuratively) a home:--(place of) rest" (Strong, p. 68).

The whole book of Ruth portrays the power of subjection. For example, Naomi told her two daughters-in-law to go back to their parents saying, "May the Lord grant that you find rest, each in the house of her husband" (Ru. 1:9).

Naomi gave God credit for giving a woman "rest" in marriage. Every woman knows that marriage doesn't give a wife physical leisure, but when a woman follows God's plan of subjection, she finds mental rest in the house of her husband. If a wife fails to enjoy this rest, she is not practicing subjection properly. God cannot give a woman rest unless she follows His instructions.

After Ruth refused to return to her parents' home, Naomi told her that she would help her find rest by helping her get married. Naomi proceeded to advise Ruth about the Jewish marriage laws of raising up an heir for the deceased (Deut. 25:5-10). As a result, Ruth went to Boaz, a near relative, at night and uncovered his feet and lay down. When Boaz discovered her and asked, "Who are you?" Ruth replied, "I am Ruth your maid. So spread your covering over your maid, for you are a close relative" (Ru. 3:6-9).

Some people imply that Ruth acted immorally when she lay down at Boaz's feet. However, she had an obligation to raise up an heir for her dead husband and a right to go to Boaz for that purpose. The Jews used the expression "spread your covering over your maid" to signified, "marry me and keep me under your protection." Ruth acted properly according to the Mosaical law.

Boaz praised Ruth because, instead of chasing young men, she denied her personal desires and sought to raise up an heir for her dead husband. He told her he would do whatever she asked, but a relative closer than he legally had the first choice of raising up an heir. Boaz proceeded to inquire of the closer relative to see if he wanted to fulfill his obligations toward Ruth. When the relative chose not to raise up an heir for another man, Boaz took Ruth for his wife.

As a submissive woman, Ruth presented the problem of raising up a lawful heir for her dead husband to Boaz and then went home and let Boaz do all the worrying and make the final arrangements. In every way, Ruth demonstrated the power and beauty of a submissive and trusting woman. God rewarded her with rest in marriage to a loving husband.

III. FALSE CONCEPTS ABOUT SUBJECTION

At just the mention of the word "subjection," a woman automatically thinks of certain concepts--often bad ones. But many of these ideas aren't really a part of true Bible subjection. As a way of summarizing subjection, the following list gives some of the false reasons many women give for refusing to be submissive:

A. NOT A DOOR MAT, BUT HONORABLE

I Pet. 3:7: "You husband likewise, ...grant her honor..."

Frightened women accuse God of wanting women to become door mats for their husbands to wipe their feet on. These women just know that if they submit to their husbands, their husbands will abuse them more than ever. Their cry of contention is, "He's selfish now and if I give in to him, he'll be more selfish than ever." To them subjection means that a wife lies down at her husband's feet and allows him to walk all over her by nodding approval instead of registering a single complaint.

But God designed women to receive honor from their husbands as the most valuable of all his possessions. What do men do with priceless treasures? Certainly, most men don't toss their jewels around any old way and wipe their feet on them. Men admire their valuables and handle them with care, placing them in a realm of security. So will a husband treat his wife if she is precious to him. If a husband wipes his feet on his wife, perhaps she fails to make herself honorable by becoming meet for his needs.

B. NOT SPINELESS, BUT STRONG.

> **I Pet. 3:4: "...but let it be the hidden person of the heart, with the imperishable quality of a gentle and quiet spirit, which is precious in the sight of God."**

Strong-willed women seem to think that being submissive will destroy their individual character and personality. One wife said, "I don't want to turn into a little replica of my husband!" Many women think that only cowardly women submit themselves.

But it takes a tremendous amount of character for a woman to control her will and feelings. A woman needs tremendous strength to stand up against popular opinion and place herself in true subjection. Contention is the easy way of life. However, God wants His women to act courageously and to demonstrate the character necessary to obey His will. Someone void of character can't become truly submissive. So if a woman seems spineless, perhaps she lacks the strength to control her emotions and practice true submission.

C. NOT IN SLAVERY, BUT LIBERATED

> **Eph. 5:28-29: "So husbands ought also to love their own wives as their own bodies. He who loves his own wife loves himself;**

**for no one ever hated his own flesh, but
nourishes and cherishes it, just as Christ
also does the church,..."**

Women everywhere criticize subjection as being a
servant of man or a live-in maid--twentieth century
slavery. Subjection, they claim, makes women the personal slaves of their husbands. They accuse men of
being tyrants at heart, wanting only to order women
around and make them do the menial jobs. They say
subjection just involves a wife waiting on her husband
and catering to his whims.

But God commands the husband to take care of his
wife physically, mentally, and spiritually. God wants
the man to direct his wife with love, looking out for
her best interest and placing her needs above his own.
True subjection liberates a wife from worries that hinder her from becoming her most creative, intelligent,
and productive self. However, when a wife forces her
husband to order her around, she enslaves herself. So
if a woman feels like a slave, perhaps she fails to
liberate herself through true subjection.

D. NOT BURDENED, BUT RESTED

**Ru. 3:1: "Then Naomi her mother-in-law
said to her, 'My daughter, shall I not seek
security [rest--KJV and NASV footnote] for
you, that it may be well with you?'"**

Alarmed women cry that subjection is being burdened. To them, subjection represents pure misery and
torture at the hands of their husbands. They view
subjection as a chain that keeps them forever locked
in suffering without hope of freedom or happiness.

But why did Naomi want Ruth to get married? So
that she could be burdened? No, Ruth was already burdened with trying to provide for herself and her
mother-in-law. Naomi wanted Ruth to find a husband so
that she could find rest. In true subjection, a wife
finds rest from unnecessary worries and responsibilities. Half-hearted subjection produces anything, but
rest. So if a woman feels burdened, perhaps she fails
to find rest through practicing subjection.

E. NOT INFERIOR, BUT BEING GREAT

> **Mt. 20:26-28: "It is not so among you, but whoever wishes to become great among you shall be your servant, and whoever wishes to be first among you shall be your slave; just as the Son of Man did not come to be served, but to serve, and to give His life a ransom for many."**

Apprehensive women denounce subjection as making wives inferior to their husbands. They claim that men use their greater physical strength to take advantage of women and to coerce them into subjection. They say subjection makes men think they are superior to women.

But Christ did not come to be waited upon, He came to serve others. He says that anyone who wants to be great must follow His example of being a servant. The ability to serve others cheerfully denotes true greatness. Thus, God appointed women to a position of prominence by giving them an opportunity to serve their husbands. Only when a woman accepts the challenge of becoming a valuable helper for her husband can she become great. If a woman feels inferior, perhaps she fails to rise to her full potential of greatness as a submissive woman.

F. NOT UNIMPORTANT, BUT VALUABLE

> **Prov. 19:14: "House and wealth are an inheritance from fathers, but a prudent wife is from the Lord."**

Many women moan that subjection implies being unimportant. They claim that men just regard them as cooks, housekeepers, lovers, and bottle washers. Many women think that their husbands don't need them as a person, but only as a body. They view themselves as an unimportant thing to be used by their husbands.

But a woman who follows God's plan for her life enjoys immeasurable worth to her husband. *Nothing* can begin to compare with her importance to him. If a woman seems unimportant to her husband, she must examine herself to see if she fails to act the way God created her to. When a woman refuses to practice subjection to her husband, her value falls to that of a hired cook and housekeeper. Thus, if a husband doesn't value his wife, perhaps she makes herself seem unimportant to him through failure to submit herself to him.

G. NOT WITHOUT RIGHTS, BUT PROTECTED

Eph. 5:25: "Husbands, love your wives, just as Christ also loved the church and gave Himself up for her;..."

Countless women reject subjection because they believe it denies them their personal rights. They say that a submissive wife doesn't possess a right to feelings of her own. Submissive women, they claim, must do everything their husbands' way without any say in matters.

But God commands husbands to honor their wives' rights and needs before their own desires. Thus, a godly husband must respect his wife's privileges of marriage even if she refuses to honor his rights. A husband who carries out his half of subjection and leadership may never get to do what he wants to do. God designed the marriage relationship to give the wife *all the rights*. Consequently, if a woman feels deprived of her rights, perhaps she rejects her right to be protected through subjection.

H. NOT POWERLESS, BUT INFLUENTIAL

Tit. 2:3-5: "Older women likewise are to...encourage the young women...that the word of God may not be dishonored."

Numerous women condemn subjection as an institution that strips women of their power and influence. Some women say that submissive women cannot even raise a cry against injustices. They claim that only leadership positions influence others and, therefore, subjection takes away a woman's voice in matters.

But God acknowledged that Eve exercised a great amount of influence over Adam when He condemned Adam for listening submissively to the voice of his wife. Countless other women, in the Bible and out, also demonstrate the power of a woman over a man for either good or evil. Unaware of their influence, many women fail to use it for good. However, men are receptive to the influence of submissive women while contention turns them off almost before the woman opens her mouth. So when a woman seems powerless to bring out the best in her husband, perhaps she fails to use her influence through subjection.

I. NOT DEGRADED, BUT A JOINT-HEIR

I Pet. 3:7: "You husbands...grant her honor as a fellow-heir of the grace of life, so that your prayers may not be hindered."

Various women slander God and the male writers of the Bible as framing and degrading women. They claim that men view all women as second-rate citizens without brains or abilities. These women consider themselves rejects in the sight of God and men.

But God warns husbands that if they degrade their wives, He will not hear their prayers. Since God planned an important role for women to occupy in the home and the church, godly men honor their wives as joint-heirs. In true subjection, the woman works with the man to glorify God. Unfortunately, few women realize the importance of their spiritual role. Consequently, both homes and the church suffer. If a woman thinks God degrades her, perhaps she fails to apply subjection to her life so that she can become a joint-heir with man.

J. NOT MOUSY, BUT BEAUTIFUL

I Pet. 3:5: "For in this way in former times the holy women also, who hoped in God, used to adorn themselves, being submissive to their husbands."

Fearful women wail that subjection makes a woman mousy or like a little brown hen. Subjection, they say, makes a woman fade into the woodwork where no one notices her. To them, subjection means the opposite of glamour and attention and equals non-existence.

But the holy women of old made themselves beautiful by submitting to their husbands. True subjection makes a woman radiantly beautiful! Women with physical beauty cannot maintain their appeal to their husbands if they lack the beauty of true submissiveness. While an inner quality, subjection affects the outer appearance. True subjection softens plain features and makes the voice's tone pleasant to the ear. If beauty defies a woman, perhaps she makes herself seem mousy by failing to practice honest subjection.

K. NOT UNINTELLIGENT, BUT PRUDENT

Prov. 19:14: "Houses and wealth are an inheritance from fathers, but a prudent wife is from the Lord."

Militant women condemn subjection as fit only for unintelligent women. They say that intelligent women use their brains and don't require men to tell them what to do. Only stupid women practice subjection to their husbands. They claim that it does not take any brains to be a wife.

But even though a man might receive a fabulous fortune from his father, that fortune cannot begin to compare with a prudent wife--God's gift to man. A woman needs intelligence or prudence to become an excellent wife, a loving mother, and a professional homemaker. A woman cannot fulfill these roles without effort. Besides that, subjection requires clear thinking to fully understand and practice it properly. If a woman feels unintelligent in the home, perhaps she fails to rise to the full challenge of prudence that God offers a woman.

L. NOT UNNEEDED, BUT MEET FOR MAN

Gen. 2:18: "Then the Lord God said, 'It is not good for the man to be alone; I will make him a helper suitable for him.'"

Unfulfilled women feel sorry for themselves with the claim that they are not needed. They think that only men are important to society. These women feel like misfits without a purpose in life. They think that men enjoy challenging work while women endure dead-end jobs in the home. To these women, only secular jobs promise fulfillment.

But God said that it was not good for the man to be alone. None of the animals could solve man's problem because man needed a special kind of helper--not just any old helper, but a unique one. God gave each woman the inherent qualities that she needs to supply man's needs. The only missing ingredient is for each woman to make herself meet for her husband. When a woman does this, she becomes a specialist with the ability to transform a house into home. Therefore, if a woman is not needed by her husband, then perhaps she fails to adapt her mood and spirit to become meet for him.

M. NOT DESPISED, BUT LOVED

Eccl. 9:9: "Enjoy life with the woman whom you love all the days of your fleeting life...this is your reward in life..."

Resentful women often claim that men force subjection on women because they despise them. They accuse men of looking down on them and just tolerating them. Wives wail, "My husband doesn't love me, he just uses me." They believe that subjection destroys a woman's self-worth.

But God tells the husband to enjoy life with the woman he loves, for this is the reward God gives a man for his labors. Love for a wife comes easy when she submits to her husband and works with him. Without her support, the husband certainly looses his motivation to excel and may even loose his desire for life itself. Subjection makes a husband cherish his wife more than ever and desire to surround her with warmth and tenderness. So if a woman feels despised by her husband, then perhaps she fails to bring his love to life through subjection.

IV. THE CHOICE

Prov. 14:12: "There is a way which seems right to a man, but its end is the way of death."

God gives every husband and wife the choice either to obey Him and enjoy happiness or to disobey Him and suffer misery. The law of subjection and leadership demonstrates that human beings lack the ability to direct their own footsteps wisely. For subjection does not make sense to a wife when her husband mistreats her--standing up for her own rights makes sense. Likewise, loving leadership does not make sense to a husband when his wife opposes everything he suggests--selfishness makes sense. Even though freewill subjection and responsible leadership often fail to make sense to the average person, they work together to make both husbands and wives happy. Refusal to apply them properly usually results in marital misery.

Basic principles for orderly conduct in relationships outside of marriage often seem illogical in the husband-wife union to many people. Instead, myths and untruths about subjection and leadership dominate people's thinking. Even when they know the truth, many people reject it because they allow their emotions instead of their intellect to govern them. Thus, married couples need to implement God's rules into their lives with diligent, honest, soul-searching prayer which rids them of all rebellion against God's word.

A. THE HUSBAND'S CHOICE

The husband and wife share equal responsibilities for making their union happy and fulfilling. But the husband's obligations for loving leadership places a tremendous burden on his shoulders. If he fails to deliberately choose to become a guardian of authority in the home, he probably makes the wrong choice by default.

1. MAKE HIS HOME FLOURISH

Prov. 14:11: "The house of the wicked will be destroyed, but the tent of the upright will flourish."

"Flourish": means "to break forth as a bud, i.e. bloom, generally to spread, specifically to fly (as extending the wings), figuratively to flourish" (Strong, p. 96).

When a husband dares to fulfill the role God assigned him of providing for, leading, and protecting his family, he reaps numerous physical, mental, and spiritual benefits. One of the greatest is a contented wife. Any man who lives with an unhappy, complaining woman at his side knows that all the physical blessings in the world seem of little value when his wife complains and refuses to be satisfied.

Just as the way Christ treats the church affects Christians, the way a husband treats his wife affects how she responds to him. Christ always seeks to bring out the best in Christians and to do what is best for them--even giving up His own life for them. Christ always focuses on the potential in His followers and helps them achieve true beauty of character. In like manner, a husband who wants a beautiful, loving, and submissive wife ever strives to become a good, loving, and considerate leader. It cannot be denied, how a husband treats his wife affects what she becomes over the years.

God gave the husband the right to lead his wife and children in the realm of opinion. Even so, God cautions him to act always in the best interest of his family. God designed the husband's leadership as one of total self-denial. Selfishness has no place in the life of a loving leader. When a husband acts in the best interest of his wife, he brings out his wife's best side and reaps benefits for himself. Truly, a husband who loves his wife as his own body loves himself.

And even if a husband lives in a humble tent, if he leads his wife with love and consideration, his home flourishes. His marriage grows more beautiful through the years like a rose slowly opening to its full beauty. Thus, God offers great rewards for the husband who obeys Him in the way that he treats his wife.

2. OR DESTROY HIS HOME

Prov. 14:11: "The house of the wicked will be destroyed, but the tent of the upright will flourish."

"Destroyed" means "to desolate:--destroy (-uction), bring to nought, overthrow, perish, pluck down" (Strong, p. 118).

One of the saddest sights to behold is a godly woman married to a man who refuses to assume his masculine responsibilities. While a wife exerts tremendous influence over what a family becomes over the years, if the man is weak and ineffective, by the very nature of her being, she cannot replace him or completely counteract all of his evil influences.

When a wicked husband provides his wife with a mansion overlooking the bay with far too many servants, it seems void of complete happiness and contentment. Yet a humble man who works hard, acts responsibly, and shows consideration finds his home flourishing. His wife glows when he rises to the full challenge of a man--a man who dares to become everything that God planned in the beginning. When a husband leads, protects, and provides the necessities of life, he reaps these benefits even if he can never afford to buy a house, but must continually live in makeshift dwellings such as tents.

If a woman's husband shows determination to act as the head of his family, (even if she thinks he is too determined and stubborn), works hard to make a living (even if she thinks he works too hard), and tells her "no" to projects that she wants to do (even if she thinks he says "no" too often), she should hug his neck and tell him how lucky she is to be his wife. Even if he is not a Christian, he still possesses the essential characteristics of a real man and can be a good influence upon their children in every realm except the spiritual one. A wise wife cherishes and loves such a man.

When a husband wants to lead, provide for, and protect his family, generally, the wife can, by making the right choice for herself, bring out a greatness in her husband that she never knew existed. On the other hand, if a woman marries a selfish man who shuns his proper role in life, then she has a greater challenge than the woman who married a considerate man. She must give more of herself to the needs of her husband to bring out his better nature. Selfishness breeds selfishness, while kindness usually breeds kindness.

B. THE WIFE'S CHOICE

Just as a husband makes his own choice, every wife makes her own choice. She can choose to submit to her husband and make him a king even if they live in a tent or she can despise him and become as rottenness in his bones even if they live in a mansion. The choice is hers alone to make:

1. HER HUSBAND'S CROWN

Prov. 12:4: "An excellent [virtuous--KJV] wife is the crown of her husband,..."

"Husband" means "lord, master, owner, possessor."[3]

"Excellent" or "virtuous" means "a force, whether of men, means, or other resources, an army, wealth, virtue, valor, strength" (Strong, p. 39).

A crown symbolizes authority; however, the authority does not lie in the crown but in the wearer. Thus, when a wife is the crown of her husband, she freely gives her husband authority over her. She regards him as her "lord, master, owner, and possessor." On the other hand, when a woman acts contentiously and determines to be her own authority, her husband cannot force her to submit to him.

The only real king who comes home to his castle from work is the husband who has an excellent wife to crown him. If a husband functions as the true head of the home, his wife makes him the head. Otherwise, he might be a tyrant who insists, "I am going to be the leader of my family." He may browbeat and terrorize his wife, but if she refuses to put her mind in subjection, he isn't a real king. He is only someone who controls by sheer force or might. If he is a real king, it is because his wife crowned him king. A woman can crown her husband as king or she can force him to take on a dictatorship, or worse yet, she can make him cower in a corner of the roof (Prov. 21:9).

Whether harmony or discord reigns in the home depends primarily upon the woman's meek and quiet

---

[3]Robert Young, *Analytical Concordance to the Bible* (Grand Rapids, MI: Wm. B. Eerdmans Publishing Company, 1964), p. 505.

spirit and her trust in God. "Excellent" refers to the strength and force found in an army. Subjection is not for weak-willed women, but women of strength of character. Weak women make the easy choice:

2. OR ROTTENNESS IN HIS BONES

Prov. 12:4: "...but she who shames him is as rottenness in his bones."

"Shames" means "properly pale, i.e. by implication to be ashamed, also (by implication) to be disappointed, or delayed" (Strong, p. 19).

"Rottenness" means "to decay (as by worm-eating):--rot" (Strong, p. 110).

Solomon contrasts the wife who crowns her husband with the one who shames him. A woman who fails to highly regard her husband and crown him as a king is continually filled with doubts about his ability to lead her properly. She feels ashamed of him and it shows, perhaps in little ways, but she shames him just the same.

Sometimes a wife disguises shame by belittling her husband with humor. She often fools other people by pretending to joke, but her husband usually gets the point of the jab. Or a wife may avoid pointing out her husband's faults to his face while she complains to her friends about what he does. She also reminds the children that they must make allowances for "Daddy." A husband senses when he cannot do anything to please his wife, even if she never says an unkind word to him.

As one of the most effective methods for demoralizing a husband, a wife bluntly points out each mistake as he makes it, tells him every move to make, and continually reminds him of his past blunders. Amazingly, few husbands fight back; most just suffer in silence when treated this way.

The art of silent shaming provides yet another method for shaming the husband. The wife simply looks at her husband with those big, sad, disappointed eyes while suffering his injustices in silence, hoping that some day he will straighten up and treat her like a queen. This method quickly makes a husband feel like a first-class heel.

Many a husband willingly comforts his wife when she cries from genuine sorrow. But tears that flow from not getting her own way can help whip a husband back into line. Such a woman may not cry deliberately to manipulate her husband; she just has not learned that when the heart stubbornly resists subjection, tears often swell in a woman's eyes. A husband greatly resents these tears and views them as a weapon for intimidating him.

Many a wife who rebels against her husband's authority ceases to enjoy taking care of her home and quickly becomes a poor housekeeper. She does the things she wants to do during the day instead of supporting her husband's role of earning a living.

Many a woman openly blames her physical ills on others. If only her husband, relatives, or friends treated her better, she would recover. While unhappy thoughts lead to depression and lack of energy, contentious living promotes stress which makes the body susceptible to real diseases. Illness, genuine or psychological, provides an opportunity to control the lives of others.

Sometimes a contentious woman treats her husband nice just to get her own way. Such a wife's sweet nothings whispered into her husband's ear are just that--nothings! This wife knows how to sweet-talk her husband into buying whatever she desires. She knows when to fix his favorite food--not when he feels beat down and discouraged, but when she fears that he might say, "No," to her request.

Along this same line, many a wife uses sex as a weapon instead of as an expression of love. When her husband is docile, she loves him passionately. But! when he exerts his will, he gets to sleep with anything from an icicle to an iceberg depending on how mad she is.

Many a manipulative woman subdues her husband by cutting off her hair, especially if her husband loves long hair on a woman. Sometimes a husband gets very upset when his wife whacks her curls off. When this happens, the wife promises to let her hair grow out again if he will yield to her demands.

Other times a wife relieves her pent-up hostilities by going on a shopping spree whether her husband can afford it or not. She believes in fighting selfishness with selfishness. The credit manager of a large department store said in a newspaper interview that one of the major causes of overbuying was a spouse going on a buying spree to get even with a marriage partner.

An alienated woman often runs home to her mother or to a hotel where her husband can't find her. If it works, this humiliates the husband into thinking he can't get along without her even if she refuses to do what he wants. After letting the husband stew for an appropriate time, the wife comes home to what she hopes is a submissive husband.

Unbelievable! A quarrelsome woman may even resort to yelling to make her husband listen to her point of view--even a woman who professes Christianity. Some of these women know that if they yell in public, their husbands cower even more quickly and give in just to quiet them. Even harder to believe, some women use foul language to make their points--even women claiming to be Christians.

Likewise, a pugnacious wife who gives in to violent temper tantrums may throw things at her husband. The old joke about the wife waiting behind the door with the rolling pin is not very funny in some households.

An unsympathetic wife often shames her husband publicly by correcting his stories, sometimes in regard to minute details that don't affect the story in any way except to interrupt it. Usually such stories are not a matter of telling a lie, but of simply being able to remember every insignificant detail.

A self-righteous wife often thinks that if her husband isn't a Christian, it gives her the right to preach to him. Such a wife frequently gives in to her husband, but she makes sure he knows that she disapproves. While she flaunts Christianity, she fails to practice it in her marriage.

Frequently, an estranged wife, either openly or in her thoughts, holds up other men as perfect examples of humanity. If her husband were only half as good as they, she would enjoy true happiness. If that fails to achieve results, she holds up *bad men* as shining examples. If that doesn't make a husband feel worthless, nothing will.

So what can a husband do when his wife shames him either through gimmicks or openly? In spite of how a husband reacts to his wife when she forsakes her feminine role and becomes a dishonest ruler behind the scenes, he pays a high price: Solomon said such a wife becomes as rottenness in his bones.

Medical science has proven over and over again that stress, whether mental or physical, causes real diseases in the body such as heart attacks, cancer, high blood pressure, diabetes, etc. For example, "Dr. Hans Gersenheim, a medical researcher in Hamburg, Germany, conducted a series of detailed, intimate interviews with 237 men who had survived their first heart attack. He found that an overwhelming majority had been consistently downgraded by nagging wives."[2]

Female dominance not only affects husbands adversely, but it also carries grave consequences for male children. In a report on female-dominated homes, Herman P. Miller concluded, on the basis of psychiatric studies, that "mental depression, dwarfism, crime, delinquency, homosexuality, diabetes, colds, asthma, arthritis, cancer, and paranoia are among the serious consequences of female dominance."[3]

A woman who refuses to submit herself to her husband so that she can work *with* him places her life at odds with his and works *against* him. A contentious woman literally undermines her husband's health like an incurable disease eating away at the life marrow of his bones. She saps his strength and his ambition and can even destroy his life.

Is it any wonder that the husband of such a wife would rather work all the time or go out with the boys until all hours, or that he doesn't feel loving toward his "better half"? While such a wife continually shames her husband, the shame belongs to her. God did not create a woman as a cancer-causing stress to her husband, but as the most emotionally desirable person on earth to him.

Vol. II: Learning to Love puts the crowning touch on the principles taught in this book and shows how to take the marriage a step further. However, it devotes the last chapter, "Sexual Problems in Perspective," to

[2]Dr. Phon E. Hudkins, "Ethology and Manpower Policy" (Washington, D.C.: Labor Department Report, 1970).
[3]"Female Dominance: Labor's New Pain," *Modern Medicine* (5/18/70), p. 33.

discussing what a wife's attitude should be toward problems beyond her control. While subjection and spontaneous love bring success to the average marriage, God does not guarantee one hundred percent success for everyone. God still allows people to make their own freewill choices. But through His love for women, God makes provisions for the wife whose husband makes her life unbearable. But until a wife applies *all of God's law* to her life, she doesn't know if following God's way will bring out the best in her husband and save her marriage.

If a wife allows herself to grow bitter on the grounds that her husband fails to make the right choice for himself, it prevents her from making the right choice for herself. Then life for them only gets worse. As long as a woman serves God, Peter says she enjoys hope (I Pet. 3:1-2). Now that the wife has learned how to appreciate marriage and be submissive, she needs to take the second step and learn how to love.

Every wife makes her own choice; her husband cannot make it for her. Every husband gambles and places his emotional welfare in the hands of his wife when he marries. His wife either becomes the best thing that ever happened to him or she becomes like worms eating away at his flesh. The choice is hers alone to make. And the choice she makes determines if love reigns in the home or if contention does.

What is YOUR choice?

———

STUDY EXERCISE

Answer all questions in your own words.

1. It has been said that when subjection is practiced properly, it makes a woman's life happy; but when it is practiced wrongly, it makes a woman's life miserable. Do you agree? Why?

2. How does Satan use women today? How can a woman keep him from using her?

3. How can God use women to serve Him?

4. What do you think is the hardest part of subjection to practice?

5. How does contention hurt both men and women?

6. How does subjection protect both men and women?

7. List three ways a wife can make her husband be a king.

8. List three ways women commonly shame their husbands.

9. Do you disagree with anything in this lesson? If so, explain in detail giving scriptures for your reasons.

PERSONAL EXERCISE

Answer the following questions to determine if you practice true Bible subjection. If you sincerely want to please your husband, ask him to answer the questions for you. Give yourself the appropriate points for how often you do each thing (4 points--every chance you get, 3 points--most of the time, 2 points--once in a while, 1 point--never):

1. Submit yourself
2. Submit to your own husband
3. Set a good example for your husband
4. Submit in everything
5. Love husband being in subjection
6. Love children being in subjection
7. Sober-minded being in subjection
8. Spend money being in subjection
9. Dress to please him
10. Chaste being in subjection
11. Worker at home being in subjection
12. Kind being in subjection
13. Calling him "lord" (mind in subjection)
14. With meekness (self-control)
15. Submit with quietness (with inward and outward peace)
16. Submit with reverence (ask him instead of telling)
17. Submit as to the Lord (even when he is not looking)
18. Submit as the church is (a picture of the bride of Christ)
19. Submit as is fitting in the Lord (obey God before man)
20. Submit without fear (not afraid of what he will do)

Score: Add up your points and to determine if you are beautiful to your husband.

    51-60 points--Beautiful
    41-50 points--Pretty
    31-40 points--Mousy
     0-30 points--Ugly

OPTIONAL CREATIVE EXERCISE

A woman who is an artist made drawings to illustrate what subjection is verses what subjection is not. Her young daughter loved them and frequently asked her to go over the pictures with her. The woman also used the drawings when she taught these lessons, and the adult women also enjoyed them.

SPECIAL PROBLEM-SOLVING EXERCISE DUE

The special exercise assigned at the end of chapter four is due at this time. It is the report analyzing a current magazine or newspaper article.

RESEARCH EXERCISE DUE

The research exercise assigned at the end of chapter 6 is due at this time. It catalogs all of a woman's duties under "love" and "subjection" along with the rewards and penalties, etc.

BIBLIOGRAPHY

Adams, Jay E. *Competent to Counsel*. Grand Rapids, MI: Baker Book House, 1970.

Astrachan, Anthony. "New York's Abortion Law Faces Serious Political Test." *The Spokesman-Review* (1/14/73).

Atkinson, Ti-Grace. St. Paul, MN: *Dispatch* (8/21/74).

Babbage, Stuart Barton. *Sex and Sanity, A Christian View of Sexual Morality*. Philadelphia: The West- minster Press, 1965. Quoting Workman, Herbert. *The Evolution of the Monastic Ideal*.

Barclay, William. *Letters of James and Peter*. Philadelphia: The Westminister Press, 1958.

Bird, Caroline. *Born Female: The High Cost of Keeping Women Down*. New York: David McKay Co., Inc., 1970.

Botwin, Carol and Parsons, Edward L. M.D. "Good Women, Bad Marriages." *Redbook* (2/87).

Chartham, Robert. *Mainly for Wives: The Art of Sex for Women*. New York: Signet Books, 1969.

"Child Divorcing Parent 'Not So Far-Fetched.'" *Amarillo Globe-Times* (4/29/80).

Daly, Mary. "A Call for the Castration of Sexist Reli- gion." Pittsburgh, PA: KNOW, Inc., 1972.

Densmore, Dana. "Chivalry—The Iron Hand in the Velvet Glove." Pittsburgh, PA: KNOW, Inc., (9/69).

Densmore, Dana. "Who is Saying Men are the Enemy?" Pittsburgh, PA: KNOW, Inc.

Dietrick, Ellen Battelle. *The Woman's Bible*. Originally published New York: European Publishing Co., 1895. Reprinted Seattle, WA: Seattle Coalition Task Force on Women and Religion, 1974.

Dillow, Joseph P. *Solomon on Sex*. Nashville: Thomas Nelson Publishers, 1977.

Downs, Robert B. *Books That Changed the World.* New York: New American Library, 1956.

Dyer, K. F. with Wischnia, Bob. "Why Men Run Faster than Women." *Runner's World* (11/83).

"Female Dominance: Labor's New Pain." *Modern Medicine* (5/18/70).

"Feminist Leaders Seek Wider Appeal Following ERA Defeats." *The Spokesman-Review* (11/13/75).

Friedan, Betty. "Being 'Superwoman' is *Not* the Way to Go." *Woman's Day* (10/13/81).

Friedan, Betty. *The Feminine Mystique.* New York: Norton, 1963.

Gardner, Jo-Ann. "Sexist Counselling Must Stop." Quoting *Personnel and Guidance Journal,* Vol. 49, No. 9 (May 1971).

Gelman, David. "Just How the Sexes Differ." *Newsweek* (5/18/81).

Gilder, George. *Men and Marriage.* Gretna, LO: Pelican Publishing Co. Inc., 1986.

Gilman, Richard. "The 'Woman Problem'--Then and Now." *Life* (8/13/71).

Gilman, Richard. "Where Did It All Go Wrong?" *Life* (8/13/71).

Goleman, Daniel. "Special Abilities of the Sexes: Do They Begin in the Brain?" *Psychology Today* (November 1978).

Gottlieb, Annie. "Men and Women: What Differences Do the Differences Really Make?" *Mademoiselle* (7/81).

Gray's Anatomy. Philadelphia: W. B. Saunder's Co., 1973.

Hailey, Homer. "Syllabus on the Song of Solomon." Temple Terrace, FL: Florida College. Unpublished class notes.

Harrell, Pat E. *Divorce and Remarriage in the Early Church.* Austin, TX: R. B. Sweet Company, Inc., 1967.

Harris, R. Laird, Archer, Gleason L. Jr. and Waltke, Bruce K. *Theological Wordbook of the Old Testament.* Chicago, IL: Moody Press, 1980.

Henderson, Robert and Gould, Ian. *Life in Bible Times.* Chicago: Rand McNally & Company, 1967.

Hendriksen, William. *New Testament Commentary,* I–II Timothy-Titus. Grand Rapids, MI: Baker Book House, 1957.

Henry, Matthew. *Matthew Henry's Commentary on the Whole Bible*, Vol. III. New York: Fleming H. Revell Co., 1710.

Hobbs, Lottie Beth. *You Can Be Beautiful (with the Beauty of Holiness)*. Ft. Worth, TX: Harvest Publications, 1959. Used by permission.

Hudkins, Phon E., Ph.D. "Ethology and Manpower Policy." Washington, D.C.: Labor Department Report, 1970.

Human Physiology. New York: McGraw-Hill Book Co., Inc., 1951.

Hunt, Morton. "Does Love Really Make the World Go Round?" *Parade Magazine* (2/8/87).

International Standard Bible Encyclopedia. Grand Rapids, MI: Wm. B. Eerdmans Publishing Co., 1939.

Jauncey, James H. *Magic in Marriage*. Grand Rapids, MI: Zondervan, 1966.

Jennings, Peter. "After the Sexual Revolution." New York: ABC News Closeup Transcript (8/1/86).

Keller, Philip. *A Shepherd Looks at Psalm 23*. Grand Rapids, MI: Zondervan, 1970.

Loesch, Julie. "Children's Liberation, The Politics of Childhood." Pittsburgh, PA: KNOW, Inc.

Luftig, Don. "The Sex Test." Condensed from a WNBC-TV Feature. *Reader's Digest* (Sept, 1977).

MacLeish, Kenneth and Launois, John. "Stone Age Cavemen of Mindanao." *National Geographic* (August 1972). Used by permission.

Maltz, Maxwell. *Psycho-Cybernetics*. New York: Pocket Books, 1960.

"Marriage and Divorce as Political Institutions: A Working Paper from Women in Transition, Inc." Philadelphia: Women in Transition, Inc.

"Mental Health." *Time* (4/12/76).

McMillen, S. I., M.D. *None of These Diseases*. Old Tappen, NJ: Revell, 1967.

Millett, Kate. *Sexual Politics*. New York: The Hearst Corp., 1970. Used by permission of Doubleday and Company.

Moberg, Verne. "A Child's Right to Equal Reading." Washington, D.C.: National Education Association.

Morgan, Robin editor. "Sisterhood is Powerful, an Anthology of Writing From the Women's Liberation Movement." SCUM.

Muller, Kal. "Taboos and Magic Rule Namba Lives." *National Geographic* (January 1972). Used by permission.

"NOW President Defends Way of Life." *Spokesman-Review* (10/26/75).

"NOW Supports Abortion, Lesbian Rights." *Amarillo Globe-Times* (10/10/79).

Pettus, Robert L. Jr., M.D. *As I See Sex Through the Bible.* Madison, TN: Pettus, 1973. Quoting Rotnavale, David N., M.D. *Medical Aspects of Human Sexuality.* April 1970, Vol. IV, No. 4.

Popular and Critical Bible Encyclopedia and Scriptural Dictionary. Chicago, IL: The Howard-Severance Company, 1902.

Porter, Sylvia. "You and Your Money: The Truth about Equal Pay." *Ladies' Home Journal* (8/82).

Pulpit Commentary, Vol. III. Grand Rapids, MI: Wm. B. Eerdmans Publishing Co., 1950.

Reville, Albert. *The Song of Songs.* As quoted by Hailey, Homer. "Syllabus on the Song of Solomon." Temple Terrace, FL: Florida College. Unpublished class notes.

Roiphe, Anne. "The Private Language of Marriage." *McCall's* (February, 1974).

Schauss, Hayyim. *The Lifetime of a Jew.* New York: Union of American Hebrew Congregations, 1950.

Septuagint Version of the Old Testament. Grand Rapids, MI: Zondervan Publishing House, 1970 Edition.

"Shop Is Stocked for Transvestites." *The Spokesman-Review* (3/5/76).

Stannard, Una, Ph.D. "The Male Maternal Instinct." Pittsburgh, PA: Know, Inc., 1970.

Steinem, Gloria. "Sisterhood." As quoted in *The First Ms. Reader.* New York: Warner Books Inc., 1973.

Strong, James. *Strong's Exhaustive Concordance.* Grand Rapids, MI: Associated Publishers and Authors Inc., n.d.

Stump, Jane Barr, Ph.D. *What's the Difference? How Men and Women Compare.* New York: William Morrow & Co., Inc., 1985.

Tavris, Carol and Jayaratne, Toby. *How Do You Feel About Being a Woman? The Results of a Redbook Questionnaire. Redbook* booklet (Jan, 1973).

Thayer, Joseph Henry, D.D. *Thayer's Greek-English Lexicon of the New Testament.* Grand Rapids, MI: Associated Publishers and Authors Inc., n.d.

Vanauken, "A Primer for the Last Revolution." Pittsburgh, PA: KNOW, Inc., 1971.

Vincent, Marvin R. *Word Studies in the New Testament.* Grand Rapids, MI: Eerdmans, 1887.

Vine, W. E. *Expository Dictionary of New Testament Words.* Westwood, N.J.: Fleming H. Revell Company, 1950.

Wallace, Irving. *The Two.* New York: Simon and Schuster, 1978.

West, Jayne. "No More Fun and Games." Pittsburgh, PA: KNOW, Inc.

"Who Are the Proponents of ERA?" San Antonio, TX: Committee to Restore Women's Rights.

Wigram. *Analytical Greek Lexicon of the New Testament.* Wilmington, DL: Associates Publishers and Authors Inc., n.d.

"Women More Thin-Skinned." *Spokane Daily Chronicle* (11/20/75).

Young, Robert, LL.D. *Analytical Concordance to the Bible.* Grand Rapids, MI: Wm. B. Eerdmans Publishing Company, 1964.

Zilbergeld, Bernie, Ph.D. *Male Sexuality.* New York: Bantam, 1978.

INDEX